Praise for *Real 802.11 Security: Wi-Fi Protected*

Jon Edney and Bill Arbaugh are both recognized experts
and they both played a significant role in the developmen
This book will provide you with a comprehensive under.
the basics of why it's needed to implementation on your Wi-Fi network. It will provide
you with the information you need to make the right security decisions in a way that is
both easy to understand and enjoyable to read.

—Dennis Eaton, Chairman, Wi-Fi Alliance, www.wi-fi.org

Real 802.11 Security provides clear descriptions of current and emerging security techniques. It will be extremely useful to product designers, network administrators, and
advanced home users. The authors handle complex topics nicely, and offer significant
clarification of IEEE draft standards. This book provides timely information about TKIP
and CCMP which is critical to understanding wireless local area network security.

—Russ Housley, founder of Vigil Security, LLC and IETF Security Area Director

Edney and Arbaugh have done a remarkable job at laying out all the details in a clear and
thorough manner. They don't hide any warts. This is certainly the definitive text on the
internals of 802.11 security!

—John Viega, chief scientist, Secure Software, Inc., co-author of *Building Secure Software*

The approach of *Real 802.11 Security* will be useful for a wide audience: IT managers
tasked with deploying WLAN, engineers keen to learn about WLAN security, as well as
curious home users. The book keeps the exposition as straightforward as possible and
enables readers to cut through the maze of acronyms, hacking tools, rumored weaknesses,
and vague vendor security claims to make educated security decisions when purchasing or
deploying WLAN. The authors are two of the leading experts on WLAN security, and
I'm particularly excited to see them working together.

—Simon Blake-Wilson, Director of Information Security, BCI

The need is there for a good book on 802.11 security, and the authors have something to
contribute. *Real 802.11 Security* is comprehensive and detailed without getting mired in
the details. I like the writing and think the book will be helpful for anyone interested in
wireless.

—Robert Bruen, Merrimack College

Real 802.11 Security is an enjoyable, informative and easy-to-read book about the intrica-
cies of 802.11-based wireless security. If you want to know about the important issues sur-
rounding 802.11-based wireless security, this book will definitely help you.

—Victor R. Garza, security consultant and author

Wi-Fi Wireless LANs are now commonplace in commerce, public places, and in the
home, but their security flaws have received wide press. WPA and IEEE 802.11i will
address these flaws, but people deploying wireless LANs need information to fully understand the security issues and have confidence in the available solutions. *Real 802.11 Security* fits this bill nicely. It brings together relevant topics and places them in context—
explaining why the solutions being developed for WLAN security are as they are.

—Simon Black, security consultant

Real 802.11 Security

Wi-Fi Protected Access and 802.11i

Jon Edney

and

William A. Arbaugh

♦♦Addison-Wesley

Boston • San Francisco • New York • Toronto • Montreal
London • Munich • Paris • Madrid
Capetown • Sydney • Tokyo • Singapore • Mexico City

Many of the designations used by manufacturers and sellers to distinguish their products are claimed as trademarks. Where those designations appear in this book, and Addison-Wesley was aware of a trademark claim, the designations have been printed with initial capital letters or in all capitals.

The authors and publisher have taken care in the preparation of this book, but make no expressed or implied warranty of any kind and assume no responsibility for errors or omissions. No liability is assumed for incidental or consequential damages in connection with or arising out of the use of the information or programs contained herein.

The publisher offers discounts on this book when ordered in quantity for bulk purchases and special sales. For more information, please contact:

U.S. Corporate and Government Sales
(800) 382-3419
corpsales@pearsontechgroup.com

For sales outside of the U.S., please contact:

International Sales
(317) 581-3793
international@pearsontechgroup.com

Visit Addison-Wesley on the Web: www.awprofessional.com

Library of Congress Cataloging-in-Publication Data

Edney, Jon.
   Real 802.11 security : Wi-Fi protected access and 802.11i / Jon Edney and William A. Arbaugh.
      p. cm.
   Includes bibliographical references and index.
   ISBN 0-321-13620-9 (pbk. : alk. paper)
   1. Wireless LANs--Security measures. 2. IEEE 802.11 (Standard) I. Arbaugh, William
A. II. Title.

TK5105.59.E36 2004
005.8—dc21

                                                                        2003049595

Pearson Education, Inc.
Rights and Contracts Department
75 Arlington Street, Suite 300
Boston, MA 02116
Fax: (617) 848-7047

ISBN 0-321-13620-9

Text printed on recycled paper
1 2 3 4 5 6 7 8 9 10—CRS—0706050403
First printing, July 2003

Contents

Preface   xv

Acknowledgments   xxi

Part I   What Everyone Should Know   1

Chapter 1   Introduction   3
Setting the Scene   3
Roadmap to the Book   5
Notes on the Book   6

Chapter 2   Security Principles   7
What Is Security?   7
Good Security Thinking   8
　　1. Don't Talk to Anyone You Don't Know   8
　　2. Accept Nothing Without a Guarantee   10
　　3. Treat Everyone as an Enemy until Proved Otherwise   11
　　4. Don't Trust Your Friends for Long   12
　　5. Use Well-Tried Solutions   13
　　6. Watch the Ground You Are Standing on for Cracks   15
Security Terms   17
Summary   19

Chapter 3   Why Is Wi-Fi Vulnerable to Attack?   21
Changing the Security Model   21
What Are the Enemies Like?   22
　　Gaming Attackers   23
　　Profit or Revenge Attackers   25
　　Ego Attackers   26

Traditional Security Architecture   27
   Option 1: Put Wireless LAN in the Untrusted Zone   29
   Option 2: Make Wi-Fi LAN Trusted   30
Danger of Passive Monitoring   31
Summary   32

Chapter 4   **Different Types of Attack   33**
Classification of Attacks   34
Attacks Without Keys   35
   Snooping   36
   Man-in-the-Middle Attack (Modification)   37
Attacks on the Keys   40
   One-Time Passwords   41
   Burying the Keys   41
   Wireless Attacks   42
   Attacking the Keys Through Brute Force   45
   Dictionary Attacks   46
   Algorithmic Attacks   47
Summary   48

Part II   The Design of Wi-Fi Security   49

Chapter 5   **IEEE 802.11 Protocol Primer   51**
Layers   51
Wireless LAN Organization   53
Basics of Operation in Infrastructure Mode   54
   Beacons   55
   Probing   56
   Connecting to an AP   56
   Roaming   56
   Sending Data   56
Protocol Details   57
   General Frame Formats   57
   AC header   58
   Management Frames   60
Radio Bits   63
Summary   65

Chapter 6   How IEEE 802.11 WEP Works and Why It Doesn't   67
Introduction   67
Authentication   69
Privacy   72
Use of RC4 Algorithm   73
Initialization Vector (IV)   74
WEP Keys   76
Mechanics of WEP   83
Fragmentation   83
Integrity Check Value (ICV)   84
Preparing the Frame for Transmission   85
RC4 Encryption Algorithm   86
Why WEP Is Not Secure   89
Authentication   90
Access Control   93
Replay Prevention   93
Message Modification Detection   94
Message Privacy   95
RC4 Weak Keys   99
Direct Key Attacks   100
Summary   101

Chapter 7   WPA, RSN, and IEEE 802.11i   103
Relationship Between Wi-Fi and IEEE 802.11   103
What Is IEEE 802.11i?   104
What Is WPA?   105
Differences Between RSN and WPA   106
Security Context   107
Keys   108
Security Layers   110
How the Layers Are Implemented   111
Relationship of the Standards   113
List of Standards   113
Pictorial Map   114
Summary   115

Chapter 8   Access Control: IEEE 802.1X, EAP, and RADIUS   117
Importance of Access Control   117
Authentication for Dial-in Users   120

IEEE 802.1X   122
   IEEE 802.1X in a Simple Switched Hub Environment   124
   IEEE 802.1X in Wi-Fi LANs   127

EAP Principles   129
   EAP Message Formats   131

EAPOL   133
   EAPOL-Start   133
   EAPOL-Key   134
   EAPOL-Packet   134
   EAPOL-Logoff   134

Messages Used in IEEE 802.1X   135
   Authentication Sequence   135

Implementation Considerations   137

RADIUS—Remote Access Dial-In User Service   138
   RADIUS Mechanics   140
   EAP over RADIUS   144
   Use of RADIUS in WPA and RSN   146

Summary   147

Chapter 9   Upper-Layer Authentication   149

Introduction   149

Who Decides Which Authentication Method to Use?   150

Use of Keys in Upper-Layer Authentication   151
   Symmetric Keys   151
   Asymmetric Keys   151
   Certificates and Certification Authorities   153

A Detailed Look at Upper-Level Authentication
   Methods   155

Transport Layer Security (TLS)   155
   Functions of TLS   156
   Handshake Exchange   159
   Relationship of TLS Handshake and WPA/RSN   164
   TLS over EAP   165
   Summary of TLS   169

Kerberos V5V5   169
   Using Tickets   169
   Kerberos Tickets   171
   Obtaining the Ticket-Granting Ticket   171
   Service Tickets   172

Cross-Domain Access   174
How Tickets Work   176
Use of Kerberos in RSN   178
Cisco Light EAP (LEAP)   184
Protected EAP Protocol (PEAP)   186
Phase 1   188
Phase 2   189
Status of PEAP   189
Authentication in the Cellular Phone World: EAP-SIM   189
Overview of Authentication in a GSM Network   191
Linking GSM Security to Wi-Fi LAN Security   192
EAP-SIM   193
Status of GSM-SIM Authentication   196
Summary   196

Chapter 10   WPA and RSN Key Hierarchy   199
Pairwise and Group Keys   199
Pairwise Key Hierarchy   201
Creating and Delivering the PMK   201
Computing the Temporal Keys   203
Exchanging and Verifying Key Information   204
Completing the Handshake   207
Group Key Hierarchy   207
Summary of the Key Establishment Process   210
Key Hierarchy Using AES–CCMP   211
Mixed Environments   212
Summary of Key Hierarchies   212
Details of Key Derivation for WPA   214
Four-Way Handshake   217
Group Key Handshake   223
Nonce Selection   224
Computing the Temporal Keys   225
Summary   229

Chapter 11   TKIP   231
What Is TKIP and Why Was It Created?   231
TKIP Overview   234
Message Integrity   235
IV Selection and Use   238

Per-Packet Key Mixing   243
TKIP Implementation Details   245
Message Integrity—Michael   249
   Countermeasures   249
   Computation of the MIC   252
Per-Packet Key Mixing   255
   Substitution Table or S-Box   256
   Phase 1 Computation   257
   Phase 2 Computation   258
Summary   259

Chapter 12   AES–CCMP   261
Introduction   261
Why AES?   262
AES Overview   264
   Modes of Operation   264
   Offset Codebook Mode (OCB)   269
How CCMP Is Used in RSN   269
   Steps in Encrypting a Transmission   270
   CCMP Header   271
   Overview of Implementation   272
   Steps in Encrypting an MPDU   273
   Decrypting MPDUs   277
Summary   278

Chapter 13   Wi-Fi LAN Coordination: ESS and IBSS   279
Network Coordination   279
   ESS Versus IBSS   280
   Joining an ESS Network   280
WPA/RSN Information Element   282
   Validating the Information Elements   283
Preauthentication Using IEEE 802.1X   283
IBSS Ad-Hoc Networks   285
Summary   289

Part III   Wi-Fi Security in the Real World   291

Chapter 14   Public Wireless Hotspots   293

Development of Hotspots   293
Public Wireless Access Defined   294
Barriers to Growth   294

Security Issues in Public Hotspots   296

How Hotspots Are Organized   297
Subscribers   298
Access Points   299
Hotspot Controllers   300
Authentication Server   302

Different Types of Hotspots   303
Airports   303
Hotels   303
Coffee Shops   303
Homes   304

How to Protect Yourself When Using a Hotspot   305
Personal Firewall Software   305
Virtual Private Network (VPN)   306

Summary   308

Chapter 15   Known Attacks: Technical Review   311

Review of Basic Security Mechanisms   311
Confidentiality   312
Integrity   314

Review of Previous IEEE 802.11 Security Mechanisms   316
Confidentiality   316
RC4 and WEP   316
Integrity and Authentication   321

Attacks Against the Previous IEEE 802.11 Security
    Mechanisms   322
Confidentiality   322
Access Control   329
Authentication   330

Man-in-the-Middle Attacks   331
Management Frames   331
ARP Spoofing   332

Problems Created by Man-in-the-Middle Attacks   333
   802.1x and EAP   *333*
   PEAP   *334*
Denial-of-Service Attacks   334
   Layer 2 Denial-of-Service Attacks Against All Wi-Fi-Based
      Standards   *335*
   WPA Cryptographic Denial-of-Service Attack   *335*
Summary   336

Chapter 16   Actual Attack Tools   337
Attacker Goals   338
Process   338
   Reconnaissance   *338*
Example Scenarios   345
   Planning   *346*
   Collection   *348*
   Analysis   *349*
   Execution   *350*
Other Tools of Interest   351
   Airsnort   *351*
   Airjack   *352*
Summary   353

Chapter 17   Open Source Implementation Example   355
General Architecture Design Guidelines   355
Protecting a Deployed Network   357
   Isolate and Canalize   *357*
   Upgrade Equipment's Firmware to WPA   *357*
   What to Do If You Can't Do Anything   *358*
Planning to Deploy a WPA Network   359
Deploying the Infrastructure   360
   Add a RADIUS Server for IEEE 802.1X Support   *360*
   Use a Public Key Infrastructure for Client Certificates   *360*
   Install Client IEEE 802.1X Supplicant Software   *360*
Practical Example Based on Open Source Projects   361
   Server Infrastucture   *361*
   Building an Open Source Access Point   *374*
   Making It All Work   *376*
Summary   383

Acknowledgments   384

References and More Information   384

Appendixes   385

Appendix A   Overview of the AES Block Cipher   387

Finite Field Arithmetic   388
   Addition   389
   Subtraction   390
   Multiplication   390
   Division   391
   Galois Field GF()   392
   Conclusion   397

Steps in the AES Encryption Process   398
   Round Keys   399
   Computing the Rounds   401
   Decryption   403
   Summary of AES   405

Appendix B   Example Message Modification   407

Appendix C   Verifying the Integrity of Downloaded Files   411

Checking the MD5 Digest   411
Checking the GPG Signature   412

Acronyms   417

References   421

Index   425

Preface

Why This Book Now?

Ask anyone with a computer whether they want to be protected against strangers reading their data or planting viruses. Not really worth the effort, is it? *Everyone* wants this type of protection. However, most Wi-Fi wireless LANs operating in 2003 have no effective security. In fact, so many Wi-Fi LANs operate without security that an entire new hobby, "war driving," has sprung up in which folks drive around detecting and connecting to unsuspecting networks for fun. There are Web sites that publish the location and details of unprotected networks that are found—there are bound to be some near you! This problem is the result of people being unaware of the danger, but you are different, right?

The fact that you are reading this preface means that you are aware of the need to take active steps to implement security. Already, you may have implemented some security approach, perhaps as recommended by the supplier of the equipment you installed. Would that this were enough. The horrible truth is that the security systems shipped with Wi-Fi systems over the period from 1999 to 2002 are completely inadequate, some would say completely broken. Any computer-literate person can now download from the Internet tools that will attack and break into the first-generation Wi-Fi systems.

This book will show you how to tip the balance back in your favor—how to establish real security within your Wi-Fi LAN. It is not just about configuring your computer correctly or choosing good passwords, although these things *are* important. There are many books that focus on "parameter setting." What we describe in this book is a whole new approach to wireless LAN security enabled by the recent development of new core technology for Wi-Fi. The new developments achieve what no amount of reconfiguration can do: they solve the problem at the source. In this book we show how the new approaches work and how they should be applied to maximum effect. Whether you are a system administrator or an advanced home user, this book will open your eyes to current weaknesses and practical, implementable solutions.

To Wi-Fi or Not to Wi-Fi

For many years, Wi-Fi or IEEE 802.11 wireless LANs were considered an interesting technology but not mainstream. This has changed. Now ordinary people and companies, not just technology addicts and experimenters in IT departments, see the practical benefits of this technology. There are two categories of users: business and home. Corporations set up Wi-Fi LANs to allow rapid network deployment, to reduce the cost of installing wiring, and to give workers more flexibility in where and when they work. Home users also want to avoid installing wiring and like the ability to use a laptop on the couch or in a comfy chair outside.

System administrators have a big problem when it comes to Wi-Fi LANs. On the one hand they recognize the benefits of wireless both for their own configuration management and for users. On the other hand, they must not deploy anything that will be a serious security threat. We say "serious" because there is always some security risk in any technology deployment. The only truly secure network is no network. So system administrators have to choose between banning Wi-Fi networks or figuring out how to obtain the needed level of security. Experienced system administrators recognize that any new system component brings both benefits and risks. The problem with Wi-Fi up to now has been how to evaluate the risk.

The Cavalry Is Here

In 2001 those few who deployed security often relied on the original Wi-Fi security method, called WEP. Regrettably, and quite suddenly, it was discovered that WEP had major security flaws and, while arguably better than nothing, customers were left without effective protection. The result, in 2002, was an unparalleled effort on the part of the industry to devise a replacement for WEP, something that would be impregnable, but which could be used to upgrade the existing installed systems. In 2003 we see the results of this effort being deployed.

The new solutions for Wi-Fi security are being delivered in two installments. The first installment is called Wi-Fi Protected Access (WPA), announced by the Wi-Fi Alliance at the end of 2002. WPA has been specifically designed to allow software upgrade of most existing Wi-Fi systems. It repairs all the security weaknesses found in older Wi-Fi systems and has been developed to provide system administrators with a solution to the security dilemma.

In time WPA will be incorporated into a new version of the IEEE 802.11 standard (IEEE 802.11i) that is incomplete at the time of writing. This will provide a flexible and extremely secure solution for all future products. WPA offers levels of security much higher than previously available. The failure of WEP was a sharp wake-up call for the industry and the prevailing mood during 2002 was "we will never let this happen again." As a result, the best experts have participated in creating the new solution and the results have been reviewed worldwide prior to completion.

Naturally, change brings questions:

"Should I implement WPA now rather than wait for IEEE 802.11i?"
"What do I do with my existing WEP equipment/Can I upgrade it?"
"Is it now safe to put Wi-Fi inside the firewall?"

These are the types of questions that this book answers. We could answer them right here: "yes," "yes," "yes," but our goal in writing is to ensure that you understand enough about the mechanics to answer these questions for yourself.

In this book we look at security issues, protocols, and applications. An overview covers all the important protocols from IEEE 802.11 and IEEE 802.1X through to authentication protocols such as RADIUS and EAP. We cover the security protocols of WPA and IEEE 802.11i in detail. We also look at the real-world tools that have been used to attack Wi-Fi systems and you will learn why these will no longer be a threat.

Audience

This book is written principally for system administrators but will also be useful to technically oriented home users and design engineers. It focuses on why the new Wi-Fi security methods are secure and how they work. You will finish with an understanding of Wi-Fi security so you will know what you are doing, and why. The book does not flood you with pages of installation and configuration instructions for specific vendor equipment, as that information changes frequently and becomes obsolete. You should use this book alongside vendor documentation to create customized security solutions.

System administrators have been badly burned in the past by assurances that Wi-Fi LANs had effective built in security, assurances that did not hold true over time. We feel that administrators will not want to take at face value statements like "the new WPA and IEEE 802.11i methods are completely secure." They should be able to see for themselves how the security methods are implemented and understand for themselves why the types of weakness that existed previously have been overcome. Only when this trust is reestablished can administrators continue deployment in comfort. This book attempts to provide all the information needed for this understanding.

If you are a design engineer in any networking field, wireless or otherwise, you will find this book relevant. The security technologies incorporated into WPA and IEEE 802.11i are the state of the art for data networking, and it is much easier to learn and understand technology when it is described in the context of a real system. It seems likely that some of the techniques incorporated into the wireless LAN area will also be applied to wired LANs in the future.

If you are just generally interested in the area, you will find lots of material describing the approach to security that is needed to provide a robust defense. You may choose to skip some of the chapters that describe the protocol and you will probably be surprised to see the real examples of hacking tools presented in the later chapters.

We assume that you have a reasonable understanding of how computer networks operate. You don't need to be an expert, especially to understand the first part of the book, but we presume you know what a Wi-Fi access point does and how it is connected to the rest of the network. We don't explain terms like Ethernet or TCP/IP in detail. There is a primer on IEEE 802.11 if you are not familiar with the protocol used to communicate over the air.

Organization

This book is organized into three parts. Roughly speaking, these parts describe:

- Things you should know about security in general
- How both the old and new methods of security work in Wi-Fi networks
- Real-world issues and examples of attack tools that have been (and continue to be) used

In Part I, "What Everyone Should Know," we review issues that everybody should know about security. Some of these issues are commonsense, but you may not have thought about them. If you are already a security expert and exploring how security works for Wi-Fi, consider skimming this material because many of the principles will be familiar.

Part II, "The Design of Wi-Fi Security," starts with a primer on IEEE 802.11 that runs through the basics of Wi-Fi systems communication. It describes the types of messages that are exchanged, usually hidden from the end user, and explains how a portable device like a laptop can find, select, and connect to an access point. The primer contains a moderate, but hopefully not oppressive, amount of detail. You need to understand the messages being sent between the Wi-Fi components to appreciate the security risks.

After the primer, the book delves into the security protocols for Wi-Fi. It describes the original Wi-Fi security approach, WEP, and explains why this method is no longer considered secure. It then covers the new approaches of Wi-Fi Protected Access (WPA) and IEEE 802.11i Robust Security Networks. Both the new methods share a common approach and are scalable from small networks of a few devices up to international corporations. The solution involves many pieces assembled in layers. This makes the approach appear complicated but, if you take one layer at a time, you can understand each part separately.

Part III, "Wi-Fi Security in the Real World," returns to practical issues. We start off with a review of security in hotspots or public access networks. Such network access is becoming increasingly popular in Internet cafes and airports; and hotspots bring their own special security risks. We then look at some of the tools available on the Web that anyone can download for attacking wireless LANs. Our philosophy here is that it is only by sitting in the cockpit of the enemy's plane that you can understand the threat it poses. Finally we make recommendations about practical actions for designing a secure network and look at an open source project that has been established to set up and test the security approaches that you will need to deploy.

We have not focused on specific vendor products. In the end each vendor will package the new security approaches in its own way. They will hide the complexity behind graphical user interfaces and try to simplify the installation and maintenance as much as possible. All this can make life easy for you if you are deploying the equipment. However, while the work required to install systems can be boiled down, we believe that the understanding of what is going on should be sharpened up. Why? Because at the end of the day, *you're* the one that gets hurt by attacks, not the vendor.

There is no "neighborhood watch" scheme for network security. The administrator or owner of the equipment must be aware of the risks and be proactive in response. Of course most people can't afford, and don't want, to spend all their time working on security issues. We all welcome shortcuts from vendors that simplify or set up the systems. However, remember that salespeople are optimists, but security people must be pessimists.

Our advice to you is simple: Be informed. Take advantage of vendor tools to simplify installation and management but understand what they are doing. Know enough to decide what is best for you and to tweak under the hood when you think it is necessary. Make better purchasing decisions and sleep well at night. Helping you meet these goals is the purpose of this book.

Disclaimer

Readers should be aware that some of the standards described in this book are still under development and may have changed by the time this book is published. The information in this book is intended to be descriptive and should not be relied upon for implementation as a substitute for the published industry standards.

Acknowledgments

Many people helped in the creation of this book. The authors wish to thank the major reviewers: Simon Black, Robert Bruen, Victor Garza, John Viega, and Dan Seth Wallach for their attention to detail and helpful input. In specific areas we greatly appreciated the insight and comments of Simon Blake-Wilson (authentication), Russ Housley (TKIP and CCMP), Nancy Cam-Winget (key hierarchy), Bernard Aboba (access control), Henry Haverinen (public access), and Mike van Opstal and Adam Sulmicki (configuration issues).

We are grateful for the cheerful but persistent support of our commissioning editor Jessica Goldstein and the work of the Addison-Wesley production team, Elizabeth Ryan, Elizabeth Collins, Maria Coughlin, and Rob Mauhar.

We also wish to acknowledge the work of IEEE 802.11 Task Group 'i' members in creating the security solutions that we have been able to document.

Finally, Jon would like to acknowledge his wife Margaret for her quiet but strong support, and Bill would like to thank his family for their understanding and support while completing this book.

Jon Edney, 2003
www.wifi-security.co.uk

William A. Arbaugh, 2003
Department of Computer Science
University of Maryland, College Park

Part I

What Everyone Should Know

Chapter 1

Introduction

Setting the Scene

Broadcast radio and, later, broadcast TV have defined wireless for two generations. The ability for radio waves and TV signals to go anywhere and be heard and seen by anyone has provided huge benefits to the general public since the early twentieth century. If you are the *receiver* this broadcast capability is very attractive, but sometimes for the *sender* these broadcast qualities can be a major disadvantage.

The military were the first to address the disadvantage of being heard by everyone. To protect communications over radio, the military adapted secret codes that had for many years been used to protect written messages. Techniques such as spread spectrum transmission were invented to try to prevent unwanted reception. Catalyzed by the need to protect wireless communication during the Cold War (1950 to 1980), huge advances were made in secure communications, but the general public did not receive any direct benefits from this work.

Because wireless technology has advanced and dropped in price, now almost everyone uses both radio receivers *and* transmitters—in mobile phones, cordless phones, Wi-Fi LANs, and a host of other equipment. However, along with this proliferation in use, over the past few years millions of people in industry and at home have had to face up to a basic conflict. They want the wireless advantage, "receive anywhere," without the wireless feature of "send to everyone."

This book specifically addresses Wi-Fi security. Wi-Fi is the most popular wireless method for networking computers, and people use it widely both in corporate locations and in the home. Typically a Wi-Fi "adapter card" is inserted into a computer so data can be sent to other computers or the Internet via a short-range radio link to a Wi-Fi *access point*. It means you can work at your desk or in a conference room, in your home office or in the family room. It provides freedom. Increasingly, Wi-Fi "access zones" in shops or hotels also provide Internet access to people "on the road."

Wi-Fi is not the only wireless technology available. For short-range communications Bluetooth or HomeRF[1] can be used. Cellular modems can also be used if a low connection speed is acceptable. However, Wi-Fi provides simple wireless broadband access and has become the market leader.

"Wi-Fi" is a brand name coined by the Wi-Fi Alliance. The purpose of the brand is to identify products that have been tested to ensure interoperability between vendors. Wi-Fi products include plug-in adapter cards, network adapters connected by USB, access points, and integrated devices such as personal digital assistants (PDAs) or even cellular phones. The Wi-Fi Alliance has established a testing program that operates all products bearing the logo in conjunction with a range of products from other vendors. As a result, customers can be confident that products will work outside the store. Wi-Fi products must be designed using an industry standard, known as IEEE 802.11.[2] There are various subgroups within IEEE 802.11, and each one is assigned a letter. For example, IEEE 802.11b is the standard on which many Wi-Fi systems are based today.

You may have used Wi-Fi systems already. Perhaps you have become addicted to the convenience of working wherever suits you best, but you are wondering how to maintain the privacy of your information and you may have tried some of the security features built into your Wi-Fi system. Because you are reading this book, you are probably still concerned about the level of protection you have. You are right to be concerned. As you read through this book, you will realize that the tools provided with most Wi-Fi systems to date are not adequate to protect you. Although some of your data might not be important enough to attract any serious attack, the availability of downloadable attack tools means that even the kid next door might be able to get at your data. Our goal is to not only guide you to a secure solution but also to ensure that you get a good understanding of the problems of security and how they are solved.

---

1. HomeRF was a market competitor during 2000–2001 but lost out to the more successful Wi-Fi technology.

2. The IEEE (Eye-triple-E) is a nonprofit, technical professional association of more than 377,000 members in 150 countries. The full name is the Institute of Electrical and Electronics Engineers, Inc., although the organization is most popularly known and referred to by its acronym.

Roadmap to the Book

We once took a tour of a well-known brewery in St. Louis, Missouri. We mention this not just because we enjoyed it, but because the tour, like this book, was divided into three parts. In the first part of our tour we were informed about the issues of beer—the difficulties of producing good flavor and the importance of good ingredients. In the second part we walked the factory floor and looked at the machinery, the tanks, and pipes involved in the production process. Finally, we met the real thing as we were given the opportunity to drink the product.

In a similar way the three parts of this book address the theory, implementations, and reality concerning Wi-Fi security. If you are not interested in the mechanics, you can skip the finer details. Likewise, you may be comfortable with the theory and want to focus on how it is put into practice. Either way, you do not have to read the book from cover to cover to realize its benefits.

Part I examines the security problem in general. Initially we look at the general principles on which security is built and then specifically at why Wi-Fi and other wireless LAN technologies are vulnerable to attack. We discuss where attacks might come from and the types of people who might carry them out. Finally we look at the types of tools that attackers use to break into systems. This section of the book is not highly technical, but it should help you understand how vulnerable a Wi-Fi system can be.

In Part II we head to the factory floor to look at the machinery that can protect you. In the overview of how Wi-Fi systems work, we do not discuss such issues as how to install the software drivers or how to plug in the USB connector. Instead, we go right into the IEEE 802.11 protocol to look at the messages being transmitted between systems. It is at this level that the attack tools work, and it is only at this level that you can get an understanding of how the security defenses work. The original IEEE 802.11 standard did provide a security method called "WEP." Many people relied on WEP for protection and were alarmed to discover that it was not effective. Part II includes a chapter that details how WEP works and why it was broken. Look here for a useful lesson in understanding security.

The remainder of Part II describes the security technologies that are being introduced to provide real protection. There are many pieces to the picture, and successive chapters deal with the solutions from the lowest layers up. You may have seen jargon words and acronyms used in relation to Wi-Fi security. You will find them explained here.

Part III moves to real implementation issues. We look at the special requirement of public access networks such as hotspot zones. We review attacks that have been performed against Wi-Fi systems and analyze how they worked. We let you sit in the attacker's seat and, if you wish, try out some of the attack tools yourself. This is a good way to test whether you can break into your own system. Finally, we look at an open source implementation of wireless LAN security. We do not provide step-by-step guides to installing particular brands of equipment. When you understand how all the pieces fit together, you will be much better positioned to understand and successfully follow the installation instructions that come with the products you purchase.

Notes on the Book

We describe many techniques for attacking Wi-Fi systems and even provide step-by-step instructions on how to use attack tools. Some people are uncomfortable with this approach, but we reject the argument that it assists people who have bad intent. Those people will find out what they need to know one way or another. It is the honest people who will be left in the dark unless these details are exposed. Unless you are familiar with your enemies' weapons, you cannot set up a proper defense.

Also, there is an emotive debate about the word "hacker." This word was originally coined to describe honest, hardworking, and very inventive programmers. It is still used with this meaning by some in the industry, who prefer the word "cracker" to describe security attackers. The general public, however, uses the word "hacker" to mean a person who attacks computers with malicious intent. We use the word "hacker" in this sense, and we apologize for any irritation this causes.

Finally, to avoid confusion, we'd like to clear up the relationships among the terms Wi-Fi, wireless LAN, and IEEE 802.11.

- **Wireless LAN** is a general term used for short-range, high-speed radio networks. Wi-Fi is one kind of wireless LAN.
- **IEEE 802.11** is the formal technical standard that defines how Wi-Fi systems operate.
- **Wi-Fi** is the industry standard for products based on IEEE 802.11 as defined by the Wi-Fi Alliance. Wi-Fi products are tested for compatibility among different manufacturers.

Broadly speaking, IEEE 802.11 and Wi-Fi refer to the same thing, but some parts of the IEEE 802.11 standard are not implemented by Wi-Fi systems and, conversely, some extensions are added. If you have any doubts, substitute "Wi-Fi" every time you see "wireless LAN" or "IEEE 802.11."

2 Chapter

Security Principles

This chapter is a guide to security thinking. Although it ends with a section defining common terms, it is not intended to be a primer on cryptography. Rather it reviews the assumptions that people make when setting up networks and generally in communication. We see how it is necessary to challenge assumptions to identify weaknesses and move toward a secure environment.

What Is Security?

The word **security** can mean different things when taken in different contexts. For instance, we talk about security in relation to national policy, personal safety, financial risk, and privacy of communication. We even use the word to describe our state of emotions. So what is the common thread that links these definitions? Why do we use the same word to describe protection from muggers and protection from hackers?

We propose to define security in the context of two groups: "the good guys" and the "bad guys." It doesn't matter if we are talking about people, robots, or computers; in our definition, if there are no "bad guys," you are secure by default. Imagine a perfect world with no crime—there would be no need for a police force. Security tries to create such a perfect world, not globally but in a controlled space; it tries to create a bubble within which there are no "bad guys" at a given time. National security performs this role for a country, personal security for the living space of an individual, and emotional security for the confines of a person's mind. If the security is implemented successfully, the entity being secured is immune from the influence of the "bad guys." It is as though the bad guys don't exist.

As we look at Wi-Fi security, keep this goal in mind: Make it as though the bad guys don't exist. It is dangerous to focus on only one mechanism of security, such as data encryption, or to concentrate on defending against a certain type of attack. Also, it is wrong to ignore security weaknesses just because they have low consequences. Suppose a virus succeeds in getting into your computer, but it does no damage. Would we say security hasn't been breached because no damage was done? No, because although there is no consequence, we still have a security breach. In the same way, solutions for Wi-Fi LAN security should prevent *any* sort of interference with, or monitoring of, your actions. This is the ultimate goal of security.

With the new Wi-Fi security measures covered in this book, we can come close to this ultimate security goal. There is only one thing we cannot achieve because we are using wireless. Someone can prevent your communications by transmitting a jamming signal; in other words, the bad guys will still be able to demonstrate their presence by blocking communication. But if we design our security protocols correctly, and install them correctly, that is *all* they can do.

Good Security Thinking

Rather than dive straight into the methods for implementing network security, let's take a high-level look at six principles of security thinking. You won't find these principles in a book such as *How to Make Friends and Influence People;* they are inevitably based on a philosophy of mistrust.

1. Don't talk to anyone you don't know.
2. Accept nothing without a guarantee.
3. Treat everyone as an enemy until proved otherwise.
4. Don't trust your friends for long.
5. Use well-tried solutions.
6. Watch the ground you are standing on for cracks.

The sixth principle is a bit cryptic. The "ground" in this context refers to the pile of assumptions we all stand on. As you will see shortly, this sixth principle is the real danger zone in security and one of the most fruitful for the enemy.

1. Don't Talk to Anyone You Don't Know

In the context of security, this means you must be 100% certain about the identity of a device or person before you communicate. Security gurus point out that it is impossible to be 100% certain of anything, but it is the job of security designers to bring you as close to 100% as you need.

To understand this principle even better, consider this analogy. Imagine you are at a wild party. You are strapped to a chair in the middle of the room and blindfolded. Nobody touches you and your nose is covered so you can't smell peoples' perfume. Well, we never get invited to these sorts of parties anyway; but if you did, you would know what it feels like to be a Wi-Fi LAN.

In this scenario, you can listen and you can speak, but you have no other means to identify the people in the room. A simpler (albeit more boring) analogy is a telephone conference call. In ordinary phone conversations, during which we can hear but not see the other person on the phone, we constantly prove to ourselves that the other person *is* who we think he *is*. In most cases, we do this subconsciously. Initially we assume the caller is who he says he is; we accept his identity as stated. However, before we open our communications channels, we test that identity. If we know the caller, we recognize the voice and we go straight to open mode. If we don't, we cautiously open up as we hear information that is consistent with the person's stated identity. Throughout the call, we continue to monitor and are alert to comments that sound strange or out of context.

Conference calls are difficult because more people are involved and you need to constantly identify who is talking. Imagine that somebody makes a comment that you don't quite hear and you say, "Could you repeat that?" The comment is repeated, but can you be sure the same person repeated it, or that what was repeated is the same as the original comment?

The only reliable solution to this quandary is to require that the identities of all the call participants be proven without a doubt for every sentence they speak.

For a Wi-Fi LAN, it is not enough to verify the identity of the other party. A Wi-Fi LAN must also verify that every message really came from that party.[1] A simple method to authenticate someone is to require that they know a secret password or key. This can be used at the start of communication to establish identity, and then the same secret key can be incorporated into each message to ensure the message's authenticity. The idea is that, even if enemies are impersonating valid network addresses and other information, they cannot substitute rogue messages for authentic ones because they don't know the secret key, which must be incorporated into every message. This approach was the basis of the original IEEE 802.11/Wi-Fi Security protocol called WEP; but, as we will see later, it was too simple to be secure in the long run.

---

1. A variation on this theme is when you want to be sure a group of messages all came from the same sender, even though you don't know the identity of the sender.

2. Accept Nothing Without a Guarantee

Like "security," the word "guarantee" means different things to different people (for instance, try taking your used car back to the dealer when things go wrong). In the context of network security, "guarantee" means a *guarantee of authenticity*. In other words, it is proof that the message has not been changed.

You know the sender must prove his identity before you accept his message, but you also need to be sure that what you receive is the message the sender intended to send and that the message has not been modified, delayed, or even replaced with a new message.

At first this seems like a small point and one that is essentially the same as proving the identity of the sender. After all, if the message has been altered, then surely the enemy must have intercepted and resent it.

Consider the following.

1. A friend sends a valid message to you.

2. An enemy intercepts the message before you receive it, modifies some bits, and then sends it on to you.

3. You receive the message and check the sender's identity; but because the enemy sent it last, you can detect the interception, right?

Well, no…there are two flaws in that conclusion, as shown in Figure 2.1. The first is that it assumes it is possible to know who sent you the message. Remember the onus is on the sender to provide proof for the receiver to check. In a wireless environment, we cannot expect the receiver to have a magic method of knowing who sent the message other than by reading its contents. Therefore, if an enemy

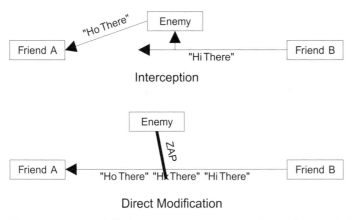

Figure 2.1   Modified Message Appears to Come from a Friend

forwards an identical copy of a message sent by a friend, how can the receiver possibly know that it has been handled in transit? Therefore, you cannot detect that a message has been handled simply by looking at it.

The second flaw is one of those hidden assumptions. We have *assumed* it is necessary for the enemy to receive and then resend the message. However, in a wireless environment, the enemy might discover a way to modify the message while the friend is transmitting it. Today, we don't know any way to do that. But you could imagine that a carefully timed burst of radio transmission from the enemy, colliding with the friendly transmission, might cause the receiver to interpret a bit to have a different value, even though the rest of the transmission came from the friend. In this case the enemy has tampered with a message without retransmitting it at all.

In practice many security protocols use a method that provides both identity proof and tamper-resistant packaging in the same algorithm. However, the rule still applies: Accept nothing without a guarantee.

3. Treat Everyone as an Enemy until Proved Otherwise

A few years ago a story circulated about a scam involving automatic teller machines (ATMs) (Neumann, 2001). We have since heard several versions of the story, so it might be urban myth, but it's interesting nonetheless. Someone obtained an old ATM that had been taken out of service. The ATM was complete and still had its bank logo attached. This person installed the ATM in a small trailer, ran it off a generator, and parked it in a busy downtown area. Shoppers assumed the bank was being proactive by introducing mobile ATMs and went to withdraw cash. The machine displayed an error message saying it was empty of cash, but it recorded the customers' ATM card information and personal identification numbers (PINs). Each day, the criminal made copies of all the ATM cards used and withdrew the maximum allowed amount from the real bank for every card, each day, until the scam was discovered and the cards were disabled. This scam succeeded because the customers assumed only the real bank would set up an ATM. The ATM cards did not have the capability to check the machine's authenticity either.[2]

This example illustrates the importance of not giving information to anyone until that person has proved identity. Arguably the customers in this example followed this rule, but their standard of proof was too low—they trusted the bank sign on the ATM!

---

2. Modern smart card devices can check that they are inserted into a valid machine.

This rule is important in Wi-Fi wireless LAN applications. In a wired LAN, for example, you have a pretty good idea where you are connected because you plug the cable into a hole in the wall, which either you or an IT department maintain. Assuming you keep your wiring closet locked, you should be safe. However, by design, Wi-Fi LANs can search the airwaves looking for networks to join. Access points advertise their availability by transmitting beacon frames with their identity. It is, of course, trivial for an enemy to start up an access point from a van and falsely advertise that he is part of your network in the hope of fooling a few WLAN cards into connecting. Later we will see how the new Wi-Fi security protocols work to ensure that you are not caught in this trap.

4. Don't Trust Your Friends for Long

"Make new friends but keep the old...." What does it mean to "keep" a friend? The word "keep" implies an active process, a process of *affirmation*. Suppose one day you are walking down the street and you meet up with your best friend from high school. This is a nice surprise because you had lost contact and you hadn't seen this person for 10 years. You grew up with this friend and shared all your secrets. After reminiscing for a while, you learn things are not going well and you hear the dreaded words, "Can you lend me some money? I absolutely promise I'll pay you back." Why do you feel uncomfortable? Ten years ago you might have forked over the money in complete confidence. Why not now? You have not reaffirmed the friendship; you don't really know who this person is anymore. You would have to take time to reestablish trust before you were comfortable again.

Applying this analogy to Wi-Fi security, friends are those devices you can communicate with and enemies are everyone else. "Friends" in a Wi-Fi LAN can be identified because they possess tokens such as a secret key that can be verified. Such tokens, whether they are keys, certificates, or passwords, need to have a limited life. You should keep reaffirming the relationship by renewing the tokens. Failure to take this step can result in unpleasant surprises.

There is a difference between policy and protocol. In simple terms, the security protocol is designed to implement the security policy. You are going to decide for your organization which people are "friends." You are also going to decide when those friends can access the network and, for multisite corporations, where they are allowed access. All these issues are part of security policy. It is then the job of the security protocol, in conjunction with hardware and software, to ensure that no one can breach the policy. For example, enemies should never get access.

In the Wi-Fi LAN context, a friend is usually a person or a computer. If you are talking to some dedicated equipment, such as a server or a network gateway, you need to establish that the equipment is considered a friend in your security policy. However, in the case of laptop or desktop computers, it might not be enough to identify the equipment. The laptop might have been stolen or left unattended. In these cases, you need to be sure the person using the computer is also legitimate. Memorizing a password is the most common way to do this.

Normally, well at least in theory, people who work for your company are friends and it is acceptable to communicate with them. In larger companies the notion of "friend" can be divided down to departments or projects. Even when you are certain of the other party's identity, you might have to check whether she has left the company or moved off the project.

Corporations have security databases that are constantly updated with the access rights or credentials of all prospective friends. Later we will look at how Wi-Fi LAN security can be linked to those databases. However, accessing such a database often requires a significant investment in time and resources, and in some cases, the database might be temporarily inaccessible.

To reduce overhead, it is common to verify another person's credentials and then assume these credentials are OK for a limited period of time before checking again. The actual amount of time can be set by the security administrator and might vary from a few minutes to a few days.

5. Use Well-Tried Solutions

A security guru will never say that something is "totally secure." So what's the best you can do? How can you ever develop trust in a security protocol?

Part of security psychology involves developing a high level of *mistrust* for anything new. To see how this affects people's attitudes, let's take encryption as an example. The object of encryption is to make the encrypted data look like perfectly random noise. Suppose you take an arbitrary message, pass it through the encryption algorithm, and send it over a communications link. Then repeat the process millions of times, sending the same message over and over but encrypting it each time before sending. If the encryption algorithm is good, every transmission will be different and look totally random. If you could do this with no gaps in the transmission, no amount of analysis on the output stream would reveal any pattern—just white noise.

Now comes the hard part. If you really did convert the message to random white noise, it would not be very useful because neither the friend nor the enemy would be able to decode it. The trick is to make it look like noise to the enemy while enabling the friend to extract the original data. Many algorithms are available for achieving this goal, but how can you tell which ones *really* work? If the message is to be decoded by the friend, it cannot be true noise—somewhere there must be some information that allows the data to be extracted. So how can you be sure an enemy cannot eventually figure out that information and decode the message?

The answer to this question has two parts. The first involves mathematical analysis called cryptanalysis. Cryptanalysis lets you determine how hard it is to break the encryption code by conventional or well-known methods. However, weaknesses can also come from unconventional methods, such as unexpected relationships between computations in the algorithm or implicit hidden assumptions. Therefore, the second part of developing confidence in a new algorithm is the good old "test of time."

There is no shortage of encryption algorithms. Occasionally, very occasionally, an algorithm will be broken—that is, someone figures out how to decode a message without using the computing power of all the computers in the universe. However, this is not the primary motivation for research into new methods. It takes a certain amount of computing power, energy, and memory to perform encryption and decryption. Different types of devices have different capabilities. For example, the computing resources of a modern desktop computer are different from those of a mobile phone. Therefore, much of the research into new methods is directed at tailoring methods to the resources of real devices. There is no problem deploying an unbreakable[3] encryption code if you have limitless computing power and energy, but creating a method that can be run on a battery-powered PDA is a challenge.

The point here is that new methods are still invented from time to time, and the question then arises whether a new method is really secure. Initially, security gurus are likely to be skeptical about the claims of any new algorithm. That is not to say that they lack interest or enthusiasm—it just means they won't give it a seal of approval until the method has a few miles on the odometer.

If you are introducing a new method, you depend heavily on the interest of the world's security experts if you want to get the method accepted widely. First of all, the method has to be publicly available and sufficiently interesting to attract experts' attention. If it is not novel, or if it includes mistakes, your method will get nothing more than a sniff. If you are a credible guru and your method has some good new tricks, the others might walk around and kick the tires. If you are really doing well, several of them will go for a test drive. But before your method can become truly accepted, it needs to be deployed in the real world for several years, hopefully in an application that attracts attacks. When a method is deployed in the public eye, both hackers and legitimate security researchers will receive kudos if they can break the system. For example, when IEEE 802.11 WEP was broken, the story reached national newspapers, and the researchers who discovered the cracks attracted much attention. But, if you survive a few years and no one has broken your method, it can achieve the status of *trusted and mature*. You probably will, too.

---

3. We use "unbreakable" here in the real world sense. Theoretically all encryption algorithms are breakable with enough time and computing power except the Vernam cipher, which uses pure random data, different for every message.

You can see why it is so hard to get new methods accepted and adopted. But you can also see why it is necessary for this process to occur and why security gurus are correct to take a wait-and-see approach. Notice also that it is not enough to invent a great method. Unless the method can attract the interest of the cryptographic research community and be deployed to attract the interests of hackers, it can never really be tested.

So what about the new Wi-Fi security methods? How can we be sure they are safe? It is true that the new security methods for Wi-Fi have not had time in the field. However, the technology used to implement them is based wherever possible on preexisting and well-tried algorithms. It's always tempting for engineers to reinvent the wheel and come up with some grand new scheme of their own. Because of the experience of the security professional involved in the new Wi-Fi approach, this temptation has been resisted. Having said that, some new concepts have been incorporated, and although they have been reviewed around the world, the "newness" risk does still apply.

We will see later how the lack of review by the security research community was one of the factors that led to problems in the original IEEE 802.11 WEP security. By contrast, the new standard has had participation and review from world-renowned experts in the field, and the principles employed, where novel, have been presented at cryptographic conferences to stimulate review.

6. Watch the Ground You Are Standing on for Cracks

Every day, we make countless assumptions. From our earliest days we have learned how to look at situations and decide which ones are safe and which ones are dangerous. Over time we perform many of these skills subconsciously; we learn to trust, and for most of us, that trust is only occasionally misplaced, sometimes painfully.

Humans automatically transfer safe assumptions from conscious memory to subconscious behavior. The key word here is *automatically*; that is, people are not aware this transfer happens. In fact, if it didn't happen, we could not function, as our minds would be cluttered with so many checks and questions. However, this essential ability for life is the open door that has been exploited by generations of con men, pickpockets, and tricksters in performing crimes. It is also the starting point for hackers who want to attack your network.

People design software, hardware, and systems. *People* write and evaluate international standards. No matter how sophisticated the design tools, or what computer-aided design software is used, the designers' assumptions still come shining through. Some are valid and some false—and, more dangerously, many are applied subconsciously or implicitly.

Consider a medieval castle. The designers could specify thick walls, deep moats, and strong gates. They could require that gallons of boiling oil be kept ready at all times. But how would the castle folk fare against a modern helicopter cruising overhead, dropping boiling oil on *them*? They would have no defense because the designers unconsciously assumed that attacks would not come from the air. This assumption is a hidden weakness of the castle design.

How is it possible to protect against things that you can't even imagine? How can you see the implicit assumptions and bring them forward for inspection and testing? There is no certain way, but these challenges mold the way of thinking for security experts.

As a result, it can be difficult to have ordinary conversations with security experts. Here is a simple test to determine whether you are talking to a security guru: Ask him to name the security system he considers to be the strongest in the world for sending secret data by any method (wireless, wire, smoke signals, whatever). Then ask the following question, "Would I be secure if I implemented this in my system?" If the answer is "yes," you are *not* talking to a real security guru.

Security gurus never say, "This is completely secure." They make statements like, "Based on the assumption that attackers are limited to computational methods and processor architectures similar to today, it is computationally infeasible to mount a [certain type of attack] and no other types of attack are known to be more effective at this time." Sometimes they are prepared to say that one method is definitely as secure as another method, but the word "definite" doesn't get too many outings in the security expert's vocabulary.

Such hedging doesn't translate well to the glossy front of a product box, where customers simply look for the words "this is secure." The best approach for a customer is to understand the strengths of the security method used and, where possible, the assumptions that were made in the design. If the assumptions are reasonable, the method is well designed, and plenty of people are using it (to ensure future support), the customer can be comfortable.

The challenge for hackers, of course, is to look for the little cracks and crevices that result from hidden assumptions. Unfortunately for the rest of us, this search is an intriguing, fascinating, and motivating challenge for hackers. Some people like to do crossword puzzles, and some people like to play sophisticated problem-solving computer games, often wrapped in a fantastical visual landscape. Hacking is another form of these mind games. When inventing a new virus or a password-cracking program, the hacker is trying to see into the mind of the designer and look for false assumptions that were made subconsciously. For example, a recent virus called "Code Red" (actually a worm) worked by exploiting the fact that when internal memory buffers overflowed in a computer, information was accidentally left in memory in a place that was accessible from outside. The system's designers made the false assumption that buffers do not overflow and that, if they do, the excess buffers are properly thrown away. Almost certainly this was a subconscious assumption; it was false and an attacker found it.

Security Terms

To set up a system in practice, we need to implement the six principles covered in the previous section using mechanisms that tend to be similar from one system to the next. It doesn't really matter whether you are implementing a system to send secret letters by pigeon or a security method for a wireless LAN. Some common processes and terms should be understood. This section briefly describes some of the main terms used in security. Sometimes words in common use have a specific meaning in security. For example, the word "encryption" tends to be used in common speech to refer to an entire security protocol, whereas in security it refers to a single specific process.

- **Threat model**: We need a means to measure whether a security system meets its goals. One way to understand the security goals in a given situation is to make a list of all the types of attack that are known. This "list" is used to create the threat model, which is the basis for designing and evaluating security. Having created the list, we then identify all those threats against which we plan to defend. From a practical standpoint, some of the threats on the list may be too low risk and too expensive to defend against. As an example, the threat model for protecting wired Ethernet LANs does not (usually) include the threat of being monitored via the tiny radiations coming from the wires. By contrast, unwanted monitoring of radio emissions is central to the threat model of wireless LANs.

- **Security protocol**: Many people use the word "encryption" in a general way to talk about security. You often hear people talking about "sending data over an encrypted link," and so on. This is dangerous because encryption is only one part of the process, albeit a very important part. Real security is provided by a set of processes and procedures that are carefully linked together. This set of procedures and processes is called the security protocol. It is important to realize that even if the most advanced encryption techniques are used, you have no security if they are used together in the wrong way.

- **Keys and passwords**: These terms are often used interchangeably, although there is a slight difference in meaning. Both refer to a piece of information that is intended to be secret to two or more parties. Conventionally, the term **password** is used to refer to keys that are chosen by humans. The term **key** is more often used to describe information generated by a machine that is usually not human-readable. You will often see references to the **length of the key**. For example, the original IEEE 802.11 had "40-bit" keys, whereas most Wi-Fi WEP systems have "128-bit keys." In general, longer keys are more difficult to crack than shorter keys, but not always—it depends on the key entropy (described next).

- **Key entropy**: What is important about passwords and keys is the number of different possible values a key can take. Theoretically, a 40-bit key has 2^{40} or 1,000 billion possible values. However, if we restrict the values that are allowed, the effectiveness of the key goes down. For example, suppose the user enters a 40-bit key as five uppercase letter symbols (assume each letter uses 8 bits, hence 40 bits total). An example of such a password is the string "LASER." Because each symbol is limited to only 26 letters, you can have only 26^5 (or about 12 million) different passwords. By limiting the type of password, you have reduced the number of possible passwords by a factor of 100,000. The number of possible key values determines the strength of the key and is known as the **key entropy**. In our earlier example, the restriction to using uppercase letters has reduced the key entropy (and hence its effectiveness) from 40 bits to 23 bits, even though the key remains 40 bits long. If we restricted ourselves to known words and names, it would be reduced even more.

- **Authentication**: The heart of security is the ability to distinguish the "good guys" from the "bad guys." If you can't be sure whom you are talking to, you can't protect yourself against attack. The term **authentication** is used at two different levels in security protocols, and this sometimes leads to confusion. The first level is user authentication and the second level is message authentication. The objective of user authentication is to prove that the other party with whom you want to communicate is who she says she is. Note that although we talk about "user" here, it could be that the other party is a computer or even a software process running on a server rather than a person. Message authentication has a different objective: to prove that a received message has not been tampered with, delayed, altered, or copied. A message is said to be **authentic** if it passes these tests. Typically, user authentication must be performed to identify the other party, and message authentication is done to ensure that subsequent communications come from that other party and are unaltered.

- **Authorization**: The process of user authentication is difficult to perform correctly. Therefore, it is discussed extensively in this book and in others. You often see statements such as, "When the mobile device is authenticated, the access point allows it to communicate with the network." This is not quite true. We saw a cartoon by Gary Larson recently in which a ghoulish specter was peeking through a partly open front door held by a security chain. The old lady inside was saying, "Ah, but how do I know you really *are* the angel of death?" The message is simple: the fact that you know who someone is (authenticate) doesn't mean you always want to give him access. The decision to "let him in" is called **authorization** and comes after authentication.

- **Encryption**: The process of combining a piece of data and a key to produce random-looking numbers is called **encryption**. It is useful only if a known key can be used to transform the random-looking numbers back to the original data. Note that we have said nothing about LANs, packets, wires, or even time. Encryption is just a computational algorithm of which there are many variants. Encryption algorithms are used to create security protocols.

Summary

In this chapter we looked into the mindset behind security systems design, as well as into the minds of computer attackers and legitimate researchers. Seeing how security gurus think and work is interesting—you don't have to become a guru to install and run a secure system. Home users need basic policy skills to run the network and basic protocol skills to make an informed purchasing choice. Managers of large networks need complex policy arrangements and can benefit from a detailed understanding of the protocols, particularly for problem diagnosis and interfacing to other systems.

The whole field of security related to computing network is huge. We have set the scene in this chapter by looking at the basic assumptions underlying security. The next chapter considers how these apply to wireless and, in particular, Wi-Fi networks. If you wish to study the more general aspects of computer security, these books provide comprehensive general coverage: Bishop (2002) and Pfleeger et al. (2002).

3 Chapter

Why Is Wi-Fi Vulnerable to Attack?

This chapter begins by asking the questions "Who is likely to attack?" and "What motivates them to attack?" By understanding the enemy, you will be better prepared to set up and evaluate defenses. We look at the technical characteristics that make Wi-Fi LANs especially vulnerable and review different system approaches that have been applied to try to provide security.

Changing the Security Model

The question in the title of this chapter seems too obvious to ask. Everyone knows that Wi-Fi LANs use radio waves, those waves propagate all over the place, and therefore anyone can listen in on your communications. So why have a chapter dedicated to this subject? Well, it's worth spending time looking at the effect that this widespread propagation has on conventional security models because this type of uncontrolled propagation creates the problems we need to solve.

In the past, security architectures were often developed on the assumption that the core parts of the network were not physically accessible to the enemy. People inside the building were considered to be friends, and friends were expected to monitor visitors. Attacks were only expected in well-defined places such as the connection to the outside Internet, where firewalls are located. Wi-Fi LANs turn these assumptions on their heads. Using radio propagation is like inviting anyone who passes by, friend or enemy, to come into your facility and plug into an Ethernet jack of his choice. This totally open scenario requires a new way of thinking about LAN security and introduces new challenges. Wi-Fi LANs are vulnerable because they don't work according to the old rules.

Another vulnerability follows from the fact that eavesdropping can lead to breaches of the network. Some people may not care if outsiders read their communications. They may feel they have nothing to hide and they aren't doing anything secret. However, everybody should care if enemies can come into their network and delete information or plant a virus. These two threats cannot actually be separated. If you allow passive listening, you open yourself to active attacks.

With that in mind, this chapter does not only answer the question in the title but also looks at the implications of this vulnerability. Specifically, this chapter considers how a network is organized in the conventional security model and how Wi-Fi conflicts with this organization. It also looks at two ways to adjust the model to include Wi-Fi using VPN and direct wireless connections. To understand these implications, however, it is important to first take a look at the types of people who are likely to try to attack your network, and discuss their motivations for doing so.

What Are the Enemies Like?

The popular media such as television, newspapers, and movies are fond of the word "hacker," which has passed into the English language and probably many others. However, there is no clear definition for what constitutes a hacker. Movies usually represent a hacker either as a nerdy, socially disconnected genius or as a 12-year-old computer wizard—and neither of these descriptions is usually true. In fact there are so many activities that can be described as "hacking" that we could probably all earn the title at some point or other. Still, there are people who specialize in attacking computer security in sophisticated ways, and they certainly merit the title of hacker. It is useful in building our defenses to try to understand the motivations of those enemies who are prepared to dedicate resources to attacks.

Hackers fall into categories of threat that you can draw like a pyramid. At the bottom are people, sometimes called "script kiddies," who have relatively weak tools. As you move up toward the top of the pyramid, the number of attackers decreases quickly but their expertise and the complexity of their tools increase. This middle section is where you would start to see cryptographic attack tools—that is, tools that seek to break into secure systems rather than just searching for systems where security is turned off. At the top of the pyramid is a small group we describe as ego hackers using the most sophisticated techniques.

Let's start with the casual sorts of privacy violations. If you peek over someone's shoulder on an airplane to read the presentation she is preparing, are you a hacker? IEEE 802.11 committee meetings involve hundreds of people using a huge Wi-Fi LAN. Even here some people forget to enable protection of their laptops. If, in a boring moment, a committee member browses around the network out of curiosity, is that person a hacker?

From the point of view of popular culture, these casual acts do not constitute hacking. But from the point of view of a security system, there is no distinction between casual and dedicated attacks, except in the sophistication of the tools that are used. *All* unwelcome network visitors must be classed as potential enemies regardless of their motivations or skills.

The enemy has choices in where and when to attack. It is the job of security policy to anticipate the possibilities and the job of security protocols to block the attacks. Correctly anticipating all the options is one of the challenges of good security. To use a crude example, there is no point in locking the front door if you leave the windows open.

Almost any attack can be explained by one of these motivations:

- Gaming: A hacker gambles her time and effort in the hope of a payoff through a successful attack. Many sports and games rely on a similar motivation. It is the cyber equivalent to fly-fishing.
- Profit or revenge: The attacker wants to steal information, damage your system because of a grievance, or alter your system to acquire a tangible reward (such as money, stock, or pension rights).
- Ego: The hacker wants to prove, to himself or his peers, that he is clever, tenacious, and brave.

The motivation determines the options the attacker considers. A revenge attacker, for example, may consider blowing up your network server with a bomb, whereas such an approach would be unlikely to provide satisfaction to the ego player.

Gaming Attackers

By far the largest number of attacks come from gaming attackers. We use this term to describe people who have too much time on their hands and enjoy playing a game called "let's see whether we can watch the neighbors without their knowing."

People can stumble into this type of activity almost accidentally by downloading a tool they found on the Web that is designed to compromise security. There are many such programs and they are easy to download, install, and run. Chapter 16 looks at a few examples. Some of these programs simply try to access every Internet (IP) address possible, looking for a response. These programs, called **scanners**, require no technical expertise and can work unattended. You download it, run it, and go to work, school, or bed. The next day you can check to see whether it found anything. These types of programs can sometimes be successful when running on a broadband connection such as cable modem or ADSL.

Performing these simple incursions requires little expense. As with any good game, players can get early, but limited, positive results such as a list of active computers. It's easy to see how these types of tools can be captivating. In most cases the fun wears off, due to lack of success or lack of interesting discoveries or fear of detection. However, for a few people the desire to make progress will become stronger, leading them to look for more powerful tools and other ways to score successes. People who attack you in this way generally don't understand security, but they do know how to run downloaded scripts.

The picture of a fresh-faced teen sliding down the slippery path to a life of obsession and ultimate destruction is, of course, more than a little sensational. But it becomes easier to understand why people get involved in security attacks, and a few really do move into the hard-core categories. Fresh faced or not, these attackers are your enemy when you are setting up network security.

While the gamers are the most numerous, they are easy to block and against. It is easy to mount this class of attack by downloading the appropriate scripts and programs. Our concern here is whether the gaming hackers are likely to attack Wi-Fi LANs. Such attacks require a different type of hardware and a greater investment in time. However, all the elements of "the game" are still there.

Even the simplest security mechanisms provide protection against low-level attacks. But many Wi-Fi LANs are running with *no security at all*. Companies and individuals are often unaware of security risks or assume that eavesdropping is the only risk. They may be concerned about security but procrastinate about taking action—leaving their system in the default unprotected state that it was in when they bought it, regularly thinking, "I must figure out that security configuration stuff sometime." Whatever the reason, there are many unprotected Wi-Fi LANs and it is quite simple to get a laptop computer and a Wi-Fi LAN adapter card and drive around a city or suburb looking for a network to join. You would be surprised how quickly a network can be found.

Even this simple attack requires more effort than running a script on your PC at home. You have to have a laptop and you have to spend time and gas driving around. This fact is enough to discourage a large percentage of the casual attackers. Furthermore, if you have any security (such as WEP) turned on, attackers will probably pass you by in search of an unprotected network. Generally, they only attack a protected network if they think you have something special. If you have broadband Internet access, you are at risk from attackers who want to use you as an Internet jumping-off point. They may be looking for free broadband access. However, there can be a more sinister purpose if the attacker wants to use your link for illegal purposes. In this scenario a person might use your account to download illegal pornography or to coordinate with other criminals or even terrorists. You are likely to be completely unaware of this type of incursion.

In rare cases, hackers who are moving up the "difficulty levels" may consider the security implemented on your system as a challenge for gaming. WEP does have weaknesses that can be exploited by special tools easily downloaded from the Internet (see Chapter 6).

Profit or Revenge Attackers

You are unlikely to suffer an attack for profit or revenge if you are a home user (unless you have a dog that likes to dig up the neighbor's lawn or something similar). In reality, attacking for profit is probably not that common. There have been cases in which credit card databases have been compromised. Stealing credit card information is actually a form of identity theft because the information can be used to make purchases while the thief is pretending to be the cardholder. Such identity thefts can usually be detected, and the culprits run a risk of being caught and sent to jail. However, there may be many more subtle attacks that are undetected. For example, if an attacker could read the financial results of a corporation before they were announced, he might be able to make money by buying or selling shares. This is an ideal attack because, providing his stock transaction is not so huge as to get attention, no one would ever know that an attack had occurred. This is why we used the word "probably" when we said profit attacks are rare. There is no good way to assess how any of these types of attack occur.

The risk of revenge attacks from disgruntled ex-employees or even customers is growing. This can show up as attempts to corrupt a Web site, plant a virus, or delete files. You can see that there is an important distinction between profit and revenge attacks. Profit attacks try to leave no trace. The point of a revenge attack is to be as visible as possible.

Profit or revenge attackers have a specific objective and a particular target, and they are prepared to invest time and money into planning. They are likely to research the best methods, think about weaknesses, and find the right tools for the attack. If you use a Wi-Fi LAN, they will consider it as an avenue for attack.

Doing reconnaissance on Wi-Fi LANs is easy. The attacker drives as close as possible to your building, starts up a laptop, finds out what networks you have running, and identifies the names of the access points. With simple tools, he can find out how many users are operating. He can quickly determine whether you are using Wi-Fi LAN security and whether it is WEP or some other system. If you have no security in operation, he can connect immediately. It may be that even if he gets on your network, you have logon passwords for all the servers; but, as has been mentioned previously, this only increases the level of sophistication of the required tools. If the attacker is smart, he will make several trips and try to remain undetected either until the job is done or until he is ready to inflict the damage.

The fact that these types of attacks can be performed over a period of time allows the enemy to go away and gradually learn more and acquire stronger tools. It is this iterative process, driven by a specific goal, which makes this category of attacker dangerous. If revenge is the goal then, when accomplished, the attacker will probably not repeat. He will have "gotten even" in some dysfunctional way of thinking. Of course, the profit attacker is very likely to repeat if undetected and poses a threat that increases over time. This is one reason why companies need to continuously reevaluate security policy and put effective monitoring in place

One interesting approach to detection of such attacks is a honeypot network.[1] This type of network is actually designed to attract attacks. A honeypot network looks like a conventional network, but it is intentionally weak and not attached to any real data. Your goal is to catch the attacker before he or she recognizes the trap.

To construct a simple honeypot network, set up an access point, attach it to an old computer, and put a load of useless junk data on the computer. Create directories with names like "Accounts" or "Personnel" that are access protected. Give the access point a different network name from that of your real network and site it near the visitors' parking. Leave WEP off or turn it on with a weak password like "admin." Make sure that all your legitimate clients are configured only to use the legitimate access points. Then watch for a wireless client attached to the honeypot access point. Most access points can log when a client connects. You may be able to use a network management program to get an audible alert. This would give you the opportunity to stroll outside to look for a suspicious person with a laptop in his car.

A honeypot network lets you evaluate the likelihood of attacks on your network and the types of attack being made. More advanced honeypot servers can gather information about attackers. If you are interested in retaliating against a serious attacker through law enforcement, you need to gather proof of the attacks and of the identity of the attacker. Some honeypot programs are not servers at all but instead smart software that emulates the behavior of a server to keep the attack going while information is gathered. 00[Sub]7, the Ultimate SubSeven Logging tool by Jeff Capes, for example, is a program that can be run on a home computer and sits on one of the ports most commonly attacked. It logs information when an attack occurs and can notify attackers of the monitoring—which usually scares them away.

Ego Attackers

At the top of the threat pyramid is the ego hacker. Ego hackers come closest to matching the image of hackers in popular culture. They are motivated by the dif-

---

1. For more information, see Lance Spitzner, *Honeypots: Tracking Hackers.* Boston: Addison-Wesley, 2003.

ficulty of the task and by the feeling that they are members of an elite group. They seek contact with other ego hackers and status within that group. Promotion in the group comes from demonstrating successful attacks and distributing inventive new methods. To be successful, a person would need to climb a long learning curve, understanding all the methods of attack and assimilating the weaknesses of existing systems. They would need to understand at a detailed level how the security protocols work on each system they wish to attack. Ultimately their knowledge and capability may put them on a par with legitimate security researchers. A few ego hackers have crossed the border and established legitimate security businesses.

Rather than wait for ego hackers to break into security systems, crypto professionals look for flaws in cryptographic systems and publish them. This is not popular with the companies that sell the equipment. For example, when the attacks on WEP were discovered, many in the industry wanted to avoid the information becoming widely known. However, legitimate security researchers know that they are in a race against the top-level ego hackers. These hackers will uncover any weaknesses that the researchers don't find first.

A more contentious issue is the publishing of hacking tools. For example, the weaknesses of WEP were published and vendors started to react. Then a software tool called AirSnort was made available on the Web (http://airsnort.shmoo.com/), rending WEP security instantly useless. What was the value in releasing such a tool? Supporters argued that ego hackers would have developed such a tool in secret and it was better to develop it in public. Whatever your stance in this debate, AirSnort certainly got everyone's attention. The much-improved Wi-Fi Protected Access (WPA) is the result.

Now we are ready to look at how Wi-Fi security can be incorporated into existing networks. Trying to attach Wi-Fi systems to a network with a conventional security architecture can cause real problems. These systems have very different characteristics from conventional wired hardware.

Traditional Security Architecture

The traditional approach for network security is to divide the network into two zones: **trusted** and **untrusted**. The trusted zone is the area under your physical control, where access is limited by the security guard at the front door (or by your family when at home). There is no need for network security protection within the trusted zone because there are no enemies present. You might have an account on your computer to prevent people from accessing your private files, but you assume that no one will mess with data going across the wires between computers.

By contrast, you regard the untrusted zone as full of enemies. Internet access or even dedicated wired links through the public network are untrusted. Where the untrusted network meets the trusted network, there is typically a firewall to

Figure 3.1   Conventional Security Architecture

prevent all the enemies getting in (see Figure 3.1). The firewall is the electronic equivalent of the security guard (Cheswick et al., 2003).

Difficulties arise when trusted people find themselves in the untrusted zone and want to access their home network. When you are traveling and staying in a hotel, you need a safe way to get back to the trusted zone in your company. One solution is virtual private network (VPN) technology. VPN extends the trusted zone out into the untrusted area through a secure tunnel, as shown in Figure 3.2. Imagine one of the old diving machines in which a diver went down into the water wearing a metal suit and with an umbilical cord bringing down air. The secure tunnel is a bit like that umbilical cord.

VPN uses a security protocol to form a connection, typically between a remote person and the home office. Helped by encryption, this connection is (theoretically) impenetrable to the enemies in the untrusted zone even though it passes right under their noses.

VPN can suffer from deployment issues. VPN software must be installed on the computer of the remote user, and it must be compatible with that of the VPN server. Because interoperability between vendors' products is not assured, you should consider buying the server and the client software from the same company. This type of VPN solution works at the Internet Protocol (IP) level and is not usually built in to network adapter cards such as Ethernet or Wi-Fi LAN PC cards. Also, because the implementation on the remote computer is usually in software, VPN may limit the speeds with which the computers can communicate (although for remote access the speed of the Internet is usually the limitation rather than the speed of the software). VPN is widely used in corporations for remote access and, in these applications, it is very effective (Norris and Pretty, 2000).

The important question is, "How does Wi-Fi LAN fit into this conventional security architecture?" Should it be deployed like the devices in the trusted

Figure 3.2   Remote User in "Trusted Bubble"

zone—connected straight to the network? Or should it be placed behind the fire-wall? Life would be much easier if the answers to these questions were clear. In fact, a Wi-Fi LAN can be deployed either way. Placing wireless LANs outside the firewall means they must connect using VPN—a disadvantage. Connect directly to the network inside the firewall means you have to ensure that the wireless LAN is inherently secure. Although we briefly discuss the first option (via VPN), this book focuses on the second option. A direct connect is more common and it places bigger security demands on the technology. WPA and IEEE 802.11i address this option.

Option 1: Put Wireless LAN in the Untrusted Zone

In some situations the Wi-Fi LAN user is clearly in an untrusted zone. For exam-ple, some airports have installed Wi-Fi wireless LAN coverage in waiting areas or lounges (for more detail, see Chapter 14). If you subscribe to the service, you can connect to the Wi-Fi LAN and have direct high-speed Internet access while wait-ing for your flight. This is a clear example of working in an untrusted zone.

Now think about sitting at your desk in your office. Although *you* are in a trusted zone, your wireless signal may be going down the corridor and out the window. You have to assume that the signal can be picked up outside the building. Therefore, even though you are sitting at your desk, you are operating in an untrusted zone just like an airport. If you have no security on your Wi-Fi LAN and your access points are connected to your internal wired LAN, you have con-verted your entire building's network into an untrusted zone!

With the possible exception of national security headquarters, offices do not have perfect screening. You may decide, therefore, that Wi-Fi LANs are *always* operating in an untrusted zone *regardless* of where you are. In some sense you have created the situation shown in Figure 3.3, wherein the untrusted area extends inside your building.

One response to this situation is to handle Wi-Fi LAN users in the same way that you handle remote users. Make them use VPN as if they were outside the building. Even though a person is sitting at her desk, all the communications from Wi-Fi LAN computers must be encrypted by VPN software before passing over the network. These communications then go to the wireless access point and on to an Ethernet connection that is *outside* the firewall. From there they go through

Figure 3.3 Wireless User Is in Untrusted Zone

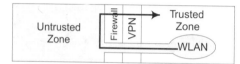

Figure 3.4 Treating a Wi-Fi LAN User Like a Remote User

the firewall and are decoded by the VPN server. Finally, the messages are placed on the trusted wired network and arrive at their destination, which might be the printer on the desk of a Wi-Fi LAN user. Figure 3.4 shows this design. There are several disadvantages with this approach:

- VPN software on the laptop can sometimes be intrusive, slowing down communication and limiting the types of operations that can be performed.
- The VPN server may have limited capacity. Often companies install servers that can handle 20 to 50 users. This is enough for remote users in the field connecting from time to time. However, if you have many internal Wi-Fi LAN users, you need a high-capacity VPN server.
- The access points must be connected to the untrusted side of the firewall. They must have dedicated wiring and cannot share with the internal Ethernet system. If there are multiple access points, you probably need a dedicated patch panel to avoid the possibility that the access point wiring and the internal wiring are connected up by mistake.

These disadvantages make this approach unattractive for many companies as well as impractical for small office and home users. Some companies have proceeded along these lines because they realized that the first generation of Wi-Fi was not sufficiently secure. Most would prefer the second approach, in which the Wi-Fi LAN becomes part of the trusted network, because it is simpler to administer.

Option 2: Make Wi-Fi LAN Trusted

The alternative to treating Wi-Fi LAN as a pariah that can never be trusted is to make the Wi-Fi LAN itself fundamentally impenetrable by enemies. Your goal is to make the LAN so secure that it can be regarded in the same way as physical wiring and treated as part of the trusted zone. Thinking along these lines led to the original security system of IEEE 802.11 being called "WEP," which stands for Wired Equivalent Privacy.

The idea runs something like this: It is very difficult, but not impossible, for an enemy to tap into a wired network in a building. There are various options, such as breaking into the building, bribing a security guard or employee, or using highly sensitive and directional radio receivers to pick up the slight emissions from the Ethernet cable connectors. The point is that it is *not* impossible to breach wired LAN security. So, the theory goes, you can make Wi-Fi LANs as trusted as wired LANs by making it very difficult to decode the wireless signals. You don't need to make it *impossible* to break the wireless security, just *more difficult* than breaking into the wired network because the enemy will always take the simplest route.

This principle that the enemy takes the path of least resistance is reasonable, but you cannot realistically compare the difficulty of bribing a security guard with the difficulty of breaking the Wi-Fi LAN security protocol. More modern thinking concludes that Wi-Fi LAN security must be evaluated on its own merits rather than by comparison to attacks on the wiring plant. The standard of security that has been set for the new generation of Wi-Fi and IEEE 802.11 is very high. It makes the signals look so random that any amount of monitoring by enemies does not provide useful information. It also prevents forgery, tampering, and other attack techniques. As a result, you can considering moving the Wi-Fi LAN back inside the trusted domain.

Once you believe that information being sent by wireless is completely inaccessible to attackers (perhaps more so than information on the wires), you can treat Wi-Fi LAN devices in the same way as regular LAN devices. The access points go right on to the regular internal LAN, and Wi-Fi LAN users who connect to them have the same rights as everybody else. Wi-Fi LAN can still be used in the untrusted zone, when people are passing through a hotel or airport, by employing VPN. WPA allows the old security model to be put back in place, making it much easier to integrate Wi-Fi into everyday networks. The same principle applies at home: you can treat Wi-Fi in the same way as you treat the Ethernet cables running across your floor. No one can get access to them but you.

Danger of Passive Monitoring

Earlier we mentioned the link between passive monitoring and active attacks. Everybody is subject to eavesdropping. People overhear conversations or peek over shoulders at laptops on planes. Business users should be sensitive to this issue and take steps with confidential information. However, there is usually a clear distinction between eavesdropping and interfering. You might not notice someone peeking at your laptop screen and you might not care if the information were not confidential. You would certainly notice if someone leaned across and typed on your keyboard.

The same is not true for an unsecured Wi-Fi LAN. Unless security is in place, you may not be able to detect when you are being attacked. The simplest form of attack is a connection to an unprotected access point. Access points send out wireless messages advertising themselves to anyone in range. If security is turned off, the enemy can request a connection just as an authorized user would. Magazine reports have written about driving around a city with a laptop and connecting directly into companies' unprotected wireless LANs (Hopper, 2002). This has become known as "war driving" and has been publicized by, among others, Pete Shipley in California. He created software, linked to a GPS receiver, that automatically logs the position of vulnerable networks (Poulsen, 2001). There is even a term "warchalking" for the practice of marking on the sidewalk where access to a Wi-Fi network has been detected.

The prospect of strangers connecting to your LAN is frightening, but surely the network operating system can protect you? Attackers can't log on to the server because it requires a username and password—right? Well, yes and no. Attackers can't log on to the server; but, if they are clever, they don't need to. They can monitor the Wi-Fi LAN to find an existing user who has already logged on, and then they imitate that user's transmissions. If the attacker copies the user's network address information, the server may not realize that it is talking to an enemy and may allow all the same access rights as the valid user has.

These examples show just how vulnerable a Wi-Fi LAN can be unless security is put in place. Even if you don't care about eavesdropping and you use your home computer only for browsing the Web, don't assume that you are safe without activating security measures. If the enemy can see you, he can always touch you.

Summary

This chapter outlines why Wi-Fi networks are vulnerable to attack and what types of attackers you might encounter. By understanding the motivations and resources of attackers, you can establish your policy on defense. Some people would argue that your policy should always be "go for the maximum defensive measures and never compromise on security." But this is too simplistic. Remember, the ultimate wireless security comes by not using Wi-Fi LAN at all! In the same way, ultimate road safety comes by staying at home. However, practical managers recognize that there are real benefits to Wi-Fi LANs and an effective policy balances risk and utility.

The second half of this chapter defines two strategies for managing security risk. One is to treat all wireless connections as if they were outside the firewall— that is, completely untrusted. This is an expensive approach in terms of equipment and performance, but one that fits well into existing security architectures. The second approach is to treat the Wi-Fi LAN as a trusted component of the network. This requires confidence in the integrity of the Wi-Fi security method. The rest of this book focuses on showing how the second scenario can be used and why the security level is now sufficient to justify your trust.

4 Chapter

Different Types of Attack

Chapter 4 provides an overview of the different types of attack that a Wi-Fi LAN must defend against. Some types of attack are quite obvious, but many are subtle and done in unexpected ways. These subtle attacks are the most dangerous because they exploit our assumptions about where the vulnerabilities lie. We focus on attack concepts. Later, in Chapter 15, we provide a much more detailed and technical analysis for certain known attacks that have been successful against early Wi-Fi systems.

As we build our defenses, it is important to understand the types of attack we may encounter. The technical approach of an attack can vary from crude to sophisticated, but the fact that an attack is crude doesn't make it ineffective. For example, if someone steals your laptop while it is logged onto the network, they have made a successful, albeit crude and detectable, security attack. More sophisticated methods of attack, however, allow an attacker to gain access without being detected—and these methods are more dangerous. Detecting a security breach is a close second in importance to preventing the breach. For example, if a security breach were detected immediately and appropriate responses taken, service might be disrupted but the damage might be considerably reduced. By contrast, if an intruder were allowed to break in multiple times over an extended period, the consequences could be catastrophic. The smarter the attacker is, the more careful they will be to avoid detection.

Classification of Attacks

Attacks can be classified into four broad categories: snooping, modification, masquerading, and denial of service. In practice, an attack may employ several of these approaches. Almost all attacks start with snooping, for example.

> More formally, attack methods are classified as "passive" and "active." Passive attacks include eavesdropping. Active attacks are subdivided into "forgery," "message modification," and "denial of service." We use a simpler list of four categories for use in the explanations here.

Snooping,[1] as the name suggests, is simply accessing private information. This information could be used for an advantage, such as getting company secrets to help your own business or stock purchase decisions. It could also be used for active assaults such as blackmail. Encryption can be used to make snooping difficult. The attacker is required either to know the secret encryption key or to use some clever technique to recover the encrypted data.

Modifications to data can be achieved in some nonobvious ways. When thinking about modification attacks, most people consider an attacker modifying e-mails with malicious content or changing the numbers in an electronic bank transfer. While such high-level modifications have been accomplished, there are more subtle ways to modify data. For example, if you can intercept a wireless transmission and change the destination address field (IP address) on a message, you could cause that message to be forwarded to you across the Internet, instead of to its intended recipient. Why would you want to do this? Because the message on the wireless link is encrypted and you can't read the content, but if you can get it forwarded across the Internet, you will receive the decrypted version. The IP header is easier to attack because it is a known format.

Masquerading is the term used when an attacking network device impersonates a valid device. It is the ideal approach if an attacker wants to remain undetected. If the device can successfully fool the target network into validating it as an authorized device, the attacker gets all the access rights that the authorized device established during logon. Furthermore, there will be no security warnings. Even an eagle-eyed IT manager scanning the traffic records won't see anything amiss unless the attacker does things that a normal user wouldn't do, such as trying to access

---

1. Also known as "footprinting" or "information gathering."

system areas. There are, of course, nonelectronic attacks based on masquerading that are equally effective—if you leave your terminal logged in and go to lunch, anyone can sit down and get your access rights. It is the same principle.

Denial of service (DoS) is quite unlike the other three categories both in technique and goals. While the other three extend extra privilege to the attacker, a DoS attack usually blocks out everybody, including the attacker. The object of a DoS attack is to cause damage to the target by preventing operation of the network. In 2000 the largest attack yet publicized occurred with a distributed DoS attack against several major Web commerce sites. The attack blocked access to the sites for hours. This attack originated from thousands of remotely controlled computers throughout the world whose owners were largely unaware of their participation. The attackers used these "zombie" computers to generate large amounts of traffic directed toward their victims, preventing them from servicing valid requests. Why did they do it? Perhaps to gain bragging rights—this is classic ego hacking culture. A more sinister reason might be to gather experience and data for some larger future event.

In principle, DoS attacks could be mounted for commercial reasons. Bringing down a sales Web site in the run-up to the holidays could inflict financial damage on a competitor. However, it is unlikely that any serious retailer has actually used such tactics. An attack by an ex-employee with a grievance is more plausible. DoS attacks are hard to prevent on the Internet and usually rely on causing the receiving server to exhaust its buffer resources so it cannot accept any valid connections for a period of time. Unfortunately for us, DoS attacks on Wi-Fi LANs are easy to mount and almost impossible to prevent.

The enemy can successfully use some of these attacks without having access to your secret network keys. However, in most cases the damage that can be done without knowing the keys is quite limited. If the attacker *can* find out your keys, then you move into a different category of danger. Unauthorized modifications to Web sites and the stealing of databases full of credit card details occur because someone has broken the keys. As we look at the types of attack that can be made against Wi-Fi LANs, we'll consider these cases separately: first, attacks against the network without the keys, and second, attacks to try to uncover the keys themselves.

Attacks Without Keys

Getting the keys is the ultimate success for an attacker, but it's surprising how much information can be obtained without ever needing to compromise the keys. In some cases it's possible to completely breach security. In this section we look at a few of the activities attackers might perform as an alternative to key attacks.

Snooping

First, consider snooping. Let's imagine you are an attacker within range of your target—a Wi-Fi LAN that is using secret keys and hence is encrypting messages in some way. Let's also assume you have a modified Wi-Fi card designed to intercept data. You have a lot of knowledge about IEEE 802.11 protocols as well as higher-level protocols like TCP/IP. "You" may be a very clever person with a PhD in communications…or in this context, "you" may be a sophisticated program running on the laptop of a total moron. Either way, the question is, what can be seen?

First of all, you can see and read all the information coming from the access points.[2] Therefore, you know the network name (or SSID). If the network name is something obvious like "accounts_department," you can get an idea of what the users on the network might be doing. You have most likely identified the manufacturer of each access point by looking at its MAC address, and you may even know the model number based on the capabilities or proprietary information that each includes in its beacons. If that model has any hidden flaws, that information might be useful. Some security advisers propose disabling SSID broadcasts; but while this step may reduce "war driving" attacks (see Chapter 3), it provides only a short-term advantage, as the information will be discovered as soon as a new user connects to an access point.

As an attacker, you may also see quite a bit of data going to and from an access point. By watching for a while, you will be able to count how many wireless devices are connected to each access point (just by looking for different MAC addresses). You will also be able to identify the manufacturer of the wireless adapter in each case from the first three bytes of the MAC address. If the network is using WEP, you might be able to see whether everyone is using the same key (shared) or whether each device has a separate key by looking at bits in the IEEE 802.11 header. That information could be useful later.

So far, it has been easy. But when you capture any of the data packets, you cannot interpret them because they are encrypted. We are not considering attempts to decrypt the packets here because that is an attack on the secret key and is covered in the next section. So if you are not going to try to crack the code, can you do anything useful?

You can, using a technique called traffic analysis. **Traffic analysis** is the study of message externals, for example, frequency of communication and size. So, the first thing is to watch the size of the packets. You should be able to identify which protocol they are using by checking the length. For example, certain TCP/IP

---

2. Access points transmit regular beacon messages advertising various pieces of information. This is covered in detail in Chapter 5, "IEEE 802.11 Protocol Primer."

messages, such as acknowledgment frames, have a fixed length and occur with a typical regularity. This applies to other protocols, too, so the length of the packets can tell you the network protocol in use. Let's suppose it is TCP/IP. You can look out for messages such as DHCP discover messages that are used to give IP addresses to the network.

You can also get information from the timing of messages. By watching messages go to the network from a user and timing when messages come back, you can probably guess whether that user is browsing the Web or working on a local server. Even the amount of data being sent around might give a clue as to what is happening. For example, a sudden increase in activity might mean that the payroll is being prepared or that a shipment is being prepared. Unfortunately, it is possible to learn a whole lot about the types of things going on in a network just by watching packet lengths and noting timing without looking inside the packets. However, you cannot see anything *really* useful, such as the message content. Like the voyeur watching the neighbor's window when the blind is down, you'll see shadows that tell you whether someone is "in the room," but nothing more.

So, by itself, snooping an encrypted LAN can only provide information about how, when, and by which devices the network is being used. This information by itself is of limited use; but combined with other information the attacker might gain from other methods or sources, it can be very helpful. So now let's look at the prospects for combining snooping and modification.

Man-in-the-Middle Attack (Modification)

Suppose two people are communicating—traditionally in security literature, they are called Alice and Bob. Alice receives messages from Bob and Bob receives from Alice. Suppose there is an attacker able to intercept and cut off the communications. Suppose that the attacker can imitate Bob while sending to Alice and imitating Alice while sending to Bob. In this case Alice and Bob are subject to a "man-in-the-middle" attack, as shown in Figure 4.1. Such attacks can be used to modify messages in transit without detection.

There are (at least) two ways to modify a message: you can modify it on the fly or you can capture, modify, and replay the message, a technique known as **store and forward**. Modification on the fly is really hard. You would need to send a burst of radio transmission at just the right moment to cause the receiver to interpret a bit incorrectly. Because of the sophisticated modulation used in Wi-Fi LANs, bits are not sent individually but in groups coded together, making it very difficult to change a single bit at a time. Therefore, we will, for the moment, assume that any modification occurs due to a store-and-forward approach by the attacker; on-the-fly modification might be possible in theory, but we won't cover the topic any further.

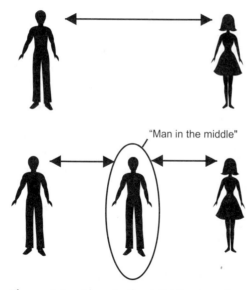

Figure 4.1 Man-in-the-Middle-Attack

The store-and-forward method is called a man-in-the-middle modification attack. The principle is simple enough in wired networks: an attacker cuts the wire, receives all the data, and is careful to send it on so the two devices at the ends don't know their data is being intercepted. There is, for example, a man-in-the-middle attack possible at every forwarding router in the Internet, which is one reason the Internet is treated as totally insecure.

In Wi-Fi LANs a man-in-the-middle attack is a little more difficult to mount because there is no wire to cut. The enemy must stop the receiver from getting the message on the initial transmission so he can then forward it after exercising his evil intent. The procedure could work something like this. To become a man-in-the-middle between mobile device (Mob) and the access point (AP), the enemy must:

1. Listen for a message from Mob to AP.

2. Read in the message up to the checkword[3] at the end.

3. Transmit a sudden burst of noise to corrupt the checkword—this causes AP to drop the message as invalid, but the attacker now has a copy of the valid message.

4. Forge an acknowledge message with AP's address and send it to Mob; now Mob thinks the message has been received by AP.

---

3. The checkword is used by the receiver to detect any errors in the data.

5. Recalculate the correct checkword and send the captured message to AP; AP thinks it came from Mob.

6. Wait for an acknowledgment message from AP and send a burst of noise so Mob ignores it and doesn't see two acknowledgments for the same packet.

Clearly, this procedure is not simple, but it is absolutely feasible and would effectively put the attacker in the middle of the communications. Neither the access point nor the mobile device would have any idea that the communications were intercepted.

Another approach—and one that is much more likely to occur—would be for the enemy to set up a bogus access point. The bogus AP identifies a real AP in advance. When an unwitting mobile device sees the bogus AP and tries to associate, the bogus AP simply copies all the messages it receives to the valid AP, substituting its own MAC address. Similarly, it copies all the messages received from the good AP back to the mobile device. By this method, it doesn't need to know the encryption keys because the MAC address fields that it modifies are not encrypted. As a result, all the data between the mobile device and the good AP goes through the bogus AP en route.

Once the enemy is established in the middle of a communication, he has the opportunity to mess with the data. Remember that this intervention is possible even when the data is encrypted and without the enemy knowing the secret keys. The question is, what can modification achieve without the attacker knowing the keys?

There is really very little that can be accomplished by modifying individual messages, unless you have some knowledge about the contents of the messages before they were encrypted. The enemy has some information about most packets because the TCP/IP header has a fixed format and some of the fields have fixed or obvious values (such as the length field). The attacker might like to modify the destination IP address to try to get the data sent out over the Internet (to him). This is a really hard attack to accomplish, however, and it is quickly detected by the sender because it would be hard (but not impossible) to get a response back.

More can be achieved if the attacker is allowed to *replay* captured messages. For example, suppose the attacker spots an ICMP message going from the mobile device to the network server. An **ICMP message** is a short administrative message sent between devices in a TCP/IP network. The attacker could guess what the ICMP message type is from the length. Many ICMP messages require a response from the server that the enemy will also see (although it is still encrypted). Remember that the enemy can't read either message but can make an educated guess at much of the content. Furthermore, if the enemy can send the same encrypted ICMP message again, the server might come back with a response every time—thinking it came from the valid device.

Now the attacker can play games. The ICMP message contains a checkword. If the attacker changes a single bit and resends the message, after decryption the checkword will indicate an error and the message will be thrown away. The attacker will notice that there was no reply from the server. So what if the attacker can modify both a data bit and some of the checkword bits? If he is allowed to try over and over, maybe tens of thousands of times, eventually the enemy will find a combination that gets a response from the server again. By playing this game, an attacker could eventually decode the message. At the end of several hours, he has found out the IP address of the mobile device and the server. For a fuller description of this attack, see Borisov et al. (2001). Although this is a potentially successful attack, it's no big deal. A lot of work would be required for a relatively small amount of information. However, even a small crack cannot be considered acceptable in a security system. As in a dam wall, small cracks can lead to real breaches and eventually the collapse of the system.

Active attacks are sometimes difficult to carry out, and they run the risk of being detected. Nonetheless, against some systems, WEP being one of them, active attacks can accomplish a great deal for the attacker. However, the new security methods of WPA and RSN are resiliant to such attacks. This is one reason why most attackers will try to get the keys. With the exception of DoS attacks, attacks without keys are generally used only as a step toward determining the keys. Once an enemy has the keys, your only hope is to detect the intruder, shut down the network, and change the lock.

Attacks on the Keys

The problem with keys in general is that there are so many ways to get at them. Let's take a simple case of a burglar who wants to break into a bank vault. The walls are thick steel and so the burglar has concluded that the only viable way in is through the vault door, which needs a key. What are the options? Well, here are a few:

- Find where the key is stored and steal it.
- Get a job in the bank and finagle a few moments of access to the key; make an impression to copy later.
- Point a gun at the manager and make him unlock the vault.
- Make lots of different keys and try them all.
- Pick the lock.

The list goes on, and a real burglar would have a few more to suggest as well. All of these attacks have an analogy in Wi-Fi LAN security, and by no means do they all involve clever cryptography. Let's get the most obvious one out of the way first. The simplest way to get a key is to look over the shoulder of a person as she enters a password or simply to ask a disgruntled employee to tell you. It is well known that thieves are able to observe and remember sequences of digits typed into a phone when a victim uses a calling card. This is a problem whenever you expose your key information to people. Humans are a weak link in security.

One solution is to keep the keys inside the computer and not visible to the human operator. The problem with this approach is that, if the computer is stolen, the key goes with it and the thief can get access by masquerading as the valid user until the theft is discovered. In general, the best protection comes from choosing good passwords and changing them regularly.

One-Time Passwords

A clever solution that avoids human weakness is the use of the **one-time password**. As the name suggests, the idea is that each and every time you log on or connect, you use a new password—hence each password is only used once. In a typical case, the user has a credit card–sized gadget that displays a set of digits. The display changes once per minute to a new number. Back at headquarters is a special server, running off an accurate clock, which knows which number is being displayed by the card at any point in time. When the user logs on, she types in the number currently displayed and the server checks that it is valid. However, five minutes later, if the same password is entered, the server will reject it. The idea is that the password, if memorized, is of very limited value and the card stays with the user even if the computer is stolen—quite a clever system.

One-time passwords incorporate a concept called liveness that is vital to good security. **Liveness** is simply the inclusion of something that changes in time so you can detect whether someone is using old (and hence probably copied) information.

Burying the Keys

If you try to hide the key information from the user, it is still vulnerable to eventual discovery by a sufficiently dedicated attacker. This is particularly true if the enemy has physical access to the equipment where the key is stored. For example, if the enemy can take a laptop home and work on it, and if he has sufficient technical skills, he can probably get the key, no matter how deeply it is buried in the software or hardware of the device. As an example, a large corporation in the United States had Wi-Fi wireless LAN adapters custom-made so the WEP key was programmed into the flash memory of the adapters before shipment and was never visible to the software on the computer. Despite this precaution, eventually someone was able to reverse-engineer the key value and publish it on the Internet. At that moment, the security of all the cards the company possessed plummeted to nothing.

Another example involves the cracking of the password on a mobile phone SIM card (Kocher et al., 1999). SIM cards are thumbnail-sized smart cards used in European and some U.S. cellular phones. The benefits of a smart card are its self-contained memory and built-in microprocessor. Therefore, the key can be stored inside and is not accessible from the outside. When you want to check whether a password is correct, you send it to the microprocessor in the card. The microprocessor does the check and simply tells you "correct" or "incorrect." It would seem an ideal solution because no one, including the manufacturer, can read the password once it leaves the factory. And yet attackers did find several ways to crack the passwords.

In one particularly clever approach, they obtained a copy of the program that the little microprocessor used. They had realized that the specific instructions that the processor executed depended on the value of the password. When the password byte presented was correct, it took one path; and when it was wrong, it took another. Astonishingly they realized that they could guess which type of instruction was being executed simply by carefully measuring the electrical current consumption used by the smart card. This meant they could try each byte of the password one at a time until they saw the card perform the "equal" test. It was like cracking a ten-digit combination lock when the lock beeps every time you enter one digit correctly. They cracked the code in very little time. Now, of course, smart cards have been modified so the instruction operation is not signaled by the current consumption, but this story once more illustrates the ingenuity of attackers.

A third example when burying the key failed concerns the protection of DVD movies. To stop people from reading DVD movies into their computers, the contents on the discs are encrypted. However, a DVD player obviously has to know the keys in order to decrypt and play the contents. Therefore, each DVD manufacturer has to sign up to very tough licensing restrictions, and those who have access to the encryption key must use special care to keep it safe. Did this work? No. As you might expect, only a couple of years passed before programs appeared that could decrypt a DVD. A Finnish teenager reverse-engineered a ROM chip from a DVD player and determined not only a valid key but also the previously unknown proprietary encryption algorithms. There is little the industry can do now because they can't change the key without making obsolete millions of consumers' DVD players. They have resorted to taking aggressive legal action against anyone who tries to distribute the program (Salkever, 2000).

One of the main lessons of these examples is the well-known security policy that you should change the master keys from time to time. We will discuss how often is appropriate in the later section on network configuration.

Wireless Attacks

Most of the things that have been said so far about protecting keys apply regardless of the type of security system you are using. They are not specific to wireless.

Wireless, of course, introduces a whole new set of opportunities for attackers trying to get keys because it is so easy to access the data streams, even though they may be encrypted. Imagine a hacker ten years ago, before the advent of wireless LAN. The hacker would like to get access to the network inside a corporation. It's very risky because access to the building is restricted; and even after the attacker got inside, there would be limited time to sample the data. "Wouldn't it be great," the hacker dreams, "if I could get in there and install a radio transmitter that sent all the data outside, where I could pick it up in safety." Today, not only has the hacker's dream come true but also someone else (the corporation) has already bought the equipment and installed it! Life's not usually like that.

The problem for the attacker is that the data is encrypted and she needs the keys. Assuming you don't change the keys, she has as much time as she wants to capture sample messages and analyze them. What to do next?

First, let's look at a couple of assumptions we need to make about what the attacker knows. To do this, we need to introduce some common terms:

- **Plaintext**: The data before encryption—this is what we want to protect
- **Ciphertext**: The encrypted version that the enemy can see over the radio link
- **Keys**: The secret value that is used to encrypt/decrypt the message
- **Cipher**: The algorithm and rules used to perform the encryption and decryption

To summarize, the ciphertext is created by processing the plaintext with the ciphersuite using the keys (see Figure 4.2). This process is sometimes written as a formula: Ciphertext = Cipher (Key, Plaintext).

Okay, coming back to our attacker. We know that she has a copy of the ciphertext because that can be snooped directly. We know that she doesn't know the key because getting it is her objective. What about the cipher and the plaintext?

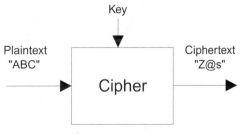

Figure 4.2 Encryption Terms

One of the rules of modern cryptography is that you should assume that the attacker knows the algorithm used for encryption.[4] Most attack methods rely on finding weaknesses in the underlying algorithm or in its implementation. If, however, the attacker does not know the algorithm, an attack is almost impossible. So it might seem that keeping the algorithm secret is a good idea. This type of thinking, also known as **security by obscurity,** has been adopted in some security systems. For example, the encryption algorithm used in most European cellular phones is a secret and may be different from one mobile phone operator to another. However, security experts feel that keeping the algorithm secret is a bad idea for (at least) two reasons:

- It is impossible to keep a secret forever, no matter how hard you try. People have to know the algorithm in order to implement it, and sooner or later someone will be bribed, get drunk at a crypto conference (yes, it could happen), or have their laptop stolen. Sooner or later, the secret will come out, and the bad guys might get the secret. That leaves all of us users vulnerable without knowing it.

- The other disadvantage of keeping the cryptographic algorithm a secret is that this approach doesn't allow legitimate researchers to look for flaws. If there is a flaw, it is better that a researcher finds it and alerts everyone before an attacker finds and exploits it. The weaknesses of IEEE 802.11 WEP were found and publicized in this way. The equipment manufacturers may not be pleased by such publication. They tend to argue that it is better to keep flaws quiet and fix them in the background. However, this is a dangerous approach—you can be sure that if only 1% of people know about the flaw, the hacker community is included in the 1% along with the manufacturers. So by publication, the public is well served.

So, now we are assuming that the attacker knows the ciphertext and the cipher. Does she have the plaintext? This might seem like a silly question because if she has the plaintext, why does she need to crack the code at all? However, consider that the objective is not to crack a single message; it is to get the keys so *every* message can be read. The hacker may know the plaintext of a single message and use that to attack the keys. So let's ask that again—could the enemy get a sample of the plaintext?

In fact, there are quite a few ways in which this might be done. The first way has already been mentioned: protocol headers. In IEEE 802.11, the MAC header is not encrypted, but all the rest of the message is (for more discussion, see Chap-

---

4. This is known as Kirchoff's criterion.

ter 5). If you are using a protocol such as TCP/IP, this means that the header portion of the TCP/IP message is part of the *plaintext* that is converted to *ciphertext*. The danger is that the header always occurs in the same place (at the start of the packet) and that some of the fields have fixed values, or values that can be easily guessed. This means that an attacker immediately has some knowledge about the plaintext. Furthermore, some IP messages are of a known format, such as DHCP discover messages used in assigning network addresses. These are encrypted but can be identified from their length. In these cases, an attacker might correctly guess the entire plaintext.

It gets worse! If a person is accessing a Web site, and the attacker can guess which Web site, he can get the plaintext just by going to the same site. Suppose that someone goes to a popular news Web site. The home page is downloaded and sent encrypted across the wireless link. If the attacker can correctly guess which frames are which, he has the plaintext as well as the ciphertext. Guessing which frames are which is not as hard as you might think because the number of bytes in certain parts of the home page, such as pictures, provides a clue. The last method for getting plaintext is the simple approach of sending e-mail. If an attacker knows the e-mail address of a user at the target, he could send the user a message that at some point might be read. The attacker has a chance to identify when his message is read from the length. Alternatively, the e-mail might persuade the user to click a link to the home page of a Web site that the attacker knows.

Because there are so many ways for attackers to guess or obtain samples of plaintext, we have to assume that they can obtain all three components: the ciphertext, the plaintext, and the cipher. Once they have all three, they can start an attack on the keys.

Attacking the Keys Through Brute Force

The first thing anyone thinks about when it comes to working out the keys is the brute force attack. We'll look at this because the statistics are fun. Basically, the **brute force method** means that an attacker tries every possible key until he finds a match. Given that he knows the ciphertext and protocol, he would start with a key value of all zeros, decrypt the message, and see whether it matches the plaintext (or any fragments he has). If he keeps adding 1 to the key value, in principle, he will sooner or later hit on the right key because all possible keys will have been tried. Well, "sooner or later" is probably "later or never" in any real encryption system. In fact, if an attacker felt lucky enough to stumble on the key this way, he should buy a ticket for the state lottery. The odds of winning are considerably higher for the lottery.

The time taken for a brute force attack depends on the key size, or more correctly the key entropy (see Chapter 2). This is one of the reasons that government export controls tend to be set according to *key length*. For example, it used to be that you could not export any security technology from the United States with a key length of more than around 40 bits. This was one reason why in the original IEEE 802.11 standard, WEP used a 40-bit key.

To crack a 40-bit key using brute force, you would, on average, have to try 2^{39} times,[5] which equals 550 billion different keys. That's a big number, but it's not impossible. Say you have a supercomputer that can conduct one test per microsecond; you could crack the key in about a week.

Because the 40-bit key is crackable, many security systems use larger keys—128 bits is common. In an attempt to strengthen security, some wireless LAN manufacturers brought out IEEE 802.11 systems using 104-bit keys, a length that was eventually adopted as a de facto standard. Most Wi-Fi systems support 104-bit keys, although strictly this has never been part of the IEEE 802.11 standard. The use of a longer key really renders brute force attacks completely ineffective, assuming the underlying cryptographic algorithm has no weaknesses. Let's suppose supercomputers become faster and we can try a hundred keys in a microsecond. With a 104-bit key, you would still need (on average) 3,200,000 billion years to find the right key. Yes, 3 million billion years—and if that doesn't put you off, then you must be an avid lottery player. If you want to check the calculation yourself, here is the formula:

$$\text{Ave Time} = 2^{103} / (\text{num tries per sec}) / (\text{num secs per year})$$

Dictionary Attacks

Given that you can so easily defeat brute force attacks by adding a few bits to the key, any attacker with an IQ in the double digits will look for another approach. Here's the idea: Instead of trying every possible key, try only those keys that you think the user is likely to use. For example, the attacker could assume that the key is made up entirely of letters and numbers, as is typical for user-chosen passwords. As we discussed in Chapter 2, this reduces key entropy. A 104-bit key is now only as effective as a 78-bit key because only 6 bits of every byte are used. However, 78 bits is still uncrackable using brute force so the attacker must narrow down further. This approach to reducing the number of keys to test brings us to the idea behind a dictionary attack (Bishop, 2002; Salkever, 2000).

In a dictionary attack, the enemy uses a huge dictionary, or database, containing all the likely passwords. This will certainly include every word in the English language and may contain other languages as well. It will contain thousands of place names and proper names. It will contain words extracted from every street

---

5. The total number of combinations is 2^{40} but on average you would only have to try half of them before finding the right one. Hence 2^{39}.

address in the United States (for example). Every name registered in the phone book, including first and last names, will be there. Every common pet name, strings of digits for every zip code, the date of every day in the year, and on and on.

The creation of such a database might seem like a formidable task, but the hacker community shares material, and bit by bit more data is added to the dictionary. Of course, in the end there will be millions of entries in the dictionary—but remember that the enemy is reducing the key space from multiple gazillions, so getting it down to a few million is a real advantage.

With such a database, if the enemy can take home a sample of ciphertext and plaintext and leave it crunching away, the password could be cracked in a few days rather than a few billion years. The availability of such attack dictionaries explains why security managers want users to define passwords that use both upper- and lowercase (in unexpected places), and to insert digits or other strange characters. The attack works only against human-readable passwords or keys derived from such passwords in a known way.

Certain security protocols are more susceptible to dictionary attack than others. It depends to some extent on how the **master password**, selected by the user, is applied to the encryption process. For example, a password such as "Vesuvius" would easily be discovered by a dictionary attack. However, if the key used for encryption were derived from "Vesuvius" through a number of processing steps, dictionary attacks would not be easy. Consider the following: A user has chosen the password "Vesuvius". But before the key is used, the letters are swapped around in a known way to give "svsuieVu". This new version is used for the key instead. Both ends of the link know how to swap the bytes around, so it is not a problem for the friendly devices; but the letter-swapping will foil a simple dictionary attack. Of course, if the enemy knows the rule for swapping the letters, he can build this rule into the attack, so you could arrange to use a different swapping pattern depending on some other information known to both ends of the link. Swapping the bytes is a simple example and not a practical secure method. However, there are much more sophisticated ways to obscure the passwords before use, some of which are used in the new IEEE 802.11 security protocol (see Chapter 10). As a result of such **key derivation**, most modern security systems are *not* susceptible to dictionary attack.

Algorithmic Attacks

If the enemy cannot mount a brute force or a dictionary attack, another approach is to try to break the algorithm—that is, to try to find a flaw in the way the encryption is performed that might expose the key value. We will see later that this was the successful attack made on WEP. It is difficult to describe these algorithmic attacks generally because they depend so much on the algorithm and understanding the weaknesses often requires that you are a cryptographic expert. However, there is a straightforward analogy with safe breaking.

In many B movies involving safe breaking, the master criminal is seen with a doctor's stethoscope, listening to the front door of a large safe and carefully turning the dial. When we were kids, we had no idea why anyone would do that and assumed that the criminal was seeing whether the safe was sick and hence easy to break into. The use of the stethoscope was never explained, as if the movie producers assumed all viewers were master safecrackers and would know what was going on. Years later, we realized that the purpose was to try to find one digit of the combination at a time by listening to faint clicking noises coming from the levers inside. This is a prime example of attacking the algorithm. The safecracker knows how the mechanism (algorithm) works and knows that it leaks information about the combination due to the noises. In particular, it leaks information about one digit at a time. By exploiting the leak one digit at a time, the combination is discovered. Furthermore, the time required goes up only in proportion to the number of digits, whereas the difficulty of a brute force attack goes up exponentially with the number of digits.

The algorithmic style of attack is very similar to that used against WEP. A weakness in the algorithm allows one byte of the key to be attacked at a time. Although it takes a while to crack each byte of the key, the total time is proportional to the number of bytes. This means that it is only slightly more difficult to crack a 104-bit key than it is a 40-bit key.

Successful attacks against the algorithm are frightening because, once the method is discovered, it is usually easy to build automatic tools to find out the keys. And, as has been observed, after the keys are discovered, your only chance is detection of the intruder.

Summary

In this chapter we have seen that there are many ways in which attacks can be mounted against security systems. Methods do not need to be sophisticated to be effective, nor does the person making the attack need to be a technical expert if he is using a tool written by such an expert. Most security attacks in the past have come from bad passwords or dictionary attacks. However, key derivation is helping to reduce this problem. Now attackers must look for flaws in the algorithms— or at least weaknesses that allow the strength of the keys to be compromised.

The special vulnerability of Wi-Fi LANs makes them susceptible to all these attacks and means that the security protections chosen must be extremely good. By the end of this book, you will see how the new Wi-Fi and IEEE 802.11 security methods are, indeed, that good.

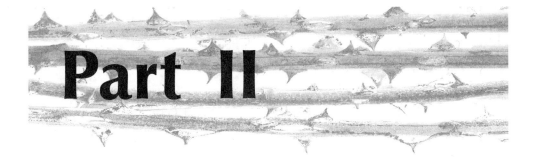

Part II

The Design of
Wi-Fi Security

5
Chapter

IEEE 802.11 Protocol Primer

This chapter provides an overview of how the IEEE 802.11 protocol operates. You may feel that understanding the way in which low-level messages are exchanged is not relevant to understanding security. If you are concerned only with setting up a secure network following the configuration instructions in the manual, you are probably right. But one purpose of this book is to explain the new security system of IEEE 802.11 in sufficient detail that you become convinced that it really has been well thought out and is thoroughly secure. Accepting that systems are secure on face value is less work but sometimes leads to disappointment. To understand the later sections of this book, you need a grounding in the basic standard. Hopefully just enough of that grounding is provided here, but not too much.

Layers

The connection between the user and the LAN is a sequence of hardware and software components, each connected through a clearly defined interface. It's useful to think of this like a very efficient government organization that goes into operation when you, the user, fill out a form for some service and hand it in. Unlike a real government organization where your application form gets used as a coffee mat for a few weeks before falling behind the photocopier, in this super efficient service, the form passes from department to department and is rapidly processed by each before being handing on to the next. Within milliseconds, your service request is satisfied or rejected.

In a computer network layers implement this department concept. Each layer performs a particular function and is responsible for certain activities. The layers close to the user are called upper layers and the layers down by the LAN are called lower layers. Most engineering students are taught about the ISO seven-layer model in which the layers are defined with particular names and meanings. We don't propose to reiterate the complete model here, partly because it is boring and partly because few practical implementations really follow it in its entirety. However, we will look at the layers of a typical real system (Davie et al., 1999).

At the top is the user—the person sitting at a terminal and hoping to get service (such as read a document from a server or copy a file). To do this, the user interacts with an application program such as Microsoft Internet Explorer. Let's look at the sequence of events required to access a remote file, as shown in Figure 5.1:

1. When the application is asked to open a file, it requests the service of a file subsystem that understands directory structures and server names.

2. If the requested file is on a network server, the file subsystem needs to talk to that server and requests the services of the network operating system to determine what type of network protocol is needed.

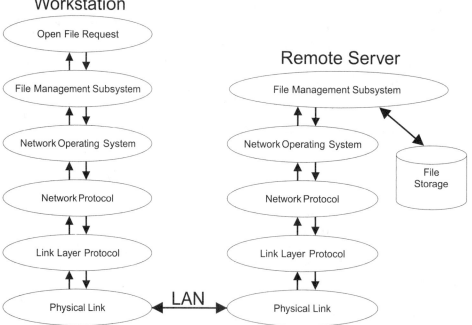

Figure 5.1 Handling a Request Through Layers

3. The network operating system forwards a message to the remote server and asks the appropriate protocol layer, such as TCP/IP, to deliver it.

4. The network protocol layer packages the message in the appropriate format and generates multiple packets of data, each usually about 100–1,500 bytes in length. Then the protocol layer asks the link layer to deliver the packets.

5. The link layer uses the services of low-level hardware and software to transport a single packet of data across a single link, which could be an Ethernet link or a wireless LAN link.

6. The physical layer is the actual electrical signals or radio waves that transfer the data in the appropriate form for the medium being used.

Message replies that arrive follow a similar path (but of course in reverse).

The notable thing about this sequence is the way in which each layer does its job: no more and no less. The link layer just delivers packets. It doesn't care what they contain or where they are eventually headed. It has to get it from here to there and if *there* is a dead end—well, that's someone else's problem. It's like the truck driver who delivers the elephant to the nunnery at 23 Main St. "That's the address on my form so that's where Jumbo gets off." The fact that there is a zoo at 32 Main St. is not in any way relevant to the truck driver.

Wireless LAN Organization

When we talk about "wireless LAN," we are generally referring to the link and physical layers of the network. The IEEE 802 standards deal with these layers for a range of different LAN technologies, including IEEE 802.3, which is commonly (but incorrectly) called "Ethernet" [IEEE 802.3]. IEEE 802.11, of course, is the very widely deployed standard for Wi-Fi wireless LAN. In most LAN technologies, the same type of LAN must exist at both ends of a link. In other words, an Ethernet cable connects an Ethernet port on a computer to an Ethernet port on a hub. The equivalent to the LAN hub in IEEE 802.11 is the access point, which acts like the center of a wheel in distributing data for most Wi-Fi LANs. When IEEE 802.11 systems work through an access point, they are said to be operating in **infrastructure mode** because the access point is coordinating the Wi-Fi LAN from a fixed point and often providing a connection to a wired Ethernet network.

In the early days of Ethernet, you could use a hub (like all systems today) or you could connect all the computers together using a single coaxial cable. In the latter case, you didn't need a hub because the single cable joined all the computers together in series. When any computer sent a message, all the others could potentially receive it, but only the recipient to whom it was addressed would actually listen. IEEE 802.11 has a similar mode called **ad-hoc mode**. In this case no access point is needed and each wireless device can transmit directly to any other. It was intended to be useful for groups of people who wanted to set up a network anywhere and share information—hence, "ad-hoc."

To summarize, IEEE 802.11 has two modes, infrastructure and ad-hoc, sometimes referred to by the technical acronyms ESS and IBSS, respectively. From a security standpoint, ad-hoc networks present quite a challenge and we will deal with them separately in a later chapter. Most people operate in infrastructure mode because they want to be able to connect to a wired infrastructure such as a local Ethernet or an Internet connection. Infrastructure mode also offers a much better platform for building security. Most of what is described in the following chapters refers to operation in infrastructure mode.

Basics of Operation in Infrastructure Mode

In the following discussion AP is the acronym for a fixed access point and STA (short for "station") refers to the wireless device, such as a laptop computer, that wants to connect to the network. The AP and STA talk to each other using wireless messages. We will assume that the AP is connected to a wired network that the STA wants to access.

To help understand the process by which the STA connects to the AP and starts to send data, we'll run through a simplified overview first. This describes the sequence of events that occur in systems that are not using security. Let's assume that the AP is already turned on and operating. The AP advertises its presence by transmitting short wireless messages at a regular interval, usually about 10 times a second. These short messages are called **beacons** and allow wireless devices to discover the identity of the AP.

Now suppose that someone powers up a laptop with a Wi-Fi network adapter installed (the STA). After the initialization phase, the STA will start to search for an AP. It may have been configured to look for a particular AP, or it may be prepared to connect to any AP, regardless of identity. There are a number of different radio frequencies (called **channels**) that could be used so the STA must tune into each channel in turn and listen for beacon messages. This process is called **scanning**. The process can be accelerated by probing, as explained later in this chapter.

The STA may discover several APs in a large network and must decide to which it intends to connect; often this decision is made based on signal strength. When the STA is ready to connect to the AP, it first sends an **authenticate request message** to the AP. The original IEEE 802.11 standard defined the authenticate messages as part of the security solution, but they are not used for this purpose in Wi-Fi (for reasons why, see Chapter 6). Because, in our scenario, we are not using security, the AP immediately responds to the authenticate request by sending an authenticate response indicating acceptance.

Now that the STA has permission to connect to the AP, it must take one more step before the connection is complete. In IEEE 802.11 the concept of "connection" is called **association**. When an STA is associated with an AP, it is eligible to send data to and receive data from the network.[1] The STA sends an **association request** message and the AP replies with an **association response** indicating successful connection. After this point, data sent from the STA to the AP is forwarded onto the wired LAN to which the AP is connected. Similarly, data from the wired LAN intended for delivery to the STA is forwarded by the AP.

This overview scenario describes the sequence of events by which an STA joins a network. Many details have been left out in the interests of simplicity. Some of the details are brought out in the rest of this chapter.

In IEEE 802.11 there are three types of messages:

- **Control**: These are short messages that tell devices when to start and stop transmitting and whether there has been a communication failure.
- **Management**: These are messages that the STA and AP use to negotiate and control their relationship. For example an STA uses a management message to request access to the AP.
- **Data**: Once the STA and AP have agreed to connect, data is sent using this type of message.

We won't discuss control messages in detail here, but management messages are important for you to understand the process of connecting to a Wi-Fi LAN. The rest of this section describes the management messages and the processes they support.

Beacons

Beaconing is the method by which the access point tells the world it is ready for action and maintains timing in the network. Beacons are management frames that are regularly sent out by the AP, typically about ten times a second. The beacon contains useful information such as the network name and the capabilities of the AP. For example, the beacon can tell the STA whether the AP supports the new security provisions of the IEEE 802.11 standard.

---

1. In the original Wi-Fi products, being associated gave you network access right away. However, as we show in Chapter 8, in the new security approach, association only allows the STA to begin the full authentication process needed for secure network access.

Probing

When a station turns on, it can listen for beacons, hoping to find an access point with which to connect. You might think that ten beacons a second would be plenty for the STA to find the right access point quickly. However, remember that there are multiple frequency channels and that if the STA has to go to each frequency and wait for 0.1 seconds, it could take a while to complete the scan (in other words, the search all the channels). Furthermore, if you are already connected and want to find a new access point because your signal strength is getting weak, you must find the new access point very rapidly to avoid disruption. For this reason, the STA has the option to send a **probe request message**. This is basically the equivalent of shouting "hello, anyone there?" when entering a dark cave. If any access points receive the probe request, they immediately reply with a probe response that looks essentially like a beacon message. In this way, an STA can rapidly learn about the access points in its area.

Connecting to an AP

Remember that the process of connecting to an AP is called association. When you want to connect, you send an association request; the access point may reply with an association response. If that response is positive, you are now associated with the access point.

Roaming

If there are multiple access points on the same network, your STA might choose to move its association from the current AP to a new one. First it should disconnect from the old AP using a **disassociation message**. Then it connects to the new AP using a **reassociation message**. The reassociation message has some information about the old AP that can be useful to make the handover smoother. The information allows the new AP to talk to the old AP to confirm that the roam has taken place.

Sending Data

Once you are associated and after authentication has been performed, you can start sending data. In most cases data is exchanged between the STA and the AP. In fact, this is the normal method even if you are sending data to another STA. First, you send to the AP and then you allow the AP to forward to the STA. Often data will go to the AP and then be forwarded on to an Ethernet LAN or to an Internet gateway. To facilitate this, each IEEE 802.11 data frame going to or from the AP has three addresses. Two may be considered the "final" source and destination, and the third is the "intermediate" address—that of the access point through which the message passes.

When you are sending from the STA to the AP, there is one source address—that of the STA that sent the message—and two destination addresses. One destination address specifies the AP and the other specifies the eventual destination for the message. Similarly data from the access point to the STA has one destination address (the STA) and two source addresses—the AP and also the originator of the message.

Protocol Details

It is not our intent in this book to present the details of how IEEE 802.11 MAC[2] protocol works. The basic operating concept is simple, as described in the previous paragraphs. However, the numerous control mechanisms for dealing with different speeds, power saving, priority of service, and retransmission run into hundreds of pages. If you are really interested in those details, there are books[3] specializing on the MAC protocol and the physical layer interfaces (in other words, the radio and modem). Much of the cleverness of the standard is in how it coordinates multiple wireless devices so they can share the available radio bandwidth and not spend all their time colliding and transmitting over the top of each other.

This book naturally focuses on the security protocols that have been built into IEEE 802.11. These security protocols have been added in two stages. The first stage was incorporated in 1997 with the introduction of the first standard. The second stage, the so-called robust security network (RSN), was developed during 2001–2003. In fact, the two approaches are quite different and require separate descriptions. However, they both depend on some features of the main IEEE 802.11 protocol that we describe here. Let's look at these details now so the explanation of the security protocol makes sense later.

General Frame Formats

Every transmission over the wireless medium has a similar form, as shown in Figure 5.2. First a special pattern is sent out called the **preamble**, which the receivers on other Wi-Fi LAN devices can identify as IEEE 802.11. By the end of the preamble, which only lasts a few microseconds, all the receivers in range should have locked on and adjusted themselves to interpret the data that is to follow. The next part of the transmission is called the **PLCP header**. PLCP stands for Physical Layer Convergence Protocol, a fact that we invite you to forget immediately because it is of no importance to security. Suffice it to say that this header contains

---

2. Medium access control.

3. For example, the *IEEE 802.11 Handbook: A Designer's Companion* by Al Petrick and Bob O'Hara, published by IEEE Press.

Preamble	PLCP	MAC	User Data	CRC

Figure 5.2   Basic Frame Format in IEEE 802.11

information relevant to the receiver logic, such as the data rate of the remaining part of the frame and the packet length. Following the PLCP header is the MAC header, followed by the user data and a **cyclic redundancy check** (CRC) to detect errors. It is the portion starting with the MAC header in which we are most interested.

MAC header

The MAC header comes in three basic flavors, depending on whether the information is a control frame, a management frame, or a data frame. The most important part of the MAC header is the addressing information. The MAC header contains the source and destination addresses to allow delivery of the frame to the correct device. As is standard for IEEE LANs, these addresses are 6 bytes (48 bits) long, and each device has a unique address assigned during manufacture. The destination address can be **unicast**, which means it must be delivered to a single device (with the matching address); or it can be **multicast**, which means that it may be delivered to several devices or possibly all devices in range. It is important to remember this concept because it has a profound impact on security. So let's restate:

- Unicast address: Deliver to one device
- Multicast address: Deliver to several devices
- Broadcast address: Deliver to all devices (special case of multicast)

Other IEEE 802 LANs also use MAC headers, although each has its own format. For example, IEEE 802.3 (Ethernet) MAC headers are quite simple and have just two addresses and a field to indicate the length of the data. IEEE 802.11 MAC headers are much more complicated and have many fields used in coordinating the Wi-Fi LAN. The MAC header of an IEEE 802.11 frame can have from two addresses to four addresses, depending on the situation. Conceptually the four addresses are:

- Transmitter address (TA): The transmitting device
- Receiver address (RA): The receiving device
- Source address (SA): The device that created the original message
- Destination address (DA): The device that eventually receives the message

A moment's thought shows why you might need different combinations. In an ad-hoc network (no AP), the devices send messages directly from one to another. In this case the device that creates the message is also the device that sends it. Similarly, the device that receives the message is also the one that processes it. So in ad-hoc frames, only two addresses are contained in the MAC header.

In an infrastructure network where an access point is operating, all the mobile devices send their frames to the AP, which then forwards them to the correct destination. In this case the mobile device creates and sends the messages; the access point receives them but is not the final destination. Therefore, three addresses are needed:

- Mobile device address (source and transmitter: SA = TA)
- Access point address (receiver: RA)
- Eventual destination (DA)

When messages are going the other way (from the AP to the mobile device), the three addresses are:

- Originating device address (source: SA)
- Access point address (transmitter: TA)
- Mobile device address (receiver: RA and DA)

In principle, all four addresses are used when one access point talks wirelessly to another access point.[4] However, this mode of operation is not fully specified in the standard and the few implementations that exist are usually proprietary to each manufacturer.

MAC addresses are relevant to security because, although the rules say that every device has a unique address, it is easy for enemies to break the rules and pretend to be someone else by copying their address. This is a classic hijack attack in which the enemy allows a legitimate device to establish a connection and then takes over the connection by masquerading as that station. Another problem with MAC addresses from a security standpoint is that they have to be visible to the outside world in order to have any meaning. Think of posting a secret letter. You can use whatever code you like in the letter; but if you also use a secret code for the address on the front of the envelope, the postal service isn't going to be impressed and isn't going to deliver it. The problem with public disclosure of your MAC address is that, in principle, someone can track where you go and where you log on even if he can't see what you are saying.

---

4. Sometimes called wireless bridging.

Apart from the addresses, the MAC header contains quite a lot of information related to efficient operation of the Wi-Fi LAN. Most of this is not relevant to security except that it may need to be protected from malicious modification. In the future, for a wireless LAN operating to the proposed IEEE 802.11e approach, the MAC header may also contain information to identify the type of data and the priority with which it should be handled.

Management Frames

Remember that there are three categories of MAC frame: control, management, and data. The control frames are very short and perform functions like acknowledgment and polling. The data frames have a simple format, as shown in Figure 5.2. The user data section carries data that came from a higher layer. The management frames deserve a little more scrutiny because these are involved in the security protocol.

The original 1997 standard listed the following management frames for use in infrastructure mode:

- Beacon (notify)
- Probe (request and response)
- Authenticate (request and response)
- Associate (request and response)
- Reassociate (request and response)
- Dissassociate (notify)
- Deauthenticate (notify)

In this list, **notify** means "sent out but no response is expected."

The body of a management frame comprises two parts. The first part is a set of fixed fields appropriate to the type of management frame. The second part contains elements. An **element** is a self-contained packet of information that may (or may not) be relevant to the receiving device. There may be a number of elements added to the fixed portion of the management message, as shown in Figure 5.3.

The fixed field contains various items of information specific to particular types of management frames. This includes, for example, flag bits that indicate whether optional features are active. Including in the fixed field area information for options that are not selected would be inefficient; instead, the fixed field just indicates whether the option is used and an appropriate element is added. The use of elements is a powerful and flexible idea with several benefits:

- The use of elements has allowed the standard to be updated more easily. For example, information required for operating the new security methods can

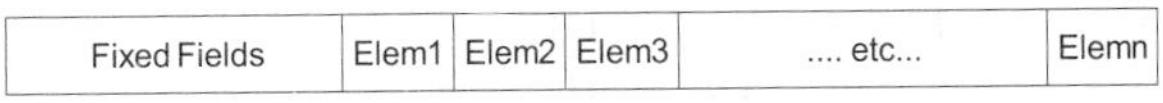

Fixed Fields	Elem1	Elem2	Elem3	.... etc...	Elemn

Figure 5.3 Management Frame Format

be put into elements. The advantage is that old systems that do not understand the new elements can simply ignore them. If the format of the fixed fields had been changed, the old system would be quite incompatible.

- Individual manufacturers sometimes take advantage of the extendibility to add elements specific to some special feature that they provide (although this is not really allowed by the standard). For example, many systems add a proprietary element in beacons that indicates, to their own brand of mobile device, how busy the access point is. This allows a feature called load balancing in which the mobile stations distribute themselves evenly across all the access points. Of course, this arrangement doesn't help mobile stations that are made by a different company than the access point because they will not understand the proprietary element and just throw it away. However, the inability to understand proprietary elements does not prevent standard operation.

Each element has a similar structure. The first byte identifies the type of element. The second byte indicates the length: how many bytes are in the element and the information in the bytes that follow. Because the type and length come first, the receiver can skip over the element if it doesn't recognize or understand the type number.

We'll get into more detail on management frames later when we look at the way the security protocols operate; but for now, let's take a quick look at beacon frames. Actually there are several variants depending on the type of wireless LAN you use, but we'll look at the most common one: IEEE 802.11b (Wi-Fi) in infrastructure mode. This beacon has three fixed fields followed by several elements, generally at least four.

The sequence of fields in a normal beacon is shown in Table 5.1. Remember that beacons are sent out by access points to advertise themselves. The information is used in two ways. First, beacons are used to locate access points with the right network name (SSID) and suitable capabilities. Then, after association, the beacons are used to let the attached devices know that the access point is still operating and in range and also to coordinate certain operations such as power save mode. Let's review each field individually:

Timestamp

This field is initialized when the AP first starts and keeps going up in microseconds. The field is 64 bits long, which means, amazingly, that even counting up

Table 5.1 Beacon Format

Contents	Type
MAC header (indicates a beacon)	header
Timestamp	Fixed Field
Beacon Interval	Fixed Field
Capability Info.	Fixed Field
SSID (network name)	Element
Supported Data Rates	Element
Radio Parameters	Element
Power Save Flags	Element

once per microsecond, it would take over half a million years to overflow! The value is used by all the attached devices to synchronize their operation.

Beacon Interval

This field tells everybody when the next beacon is expected to follow. The usual default for beacon interval is around 0.1 second.

Capabilities Information

This field identifies whether the AP supports various optional features. The original standard only had five bits defined; but as more and more features have been added to the standard, the number has increased dramatically. This field is important to security because it allows the access point to advertise that it supports the new RSN operation.

SSID

The SSID (or network name) gives the identity of the network to prospective wireless devices. There is no security in this—any rogue access point can advertise your SSID and most wireless devices have an option to allow use of any and all SSIDs they find in an area. When there are several Wi-Fi LANs operating in the same space, SSID helps you to choose which one to join. Do not labor under the misconception that choosing an unusual SSID provides some sort of security. This is *absolutely not the case.*

Supported Data Rates

This element indicates what speeds the access point can support. For example, an old access point might only support rates of 1 or 2Mbps. An IEEE 802.11b access point supports 1, 2, 5.5, or 11Mbps; and an IEEE 802.11g access point rates up to 54Mbps. An IEEE 802.11g device will prefer to associate to an AP that could support its highest data rate so this information is needed in advance. Note that because this is an element and not a fixed field, it can be extended in the future.

Radio Parameters

This element indicates the radio frequency that is being used by the access point. You might think that if you were able to receive the message in the first place, you must know which frequency you have selected. However, in some cases it is possible to be on a nearby frequency and still receive a message from an adjacent channel (although poorly). The effect is similar to hearing a noisy distorted version of a nearby FM radio station when you are not quite tuned in.

Power Save Flags (TIM)

These flags are used to tell sleepy wireless devices that there is data waiting for them. Power-saving devices turn off between beacons and then wake up to check these flags. If there is no flag set for them, and they have nothing they want to send, they can go back to sleep until the next beacon.

Others

It is really important to remember that many new elements have been added over the years as the standard has developed. The ones shown in Table 5.1 are just those in the original standard. When we look in detail at the security protocol, you will see that security-related information is added using elements

Radio Bits

This section has been left until last because it is really not relevant to security at all. In fact, if your only interest is security, skip to the next section. However, a brief overview of the radio side seems relevant to a book focused on wireless LANs. We have seen that the MAC layer produces a frame of data that it desires to be transmitted over the radio waves. From the point of view of the radio, this is just a long stream of bits. It is the job of the radio to take the bits and generate a few electromagnetic waves that can be picked up somewhere else and converted back to the same bits. Simple, huh? Well, actually, no.

Currently (in other words, as of 2003), there are two frequency bands that are available for sending IEEE 802.11 data; these are referred to as the 2.4GHz band and the 5GHz band. Band allocation is a very complicated area because governments jealously guard and control the use of radio spectrum, especially after they discovered the value of spectrum auctions in the late 1990s. Different countries and regions of the world have different rules, and we could easily fill a book on this topic alone. Here we will limit ourselves to observing that these two bands exist and, at any point in time, your radio operates in one or the other.

Having determined the radio spectrum that is available, the designer needs to figure out how to convert the digital bits into a high-frequency analog signal that can be amplified into an antenna to generate electromagnetic waves. Converting from bits to analog is the same task that a regular telephone modem performs—and, in fact, the portion of the radio that converts bits into analog is called the modem. The radio can be considered as two bits. The first part contains the modem, sometimes called the **baseband** section, and the second part contains all the very high frequency electronics to drive the antenna, usually called the **radio frequency** (RF) section. RF design is very specialized, and we salute the designers and discuss no further. The MODEM deserves more of a look.

Remember that the object is to convert digital bits into analog signals. One of the simplest modem techniques is called **frequency shift keying** (FSK): Send one frequency for a 0 bit and another for a 1 bit. You could use such a scheme to send Morse code for example—if you only needed a few bits a second! Having invented our first simple scheme, now apply 50 years of research and stir in a large consignment of top-quality gray matter and you might arrive at the very sophisticated techniques used in today's wireless LANs, such as orthogonal frequency division multiplexing (OFDM) and convolutional coding.

According to natural laws, there is a limit to how much information can be sent in a given amount of radio bandwidth. Furthermore, as you increase the information rate toward the theoretical limit, you become more susceptible to corruption by random noise. The sophisticated mathematical techniques that have been applied to wireless LAN are designed to get the optimum balance between high data rate and range. Put the data rate too high and you are susceptible to noise—hence the range becomes too short. But use the right mathematical technique, and you can increase the data rate without sacrificing range.

Improvements in modem techniques (and some changes to the regulations) have resulted in successive versions of IEEE 802.11 offering higher speed. The original 1997 standard only provided 2Mbps in the 2.4GHz band. IEEE 802.11a allowed an immediate leap to 54Mps in the 5GHz band, partly due to better modem technology and partly due to more available spectrum. However, 802.11a implementation was not practical at the time the standard was completed and product didn't appear until 2002. In 1999, IEEE 802.11b increased the speed to 11Mbps in the 2.4GHz band and set the stage for rapid growth of the wireless LAN market. Recently IEEE 802.11g has increased speeds again in 2.4GHz by introducing more sophisticated modem techniques. Soon we can anticipate new versions in the 5GHz band that might push data rates up to 100 or 200Mbps.

Well, interesting as all this is, none of it is relevant to security. The same security techniques can apply whether you are using 100Mbps or going back to your Morse code transmitter.

Summary

A broad understanding of how Wi-Fi networks operate is important for you to understand how the security mechanisms work. This chapter has reviewed IEEE 802.11 from the basic topology down to an outline of the protocol messages. We have seen how the Wi-Fi LAN fits into a stack of layers between the operating system and the wireless medium. Wi-Fi provides the lower layers of communication, while higher layers such as TCP/IP ensure delivery of data from end to end.

We looked at the way Wi-Fi LAN are organized, showing how there are two modes of operation—ad-hoc (IBSS) and infrastructure (ESS). The most common mode is ESS, which uses an access point.

Operation of the Wi-Fi LAN is coordinated by a stream of management and control messages in addition to data messages. This chapter has reviewed the main message types and how the management messages enable wireless devices to find each other and form connections. The security mechanisms are tied up with the process of making connections and passing data. The next chapter looks in detail at the original security method WEP, whose operation was closely tied to the Wi-Fi management messages.

6 Chapter

How IEEE 802.11 WEP Works and Why It Doesn't

This chapter is dedicated to failure. It focuses entirely on WEP, the security method originally employed with Wi-Fi LANs and which has now been discredited due to its numerous security weaknesses. It may seem strange to devote so much space to a protocol that will soon be consigned to history. However, an understanding of WEP and its failure modes is very educational as a case study and highlights the areas that need to be addressed for real security. The first half of the chapter looks at the design of WEP and the second half shows why it fails to meet its security goals.

Introduction

For the first five years of its life, IEEE 802.11 had only one method defined for security. This was called **Wired Equivalent Privacy** or WEP (often misidentified as Wireless Effective Privacy and other variants). In 2000, as Wi-Fi LANs increased in popularity, they attracted the attention of the cryptographic community, who rapidly detected cracks in the WEP approach. By the end of 2001, tools were available on the Internet designed to crack open WEP in a fairly short time.

For many people, WEP is the only choice until the new security methods added to the IEEE 802.11 standard become established. Even with its weaknesses,

WEP is still more effective than no security at all, providing you are aware of its potential weaknesses. It provides a barrier, albeit small, to attack and is therefore likely to cause many attackers to just drive on down the street in search of an unprotected network. Most of the attacks depend on collecting a reasonable sample of transmitted data so, for a home user, where the number of packets sent is quite small, WEP is still a fairly safe option. This section looks at how WEP works in detail, what its weaknesses are, and what an attacker has to do to break in.

Some people criticize the designers of the original IEEE 802.11 standard for creating WEP with inherent weaknesses. However, there are a few things that need to be taken into account. The first is that, at the time WEP was designed, it was not intended to provide military levels of security. As the name suggests, WEP was intended to make it difficult to break in—in the same sense that it is difficult to break into a building to connect to the wired LAN—but not impossible to break in. Section 8.2.2 of the 1999 IEEE 802.11 standard states the following as the objectives for WEP (quoted verbatim):

- It is reasonably strong: The security afforded by the algorithm relies on the difficulty of discovering the secret key through a brute-force attack. This in turn is related to the length of the secret key and the frequency of changing keys. WEP allows for the changing of the key (K) and frequent changing of the Initialization Vector (IV).

- It is self-synchronizing: WEP is self-synchronizing for each message. This property is critical for a data-link-level encryption algorithm, where "best effort" delivery is assumed and packet loss rates may be high.

- It is efficient: The WEP algorithm is efficient and may be implemented in either hardware or software.

- It may be exportable: Every effort has been made to design the WEP system operation so as to maximize the chances of approval, by the U.S. Department of Commerce, of export from the U.S. of products containing a WEP implementation. However, due to the legal and political climate toward cryptography at the time of publication, no guarantee can be made that any specific IEEE 802.11 implementations that use WEP will be exportable from the USA.

- It is optional: The implementation and use of WEP is an IEEE 802.11 option.

Notice that the requirements try to balance "reasonably strong" against the need for simple implementation and exportability. The issue of self-synchronization is really important for Wi-Fi LAN. Basically, what it says is that each packet must be separately encrypted so, given a packet and the key, you should have all the information you need. Clearly, you don't want a situation in which a single dropped packet makes all the following ones indecipherable.

The IEEE 802.11 standard only ever specified the use of 40-bit keys. As we have seen, 40 bits is too short to withstand serious brute force attack, which was why it was acceptable under export rules. The rationale was that if, say, a bank was intending to use wireless LAN, it would have its own security protocol running over the top of WEP and this security would be much higher, as appropriate to its application.

In retrospect, accepting this concept of a "reasonable" level of security was a mistake. Some people will argue that there are only two types of security: strong and none. The standard should probably have incorporated a really strong solution or taken a position that security had to be provided by some other means (like virtual private networking (VPN), for example). However, the power of marketing came to play and, in the promotion of IEEE 802.11 to the world, somehow the word "reasonably" was dropped in the brochures and WEP was simply described as secure. Furthermore, after export restrictions were relaxed, manufacturers made nonstandard extensions by using 104-bit keys. This step made them feel justified in adding adjectives like "extremely" and "absolutely" to the brochure. WEP was now *completely* secure, at least in the minds of the marketing managers. The long key extensions were adopted as part of the Wi-Fi specification and became the norm in the industry in 1999.

For the moment, let's step back from the marketing hype and look at how WEP works. To do that, we need to get back to the low-level IEEE 802.11 messages, some of which are covered in Chapter 5. All of the following refers to the 1999 standard. We cover the new security protocols in depth in a later section.

The IEEE 802.11 (1999) defined two levels of security: open and shared key. **Open security** really means *no* security. It is used in the same way that one would say, "I went to work and left the front door of my house open." Most people have figured out this is not a good security policy for their homes, and you probably feel the same way about Wi-Fi LANs. **Shared key** simply means that both ends of the wireless link know a key with a matching value. To be useful, this must be a secret shared only between trusted parties.

Authentication

There are two parts to WEP security described in the standard. The first is the authentication phase and the second is the encryption phase. The idea goes roughly as follows: When a new mobile device wants to join to an access point, it must first prove its identity. Ideally, the mobile device would also like the access point to prove itself as well. This phase is known as **authenticating** each other's identity. We need to delve into the concept of authenticating a bit more deeply here because authenticating in a WEP environment is a bit of a fool's errand.

The purpose of authentication is for each party to prove that he is who he claims to be. When you sign a check, you are authenticating yourself to the recipient, who will then use the signature to prove to the bank that you really wrote the check. In a LAN environment, every device has a (supposedly) unique number called the MAC address. Every transmission from a device on the LAN contains its MAC address so the identity of the sender can be checked. But how do you know that someone else didn't forge a message with a fake MAC address? One approach is to authenticate a device when it first joins the LAN and agree to a secret code that will be used to protect every subsequent message. Because only the true device and the access point know the secret code, each message can be validated as authentic when it is received. This is the purpose of authentication.

Now let's go back to IEEE 802.11 WEP. It has an authentication phase in which a new device proves that it is a trusted member of the group. We will look at how that is done in a moment. The access point reasons that, if the device can prove that it is trusted, it is reasonable to believe that the device's MAC address is true. Based on this trust, it will let the new device join. Unfortunately, however, in WEP no secret token is exchanged upon authentication. So there is no way to know whether the subsequent messages come from the trusted device or from an impostor. This authentication is really a rather embarrassingly pointless exercise and, in fact, was completely dropped from the Wi-Fi specification, despite being in the IEEE 802.11 standard.

As an analogy, imagine you hear a knock at the door and open it to find a man who has come to repair a utility fault inside your home. The man is wearing a utility company uniform and a mask with two holes for the eyes (okay, okay, bear with us for a moment). You ask for identification and he hands you a utility company badge. You even call up the utility company and confirm that he is scheduled to visit. The man comes in and then says he needs to go out to his van for a few minutes. In 30 seconds, a figure appears wearing the same uniform and mask and walks into your house. Question: How do you know it is the same guy? You don't know for sure. *So what was the point of checking in the first place if you can't positively identify the man every time he walks in?* You can now see the point of the mask in the analogy: In real life, we use our recognition of a person's face to confirm a person's authentication. But in a Wi-Fi LAN, there is no inherent way to do this. We will see later that the new security methods do provide this type of guarantee.

Despite its weakness, some systems still do use the "authentication" phase of the original IEE802.11 standard, so let's look at the messages that are exchanged. In the primer section, we point out that IEEE 802.11 uses three types of message: control, management, and data. The authentication phase uses management frames, as shown in Figure 6.1. For open authentication, the mobile device sends one message requesting authentication and the access point replies with a success message. For WEP-based authentication, an exchange of four messages occurs. First the

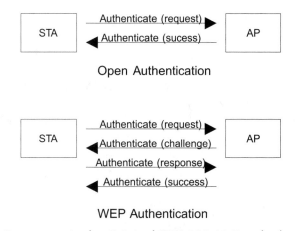

Figure 6.1 Authentication Sequences in the Original IEEE 802.11 Standard

mobile device requests authentication, and then the access point sends a challenge message. The mobile device responds to the challenge to prove that it knows a secret key and, if the proof is accepted, the access point sends the success message.

In principle, if the access point is operating in open mode, it always accepts the authentication request and responds with an authentication success message. This is the definition of open system operation. However, in practice many systems provide proprietary screening methods, the most popular being MAC address lists. The access point has a list of the MAC addresses that it will allow to join the network. This list is created by the manager and programmed in. The authentication is refused unless the mobile device's MAC address is found in the list. This doesn't protect against MAC address forgery, but it gives basic protection against very simple attacks using an off-the-shelf Wi-Fi LAN card, or even against accidental connection to the wrong network or another person's system.

WEP authentication is intended to prove to a legitimate access point that the mobile device knows the secret key. When the mobile device requests authentication, the access point sends a random number called **challenge text**. This is an arbitrary 128-bit number (preferably random). The mobile device then encrypts this number with the secret key using WEP and sends it back to the access point. Because the access point remembers the random number previously sent, it can check whether the result sent back was encrypted with the correct key; the mobile device must know the key in order to encrypt the random value successfully. Notice that this does nothing to prove to the mobile device that the access point knows the key. Notice also that if an attacker is listening, you just handed them a matching sample on which to start work because the challenge contains the plaintext and the response contains the ciphertext. You can start to see why the organization defining interoperability, the Wi-Fi Alliance, dropped the use of this exchange altogether.

The one benefit of the authentication exchange in a legitimate network is that it prevents stations joining the network unless they know the WEP key. There is a time savings in rejecting mobile devices that cannot communicate after associating. This is a management feature rather than a security feature. For example, if someone were to mistakenly enter the wrong key value, or fail to update his keys, the access point would reject the authentication and the user would be notified of the failure. Without the authentication phase, the mobile device is accepted, but every frame it sends is discarded by the access point due to decryption failure. From the mobile side, it is hard to distinguish this failure from failure due to interference or being out of range.

For completeness, let's look at the frame of the authentication messages used in this phase. Although multiple messages may be sent, they all have the same general format, as shown in Figure 6.2.

- The Algorithm Number indicates the type of authentication being used:
  0 – Open system
  1 – Shared key (WEP)
- The Transaction Sequence indicates where we are in the authentication sequence. The first message is 1, the second 2, and the third message (only used with WEP) is 3.
- The Status Code is sent in the final message to indicate success or failure of the authentication request.
- The Challenge Text field is used in the shared key (WEP) authentication, as described previously.

Privacy

If asked "What is the purpose of wireless LAN security," many people identify privacy as the key issue. It means preventing strangers from intercepting and understanding your data. Privacy is only one component of a security protocol and is not always needed, as the earlier analogy with signing a check shows. However, for Wi-Fi LAN security, privacy is a very desirable attribute, and was central to WEP's objectives.

Algorithm Num	Transaction Seq.	Status Code	Challenge Text

Figure 6.2 Authentication Message Format

Use of RC4 Algorithm

When WEP is enabled, the data messages are encrypted so an attacker who listens in cannot understand the contents (at least this is the intent). To decode the message, you have to know the secret key. The original IEEE 802.11 standard specified a two-phase approach: First you authenticate, and then you encrypt the data. As we have seen, the authentication method is next to useless; in fact, it is worse than useless because it gives an enemy information to use in an attack. Therefore, most Wi-Fi systems use open authentication and then switch on encryption after association. The fact that you effectively skip the authentication phase doesn't give the enemy any advantage in this case because, although he can join the network unchallenged, he can't send or receive any data without knowing the WEP keys for encryption.

The management of WEP keys is confusing because there are several of them used in different situations. We look at this in detail later; but for this section, let's assume that both the access point and the mobile device know the keys and that the mobile device has successfully associated (with or without authentication).

Security systems can be based around stream ciphers or block ciphers. A **stream cipher** takes a sequence of ordinary data (plaintext) and produces a sequence of encrypted data (ciphertext). It's like a sausage machine—you keep feeding plain bytes in one end and encrypted bytes come out the other end in a continuous process. A **block cipher** handles a single block of data at a time. It is more like a bakery—the dough is broken into lumps and each lump is processed separately to produce a loaf. In the case of data, fixed-length blocks are formed (typically 8, 16, or 32 bytes). Each block goes into the encryption algorithm and emerges as a completely different block of the same length. An important distinction between stream and block ciphers is that the internal state of a stream cipher is continuously updated as data is processed. By contrast, the state of a block cipher is reset for each block prior to processing.

WEP uses a stream cipher called RC4 to encrypt the data packets (Schneier, 1996). At the highest level, RC4 is a black box that takes in one byte from a stream at a time and produces a corresponding but different byte for the output stream, as shown in Figure 6.3. As with all encryption streams, the output stream is intended to look like a sequence of random numbers regardless of what the input stream looks like. Decryption is the reverse process and uses the same keys as for encryption (hence this is called a **symmetric algorithm**).

Figure 6.3 Stream Cipher

One of the advantages of RC4 is that it is fairly easy to implement and does not use any complicated or time-consuming operations like multiplication. Generally, this is the challenge for designers of an algorithm—to make it both secure and easy to implement. There are two main phases to RC4's use. In the first phase, initialization, some internal data tables are constructed based on the key value supplied; and in the second phase, the data runs through and is encrypted.

In the case of WEP, both the initialization phase and the encryption phase occur with each packet. That is, each packet is treated as if it were a new stream of data, which ensures that if one packet is lost the following packet can still be decrypted. This is both a strength and, as we shall see later, a source of weakness.

Initialization Vector (IV)

Before looking at the algorithm itself, we need to consider the encryption key again. As we mentioned previously, the original key length was 40 bits, which most manufacturers have increased to 104 bits. Manufacturers often refer to their 104-bit key solutions as "128-bit" security. So what happens to the extra 24 bits? The answer lies in the initialization vector.

There is a problem in using a fixed key value. Although the key may be updated from time to time, it is fixed relative to the flood of data packets running through the system. Effectively all the data packets are encrypted using the same key value. Suppose you initialize the RC4 algorithm with your key and run the message "qwertyuiop" into it. Suppose you get the encrypted result "b%fP★aF$!Y". This looks good and undecipherable. However, if the key is fixed, every time you run the same text "qwertyuiop" after initialization, you get the same result. In one sense, this is good—if you were to get a different result every time, it might make decryption somewhat tricky. But in another important way, this is very bad because it gives an attacker information. If she spots the same encrypted bytes in a given position, she knows that the original plaintext is being repeated.

How might this ability to spot repeated text be useful? Well, for example, the IP address always falls in the same place in a packet. So if you see the same encrypted bytes in that location, you know the message is from the same IP address (or going to the same IP address) as a previous message. You could think up lots of examples, but the basic principle is that you are giving information to the attacker and that is bad.

The solution to this problem is the **initialization vector (IV)**. This is a very simple concept. Instead of just using the fixed secret key to encrypt the packets, you combine the secret key with a 24-bit number that changes for every packet sent. This extra number is called the IV and effectively converts the 104-bit key into a 128-bit key. In our opinion, calling this 128-bit security is a minor con trick because the value of the IV is not secret at all but is transmitted openly with the encrypted frame.

To prevent the use of a fixed key for encryption, the actual key used to initialize the RC4 algorithm is the combination of the secret key and the IV, as shown in Figure 6.4.

Because the IV value always changes, the key used for encryption effectively changes with every packet so even if the input data (plaintext) is the same, the encrypted data (ciphertext) is always different.

The initialization vector is not a secret. In fact, it is sent openly as part of the transmission so the receiver knows which IV value to use in decryption. Any attacker can read the IV as well. In theory, knowledge of the IV is useless without knowledge of the secret part of the key. To be effective, the same IV value should *never be used twice* with a given secret key. Because the attacker can read the IV value, he could keep a log of the values used and notice when a value is used again. This would be the basis for an attack.

Unfortunately the IV in IEEE 802.11 WEP is only 24 bits long. This seems like quite a long number, but a few calculations show that it is not really enough. A 24-bit number has values from 0 to 16,777,216—so there are about 17 million IV values possible. A busy access point at 11Mbps is capable of transmitting/receiving about 700 average-sized packets a second. If a different IV value were used for every packet, all the values would be used up in less than seven hours! Because few people change their keys every day, IV values are bound to be reused.

There are other causes of IV reuse due to implementation issues. For example, many systems always start with the same IV value after a restart, and then the IV follows the same sequence as it is updated for each packet. Many systems change the IV according to a pseudorandom sequence—that is, a sequence that is superficially random but always follows the same sequence of numbers when started with a given value. If there are 20 mobile devices turned on in the morning, and they all start with the same IV value and follow the same sequence, then *the same IV value will appear 20 times for each value in the sequence.*

The problems with the IV illustrate that it is hard to design security protocols based on stream ciphers because the internal state of the encryption process is not

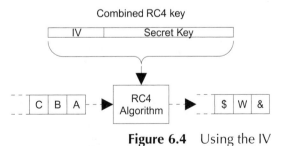

Figure 6.4   Using the IV

reset during a stream. Chapter 11 illustrates that the new version of WEP, called TKIP, which is also based on RC4, avoids IV reuse as an important part of the design.

WEP Keys

The way in which WEP keys are used is a great source of confusion to many people. Awkward terminology in the standard makes this situation even worse. The different types of keys in the standard have names that are confusing and misleading and, as a result, many manufacturers have tried to "help" by inventing new terms that are more easily understood. This is a double-edged sword because, while the new terms are better, they are not consistent across manufacturers, with the result that there are now multiple names in use for the same concepts. No wonder people have difficulty in understanding WEP keys.

So as not to propagate this confusion, **we only use the terms used in the original standard**, so you need to do some homework: Learn the official terms and, if required, cross reference them to the names used in the system you have installed. There are only two types of WEP keys mentioned in the standard. The correct terms are:

- Default key(s)
- Key mapping key(s)

Table 6.1 is a translation table showing the user-friendly names manufacturers use for these terms.

WEP keys have the following characteristics:

- **Fixed length:** Usually 40 bits or 104 bits
- **Static:** No changes in key value except by reconfiguration

Table 6.1 Manufacturer Names for WEP keys

Standard Term	Manufacturer's Term
Default key	Shared key
	Group key
	Multicast key
	Broadcast key
	Key
Key mapping key	Individual key
	Per-station key
	Unique key

- **Shared:** Access point and mobile device both have copy of the same key(s)
- **Symmetric:** Same key used to encrypt and decrypt information

The keys are static, and both the mobile device and the access point must have a copy. So the question arises how to configure the key into both devices in a way that does not risk the key being discovered. The IEEE 802.11 standard conveniently bypasses this problem with the words *"The required secret is presumed to have been delivered to participating STAs via a secure channel that is independent of IEEE 802.11."* This is not an unreasonable position because the method of installing the keys is bound to vary for different types of devices. You can install the keys on a laptop computer, for example, by typing them or using a floppy disk. However, if you have a mobile phone with Wi-Fi LAN built in, you need to use a different approach—for example, using a smart card.

Although skipping the issue of key distribution is reasonable for the standard, it doesn't make the job any easier for the system manager. At home, it is relatively easy. Just bring up a configuration utility provided with the system, choose the key values, and type them in. You can easily manage a few tens of users in this way. However, in a corporation with dozens or even hundreds of users, installing the keys to all the mobile devices and access points is an absolute nightmare—especially because it is essential to avoid unscrupulous people finding out the key values. Changing the keys can also be a major undertaking, so it doesn't help when the security guru tells you to change keys every seven hours to avoid IV reuse! In practice, each vendor tends to use a different approach to solve this problem. Most allow the simple option of typing in the key value using a utility or via the client driver interface. Some allow keys to be distributed to the mobile stations on a floppy disk that contains the keys in some obscured format. Sophisticated methods for secure key distribution have been invented, but these are not included in the WEP specification. If you are using WEP, you'll probably have to put up with typing the keys in for now.[1]

There are two different approaches to using keys under WEP. Usually when there are two ways to do something in a standard, you can figure there was a technical argument in the standards committee that neither side could win. In the end, they included both approaches and assumed the market would decide which to use. In fact, in the case of WEP, both approaches are useful in different circumstances.

- In the first case, all the mobile devices and the access points use a single set of keys. These keys are called **default keys.**

---

1. A few vendors have attempted to provide key distribution with WEP, notably Cisco LEAP (see Chapter 9).

- In the second case, each mobile device has a key that is unique. In other words the key used between each mobile device and the access point is specific to that connection and not known to other mobile devices. These keys are called **key mapping keys.**

The two modes are shown diagrammatically in Figure 6.5. Note that in the first case all the devices need to know only one key between them. In the second case, the mobile devices each know one key, but the access point has to have a table of all the keys. You can see that the names "default" and "key mapping" used in the standard don't relate very well to the function, which is why manufacturers have coined new terms in their documentation. Just remember default keys are shared, and mapping keys map to a specific device.

Default Keys

Consider a scenario in which you want all the mobile devices to share the same secret key, as in a home installation and in most small- to medium-sized commercial organizations. You decide to use the default keys. In fact, many manufacturers only support default key operation so this may be your only option. When you go to enter your key, you are surprised to find that there is not one, but four, default keys in the system. The IEEE 802.11 standard specifies that there should be four

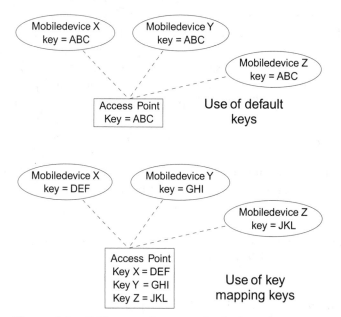

Figure 6.5   Difference Between Default and Key Mapping Keys

default keys for each device. This is another great source of confusion—do you need to enter all four? Do you need the same four on every mobile device as well? The level of confusion is so high that some users get as far as this configuration screen and give up, opting to take a chance without using WEP.

As with many things, these options make sense when you understand why you have them. Here are two key facts that help:

1. Only one default key is needed for security to work.
2. Multiple default keys are supported to help you change keys smoothly.

Let's suppose there was only one default key available system-wide. When you install your Wi-Fi LAN system, you choose a key and program it into the access point. You program the same key into each of the mobile devices and into new ones that you add later. Everything is fine until, like a good security manager, you decide it is time to change the key value. How do you do it? If you change the key in the access point, all the mobile devices will be disconnected immediately. Then you will have to track down all the users and reprogram their mobile device with the new key. This step could take hours, or days if people are out of the office. You could send out a memo telling everyone that from 9:00 Monday the key is changing and they need to update their computers. However, at least half the people will forget and be on the phone complaining their Wi-Fi LAN connection is broken and, in any case, you can hardly publish the key value in the memo for them to type in. If there were only one default key, changing its value would be a real pain in the neck.

The answer is to use two default keys "simultaneously." It works like this: When there are two default keys defined, all transmissions are encrypted using a single key that you select. This is called the **active key**. However, received frames can be decrypted using either of the two keys as appropriate. In summary, if you have multiple default keys you always encrypt using the active key but you can decrypt using any default key that is appropriate.

This technique of multiple keys makes key change much easier. The key change works as shown in Figure 6.6 (A–D).

In Figure 6.6A, the mobile station and access point are communicating using the first default key ABCDEF. The second default key is not assigned (this is called a null key). Now the manager decides to change the key. The first thing to do is to program the new key JKLMNP into to the access point as the second default key, as shown in Figure 6.6B. Note that the access point still transmits using ABC-DEF—that is still the active key. By the way, you should never use such weak key values as these in a real system!

The next stage in the change is to notify all the users that they need to have their keys updated. Perhaps you go to their desks or ask them to come to you. In

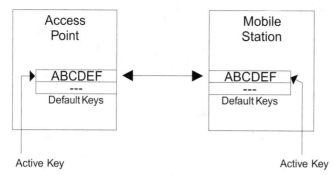

Figure 6.6A   Before Changing Keys

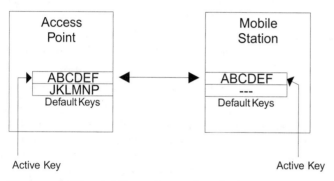

Figure 6.6B   Adding a Second Default Key

each case you install the new secret key and *make the new key active on their devices.* Now the users whose devices have been updated will be transmitting using the new key, as shown in Figure 6.6C.

Notice that the access point is still sending using the old key, but the active key on the mobile has been changed. The access point must use the old key because some users have not been updated yet and don't know the new key. Access point transmissions using the old key are accepted by mobile devices that have not been updated and also by the ones that have the new key. The mobile devices with the new key still have a copy of the old key available. In the same way the access point can accept messages from both updated and un-updated mobile devices because it also has both keys available.

After all the users' devices have been updated, or after a cut-off date for the change, you move the access point over to the new key and the old key is deleted, as shown in Figure 6.6D. You can see how this key change has been possible with relatively little disruption because of the availability of multiple default keys. You

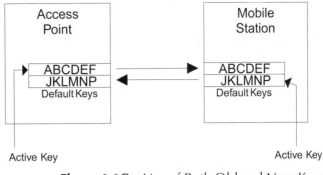

Figure 6.6C Use of Both Old and New Keys

need only two default keys to make this transfer work, so why are there four default keys? Was the Standards committee feeling generous on that day or is there some other reason?

We have assumed so far that the keys are used *bidirectionally*. In other words, the same key is used to receive and to transmit (except during a key change). With four keys, you can operate with different keys in each direction. Remember that transmitted frames are always encrypted using the active key. The active key is identified using a number: 0, 1, 2, or 3. So, for example, the AP might transmit using default key 0. However, there is no reason why the mobile devices have to transmit using 0. The mobile devices might all be configured with an active key of 2. Think about what that means—the AP encrypts its messages using key 0, but the mobile devices encrypt using key 2. Key 2 on the AP has to match key 2 on the mobile device and key 0 on the mobile has to match key 0 on the AP. However, key 0 is different from key 2. This is called **directional key use**.

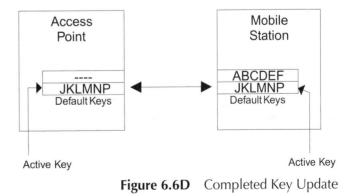

Figure 6.6D Completed Key Update

If you think directional key use gives more security, you could decide to always use keys 0 and 1 for AP transmissions and keys 2 and 3 for mobile device transmissions. You need two keys in each case to allow the key change to occur for each direction separately, making a total of four keys in use.

The key number (0, 1, 2, or 3) that is used for transmission has to be notified to the receiver so it knows which key to use for decryption. This is done by sending the information, called the **KeyID bits**, in each encrypted frame.

Now you know why there are four keys available. Remember that you are not obliged to use all four. You can operate quite happily with only one default key, provided you don't mind disruption when changing the value. There is one more use for default keys, which is needed when you use the key mapping keys, as described in the next section.

Key Mapping Keys

The basic principle of key mapping keys is to give each mobile device its own key value. The benefits of this approach are obvious in a large organization. If you have 1,000 users on a site and they all share a single default key, you will have a very hard time keeping that key secret and performing key updates. If instead each user has a unique key, you can change an individual key and enable or disable single users if, for example, a laptop is lost or stolen.

Not all manufacturers support key mapping keys because of the complexity of configuring and maintaining them. If you want to use this feature, you may need to shop around (and if you are shopping around now, we suggest you skip WEP and go straight to the new security approach of Wi-Fi WPA). Anyway, we briefly run through the issues here for completeness.

Using different keys per mobile device introduces a small but important complication related to broadcast handling. The architecture of most LANs derives from the idea of *sharing* a communication channel. For example, early wired LANs used a coax cable, rather like the antenna cable on a TV, to connect all the computers in series. The cable was shared between all the computers. Even today with modern Ethernet cabling, LAN hubs usually connect all the ports together so that they act like a single wired connection. In the wireless environment, radio transmissions are obviously shared due to the fact that anyone can receive them. In a shared LAN, three types of message operate: **unicast messages**, which are sent to a single destination, **group messages**, which are sent to several destinations at once and **broadcast messages**, which are sent to everyone. The last two cases are collectively called multicast messages.

Here's the rub: If every mobile device uses a different key, how does the AP send a broadcast message? Which key should it use for encryption? The solution is that all multicast traffic is sent using a default key that is shared by all the mobile devices. Only unicast messages are sent using the mapping key that is specific to the receiver. You need to program a minimum of two keys into each mobile device.

Apart from the need for two keys, implementing key mapping keys at the mobile device end is the same as for default keys. You must, for example, put the special key for this device into key number 0. The broadcast key goes into one of the other locations, say key number 2. You would set key 0 as the active key; mobile devices do not sent broadcasts, they only receive them.

The access point is much more complicated because it needs to know the special key for every possible station that might want to associate. Potentially this means keeping a table of hundreds of entries. Whenever the AP receives a frame, it has to pick out the sender's MAC address and use it as an index into the table to find the right key to use for decrypting. Similarly, before transmitting, it has to look up the correct key based on the destination address. This is tough work for the AP and you can see why some manufacturers opted not to provide support. The other problem is that the list of keys takes up memory space and, if there are several APs, they all have to have the same copy of the list. This makes management in a large system difficult and error prone.

The key mapping key option is a good idea, but it is not supported by all AP vendors and therefore has not been widely deployed. If you are interested in this type of approach, you will find that the new security methods such as WPA do provide these capabilities—and the ability to manage the key lists in a much more effective way.

By the way, the AP can operate with default keys and key mapping keys simultaneously; you are not required to switch between one or the other modes. When the AP receives a frame (or wants to send one), it looks in the key table to see whether there is an entry corresponding to the MAC address of the mobile. If it finds an entry, it uses it. If not, it uses the default key instead. *Eureka! That is why it is called the default key.* And that is why almost no one uses the term "default key" outside the standard (and this book).

Mechanics of WEP

So far we have discussed the original goals of WEP and given an overview of the design and use of keys. Now we will look in much more detail at the way in which WEP is implemented. You need to understand where the weaknesses of WEP arise.

Fragmentation

We are used to using the telephone. There was a time when all telephones looked the same. This was partly due to the monopoly of the telephone companies but probably was also due to the need for people who had not grown up with telephones to feel comfortable with the user interface they had learned. Today, telephones are part of our psyche. We can handle phones in any shape or size as naturally as catching a ball or walking on unfamiliar ground. We pick up the phone, dial the number, and talk to the other person with little effort. We don't care about the many complicated processes that occur between our lips and the ear of the receiver (that sounds a bit weird. but we're talking about electronic processes). A similar situation has evolved for application programs. There was a time when a programmer needed to know about the details of the network protocols and hardware that were used for communication. Today, the operating systems environment allows application programs to make a connection and communicate data with ease and without knowledge of the network implementation.

If a network includes a Wi-Fi LAN link, data from the operating system or a driver needs to pass to the IEEE 802.11 MAC service layer. In other words, a packet of data arrives at the Wi-Fi LAN with instructions to send it out. This packet of data is called an MSDU (MAC service data unit). If things go well, this MSDU will eventually pop out of the MAC service layer on the destination device and be passed to the operating system or driver for delivery to the target application. Before it reaches the radio for transmission, however, the MSDU may be broken up into several smaller pieces, a process called **fragmentation**. Each fragment is processed for WEP encryption. A MAC header is added to the front and a checkword added to the end.

You can see that the original MSDU may now be spread across several smaller messages and have had more bytes added on—quite apart from the fact that it will now be encrypted. Each one of the smaller messages is called an MPDU (MAC protocol data unit). We'll look at the last few stages, during which an MPDU encounters the encryption process.

The process treats the data as a block of unformatted bytes; the size depends on the original MSDU contents and the fragmentation settings. It is typically in the range of 10–1,500 bytes. The first step in encryption is to add some bytes called the **integrity check value (ICV)**.

Integrity Check Value (ICV)

The idea behind the ICV is to prevent anyone from tampering with the message in transit. In both encrypted and unencrypted messages, a check is made to detect whether any bits have been corrupted during transmission. All the bytes in the message are combined in a result called the CRC (cyclic redundancy check). This 4-byte value is added on to the end of the frame immediately prior to processing for transmission. Even if a single bit in the message is corrupted, the receiving device will notice that the CRC value does not match and reject the message.

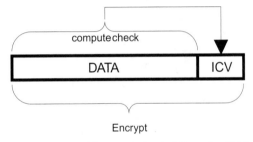

Figure 6.7   Adding the ICV

While this detects accidental errors, it provides no protection from intentional errors because an attacker can simply recompute the CRC value after altering the message and ensure that it matches again.

ICV is similar to the CRC except that it is computed and added on *before* encryption. The conventional CRC is still added after encryption. The theory is that, because the ICV is encrypted, no attacker can recompute it when attempting to modify the message. Therefore, the message is rendered tamper-proof. Er... well, only in theory, as we'll see shortly that clever people found a loophole. For now, let's suppose it works as intended.

So the ICV is computed by combining all the data bytes to create a four-byte checkword. This is then added on the end, as shown in Figure 6.7.

Preparing the Frame for Transmission

After the ICV is appended, the frame is ready for encryption. First, the system must select an IV value and append it to the secret WEP key (as indicated by the active key selection). Next, it initializes the RC4 encryption engine. Finally it passes each byte from the combined data and ICV block into the encryption engine. For each byte going in, an encrypted byte comes out until all the bytes are processed. This is a **stream cipher**.

For the receiver to know how to decrypt the message, the key number and IV value must be put on the front of the message. Four bytes are added for this purpose. The first three bytes contain the 24-bit IV value and the last byte contains the KeyID number 0, 1, 2, or 3, as shown in Figure 6.8.

Finally, the MAC header is attached and the CRC value placed at the end to detect transmission errors. A bit in the MAC header indicates to the receiver that the frame is WEP encrypted so that it knows how to handle it.

The receive process follows logically. The receiver notes that the WEP bit is set and therefore reads and stores the IV value. It then reads the key ID bits so it can select the correct WEP key, append the IV value, and initialize the RC4 encryption

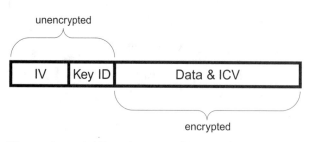

Figure 6.8   Adding the IV and KeyID bits

engine. Notice that with RC4 there is no difference between the encryption and decryption processes. If you run the data through the encryption process twice, you get back to the original data—in other words, the second encryption cancels out the first. Therefore, you need only one engine for both encryption and decryption. After the encryption engine is initialized, the data is run through one byte at a time to reveal the original message. The final step is to compute the ICV and verify that the value matches that in the received message. If all is well, the data portion is passed up for further processing.

RC4 Encryption Algorithm

RC4 is the name of the encryption algorithm used by WEP. An encryption algorithm is just a set of operations that you apply to plaintext to generate ciphertext. Obviously it is not helpful unless there is a corresponding decryption algorithm. In the case of RC4, the same algorithm is used for encryption and decryption. The value of an encryption algorithm lies partly in how strong it is and partly in how easy it is to implement. The strength of an algorithm is measured by how hard it is to crack the ciphertext. There certainly are stronger methods than RC4. However, RC4 is remarkably simple to implement and considered to be very strong if *used in the right way.* This last point is important because we will see all the weakness of WEP later, and those weaknesses do not derive from faults in RC4, but in the way it is applied in the case of WEP.

RC4[2] is a proprietary stream cipher designed in 1987. While the algorithm has received a great deal of public attention, RSA Labs, Inc. regards the description of the algorithm as a *trade secret. Implementers should consult RSA Labs about this issue. However, the algorithm was reverse-engineered and made public anonymously in 1994.*

Fortunately, because RC4 is simple to implement, it is also simple to describe. The basic idea behind RC4 encryption is to generate a pseudorandom sequence

---

2. RC4 stands for the fourth cipher designed by Ron Rivest (Rivest Cipher 4).

of bytes called the **key stream** that is then combined with the data using an exclusive OR (XOR) operation. For those not familiar with the XOR operation, it combines two bytes and generates a single byte. It does this by taking and comparing corresponding bits in each byte. If they are equal, the result is 0; if they differ, the result is 1. An example is shown in Figure 6.9.

XOR is often written mathematically using the symbol "$\oplus$" so the example shown in the figure would be written:

```
00110101 ⊕ 11100011 = 11010110
```

One important characteristic of XOR is that if you apply the same value twice, the original value is returned:

```
00110101 ⊕ 11100011 = 11010110
11010110 ⊕ 11100011 = 00110101
```

In other words, if $A \oplus B = C$, then $C \oplus B = A$. You might guess that in the case of RC4, this property is exploited as follows:

```
Encryption: Plaintext ⊕ Random = Ciphertext
Decryption: Ciphertext ⊕ Random = Plaintext
```

It is necessary that "random" looks random to an attacker but that both ends of the link can generate the same "random" value for each byte processed. It is therefore called **pseudorandom** and is generated by the RC4 algorithm.

The most important property of a pseudorandom key stream is that you can calculate the next byte in the sequence *only* if you know the key used to generate the stream. If you don't know the key, it really looks random. Note that the XOR operation completely hides the plaintext values. Even if the plaintext is just a long series of 0 values, the ciphertext still looks random to an attacker.

XOR is a trivially easy operation for a computer to implement so the only challenge is to generate a good pseudorandom number stream. You need one

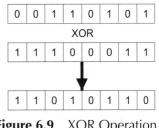

Figure 6.9 XOR Operation

pseudorandom byte for each byte of the message to be encrypted. RC4 generates such a stream.

There are two phases in RC4: key setup and pseudo-random generation. The first phase, the key setup algorithm, establishes a 256-byte array with a permutation of the numbers 0–255; that is, all the numbers are present in the array but the order is mixed up. The permutation in the array, or S-box, is established by first initializing the array with the numbers 0–255 in order. The elements in the S-box are then rearranged through the following process. First, a second 256-byte array, or K-box, is filled with the key, repeating as needed to fill the array. Now each byte in the S-box is swapped with another byte in the S-box. Starting at the first byte, the following computation is made:

```
j = (Value in first byte of S-box ) + (Value in first byte of K-box)
j is a single byte value and any overflow in the addition is ignored.
```

Now j is used as an index into the S-box and the value at that location is swapped with the value in the first location.

This procedure is repeated another 255 times until each byte in the S-box has been swapped. The process is described by the following pseudocode for people familiar with programming:

```
i = j = 0;
For i = 0 to 255 do
   j = (j + S_i + K_i) mod 256;
Swap S_i and S_j;
End;
```

Once the S-box has been initialized, the next phase in RC4 is the pseudorandom generation phase. This phase involves more swapping of bytes in the S-box and generates one pseudorandom byte per iteration (R). The equations for the iterations are shown here.

```
i = (i + 1) mod 256
j = (j + S_i) mod 256
Swap S_i and S_j
k = (S_i + S_j) mod 256
R = S_k
```

To generate the ciphertext, each byte of plaintext is XORed with a value of R as produced by the RC4 algorithm. Notice how the whole process has been done using byte length additions and swaps—very easy operations for computer logic.

Theoretically, RC4 is not a completely secure encryption system because it generates a pseudorandom key stream, not truly random bytes. But it's certainly sufficiently secure for our application, if applied correctly to the protocol.

Using XOR in this way is similar to a Vernam cipher (Vernam, 1926). Gilvert Vernam developed this cipher during World War I while working for AT&T. However, it is only completely secure if R is a *true* random byte (Menenez et al., 1996). What constitutes a *true random byte* is a philosophical debate we won't open here. But suppose that you generated a huge table of random numbers by sampling cosmic noise or some genuinely random physical event rather than using a pseudorandom algorithm such as in RC4. You could use your random numbers by sending a secret copy to your friend for use with the Vernam cipher. This has the advantage that the numbers are truly random *and* known to both ends of the link. This approach is very secure, but you would be allowed to use the table only once. Then you would have to eat it or otherwise dispose of it—it is a **one-time pad**. Ensuring that a one-time pad system is completely secure requires never reusing the same series of random bytes twice. Because the former Soviet Union made this serious mistake following World War II, the American National Security Agency (NSA) was able to decrypt a number of enciphered messages sent by Soviet agents in a project code named VENONA (U.S. NSA, 1999).

Why WEP Is Not Secure

WEP was included in the original IEEE 802.11 standard in 1997, but it was not until 1999 that systems were widely deployed when IEEE 802.11b and Wi-Fi became established. Most vendors added key extensions allowing a 104-bit key to be used (128 bit if you count the IV), and this was also adopted by Wi-Fi.

The industry started to have concerns about WEP security as designs were made and engineers started to point out some problems. In particular, the weakness of the authentication method was noted, as described earlier, and the authentication phase was dropped altogether. However, the manufacturers' concerns related to the strength of the security rather than the overall integrity. In other words, they were concerned that a serious and major attack might succeed. Nobody thought that it would be easy to break WEP.

Because of these concerns and also because of the difficulties in key management discussed in this chapter, the IEEE 802.11 Standards Committee launched a new task group to look at upgrading the security approach. The IEEE 802.11 committee is, essentially, a voluntary organization. Meetings are held roughly six times a year and the meetings are open to any industry members. The process involves technical presentations, discussions, drafting text, and a lot of voting. It is a democratic and parliamentary process. As a result, new standards do not develop quickly. Major modifications such as the security subsystem take years rather than months.

While the IEEE 802.11 group was considering a new approach, the security research community was also looking at WEP. In the early days, security gurus had not paid much attention because wireless LAN was not a widespread technology. But by 2000 it was appearing everywhere and many universities had installations. Security researchers had direct contact with Wi-Fi LAN. As did most people, they realized the potential advantages; but, unlike most people, they immediately questioned whether the security provisions were bomb-proof.

The answer came in 2000 as a series of reports emerged highlighting weakness after weakness (Walker, 2000; Arbaugh et al., 2001; Borisov et al., 2001). Finally, an attack was published showing that the keys could be extracted in a busy network within hours, regardless of the key length. The press were ecstatic. Security weakness and security breaches sell copy, and headlines appeared around the world. Even the main public media channels covered the event. This was a measure of how far IEEE 802.11 had come that it was considered of interest to the general public. However, there were lots of red faces—embarrassed manufacturers and angry customers.

This section looks in detail at the attacks on WEP that have been identified. WEP is a general term that covers a number of security mechanisms. As a basis for evaluating WEP, let's review the mechanisms that are needed for security:

- Authentication
- Access control
- Replay prevention
- Message modification detection
- Message privacy
- Key protection

Unfortunately, WEP fails to perform in all these areas. We'll look at each one separately.

Authentication

Authentication is about one party proving to the other that he really is who he claims to be. Authentication is not a one-time process—in other words, it is not enough to prove once that you are authentic. It is only useful if you can prove it every time you communicate. The process of authentication is often time consuming, and so a common approach is to perform full authentication on first contact and then provide a limited-life "identity badge." Ideally, the identity badge is such that it cannot be transferred to someone else. A photo ID is an example in which the government or corporation authenticates you.

In the wireless world, you usually need *mutual* authentication. The network wants proof about the user, but the user also wants proof that the network really is the expected one. This is important for Wi-Fi LANs because it is so inexpensive to set up decoy access points.

Finally, security experts point out that it is essential to use different secret keys for authentication than you use for encryption.[3] The use of derived keys is recommended because master keys should rarely or never be exposed directly to attack. In summary, the basic requirements for authentication in wireless LANs are:

1. Robust method of proving identity that cannot be spoofed
2. Method of preserving identity over subsequent transactions that cannot be transferred
3. Mutual authentication
4. Independent keys independent from encryption (and other) keys

Unfortunately, WEP fails on all counts. As a reminder, WEP authentication relies on a challenge–response mechanism. First, the AP sends a random string of numbers. Second, the mobile device encrypts the string and sends it back. Third, the AP decrypts the string and compares to the original string. It can then choose to accept the device and send a success message.

The key used for this process is the same WEP key used for encryption, thus breaking rule 4. The operation does not authenticate the access point to the mobile device because a rogue access point can pretend it was able to check the encrypted string and send a success message without ever knowing the key. Hence rule 3 is broken.

Rule 2 is broken because there is no token provided to validate subsequent transactions, making the whole authentication process rather futile.

Rule 1 is rather irrelevant given the weaknesses already pointed out, but it's quite interesting to look at why this also fails.

During authentication the access point sends a random string of 128 bytes. The way in which this "random" string is generated is not defined, but one would hope at least that it was different for each authentication attempt. The mobile station encrypts the string and sends it back. Sounds good, but hang on a moment— WEP encryption involves generating a sequence of pseudorandom bytes called the key stream and XORing it with the plaintext. So any one watching this transaction now has the plaintext challenge and the encrypted response. Therefore,

---

3. It is acceptable to cryptographically derive two separate keys from a single master key. If done correctly, the two keys are effectively independent.

simply by XORing the two together, the enemy has a copy of the RC4 random bytes. Remember the basic equation:

$$P \oplus R = C \quad \text{(Plaintext XOR Randombytes = Ciphertext)}$$

And remember that XORing twice gets you back to the original value (that's decryption):

$$\text{If } P \oplus R = C \text{ then } C \oplus R = P$$

By the same argument, XORing the ciphertext with the plaintext gives you the random key stream:

$$\text{If } P \oplus R = C \text{ then } C \oplus P = R$$

Whoops, the game's over! The attacker now knows the key stream corresponding to a given IV value. Now the attacker simply requests authentication, waits for the challenge text, XORs with the previously captured key stream, and returns the result with the previously captured IV.

To check the result, the access point appends the IV (chosen by the attacker) to the secret key and generates the RC4 random key stream. These will, of course, be the same bytes that the attacker worked out because the key and IV are the same as last time. Therefore when the access point decrypts the message by XORing with the RC4 key stream, surprise, surprise, it matches. The attacker is "authenticated" without ever knowing the secret key. Hopeless!

Although an attacker can get authenticated in this way, she can't then communicate because frames are encrypted with WEP. Therefore, she needs to break WEP encryption as well. However, there is even more bad news. For some of the methods of attacking encryption keys, the enemy needs a sample of matching plaintext and ciphertext. Sometimes this can be quite hard for an attacker to get, and there are various tricky methods that she might use to try to get such a sample. What a gift! The WEP authentication method provides a 128-byte sample free of charge. Worse, it is a sample of the first 128 bytes of the key stream, which is the most vulnerable to attack.[4] So not only does this approach *not* authenticate, it actually assists the enemy to attack the encryption keys. Hmmm... we better move on. Most systems today don't use the futile WEP authentication phase anyway.

---

4. We will look at this vulnerability in more detail in Chapter 11 on TKIP.

Access Control

Access control is, rather obviously, the process of allowing or denying a mobile device to communicate with the network. It is often confused with authentication. All that authentication does is to establish who you are; it does not follow that, because you are authenticated, you should be allowed access.

In general, access is usually controlled by having a list of allowed devices. It may also be done by allowing access to anyone who can prove he has possession of a certificate or some other electronic pass.

IEEE 802.11 does not define how access control is implemented. However, identification of devices is only done by MAC address, so there is an implication that a list of acceptable MAC addresses exists somewhere. Many systems implement a simple scheme whereby a list of allowed MAC addresses can be entered into the access point, even when you are operating without WEP. However, given the ease with which MAC addresses can be forged, this cannot be considered as a serious security mechanism.

If you can't trust the MAC address, the only thing left to WEP is the encryption key. If the mobile station doesn't know the correct WEP key, then the frames it sends will produce an ICV error when decrypted. Therefore, the frames will be discarded and, effectively, the device is denied access. This last line of defense is really all that the original IEEE 802.11 standard has to offer.

Replay Prevention

Let's suppose you are an attacker with a wireless sniffer that is able to capture all the frames sent between an access point and a mobile device. You observe that a new user has turned on her laptop and connected to the network. Maybe the first thing that happens is that the server sends her a login message and she enters her user name and password. Of course, you can't see the actual messages because they are encrypted. However, you might be able to guess what's going on, based on the length of the messages.

Later on, you notice the user has shut down and gone home. So now is your chance. Bring up your own client using her MAC address and connect to the network. As we have seen earlier, that part is easy. Now, if you are lucky, you'll receive a message to log in. Again, you won't be able to decode it, but you can guess what it is from the size. So now you send a copy of the message the legitimate user sent at that point. You are *replaying* an old message without needing to know the contents. If there were no replay protection, the access point would correctly decode the message; after all, it was originally encrypted with a valid key before you recorded it. The access point passes the message to the login server, which accepts it as a valid login. You, as an attacker, just successfully logged into the network and the server. It's not clear where you would go from there. However, from a security standpoint, this is a serious breach.

There are many other examples in which a replay attack can breach security unless the network is designed specifically to detect and reject old copies of messages. The wireless security protocol should allow only one copy of a message to be accepted. *Ever.*

By this time, it may come as no surprise to discover that WEP has no protection against replay at all. It was just not considered in the design. There is a sequence number in the MAC frame that must increase monotonically. However, it is not included in the WEP protection so it is easy to modify the sequence number to be valid without messing with the encrypted portion on the frame.

Replay protection is not broken in WEP; it simply doesn't exist.

Message Modification Detection

WEP has a mechanism that is designed to prevent message modification. Message modification can be used in subtle ways. The first thing people think about when message modification is proposed is to change the contents of the message in an obvious way. For example, changing the destination bank account number on a deposit or changing the amount transferred. However, in reality such large-scale modifications would be very hard to mount and assume that you can read the original message and effectively forge new messages.

If you are unable to decrypt the message, it is not obvious how modifying the ciphertext would be useful. However, even in this case modifications can be used to extract information. A technical paper by Borisov et al. (2001) proposed a method to exploit "bit flipping" in which a few bits of the ciphertext are changed at a time. They pointed out that the position of the IP header is usually known after encryption because WEP does not rearrange the byte positions. Because the IP header has a checksum, changing one bit in the header causes the checksum to fail. However, if you *also* change bits in the checksum, you might get a match. The researchers showed that, by flipping a few bits at a time and seeing whether the IP frame was accepted, based on whether responses came back, they could eventually decode portions of a frame.

To prevent tampering, WEP includes a checkfield called the integrity check value (ICV). We looked at this briefly in the previous section on frame formats. The idea behind the ICV is simple: compute a check value or CRC (cyclic redundancy check) over all the data to be encrypted, append the check value to the end of the data, and then encrypt the whole lot. If someone changes a bit in the ciphertext, the decrypted data will not have the same check word and the modification will be detected. The thinking is that, because the ICV is encrypted, you cannot go back and correct its value to compensate for the other changes you have made. It is only intended to provide protection to the ciphertext. If an attacker already knows the keys, he can modify the data and recompute the ICV before re-encrypting and forwarding the frame. So use of the ICV protects the ciphertext from tampering—right?

Wrong again! Borisov et al. pointed out a flaw in the logic. The CRC method used to compute the ICV is called a **linear method**. It turns out that, with a linear method, you can predict which bits in the ICV will be changed if you change a single bit in the message. The ICV is 32 bits. Let's suppose the message is 8,000 bits (1,000 bytes) and you flip bit position 5244. You can then compute which bits in the ICV will be changed as a result. It is typically not a single bit but a combination of bits that will change. Note that we used the word "change," not "set" or "clear." You don't need to know the actual value of the plaintext; you just need to know that if you flip the value of a certain bit in the data, you can keep the ICV valid by also flipping a certain combination of its bits. Unfortunately, because WEP works by XORing the data to get the ciphertext, bit flipping survives the encryption process. Flipping a bit in the plaintext always flips the same bit in the ciphertext, and vice versa.

If you've hung in through the argument in the last paragraph, you will see that, because of the fact that bit flipping survives encryption; the assumption that the ICV is protected by encryption just doesn't hold water. Its actual value is protected, but you can reliably flip its bits. And because you can work out which bits to flip corresponding to a change in the data, you can completely defeat its protection.

With a muffled thump, another of WEP's protections just hit the floor. The reality is that WEP provides no effective protection against ciphertext modification.[5]

Message Privacy

This is the big one: attacking the encryption method of WEP. We have seen that the other protections have already been stripped away; but, at the end of the day, if the encryption method holds up, then the attacker is very limited in what he can do. So far, it's just watching shadows or throwing rocks at the window; but if the encryption can be breached, the attacker is inside the house.

There are two main objectives in attacking the encryption: decode a message or get the keys. The ultimate success is to get the keys. Once an attacker has the keys, he is free to explore and look for the valuables. Possession of the keys doesn't automatically mean access to confidential information because there are other layers

---

5. In fact, in the general case, no integrity check word can be used successfully with RC4 unless it is created using a key generated specifically for integrity checking (as distinct from the encryption key).

of security inside, such as server passwords and operating system protections. However, the issue of network access is put aside. Furthermore, if an attacker can get the keys, he can probably go undetected, which is important to buy the time to find useful information. If an attack is detected, the WEP keys can be changed, putting the attacker back to square one.

The next best thing to getting the keys is to be able to get the plaintext. If you can get the plaintext in a reasonably fast and reliable way, you have access to a range of other types of attacks using message modification and replay. That information can also be used as a stepping-stone to getting the keys.

There are three weaknesses in the way RC4 is used in WEP and we will look at each case separately:

- IV reuse
- RC4 weak keys
- Direct key attack

IV Reuse

One of the first cryptographers to point out weaknesses in WEP was Jesse Walker of Intel. In October 2000 he wrote a submission to the IEEE 802.11 Standards Committee entitled "Unsafe at any key size: An analysis of the WEP encapsulation." This title was designed to get attention—and it did. Walker pointed out a number of potential weaknesses, but especially focused on the issue of IV reuse.

Let's quickly review how the IV is used. Instead of using a fixed secret key, the secret key is appended to a 24-bit IV value and then the combined IV/ secret is used as the encryption key. The value of the IV is sent in the frame so the receiving device can perform the decryption. One purpose of the IV is to ensure that two identical messages don't produce the same ciphertext. However, there is a second and more important purpose related to the way WEP uses XOR to create the ciphertext.

Let's suppose for a moment that there was no IV and only the secret key is used for encryption. For every frame, the RC4 algorithm is initialized with the key value prior to the start of the pseudorandom key stream generation. But if the key were to remain fixed, the RC4 algorithm would be initialized to the same state every time. Therefore the key stream produced would be the *same sequence of bytes* for every frame. This is disastrous because, if the attacker can figure out what that key stream is, he can decode every frame simply by XORing the frame with the known sequence. He doesn't need to know the key.

By adding the IV value to the key each time, RC4 is initialized to a different state for every frame and so the key stream is different for each encryption—much better. Let's review that statement because there is an implicit assumption: The IV value is *different for every frame*. If the IV is a constant value, you are no better off than in the static key case.

So we see that constant IV is useless. We can also see that using a different IV for every frame, and I mean *every* frame, is a good idea. What about the middle ground? There are a limited number of possible IVs so it is acceptable to use a different IV for most frames but eventually start reusing IVs that have been used in the past. The simple answer is that this is not acceptable—but it is precisely what WEP does.

Let's look at why IV reuse is a problem. We have said that the IV should be different for every frame. However, the original IEEE 802.11 standard did not say how it should be generated (actually it did not require that it be changed at all!). Intuitively you might think that the best approach would be to generate a random value. However, with random selection there is a good chance that you will get a repeating IV quite quickly. This is known as the **birthday paradox** (see sidebar).

In the case of IVs, it means that you are likely to get a duplicate IV sooner than you expect if you pick random values.

The best way to allocate IVs is simply to increment the value by 1 each time. This gives you the longest possible time before a repeating value. However, with a 24-bit IV, an **IV collision** (use of a previous value) is guaranteed after 2^{24} frames have been transmitted (nearly 17 million). IEEE 802.11b is capable of transmitting 500 full-length frames a second and many more shorter frames. At 500 frames a second, the IV space would be all used up in around seven hours.

In reality a collision is likely much sooner because there may be many devices transmitting, each incrementing a separate IV value and using it with the same key (assuming default keys are in use). Implementation errors can compound the problem. At least one major Wi-Fi LAN manufacturer always initializes the IV counter to 0 when the system is started up. Imagine that ten users come into work and start up their laptops. Depending on who does what, the IV counter of some will get ahead of others, but there will be a rich harvest of IV collisions to be had by an observer. IV collisions are a fact of life for WEP so let's look again at why collisions are a problem.

The Birthday Paradox

When you meet someone, there is only a 1 in 365 chance that the person has the same birthday as you. However, the chance of meeting someone with your birthday increases surprisingly fast as you meet more people. In fact, there is a 50% chance that you will find someone with a matching birthday within the first 25 people you meet. This is a surprising fact, which is probably why it is called a paradox.

If you know the key stream corresponding to a given IV value, you can immediately decode any subsequent frame that uses the same IV (and secret key). This is true regardless of whether the secret key is 40 bits, 104 bits, or 1,040 bits. To decode every message, you would have to know the key stream for every possible IV value. Because there are nearly 17 million possible IV values, that seems like a daunting task. However, it's not impossible: If you want to store a 1,500-byte key stream, for every possible IV you need a storage space of 23Gbytes—quite feasible on the hard disk of an everyday computer. With such a database, you could decode every message sent without ever knowing the secret key. However, you still have to find out all those key streams and that's not so easy.

Suppose you have captured two messages encrypted using the same IV and secret key. You know that the key stream is the same in both cases, although you don't know what it is yet. Using our simple notation:

$C_1 = P_1 \oplus K_S$ (Ciphertext msg1 = Plaintext msg1 XORed Keystream)

and

$C_2 = P_2 \oplus K_S$ (KS is the same in each case)

If you XOR C_1 and C_2, K_S disappears:

$$C_1 \oplus C_2 = (P_1 \oplus K_S) \oplus (P_2 \oplus K_S) = P_1 \oplus P_2 \oplus K_S \oplus K_S = P_1 \oplus P_2$$

This is true because XORing the same value twice takes you back to your original value.

So the attacker now has a message that is the XOR of two plaintexts. Is that useful? No not yet. However, some of the values of plaintext are definitely known, such as certain fields in the header. In other fields the value is not known, but the purpose is known. For example, the IP address fields have a limited set of possible values in most networks. The body portion of the text often encodes ASCII text, again giving some possible clues.

Over a period of time, if you collect enough samples of duplicated IVs, you can probably guess substantial portions of the key stream and hence decode more and more. It's like a collapsing building: Each block you knock away makes it more likely that the whole lot will fall down. It's hacker's celebrity squares in which you have some of the letters in a word and you try to guess the whole sentence. But once you succeed for a given IV, you can decode every subsequent frame using that IV and generate forged frames using the same IV. All without knowing the key.

This characteristic of WEP was worrisome and resulted in IEEE 802.11 undertaking the new security design. However, it was not considered a major threat to everyday use. After all, it would take a huge effort to decode a significant number of frames and the need for intelligence in guessing the plaintext makes it hard to create an automatic script tool. So the cryptographers cringed and the manufacturers worried, but the world went on after this attack was publicized. But there was worse to come.

RC4 Weak Keys

The fundamental part of RC4 is not encryption but pseudorandom number generation. Once we have a string of pseudorandom bytes, we can use them to encrypt the data by the XOR function. As we have seen, using this simple XOR function is a source of weakness if it is not applied correctly; but for the moment, let's concentrate on the pseudorandom sequence, or key stream.

RC4 works by setting up a 256-byte array containing all the values from 0 to 255. That is, each value from 0 to 255 appears once and only once in the array. However, the order in which they appear is "randomized." This is known as a permutation of the values. What's more, the values are reorganized continuously as each pseudorandom byte is generated so there is a different permutation of the array each time.

Each pseudorandom byte is generated by picking a single value from the permutation based on two index values, i and j, which also change each time. There are very many permutations (or arrangements) of 255 values that can be made. In fact, combined with the two indices, there are $512 * 256!$ (factorial) possibilities, a number too big to compute on any calculator we have, even using scientific notation.

This property of RC4 makes it very powerful despite its simple implementation. It is amazingly hard to distinguish an RC4 pseudorandom sequence from a real random sequence. RC4 has been studied by many cryptographers and yet the best known method for distinguishing an RC4 stream from true random data requires a continuous sample of 1Gbyte of the stream before it can reliably decide that the stream was generated by RC4. For WEP, of course, we already know RC4 is used, but this fact gives you some idea how effective RC4 really is once it gets going.

The phrase "once it gets going" in the last sentence is important. It signals the fact that RC4 has a potential weakness. To understand the weakness, let's quickly review how RC4 works. First it creates a table (the S-box) with all the values 0–255. Then it creates a second 256-byte table with the key, repeated over and over until the table is full. Then it rearranges the S-box based on values in the key table. This is the initialization phase. The first pseudorandom byte is generated by rearranging the S-box again and picking a byte.

The problem here is that there are not many rearrangements between the initial setup of the key table and the first pseudorandom byte. Fluhrer et al. (2001)

analyzed this fact, resulting in their now famous paper "Weaknesses in the Key Scheduling Algorithm of RC4." They showed that for certain key values, which they called **weak keys**, a disproportionate number of bits in the first few bytes of the key stream (pseudorandom bytes) were determined by a few bits in the key itself.

Let's look at this weakness in another way: Ideally if you change any one bit in the key, then the output key stream should be totally different. Each bit should have a 50% chance of being different from the previous key stream. The paper showed that this was not the case. Some bits of the key had a bigger effect than others. Some bits had no effect at all (on the first few bytes of key stream). This is bad for two reasons. First, if you reduce the number of effective bits, it is easier to attack the keys. Second, the first few bytes of plaintext are usually easier to guess. For example, in WEP it is usually the LLC header that starts with the same hexadecimal value "AA". If you know the plaintext, you can derive the key stream and start attacking the key.

There is a very simple way to avoid the weakness: Discard the first few bytes of the RC4 key stream. In other words, wait until the RC4 algorithm gets going before starting to use the output. A recommendation from RSA Labs is to discard the first 256 bytes of the key stream, but of course WEP does not do this and such a change would mean that old systems would no longer interoperate.

You might think that this is not so bad. After all, you might not be using a weak key; or if you know which keys are weak, you could avoid them, right? Think again. Remember the IV is added to the secret key. And the IV is always changing. So sooner or later, the IV guarantees that a weak key is generated. It brings tears to your eyes, doesn't it! But there's worse to come.

Direct Key Attacks

In their landmark paper, Fluhrer et al. showed that using a public IV value appended to the secret key generated a huge weakness because it allowed the attacker to wait for a potentially weak key and directly attack the key. There are two cases, one in which the IV is appended (after the secret key) and one in which the IV is prepended (before the secret key). The prepend case is the more vulnerable—and it's the relevant case for WEP, which, by now, should come as no surprise to you.

If you are interested in how the attacks work, get a college degree in mathematics and read the paper. But in overview, the idea is based on exploiting the weak key problem in the first bytes. First assume that you know the plaintext for the first few bytes, which you do for IEEE 802.11 because it is usually an IEEE 802.1LLC SNAP header. Watch transmissions looking for a weak key generated by the IV. Now you know that there is a correlation between the ciphertext, the plaintext, and the secret key bytes. There are only a limited number of possible values for the first secret key byte that could match the plaintext and ciphertext. After capturing about 60 such messages, the attacker can guess the first key byte with reasonable certainty.

The method can be tuned to attack each secret key byte in turn so eventually the entire secret key can be extracted. Note that increasing the key size from 40 bits to 104 bits only means that it takes 2.5 times longer to extract the key—in other words, the time to crack the key goes up linearly with key size rather than exponentially.

All the previous weaknesses of WEP pale into insignificance compared to this attack. Remember that extracting the keys is the ultimate goal of an attacker, and here is a method that directly extracts the keys in linear time. This attack blew apart the remnants of WEP security. Worse, because it used a fairly mechanical approach, it was feasible to create a script tool that would do the job unattended.

Within months, some "helpful" person invested their time into generating a cracker tool. Publicizing the threat was a service to everyone, but I leave it as an exercise for the readers to determine what satisfaction is obtained by the authors of tools that turn threat into reality and lay waste to millions of dollars of investment. However, the tool was published, it is available on the Internet, and attackers can use it to crack WEP systems open at will.

Summary

This chapter explains in detail how WEP works and then explains why you shouldn't use it. If you are currently using WEP, this chapter shows why you need to change. When the original IEEE 802.11 standard was published, Wired Equivalent Privacy (WEP) was included as a method to provide secure communications. However, as this chapter describes, WEP fell short of real needs in a number of areas.

The methods of key management were weak and did not scale to large networks. The key length was too small and some vendors introduced extensions to try to "improve the security." The final straw that broke the camel's back was the discovery of an attack that could successfully retrieve the secret keys by traffic monitoring.

It is said that those who don't read history are doomed to repeat it. This chapter provides the history. WEP is an interesting case study in the problems that can occur when security protocols are developed without proper review by security experts. Mostly the chapter is worth reading because it points out so many of the pitfalls that have been overcome in the new methods. Understanding WEP's failings before moving on will help you understand why the next-generation security methods are so much stronger.

7 Chapter

WPA, RSN, and IEEE 802.11i

Chapter 7 introduces the new security protocols that replace WEP and provide real security. In the next few chapters we delve into details regarding how the new protocols work and are applied to real installations. In this chapter, we define the terms and explain the process under which the protocols developed. We look at the importance of keys to the solution and how the keys are used within the context of a secure system. Finally, prior to diving into detail in Chapter 8, we provide a roadmap of the many standards used in the new security solutions.

Relationship Between Wi-Fi and IEEE 802.11

The Institute of Electrical and Electronics Engineers (www.IEEE.org) operates a group called the Standards Association (SA). Among many other standards, the IEEE-SA is responsible for the IEEE 802 family: "Local Area and Metropolitan Area Networks." IEEE 802 is divided into working groups, each of which produces standards in a specific area, as shown in Figure 7.1. The ".11" working group produces standards for wireless LANs.

The original IEEE 802.11 standard was ratified in 1997 and became an international standard in 1999. Work continues and updates to the base standard are made from time to time. Some of these, such as 802.11b and 802.11a, are complete while others are still in development. At the time this book was written, 802.11i had not been ratified and was still in draft form. Note that updates such as IEEE 802.11b

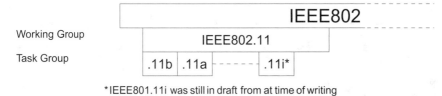

*IEEE801.11i was still in draft from at time of writing

Figure 7.1 IEEE 802 Standards Working Group

are not whole new standards; they are addendums to the existing standard. Care is taken to ensure that older equipment is not made obsolete by any changes.

Standards allow manufacturers to produce products that have known physical characteristics. For example, two wireless LAN systems could not communicate with each other unless they use compatible radio frequencies and modulation methods. The standard specifies such things in detail. The IEEE 802.11 standard also defines protocol messages and operating algorithms (see Chapter 5).

Standards are very useful to manufacturers because they create a technical specification from which designs can be made. However, end users—that is, the customers who buy the products—have a different concern. IEEE 802.11 might tell them the characteristics of the product, but it does not guarantee that a product from vendor A will completely interoperate with a product from vendor B.

IEEE 802.11 is a long and complicated standard. Despite the best efforts of the standards body, there are bound to be areas that are ambiguous or not fully defined. Also there are a number of features that are optional and different manufacturers might make different choices in their designs. To avoid interoperability problems, the Wi-Fi Alliance was formed by a group of major manufacturers and the logo "Wi-Fi" was created.

To obtain Wi-Fi certification, a manufacturer must submit its product for testing against a set of "gold standard" Wi-Fi products. The Wi-Fi Alliance created its own test plan based on IEEE 802.11. Some features of IEEE 802.11 are not required for Wi-Fi certification. Conversely, there are some requirements that are additional to the standard. Where there is ambiguity in the standard, the correct behavior is defined by the way the gold standard products work. In this way interoperability is ensured. In summary, Wi-Fi defines a subset of IEEE 802.11 with some extensions, as shown in Figure 7.2.

What Is IEEE 802.11i?

The addendum to the standard that specifies the new generation of security is called IEEE 802.11i. At the time of writing, no such standard has been released, but a draft of the standard is under discussion by Task Group i of the working

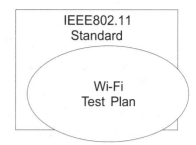

Figure 7.2   Relationship of Wi-Fi to IEEE 802.11

group. The draft is fairly complete and is unlikely to change substantially before release, but changes are certainly possible.

IEEE 802.11i defines a new type of wireless network called a **robust security network** (RSN). In some respects this is the same as the ordinary or WEP-based networks. However, in order to join an RSN, a wireless device has to have a number of new capabilities, as described in the following chapters. In a *true* RSN, the access point allows only RSN-capable mobile devices to connect and places rigorous security constraints on the process. However, because many people will want to upgrade over a period of time and use pre-RSN equipment during the upgrade, the IEEE 802.11i defines a **transitional security network** (TSN) in which both RSN and WEP systems can operate in parallel.

At the time of writing, no RSN-capable products are on the market. Such products cannot be released until the standard has been completed. Most existing Wi-Fi cards cannot be upgraded to RSN because the cryptographic operations required are not supported by the hardware and are beyond the capability of software upgrades. Therefore it will be some time before full RSN networks become operational. By contrast, WPA networks can be implemented immediately.

What Is WPA?

Remember that the definition of Wi-Fi came after completion of the IEEE 802.11 standard. However, the major Wi-Fi manufacturers decided that security was so important to end users that it had to move as fast as possible to deliver a replacement for WEP. Furthermore, they concluded that customers would not be prepared to just throw away all their existing Wi-Fi equipment in order to switch to RSN; they would want to upgrade their products through software. To address this need, Task Group i started to develop a security solution based around the capabilities of existing Wi-Fi products. This led to the definition of the Temporal Key Integrity Protocol (TKIP), as described in Chapter 11. TKIP is allowed as an optional mode under RSN.

The development of TKIP was a great help to allow upgrade of existing systems, but the industry couldn't wait until the lengthy process of standards ratification was completed. Therefore, the Wi-Fi Alliance adopted a new security approach based on the draft RSN but only specifying TKIP. This subset of RSN is called Wi-Fi Protected Access (WPA). Many leading vendors have now produced software upgrades so existing product can be converted to support WPA and most new products are now shipped with WPA capability. The Wi-Fi Alliance has created a test plan for WPA so vendors can ensure interoperability.

Cases in which the industry has run ahead of standards are not that uncommon. This has happened a number of times in modem technology and sometimes has led to two factions of the industry selling incompatible products. Fortunately, the Wi-Fi Alliance has avoided this type of a split and most manufacturers are supporting the Wi-Fi WPA specification.

Differences Between RSN and WPA

WPA and RSN share a common architecture and approach. WPA has a subset of capability focused specifically on one way to implement a network, whereas RSN allows more flexibility in implementation. RSN also supports the AES[1] cipher algorithm in addition to TKIP, whereas WPA focuses on TKIP.[2] Because WEP is more commonly found in corporations today, a natural approach is to implement WPA now, upgrade installed systems as required, and then move towards a full RSN solution over a period of time as new products are deployed. Eventually, as the older products are retired, this will lead to a system based entirely on IEEE 802.11i. In this way, WPA provides for the needs of all the current Wi-Fi LAN users in the most common configurations, while in the long term the full RSN allows more flexibility.

RSN and WPA share a single security architecture under which TKIP- or AES-based security protocols can operate. This architecture covers procedures such as upper-level authentication, secret key distribution, and key renewal—all of which are relevant to both TKIP and AES. The RSN architecture is quite different from that of WEP and quite a bit more complicated. However, it provides a solution that is both secure and scalable for use in large networks. One of the huge problems for WEP, from the earliest days, was that it was impractical to manage key distribution once you had more than a few tens of users. That problem has been addressed by both RSN and WPA.

Nobody can ever (legitimately) claim that a security system is unbreakable. However, it is fair to say that the RSN/WPA approach was devised with the

---

1. "AES" stands for Advanced Encryption Standard; see Chapter 12 for details.

2. TKIP stands for Temporal Key Integrity Protocol; see Chapter 11 for details.

involvement of specialist security experts and received far more scrutiny from the cryptographic community than WEP did when it was being developed. WEP received this kind of scrutiny only after it was deployed and the result was humiliation. The design of RSN/WPA has had the full participation of security experts. That doesn't guarantee that it will not be broken next week. But we doubt it will and we wouldn't be wasting time writing this book if we thought otherwise.

> Note that most of the discussion about RSN here assumes that you are operating in IEEE 802.11 *infrastructure mode* and that you have an access point. RSN (but not WPA) can also apply to *ad-hoc* mode in which there is no access point. Ad-hoc mode is sometimes referred to as IBSS (Independent Basic Service Set) mode. We cover the special issue of IBSS mode in Chapter 13; in this chapter, the discussion assumes that you, like most people, are using infrastructure mode.

Security Context

IEEE 802.11 Task Group i had two objectives: to create a new scalable security solution and, of course, to provide effective protection against all known passive and active attacks. It was assumed that the new solution would completely replace WEP over time. Therefore, the solution developers started from scratch. The first and most important change in approach was the separation of the user authentication process and message protection (integrity and privacy). Authentication is the process by which you prove that you are eligible to join a network (and that the network is legitimate); and message protection ensures that once you have joined the network, you can communicate without risk of interception, modification, or any of a host of other security risks. Separation of user authentication and message protection allows a solution that can be scaled from small systems to entire corporations. However, the two parts must be linked together into a security context.

The concept of a security context is important to grasp and lies at the heart of the RSN.[3] However, the idea of a security context is by no means unique to data communications. One simple example of a security context is your travel passport. The main purpose of a passport is for government officials to check who is entering and leaving the country. Countries want to allow their own citizens to come

---

3. We use RSN here and in the rest of the chapter because it is the overall model for security. WPA is derived from the RSN model so all the same comments can be applied to the WPA design.

and go, hopefully freely. To do this, they need to provide their citizens with tangible evidence that they are, in fact, citizens.

When you first apply for a passport, you are required by your country's government to provide proof of your identity. This is at the heart of the passport system. In the context of people, it's not obvious how to go about this proof of identity. To some extent possession of special documents such as birth certificates and so on might help, but these are easily forged or stolen. Many countries rely on the evidence of other people to confirm who you are. For example, in Britain you are required to get a signed statement by a nonrelative of "suitable stature." The list of qualifications for "suitable stature" is rather strange, but generally a minister of religion or a police officer would be an example. This person must have known you for a few years and sign the form to say so. The person's role is as a sort of certification authority trusted by you and the government.

So far so good—you have been authenticated, you sent in the forms, and the government has filed your picture in a large dusty vault and agrees that you exist. Now it is necessary that you have some token to prove that fact and, more importantly, that you are the person that was originally authenticated. This is the passport document. Most countries validate the passport by embedding the authenticated photograph. Some include fingerprints or descriptions of obvious features such as "no nose" or similar. Passports also have a limited duration, after which they are no longer valid.

When the government accepts your form, it establishes a **security context**. The passport proves that the context exists and that it refers only to you. Of course, this proof of context is extremely weak. It is relatively easy to fool the authentication process or modify the passport document. In particular, you can take over someone else's context by changing the picture in the passport. There are a lot of implicit trust relationships here. The immigration officer trusts the passport office not to issue fake passports, and the government agency trusts the immigration officer to perform a real check. This brings out the point that in authentication, you often have to trust other parties.

An RSN's security context has to be far stronger than that of a passport. However, the general concept is the same—an authentication process followed by a limited-life security context giving rights to the participants. A lot of the architecture of RSN relates to how to establish and maintain a security context between wireless LAN devices (usually a mobile device and an access point). The backbone of this context is the secret key.

Keys

Security relies heavily on secret keys. And security is completely lost if the keys are copied or stolen. In the passport example, the passport document is the rough equivalent of a key. It is not used for encryption or any such functions, but the assumption is that it cannot be copied (in other words, forged) and it will not be stolen or willingly given up. If either of these events occurs, the whole system breaks down.

In RSN the security context is defined by the possession of limited-life keys. Unlike with WEP, in RSN there are many different keys forming part of a **key hierarchy**, and most of these keys are not known before the authentication process completes. In fact, the creation of the keys is done in real time as the security context is established after authentication. Because they are created in real time, they are referred to as **temporal keys**. These temporal keys may be updated from time to time, but they are always destroyed when the security context is closed.

A key is basically a shared secret between two or more parties. Perhaps it would be more accurate to say that a key is any shared data that is useful only if it is kept secret. The magic word abracadabra is not very magical because everyone knows it and, by saying it, you're not actually doing anything. A *real* magic word is one that only a special group knows and that gives the group privileges or power. So it is with keys.

Keys can be used in two distinct ways. They can provide proof of your identity (such as a passport) and they can give access to services (such as the key to your car). Purists will point out that this is really the same thing because you get access to the service by proving that you are the person who has permission. However, the distinction is useful when looking at the way keys are used.

During the authentication phase, you have to prove your identity by demonstrating that you have knowledge of a secret. Passing this test entitles you to receive the other keys—those that open doors and start engines, for example. In the case of RSN, correctly authenticating enables you to receive or create the keys that are used for encryption and data protection. These useful keys are sometimes called the **temporal** or **session keys** because they work only so long as the security context is in place.

In principle, temporal keys can be created out of thin air. For example, when encrypting messages between two parties, you simply require that both parties (and *only* these parties) have the same key value. You don't care what that value is, so if you have a way that two parties can separately generate the same "random" number at roughly the same time, you can use that as the key. When you have finished communicating, you can just throw away the key.

Authentication is based on some shared secret information that cannot be created automatically. An authentication key must be created by someone trusted and attached to the holder in such a way that it can't easily be copied or stolen. And, of course, the trusted key giver has to be certain of the identity of the key receiver. The basis of all authentication methods, therefore, is that the entity that is to be authenticated possesses some special information in advance, which is called the **master key**. Using the master key in a way that protects it from discovery is very important. As a general rule, the master key is rarely, if ever, used directly; instead, it is used to create temporal keys. (WEP, of course, rode through this rule by using the master key both in authentication and encryption.)

In summary, there are two types of keys: a fixed or master key that provides proof of identity, and any number of temporal keys that are created or derived from the master key for use in the security protocol. Understanding this distinction helps to understand the way in which RSN is designed.

Security Layers

Despite the best efforts of social reformers, humans tend to organize things into layers when it comes to management. There was a fashion in the 1980s for start-up companies to be organized on a communal basis in which everyone was equally important and all meetings were open. Nice touch, but the reality is that every one of those companies that grew beyond a handful of people coalesced into a layer management structure very rapidly. People must have a limited scope of control in order to be effective. Therefore, if the organization is to scale up in size, you have to allow specialization of function and different levels of policy control.

So what's this got to do with Wi-Fi LANs? Well, in some ways, WEP was like the trendy start-up. All the security issues were bundled into a single simple package of measures and all were defined within a single standard. Quite distinct from the technical failings of WEP, this resulted in a solution that could not be scaled beyond a handful of devices. Some functions, such as encryption, are very local affairs and are only relevant to the Wi-Fi LAN hardware that is doing the actual communication. But other issues, in particular the decisions about who is allowed to access the network, have very wide importance and need to be consistent across an entire network.

For these reasons, it is necessary to identify and implement management layers in the security solution. This can be seen in the passport control system that involves layers of government from the immigration officer at the airport desk, through the passport administration center and up to the immigration policy decision makers in the Cabinet.

In the context of wireless LAN security, three layers are clearly identified. In fact, these layers are not specific to wireless LAN, but apply to any LAN-related security system. An advantage to choosing this layered model is that the RSN solution can fit into existing security architectures that have been deployed for other purposes and also leverage the standards that already exist.

The three layers of security are:

- Wireless LAN layer
- Access control layer
- Authentication layer

The **wireless LAN layer** is the worker. It is the job of this layer to deal with raw communications, advertising capabilities and accepting applications to join the network. The wireless LAN layer is also responsible for encrypting and decrypting the actual data once a security context is established.

The **access control layer** is the middle manager. It is the job of this layer to manage the security context. It must stop any data passing to or from an enemy. Here an "enemy" is defined as anyone who does not have a current security context established. The access control layer is fickle, and you can immediately change your status from enemy to friend when authentications occur and the security context is established. The access control layer talks to the authentication layer to know when it may open the security context and it participates in creating the associated temporal keys.

The most senior layer is the **authentication layer**. At this layer the policy decisions are made and proofs of identity are accepted (or rejected). In effect the authentication layer has power of veto over anyone who wants to join the LAN and delegates power to the access control layer once it approves the application for someone to join the LAN. The wireless LAN layer obviously resides in the wireless device contained in the access point. Usually the access control layer resides completely in the access point. Although in small systems the authentication layer might be in the access point also, in larger systems, the authentication layer is usually implemented in an authentication server quite separate from the access points. This ability to centralize the authentication server provides a scalable way to manage the user database. In other words, it solves the key management problems of WEP and makes it easier to integrate Wi-Fi LANs into the overall corporate security management system.

On a mobile station, there are similar layers. Typically, the wireless LAN layer is implemented in the Wi-Fi adapter card and its associated software drivers. The access control and authentication services may be implemented in the operating system or, for older systems, in the application level software provided by the manufacturer. Remember that it is very important that the mobile device also authenticates the network to ensure that it is not joining a fake network set up by an attacker. Figure 7.3 shows the relationship of all the layers and a typical example of where the layers operate. Note that in the figure "supplicant" refers to the part of the mobile device's operating system that makes the request to join the wireless LAN.

How the Layers Are Implemented

The IEEE 802.11 standard covers only wireless LANs, and the standards group is not chartered to define the behavior of systems outside this specific area. This presents a problem when designing systems that need the cooperation of various layers to

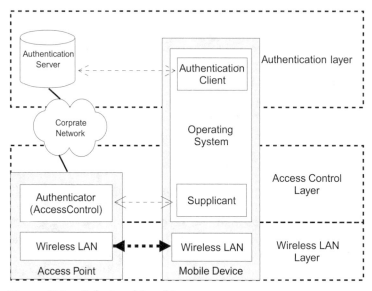

Figure 7.3 Relationship of Layers

work. This is one of the reasons that the original WEP standard tried to define all the security issues within the wireless LAN layer. When designing RSN, the standards task group avoided this problem by referencing existing standards developed outside IEEE 802.11, especially for the access control and authentication layers. In the few cases in which these other standards needed to be modified, the IEEE 802.11i group contacted the other relevant standards and requested changes to be made.

There seemed to be a perfect existing candidate for the access control layer. As early work progressed on the security standard, another standards group, IEEE 802.1X, was putting the finishing touches on a standard designed specifically to deal with access control (IEEE, 2001) IEEE 802.1X was selected as most appropriate for access control with (almost) universal approval, although this, too, had to be modified later to meet all the needs of security identified by the TGi group.

The authentication layer was much more problematic. The difficulty here was that there are many possible candidates. The purpose of having the authentication done by this upper layer was so that corporations could integrate the authentication into their existing security approach. But it turns out that there are quite a few different methods in use. And, of course, each corporation believes that the approach it is using is the best one.

In the end the decision was made that IEEE 802.11i would not specify any mandatory upper-layer authentication method, but that the RSN approach would be designed in such a way that any of the existing "good" methods could be applied. The word "good" here underlines the fact that the standard places requirements on the security capabilities of acceptable methods. For example, all methods must support mutual authentication.

In the following chapters, we look in more detail at the way in which the authentication, access control, and wireless LAN layers are implemented and how they interact. Because there are layers and different standards are employed at each layer, it might seem that RSN is very complicated. There is no doubt that it is a formidable task to read all the standards that are incorporated directly or by reference. What we intend to achieve in this book is an overview of the relevant parts of each standard so you don't need to undertake this task. Then those standards should be much more accessible should you choose to dive in.

Relationship of the Standards

The next few chapters cover a bewildering number of standards, mostly those of IEEE 802 and IETF (RFCs). The following reference list of all the standards that we mention should help you keep track of these standards and serve as a roadmap to indicate if and where they fit into the RSN picture. You may find you want to refer back here as the picture starts to form in your mind.

List of Standards

Here is a list of all the standards mentioned in Chapters 8 through 12.

Name	Title or Description
IEEE 802.1X	Port access control
IEEE 802.3	Wired LAN
IEEE 802.11	Wireless LAN
IEEE 802.11e	Wireless LAN with Quality or Service Management (in development)
IEEE 802.11i	Wireless LAN Security (in development)
RFC 1321	MD-5 Message Digest Algorithm
RFC 1510	Kerberos V5
RFC 1661	Original PPP standard
RFC 1964	GSSAPI Kerberos Protocol Mechanism
RFC 2058	Earlier RADIUS spec. (superseded)
RFC 2104	Hash Message Authentication Code
RFC 2138	Earlier RADIUS spec. (superseded)
RFC 2246	Transport Layer Security (TLS)
RFC 2284	PPP Extensible Authentication Protocol (EAP)

Name	Title or Description
RFC 2548	Microsoft Vendor Specific RADIUS Attributes
RFC 2716	PPP EAP TLS Authentication Protocol
RFC 2743	Generic Security Service Application Programming Interface
RFC 2865	RADIUS
RFC 2866	RADIUS Accounting
RFC 2869	EAP over RADIUS
RFC 2945	The SRP Authentication and Key Exchange System
draft-ietf-pppext-rfc2284bis	Updates EAP
draft-aboba-radius-rfc2869bis	Update to RFC2869
draft-josefsson-pppext-eap-tls-eap	PEAP
draft-haverinen-pppext-eap-sim	GSM-SIM over EAP
Cisco LEAP	Proprietary Vendor protocol for Wi-Fi Security
RC4	Encryption Cipher
AES	Encryption Cipher

Pictorial Map

Figure 7.4 shows a pictorial map of the main standards used in an RSN solution based on TLS authentication. Inevitably the picture is a bit simplistic, but it shows how the TLS authentication process is buried inside a set of standards that provide the communications first between the mobile device and the access point and then between the access point and the authentication server. The links are shown as a set of concentric tubes; the outer tube is the communications medium and successive inner tubes are the encapsulations used to transport the information. As we said at the beginning of this section, we do not expect you to understand the whole picture from looking at Figure 7.4, but we hope it will form a reference point to which you can return.

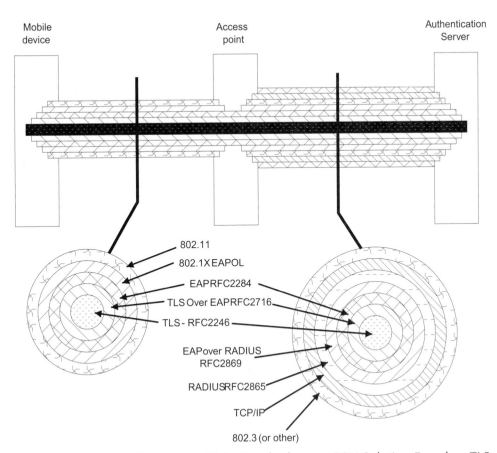

Figure 7.4 Main Standards in an RSN Solution Based on TLS

Summary

In earlier chapters we alluded frequently to "the new security solutions." We talked a lot about the difficulty of implementing good security and explained how the existing Wi-Fi security solutions had fallen short of what was needed. In this chapter we introduced IEEE 802.11i RSN and Wi-Fi Protected Access (WPA). This new generation of security methods will take over from WEP and finally meet the needs of both high security and scalability for large systems.

Systems based on RSN and WPA need not be complicated to install if the vendor has delivered all the pieces correctly. However, many pieces are required, and a full explanation takes some time. In this book we devote Chapters 8 through 12 to describing all the pieces and the way in which they depend on each other. To ease the learning process, in this chapter we have described a layered approach to thinking about the various components and have provided a map to show how the numerous standards fit together in an implementation.

As with many complicated systems, when all the pieces are put together it is not hard to understand what is going on. The difficulty is that in the beginning you can be overwhelmed by the number of pieces. To ease you through this burden, in the following chapters we lead you through the core access control descriptions first, and then look at the higher layers that provide the authentication. Finally we return to the wireless level to look at key distribution and implementation of the actual Wi-Fi security protocols.

8 Chapter

Access Control: IEEE 802.1X, EAP, and RADIUS

This chapter introduces some of the protocols that are central to the new security solutions. One of the most basic functions needed for security is access control and the new security solutions are built around a standard, IEEE 802.1X, which is specifically designed to implement access control. This chapter starts by describing the need for access control and then shows how the control techniques developed for dial-up modem pools have been reused in conjunction with WI-Fi LANs. As we will see, the combination of IEEE 802.11, IEEE 802.1X, EAP, and RADIUS provide a solution scalable from home networks all the way to large corporate networks.

Importance of Access Control

Access control is one of the most important elements of security. The object of security is to separate the world into "good guys" and "bad guys." It follows that you cannot achieve security unless you have a mechanism to perform this separation. That mechanism is **access control**.

On the surface, maintaining control is straightforward. All situations have the following elements:

- An entity that wants to have access—the **supplicant**
- An entity that controls the access gate—the **authenticator**
- An entity that decides whether the supplicant is to be admitted—for now, we will call this the **authorizer**

Suppose a visitor knocks on your front door and your child opens it (with the security chain on). The visitor is the supplicant, your child is the authenticator, and you are the authorizer. Only if you say it's okay will your child take off the security chain and let the visitor in (don't you wish you really had such power!). If you answer the door personally, you take the role of both authenticator *and* authorizer.

The steps involved in access control follow a similar pattern:

1. Authenticator is alerted by the supplicant.
2. Supplicant identifies himself.
3. Authenticator requests authorization from the authorizer.
4. Authorizer indicates YES or NO.
5. Authenticator allows or blocks access.

These steps work to control access; but as we discussed in earlier chapters, if the supplicant wants to come and go repeatedly without going through this procedure each time, he needs to obtain some sort of token that proves that he has been authorized. In the case of a corporation, for example, that might be a swipe card that opens the employee entrance door.

So if access control is really this simple, why devote a whole chapter to it? Well, the reality is that while the concept and goals of access control are simple, designing a system that is immune to attack is very difficult. Most of the access control systems dealing with people are trivially easy to fool by an intelligent con man. How many of us have left our swipe card at home one day and, upon arriving at work, just walked in behind another employee? For Wi-Fi LANs, we can't allow even the slightest flaw in the access control method, or else hacker tools will appear on the Internet within months. Getting it right is hard.

This chapter focuses on the three protocols that are used to implement access security in WPA and RSN:

- IEEE 802.1X
- EAP: Extensible Authentication Protocol
- RADIUS: Remote Authentication Dial-In User Service

The first two protocols are mandatory for WPA and RSN. RADIUS is the method of choice for WPA and is an option for RSN.

There is much confusion about IEEE 802.1X and what it does. Because it is difficult for customers to fully understand all the elements of security, vendors tend to talk about IEEE 802.1X as if it were the entire security solution for Wi-Fi LANs. In reality, as we will see shortly, IEEE 802.1X is only a small part of the solution, albeit an important one. IEEE 802.1X is the foundation of both WPA and RSN.

IETF Standards

Many of the standards in this chapter and in Chapter 9, "Upper Layer Authentication," were developed by the Internet Engineering Task Force (IETF), an organization that is completely different from the IEEE (although both often involve the same people). All the most basic protocols used on the Internet, starting with the Internet Protocol (IP) itself, have been defined by the IETF. The organization, which operates more on technical consensus and less on formal voting, creates documents called RFCs, short for "Request for Comments." The RFC number for EAP is RFC2284, for example. Despite the title, most RFCs are quite stable and not subject to much change. Perhaps these should transition to NMCTs (No More Comments Thank you), but this would not be in the spirit of continuous technical review, which the IETF encourages.

The stability of RFCs allows vendors to implement and deliver products. New ideas in the IETF are floated using *draft* documents, which are circulated for discussion. Rather than having a number, these drafts have a name incorporating the subject and main author. For example, "draft-haverinen-pppext-eap-sim-03.txt" describes draft three of a proposal written by Henry Haverinen to use EAP with GSM phone systems using a SIM smart card. Proposals that become group work items use the generic "ietf," such as "draft-ietf-pppext-eap-ttls-00.txt," which describes how to use EAP in conjunction with Tunneled TLS authentication.

Many drafts are dropped due to lack of interest, but those that get support from the group eventually move on to become RFCs. This is relevant to EAP because, at the time of this writing, most of the new EAP methods were in the form of draft IETF submissions. In addition, a revised version of EAP was in the works (draft-ietf-pppext-rfc2284bis-02.txt) and expected to supersede the current version. The revision, of course, does not change the existing protocol, but extends and clarify its capabilities. By the time you read this book, this draft might have become a new RFC. All the RFCs and current drafts are publicly available from www.ietf.org.

Before we look at IEEE 802.1X, let's take a diversion and look at the history of dial-in modem support. "Why now?" you may say. The fact is that the main protocols of EAP and RADIUS were both developed in the context of dial-in access.[1] It turns out that dial-in access control is organized in a very similar way to IEEE 802.1X, which is why the same protocols, EAP and RADIUS, can be applied to both. By reviewing the dial-in case first, you will find that the WPA and RSN cases make more sense.

Authentication for Dial-in Users

Millions of people use dial-up access for Internet connectivity every day. Each person's computer is configured with the phone number of the Internet service provider (ISP), a user name and a password; management of the connection is done automatically. Behind the scenes, the majority of these connections use a protocol called Point-to-Point Protocol (PPP), reflecting the fact that the connection is just that—a point-to-point connection between two modems that between them provide an unformatted byte-by-byte link. PPP converts the unstructured modem link into a packet-based environment suitable for transporting the IP packets. Importantly, it deals with initial handshaking during which the two ends can negotiate a common feature set. It also has a mechanism for user authentication that we are interested in here. The original PPP (RFC1661) described simple methods to authenticate the user that are still implemented by many ISPs today. When you initiate dial-up access on your computer, you may see a little box on the screen saying, "authenticating..." while this occurs. You might also be asked to enter a password during this phase. These events typically happen during the PPP negotiation.

PPP has two authentication methods described in the original standard; but by current opinion, neither method is considered very strong. In fact, the simplest method, PAP, which is still used by many ISPs, actually sends the user name and password in clear text so any snooper on the link can steal it. The other popular method, CHAP, uses a challenge response mechanism, somewhat similar to the original WEP method. This is much better than PAP but still not considered very strong.

In the dial-up case, the authentication method doesn't need to be very strong. Generally, the worst that happens if someone steals your password is that they get free access to the ISP for which you may be paying. In addition, dial-up lines are much harder to intercept than LANs. However, in some situations a stronger

---

1. Strictly, EAP was developed to support Point-to-Point Protocol (PPP), which is very widely used in dial-up networks but also has other applications.

authentication method is needed and the fact that PPP specifies only two weak methods presents a problem. Any new PPP authentication methods would have to be registered with the IANA (Internet Assigned Numbers Authority), and this would create a problem for existing deployed systems that are already "PPP compliant."

To solve this problem, IETF members decided that a more *extensible* method was needed for PPP. Therefore, the option of EAP was added alongside PAP and CHAP. EAP allows full authentication to be delayed until after the preliminary PPP link is established. RFC2284 "PPP Extensible Authentication Protocol (EAP)" describes how this modification is applied and used with PPP; it says nothing about IEEE 802.1X or wireless LAN (neither of which existed when RFC2284 was written). Recognition of LAN applications is one of the changes proposed in the draft update (draft-ietf-pppext-rfc2284bis-02.txt). This will include references to IEEE 802.1X and IEEE 802.11 in the EAP definition.

The intent of EAP is to enable the use of an authentication algorithm between the supplicant and the authorizer. EAP is designed to allow different types of authentication methods to be used —that is why it is called extensible. The object is to enable the supplicant to prove his identity to the authorizer. Many methods allow mutual authentication so both parties prove their true identity to the other.

It is common in dial-up networks to have a modem pool in each local phone area to provide cheap access, often called a **point of presence** (POP). However, the service provider doesn't want to keep a copy of their user database at every POP; they want a central database. This creates a three-party situation that is very similar to that of a corporate Wi-Fi LAN. Using the terminology in our introduction, the user is the supplicant, the POP is the authenticator, and the central database is the authorizer. The protocol used between the POP and the central database to get permission to allow a dial-in user access to the network is called RADIUS (Remote Access Dial-In User Service). We look at RADIUS in more detail later in this chapter.

The organization of a typical dial-in network is shown in Figure 8.1.

Three parties are shown in Figure 8.1:

- **Users** (supplicants)
- **Network access server** (NAS), located in the POP; authenticator
- **Authentication server** (AS), which can be located centrally; authorizer

Note that the term "authorizer" is not an official term, but one that we invented in the introduction to aid in understanding the roles of the parties. From here on, we use the term "authentication server" rather than authorizer because this is most widely used to describe the authorizing entity.

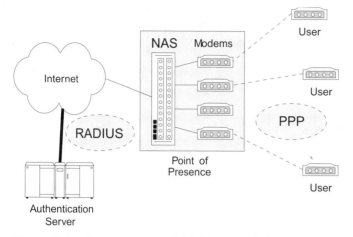

Figure 8.1 Organization of Dial-in Network

EAP allows a flexible approach so arbitrary and complicated authentication protocols can be exchanged between the supplicant and the authentication server. To allow this, RADIUS has been extended to enable EAP messages to be forwarded by the NAS. The NAS acts as a sort of middleman in the authentication process, just relaying EAP messages between the supplicant and the server until the authentication process completes. When the authentication server makes a decision, the result gets sent to both the NAS and the supplicant in RADIUS/EAP messages. This enables the NAS to either allow access or disconnect the unauthorized user.

This three-party model is in use in thousands of POPs around the world (although few use EAP at this time). This is relevant because the situation in corporate Wi-Fi LAN looks rather similar to Figure 8.1. The supplicant is the Wi-Fi user that wants network access. The equivalent of the NAS is the access point, and there is an authentication server that controls the authorization process. The difference is that IEEE 802.11 provides a structured packet network so that PPP is not needed. In the next section we see that the role of IEEE 802.1X is to provide a similar access control function to that performed by the NAS in Figure 8.1.

IEEE 802.1X

IEEE 802.1X is very simple in concept. Its purpose is to implement access control at the point at which a user joins the network. It divides the network universe into three entities along the lines we discussed in the previous section:

- Supplicant, which wants to join the network
- Authenticator, which controls access
- Authentication server, which makes authorization decisions

The point at which a user connects to the network is called a **port**. A network may have many ports; for example, in a switched LAN hub,[2] each Ethernet connector would be one port. There is a one-to-one relationship between a supplicant and a port, and each port has an associated authenticator to control its state. There is a many-to-one relationship between the ports and the authentication server. In other words, a single authentication server is usually responsible for many ports, each with its own controlling authenticator.

Although wireless is our primary concern, IEEE 802.1X was not originally designed with wireless communication in mind. In fact, work was started on IEEE 802.1X before the first version of IEEE 802.11 was completed in 1997. The opening paragraph of IEEE 802.1X says:

> IEEE 802 Local Area Networks are often deployed in environments that permit unauthorized devices to be physically attached to the LAN infrastructure.

Note that the word "physically" implies a wired connection. The original thinking behind IEEE 802.1X was to protect ports such as might be found on a switched Ethernet hub. The idea was to prevent *just anyone* from connecting to the network by plugging an Ethernet cable into a hole in the wall and, instead, require that a potential user's identity and authorization status be checked. As IEEE 802.1X moved toward completion, people recognized that the same principle could be extended from wired ports to wireless connections. Cisco incorporated the concept into its products first, and the approach was adopted for RSN in IEEE 802.11i and, subsequently, by the Wi-Fi Alliance for WPA.

The main point of providing port security is to protect network connections where those connections might be accessible in a nonsecure area, such as a lobby or conference room. For most corporations this is a small number of ports. But for wireless, it is potentially every connection, because the nature of wireless makes almost all links publicly accessible. This is why IEEE 802.1X is so appropriate for IEEE 802.11.

---

2. Because each port must act independently, IEEE 802.1X can only be supported by a LAN switch, not a conventional shared LAN hub.

IEEE 802.1X in a Simple Switched Hub Environment

Before looking at its application in WPA/RSN, let's get an overview of what IEEE 802.1X does in a simple switched hub environment. Control is based around the concept of a switch on each port that is normally open (no connection). The switch is closed only when the supplicant is authorized. As shown in Figure 8.2, the hub ports are all disconnected initially. If anyone plugs in, he doesn't automatically get network access. It is important to note that it would be most unusual for the switches to be implemented as actual physical contacts. The switch here is only logical, like software or logic gates. When the switch is "open," data packets are not forwarded to or from the port. When it is closed, they are sent. The Ethernet port remains electrically active all the time.

One of the obvious problems in the diagram shown in Figure 8.2 is that it doesn't provide any way for the devices to ask the switched hub for permission to connect. It's like forgetting to put a doorbell on your front door. No one can ring to ask to come in. Remember that each port has an authenticator that is responsible for opening and closing the switch, so IEEE 802.1X provides a way to talk to the authenticator even when the switch is open.

This is like the security guard at the front door of an office building. When you arrive you are not allowed in, but you are allowed to talk to the security guard to ask for entry. In the terminology of IEEE 802.1X, the **authenticator** has control over the **port state** (whether the switch is open or closed), as shown in Figure 8.3. Here we see that the device on port 0 has been accepted and is connected to the network; another device is in the process of requesting access to the authenticator on port 1 but does not have access yet. The protocol used to communicate between the supplicant and the authenticator is based on EAP.

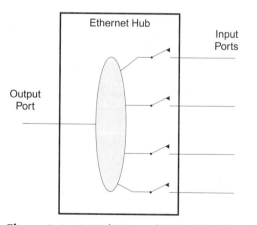

Figure 8.2 Initial State of IEEE 802.1X Switched LAN Hub

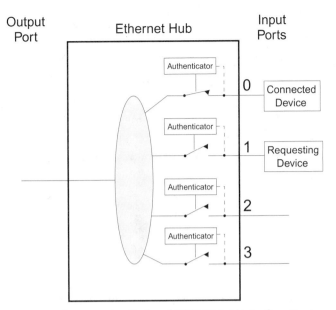

Figure 8.3   Role of IEEE 802.1X Authenticator

In Figure 8.3, it looks as if the authenticators are making the decisions about who is allowed access. In reality, the decision to admit or reject an applicant is usually based on an authentication database controlled and managed by an administrator. For this, the authenticator must communicate to an authentication server in order to get the answer "accept" or "reject" when a supplicant applies to join the network.

The authenticators in Figure 8.3 act like a security guard that has no authority. For every person who comes to the door, the guard has to call upstairs to the boss to find out whether it is OK to allow access. In a small system, the authentication server (the boss) could reside right in the switched hub and would simply have a list of users allowed access. Typically, the list of users would be configured by the system administrator in advance. This approach is impractical except for the smallest networks because each hub would have to be configured separately. Therefore, the authentication server is typically located at some central place in the network, as shown in Figure 8.4.

In Figure 8.4, all four authenticators for the hub shown communicate with the authentication server. In practice, the same would be true for all hubs on the network so the authentication server could be making decisions for many thousands of ports (hopefully not at the same time).

Although we have used a picture of a multiport switched LAN hub in these examples, the IEEE 802.1X standard is really only concerned with one port at a

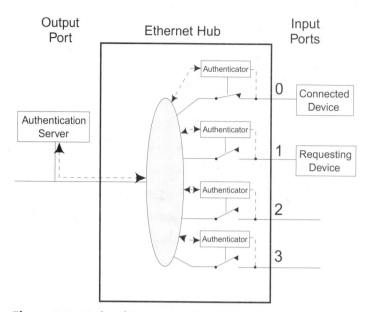

Output Port · Ethernet Hub · Input Ports

Authentication Server

Authenticator

0 Connected Device

Authenticator

1 Requesting Device

Authenticator

2

Authenticator

3

Figure 8.4 Role of Remote Authentication Server

time. Each port has its own state independent of any others in the box. Figure 8.5 shows a picture extracted directly from the IEEE 802.1X specification illustrating the relationships among the entities.

Figure 8.5 again shows the three players: supplicant system, authenticator system, and authentication server system. The supplicant is the device that wishes to get connected. Note that the switch connects through to "services offered by the authenticator's system." Usually we assume this means "connected to the network," but it could be some other service. PAE means port access entity, the full name for a port.

Figure 8.5 includes a reference to a higher-layer protocol between the authenticator and the authentication server. The EAP protocol is used by the various parties to communicate with each other. EAP messages go between the supplicant and the authenticator. The authenticator may also forward them to the authentication server as part of the process of authorization in a similar way that the NAS does in a dial-in network. If the authentication server is in a remote location, these messages need to be sent over a network using some higher-layer protocol. This is where RADIUS can be called into action to transfer the requests over an IP network. RADIUS was designed to perform this job in the dial-up user case, and now we can reuse it for IEEE 802.1X support. WPA specifies RADIUS for this purpose, although other protocols are also possible.

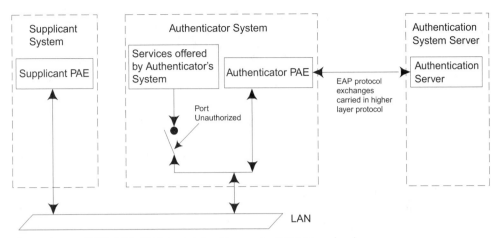

Figure 8.5 IEEE 802.1X Model As Shown in IEEE Standard

One of the differences between dial-in networks and IEEE 802.1X is that, with IEEE 802.1X, there is no need to use PPP because IEEE 802 LANs are designed to send data packets. However, it is still necessary to have some sort of protocol so the receiver can identify the information, and that protocol is called EAPOL (EAP over LAN). As described later in this chapter, EAPOL has several types of messages. Apart from the one that delivers the EAP messages, there are several additional ones that are useful for actions like attracting the attention of the authenticator (the doorbell analogy). Also there is a message for transferring key-related information.[3] WPA and RSN use a similar message in the process of establishing an encrypted link (see Chapter 10).

IEEE 802.1X in Wi-Fi LANs

Given that IEEE 802.1X is designed to control individual LAN ports, how does it map to the wireless case in which there is a single access point supporting many devices? We have to treat each wireless connection between a mobile device and the access point as if it were an independent connection. In effect, we replace the physical connections of a switched LAN hub with logical connections formed by the wireless communications.

In the context of IEEE 802.1X, each mobile device is a supplicant wanting to be provided with the services of the access point (which typically means connection to a wired network). To accomplish this, the access point must create, for

---

3. This message has no use on wired 802 LANs because they do not support cipher suites.

each supplicant it encounters, a logical port complete with an authenticator. Each authenticator is responsible for controlling access for the mobile supplicant to which it has been assigned. Along with the logical port and authenticator, there is also a logical control switch. As you would expect, the control switch starts in the open position.

A new wireless device, acting as a supplicant, has to apply for access by sending messages to the authenticator, which controls its connection inside the access point. All this is done in software. There is no physical authenticator or switch, so the number of IEEE 802.1X entities in operation is the same as the number of associated mobile devices, regardless of how many that might be (Figure 8.6).

It is a common misconception that IEEE 802.1X is only relevant to big corporate environments in which there are dedicated authentication servers. However, in practice, the authentication server could be a simple process inside the access point—just a list of user names and passwords, for example. This means that the same principles of IEEE 802.1X that apply for huge networks can also apply to home networks. If the authentication server is built inside the access point, there is no need to use RADIUS because the authenticator and authentication server do not need to talk over the network; they are in the same box! However, in this case the number of supported authentication methods would be limited to those selected by the equipment vendor.

So far we have mostly talked about IEEE 802.1X in the context of access control. This has been described as a sort of one-time operation: The supplicant requests access and the authenticator grants it after referring to the authentication server. This may be sufficient for dial-up access or for Ethernet LAN ports because there is a physical connection for each supplicant and it is very hard for an attacker to take over that connection once it is authorized. Clearly the same is not true for

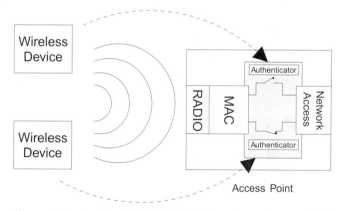

Figure 8.6   Logical IEEE 802.1X Ports in an Access Point

Wi-Fi LANs. Without protection, it would be trivially easy for an attacker to wait until a valid user was granted access and then start using the connection by stealing his identity. Therefore, for Wi-Fi LANs, we have to bind the authorization to a mechanism that prevents this type of session hijack. This is accomplished by incorporating message authentication (integrity) as part of the authorization process. We must be sure that both the access point and the mobile device have their secret keys in place by checking message authenticity and that they have turned on encryption before granting access to the network. This important difference greatly complicates the process and resulted in some minor changes to IEEE 802.1X to ensure synchronization of the process. A new standard, IEEE 802.1AA, is being developed at the time of writing to update IEEE 802.1X partly as a result of its application to IEEE 802.11i. To explore the way that synchronization is achieved, see Chapter 10.

EAP Principles

In some ways EAP performs the role of an actor's agent. When an actor is looking for work, the agent takes her to a movie director and introduces them. The agent sits back while the actor and director talk about the job, but jumps in again at the end to close the deal.

EAP has a set of messages that it uses to make the introductions and to close the deal. These are used with all upper-layer authentication methods.[4] EAP also allows two parties to exchange information that is specific to the authentication method they want to use. The content of these authentication-specific methods is not defined in EAP. In fact, they can be completely proprietary authentication methods or newly invented ones. EAP's ability to handle part of the communication in a standardized way and part in a specific way is the key to its extensibility. We refer to these authentication-specific messages as "middle messages" because they occur after the introduction and before the closing.

Quite a lot of these middle messages can be exchanged before the authentication is completed. The reason why EAP is extensible is that the details of these special messages are left to other RFCs to fill in. For example, there is an RFC saying how to use Transport Layer Security (TLS) over EAP; another (draft) says how to use Tunneled TLS (TTLS) over EAP, and so on. It also means that if you invent a new method later on, you can write a new draft called "mymethod over EAP"; and if it becomes popular, other people can implement it on existing systems.

---

4. Upper-layer authentication methods are discussed in Chapter 9 and include methods such as SSL, TLS, and Kerberos V5.

RFC2284 (EAP) is a very short document as these things go. In fact, not counting references, acknowledgments, definitions, and so on, it is only nine pages long. RFC2284 (EAP) specifies that four types of message can be sent:

- **Request**: Used to send messages from the authenticator to the supplicant
- **Response**: Used to send messages from the supplicant to the authenticator
- **Success**: Sent by the authenticator to indicate access is granted
- **Failure**: Sent by the authenticator to indicate access is refused

Note that these messages are described here in terms of the authenticator. However, in the IEEE 802.1X scenario, the authenticator forwards the messages on to the authentication server, most likely using RADIUS. In this case it is the authentication server that generates request, success, and/or failure messages and the authenticator just relays them to the supplicant.

Request and response messages are further subdivided using the EAP Type field. The Type field indicates what information is being carried in the EAP message. The first six message types are defined in the standard; all the others are reserved for specific authentication methods. The most important predefined type is Identity (type value 1). Typically, this is used as part of the EAP introduction phase: the message **EAP-Request/Identity** is sent by the authenticator to a new supplicant. The supplicant replies with the message **EAP-Response/Identity** containing its user name or some other identifier that will be understood by the authentication server.

Type numbers higher than 6 are not defined by RFC2284 (EAP), but they are issued (uniquely) by IANA for each new authentication method that is introduced. Some are even issued for vendor-proprietary methods. The type number for TLS, for example, is 13, which means that all EAP-Request and EAP-Response messages with this type field contain information that is specific to the TLS upper-layer authentication method.

The use of the Type field is a bit inconsistent. For the most part, it indicates the authentication method. But in a few cases, it defines a special-purpose message. For example, a message with a type value of 2 is called a **notification** message and is used to send some user-displayable text. This could be anything from "Please enter your password" to "Prepare to meet thy maker"—it really doesn't matter. The message is intended to appear on the screen of the user's system (although few systems actually support this). A message with a type value of 3 is called a NAK and is used when a request is made for an authentication method that is not supported. If an EAP request with type TLS is sent to a peer that doesn't support TLS, it can respond with a Type field of NAK.

Type value 1 **Identity** could be considered a special-purpose message or it could be considered a very simple authentication method. Under IEEE 802.1X, this request is often the first thing sent and the supplicant will reply with a response message giving its identity information. Originally this was treated as a special type to be used prior to the main authentication phase. However, this has been subtly changed in the revised EAP draft (while remaining compatible with the previous version). The simplest authentication exchange could go:

- EAP-Identity request (from authenticator)
- EAP-Identity response (from supplicant)
- EAP-Success (from authenticator)

Here the device has been "authenticated" on pure trust: "I choose to believe that you are who you say with no proof." Or perhaps proof is available by some other means. For example, the identity might be generated by a smart card that changes every second, synchronized to the authentication server.[5] This type of null authentication can be used with simple wireless LAN networks that have preloaded secret keys (called **preshared** keys) and then rely on the encryption to prevent unwanted communications.

Because the EAP-Identity exchange can be considered a complete authentication method by itself, when you do the identity exchange followed by another method such as TLS, you are really running two authentication methods in sequence. This concept of **serial authentication** has been generalized in the new EAP draft, which simply lists the EAP-Identity message as a basic authentication method and then says that you are allowed to run as many authentication methods in sequence as you wish prior to the final EAP-Success or EAP-Failure message.

This ability to run multiple authentication methods in sequence can be exploited in new approaches that allow the client to authenticate the network before revealing its identity. One approach, PEAP (Protected EAP), is discussed in more detail in Chapter 9.

EAP Message Formats

All EAP messages have a similar basic format, as shown in Figure 8.7. **Code** is one byte indicating the type of message:

- Request (01)
- Response (02)

---

5. This is often referred to as a *one-time password*.

Code	Indentifier	Length	Data

Figure 8.7 EAP Message Format

- Success (03)
- Failure (04)

Identifier is a value in the range 0–255 and IEEE 802.1X indicates that it should be incremented for each message sent. When a response is sent, the identifier is set equal to that in the request. This helps for checking which response goes with which request. **Length** is the total number of bytes in the EAP message (including Code and so on). It is a 16-bit value. Finally, **Data** is the actual request or response data being sent.

We have already discussed the Success and Failure packets. These messages are short and contain no data. One of these messages is used at the end of the authentication process to signal the result. Because the Success and Failure are common across all authentication protocols, intermediate devices (such as the access point) can detect when an authentication completes without understanding all the details of the authentication method. The access point should wait for the RADIUS Accept message before making any decision about access rights.

The details of the authentication method are sent in the request and response messages. These have an extra field called Type. The format of an EAP-Request or EAP-Response message is shown in Figure 8.8.

You can see the Type field, which is used to identify the request or response. The Type field is essential to separate all the different authentication methods. In fact, it is the key to the *extensibility* of EAP. Each new authentication method is assigned a unique value so the system knows whether the request contains information relevant to, for example, TLS or PEAP.[6]

Code	Indentifier	Length	Type	Rq/Rsp Data

Figure 8.8 EAP-Request/Response Message

---

6. These authentication methods are described in Chapter 9.

EAPOL

The EAP RFC does not specify how messages should be passed around. It does not, for example, specify transport over the Internet using IP. In fact, EAP *is not a LAN protocol at all* because EAP was originally designed for use with dial-up authentication via a modem. So if we are going to get EAP messages passed around our network, we have to find a way to *encapsulate* the EAP messages during their journey. IEEE 802.1X defines a protocol called **EAP over LAN** to get EAP messages passed between the supplicant and the authenticator.

IEEE 802.1X provides the description for EAPOL. It describes frame formats for Ethernet (IEEE 802.3) and token ring LANs but not for IEEE 802.11. If you just wanted to encapsulate the EAP message, you could prepend an Ethernet MAC header on an EAP message and send it over the LAN. But the IEEE 802.1X committee decided to add a few more useful messages and fields while it was defining EAPOL. Not all EAPOL frames actually carry EAP messages; some are used to perform administrative tasks. The five types of EAPOL messages are:

- EAPOL-Start
- EAPOL-Key
- EAPOL-Packet
- EAPOL-Logoff
- EAPOL-Encapsulated-ASF-Alert

We won't deal with the last message type here. It is connected with what we think is the rather dangerous idea of allowing an unauthorized device to send management alerts to the system. This message is not used by WPA/RSN.

EAPOL-Start

When the supplicant first connects to the LAN, it does not know the MAC address of the authenticator. Actually it doesn't know whether there is an authenticator present at all. To help get things going, IEEE 802.1X defines a message called EAPOL-Start. By sending this message to a special group-multicast MAC address reserved for IEEE 802.1X authenticators, a supplicant can find out whether an authenticator is present and let it know that the supplicant is ready. In many cases the authenticator will already be notified that a new device has connected from some hardware notification. For example, a hub knows that a cable is plugged in before the device sends any data. In this case the authenticator may preempt the Start message with its own message. In either case the authenticator sends an EAP-Request Identity message using the EAPOL-Packet frame (perhaps twice, if both send the initial message at the same time).

EAPOL-Key

Using this message type, the authenticator sends encryption (and other) keys to the supplicant once it has decided to admit it to the network. Of course it is necessary to encrypt the keys themselves before sending them, and IEEE 802.1X does not specify how this is done.[7] In fact, IEEE 802.1X offers little help when it comes to combining encryption with the authentication process. This was a major obstacle that had to be overcome in the WPA/RSN network design. Chapter 10, "WPA and RSN Key Hierarchy," outlines how a slightly modified EAPOL-Key message is used to establish encryption keys and also to validate that both sides have correct keys before allowing access.

EAPOL-Packet

This EAPOL frame is used for sending the actual EAP messages. It is simply a container for transporting an EAP message across the LAN, which was the original objective of the EAPOL protocol.

EAPOL-Logoff

This message type indicates that the supplicant wishes to be disconnected from the network.

For reference, the format of an EAPOL frame for use by Ethernet is shown in Figure 8.9. All of the packet types listed above fall into this format.

- The protocol version is always 1 (this could change in the future).
- The packet type number indicates start, key, and so on.
- For some message types, no further information is needed and the packet body length is set to 0 (and the body is omitted). However, if there is a packet body, such as an EAP message, its length and data are added on as appropriate.

Ethernet MAC Header	Protocol Version	Packet Type	Packet Body Length	Packet Body

Figure 8.9 EAPOL Frame Format

---

7. This is rectified in IEEE 802.1AA.

Messages Used in IEEE 802.1X

Messages must pass between three parties: the supplicant, authenticator, and authentication server. IEEE 802.1X uses EAP, or more specifically, EAPOL, to pass these messages between the supplicant and the authenticator. Let's start by following through the sequence of events when a new supplicant arrives.

Authentication Sequence

An outline of the authentication sequence is shown in Figure 8.10. When a supplicant wants to connect, it must first attract the attention of the authenticator. In most cases the authenticator is alerted by the connection process. It might be that the act of plugging in the cable or, in the case of wireless, associating with the access point is enough. Otherwise, the EAPOL-Start message can be used.

The authenticator first responds with an EAP-Request/Identity message. This is a standard EAP message that is equivalent to shouting, "Who's there?" The authenticator is allowed to skip this step if it knows the identity of the supplicant by some other method. The supplicant must respond with an EAP-Response/ Identity message. This raises an interesting issue because so far the supplicant can't be certain whether the authenticator can be trusted, especially in a wireless network. Suppose the authenticator is a rogue access point set up by an attacker. The supplicant might not want to reveal its identity at that time and uses a pseudonym instead.

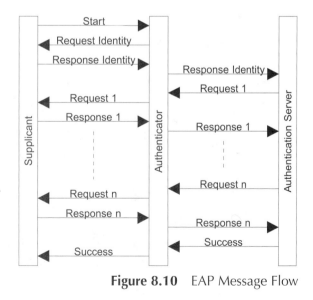

Figure 8.10   EAP Message Flow

Some schemes support the use of pseudonyms[8]; but, for the moment, let's assume the supplicant is not shy and is prepared to send its identity to the authenticator.

So far all the messages we have discussed have gone between the supplicant and the authenticator (in IEEE 802.11, this would be the mobile device and the access point). The authentication server has not been involved until now. It is important not to waste the authentication server's time until the supplicant has shown that it actually speaks IEEE 802.1X by responding to the first EAP-Request. Having obtained the identity of the supplicant, the authenticator needs to contact the authentication server to find out whether this supplicant is to be allowed in. The authentication server can't make this decision until it has verified that the supplicant really corresponds to the identity it has given. This is the whole point of authentication. To avoid the need for the authenticator (in the access point) having to know all the authentication methods, the EAP messages used for authentication are passed directly to the authentication server.

In effect, during this phase the supplicant and the server are talking directly. In our earlier office building analogy, the security guard has opened the door and asked the person's name, but not let him in yet. Then the guard calls his boss and says, "Can we let Harry Acker in?" The boss runs through a set of questions, which the security guard asks Harry one by one. The guard passes the answers back to the boss. The guard just relays the questions and answers and, in the end, the boss makes a decision on entry. Note that during this phase, the guard might not understand the purpose of the questions as in the following scenario:

Harry to guard: Hello, can I come in?

Guard to Harry: Who are you?

Harry to guard: I'm Harry Acker.

Guard to boss: Harry Acker wants to come in.

Boss to guard: Ask him whether the oak tree is a mammal or a marsupial.

(Guard asks Harry)

Harry to guard: It is a marsupial.

(Guard tells boss)

Boss to guard: Don't let him in.

Guard to Harry: You can't come in.

Note that the questions and answers relayed by the guard made no sense to him but clearly enabled the boss to make a decision that the guard then put into effect.

---

8. For example, PEAP.

During the authentication process, the authenticator takes a quick look at each EAP message that is passed between the supplicant and authentication server. It is watching for certain messages that it understands. In particular, it is looking for an EAP-Success or an EAP-Failure. It must wait until the authentication server indicates whether the supplicant has been accepted or rejected. A RADIUS message provides the indication when RADIUS is being used.

Implementation Considerations

So much for the theory, but where does IEEE 802.1X reside in real systems? For most Wi-Fi LANs, the logical place to put IEEE 802.1X is in the access point. In fact the close coupling between IEEE 802.1X and key management makes it hard to place it anywhere else. There were proposals in the standards work that would allow the key management and wireless access point functions to be separated so IEEE 802.1X could be placed on a separate access box to which the access point was connected. This approach was not adopted for WPA/RSN.

It is possible to build wireless LANs without an access point using IBSS or ad-hoc mode. In this case, it is necessary for every mobile device to have both a supplicant and an authenticator operating in parallel (see Chapter 13).

Some operating systems such as Microsoft Windows XP have support for IEEE 802.1X supplicants built in. When configuring the clients, you only need to enable IEEE 802.1X-based authentication and choose the authentication method. Of course the choice of authentication methods may be limited and you may have to install additional software to get the method you need. In older operating systems, IEEE 802.1X is probably not built in and you will need to install special drivers from the manufacturer of the Wi-Fi equipment you are installing. In all cases, supporting generic IEEE 802.1X is not enough for Wi-Fi LAN. There are other special requirements of WPA/RSN related to key management that must be built into the IEEE 802.1X implementation. In general the manufacturer of the adapter card provides all the necessary hooks and drivers to implement this extra stuff when the operating system does not. You should confirm that when a vendor advertises RSN or IEEE 802.11i compatibility that it does properly integrate with the operating system you intend to use. Systems labeled "Wi-Fi WPA" are likely to have the necessary software and will have been tested for interoperability with other vendors.

IEEE 802.1X can also be used in embedded mobile devices such as mobile phones or PDAs. In this case, the operating system may not be visible to the user. If the device supports IEEE 802.11i RSN or WPA, all the integration issues should be taken into account in the device. However, you will probably have little or no flexibility on the authentication method available. Be sure to find out what authentication method is used on such a device and confirm that your authentication server can support it.

As a final note, remember that IEEE 802.1X itself does *not* define the way that EAP messages are passed between the authenticator and the authentication server. However, it strongly hints that RADIUS is a good way to go in IP networks. It even includes an annex section outlining how RADIUS might be used. RADIUS has already been mentioned and is covered in the next section. Remember that RADIUS is needed only if the authentication server is remote to the authenticator. IEEE 802 deals with LAN protocols generally and is applicable to LANs regardless of whether they use TCP/IP. IEEE 802.1X does not specify RADIUS because it is based on IP packets, which are part of the TCP/IP protocol family. In reality, IP networks are by far the most common, but this was not always the case and IP still isn't used everywhere. Here we assume that you *are* using an IP network and we focus on RADIUS where there is a network connection between the authenticator and the authentication server. WPA goes further and defines RADIUS as a mandatory implementation choice to help ensure interoperability.

RADIUS—Remote Access Dial-In User Service

Although RADIUS is not specifically part of the IEEE 802.11i standard, many practical corporate implementations use it to communicate between the access point and the authentication server. Small office or home installations are very unlikely to use RADIUS because the authentication server is probably inside the access point. So what exactly is RADIUS? Is it a protocol or type of product? You will often hear the term RADIUS server. Is this something you can buy, or can you go to your PC shop and say, "I'd like to buy a RADIUS server please"?

The exact definition of a RADIUS server is a source of confusion. There are companies that make and sell authentication servers. You can make your own authentication server by installing a commercial software package on a conventional PC. However, there is no standard definition for the features of such servers. Some authentication servers are dedicated to specific authentication methods. Others may have special capabilities such as redundant or distributed operation. A **redundant server** has standby units that take over seamlessly if the primary server fails, and a **distributed server** has many servers operating in different locations while it keeps a common authentication database updated and consistent between all sites.

RADIUS defines two things. First, it defines a set of functionality that should be common across authentication servers. Second, it defines a protocol that allows other devices to access those capabilities. When we talk about a RADIUS server, we are talking about that subpart of the authentication server that supports the RADIUS capabilities; and when we talk about RADIUS, we are generally referring to the protocol used to talk to the server.

RADIUS is specified by the IETF and is designed for use with TCP/IP type networks; it assumes that devices use an IP network to talk to a RADIUS server.

As with many aspects of the Internet, the capabilities and needs of systems are continuously evolving, and RADIUS has been stretched and bent by various additions over the years. Therefore, when you buy an authentication server that includes RADIUS capability, you need to ensure that it supports any new bells and whistles that you might need. For example, EAP over RADIUS (RFC 2869) is needed for IEEE 802.11i RSN security, but it was not included in the original RADIUS specification (RFC 2865). RADIUS allows the definition of vendor-specific attributes for special features that the server might provide. One such special feature, Microsoft's MS-CHAPv1/v2 authentication method, is used widely and has almost become a standard requirement.

The first RADIUS RFC (specification) was RFC2058, issued in 1997, although this was superceded almost immediately by RFC2138. In 2000 RFC2138 was further updated and replaced by RFC2865. As noted at the start of the chapter, one motivation behind RADIUS was the support of dial-in modem pools. An ISP might want to provide dial-up access over a substantial area or even nationwide. Customers don't want to pay long-distance phone call charges, so the ISP has to set up a modem pool in each local phone area so users can connect cheaply (or for free). At each modem pool site is a dial-in server that answers the calls, authenticates that the user is a valid customer, and then runs the PPP to allow connection to the Internet. The problem is that each modem pool server needs to know all possible valid users in order to perform the authentication step. The motivation for RADIUS is to have a central authentication server that knows all the customers and allows the modem-pool servers to forward the authentication information to the central site for checking. In RADIUS terms, the modem pool server is the NAS (network access server) and the authentication server (AS) is the RADIUS server.

The analogy with a Wi-Fi LAN is clear. In our case the access point is like the NAS. There may be many of them dotted about the place, and we don't want each one to have to know the authentication database. We can use the RADIUS server, as was intended, to provide centralization of the authentication decisions. If you want to read the specifications, the ones that are relevant to WPA/RSN are:

- RFC2865: Remote Authentication Dial-In User Service (RADIUS)
- RFC 2866: RADIUS Accounting
- RFC 2867: RADIUS Accounting for Tunneling
- RFC 2868: RADIUS Authentication for Tunneling
- RFC2869: RADIUS Extensions
- RFC 3162: RADIUS over IP6
- RFC 2548: Microsoft Vendor-Specific RADIUS Attributes

RFC2869 is relevant because it contains information on how to use EAP over RADIUS. Note also that at the time of this writing, there is a draft RFC potentially updating RFC2869 This draft is called Draft-aboba-radius-rfc2869bis-10: RADIUS Support for Extensible Authentication Protocol (EAP). This draft update recognizes that EAP is now also used in IEEE 802.1X applications in addition to PPP dial-up modems. The original RFC gives examples based on PPP, but this has been generalized in the update.

RADIUS Mechanics

This section reviews how RADIUS works at the protocol level. The basic message set for RADIUS is deceptively simple. Most of the complexity lies with messages called attributes.

Core Messages

The core protocol of RADIUS is very simple. There are just four relevant messages:

- Access-Request (NAS $\rightarrow$ AS)
- Access-Challenge (NAS $\leftarrow$ AS)
- Access-Accept (NAS $\leftarrow$ AS)
- Access-Reject (NAS $\leftarrow$ AS)

In the WPA/RSN case, the access point is the equivalent of the NAS and AS is the RADIUS authentication server.

These four messages reflect the fact that PPP, the dial-in modem protocol, has two options for authentication: PAP and CHAP. PAP is a simple user name/password approach. CHAP requires that the server send random data called a **challenge**, which the dial-in system must encrypt and return for checking. Let's consider how this works with dial-in.

First we'll tackle the PAP case, as shown in Figure 8.11: The user dials in and the NAS answers and indicates that it is using PAP authentication. The user's system then responds by sending the user name and password for the account. The NAS now sends an Access-Request message to the RADIUS server containing

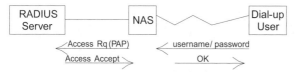

Figure 8.11 PAP Operation

the user name and password information.[9] The RADIUS server responds with either Access-Accept or Access-Reject and the NAS acts accordingly. This is a very simple approach and, of course, it is subject to a wide range of attacks. The worst part is that the password is sent unencrypted over the phone link so anyone monitoring the link can copy it. It is about as secure as one of those little padlocks that come with cheap suitcases—just pretend security, really.[10]

CHAP is a little better, and makes an attempt at secure authentication, as shown in Figure 8.12. Rather than sending the password unencrypted across the phone link, the user sends only its user name to the NAS. The NAS now needs to respond with a challenge. To get the challenge data, the NAS could send the user name to the server using an Access-Request, whereupon the server would send the challenge data using Access-Challenge. However, in most implementations the NAS avoids disturbing the server and generates the challenge by itself, as shown in Figure 8.12. The challenge is passed back to the dial-in user's system, which is required to encrypt the challenge with the password and send it back. Finally the NAS is able to send the challenge, response, and identity to the AS, indicating that it is using CHAP.

This approach means that the password is not sent unencrypted; it also provides some liveness because the challenge changes on each access attempt. However, it is still subject to dictionary attack because both the unencrypted and encrypted versions of the challenge are accessible to an attacker.

Partly because of the dictionary attack weakness, Microsoft implemented a modified version of CHAP called MS-CHAP that is now used widely in corporate dial-up pools. Microsoft "standardized" their attribute definitions through RFC2548, Microsoft Vendor-Specific RADIUS Attributes.

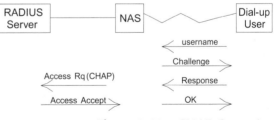

Figure 8.12 CHAP Operation

---

9. Actually, it sends an encrypted version using the "hiding" algorithm in RFC2865.

10. In defense of PAP, the threat model for PPP assumed that the telco wire was secure. This is generally a pretty good supposition, in which case there is nothing so bad about passwords in the clear.

RADIUS was specifically designed with two PPP authentication scenarios in mind: simple password request PAP and challenge response CHAP. In WPA/RSN, we need to use RADIUS in conjunction with a security protocol that is state of the art—far more complex (and secure) than the simple PAP and CHAP methods. To do this, we need to change the purpose of some of the messages in RADIUS. For example, to support EAP we will use the access-challenge method, not as a challenge, but as a way to send EAP requests and responses. The good news is that RADIUS is flexible enough to accommodate these changes. One of the reasons it is flexible is because of its use of attributes.

Core Message Format and Attributes

Although essentially only four messages are used for authentication via RADIUS, the meaning of the messages can be changed extensively through different message attributes. Figures 8.11 and 8.12 show how the Access-Request message can mean three different things at different times. The attributes the message carries are different in each case. The main body of the RADIUS message is composed of a series of **attributes**; each is a self-contained package of information that (hopefully) has meaning to both communicating parties.

Every RADIUS message has the same basic format, as shown in Figure 8.13. We will work through each field to explain its use and meaning.

The Code byte indicates the type of message:

- Access-Request: 1
- Access-Accept: 2
- Access-Reject: 3
- Access-Challenge: 11

The Identifier is an arbitrary number used to match up requests and replies, and the Length word indicates the total number of bytes in the message. The Authenticator is much more interesting because is has a bearing on security. The Authenticator is 16 bytes (128 bits) long and its use depends on the type of message:

In the Access-Request message, the authenticator contains a 16-byte nonce value. A nonce is a number whose value is never used twice in two different requests. In RADIUS, the nonce is used for two purposes. First, if the Access-Request message is sending a password value in an attribute, the password value is

Code	Identifier	Length	Authenticator	Attributes.......

Figure 8.13 Basic Format of RADIUS Message

encrypted using a combination of a secret key and this nonce. Second, reply messages use the nonce value in deriving an integrity check value, as described in the next paragraph.

One of three messages—Access-Accept, Access-Reject, and Access-Challenge—is sent in response to an Access-Request message. It is important to check that the reply came from the legitimate RADIUS server and has not been modified in transit. To accomplish this, an integrity check value (16 bytes) is computed and inserted into the Authenticator field of the reply.

The NAS and the RADIUS server share a secret key between them. To create the check value, the RADIUS server combines the entire reply message with the secret key. Before the computation, it inserts the nonce from the request message into the Authenticator position of the reply message and when the integrity check value has been computed, it overwrites the nonce to form a new Authenticator value. It is not practical to forge a reply that will match the request message without knowing the secret key and the use of the nonce reduces[11] the opportunity to replay an old message.

Attributes

The useful information carried in RADIUS messages is contained within attributes. Each message can carry one or more attributes and each is a self-contained package of information. It will come as no surprise that the ability to extend RADIUS depends on the ability to define and support new attributes. For a RADIUS server to be useful to you, it must support the attributes you need in your application (and the services accessed through the attributes). This is where an industry definition like WPA is useful because you can simply ask the vendor if the server conforms to the requirements of WPA. Because WPA has been designed around some common existing attributes (albeit proprietary extensions), this should not be a problem in practice, providing your RADIUS server has the required support.

Each attribute has the same format:

- A 1-byte Type field to identify the attribute
- A 1-byte Length field that indicates the number of bytes in the whole attribute
- Attribute specific data (if any)

---

11. We say "reduces" rather than "eliminates" because the creation of the nonce is implementation dependent and cannot be guaranteed to be unique in the true meaning of the word "nonce."

Table 8.1 Examples of RADIUS Attributes

Attribute Type Value	Name	Description
1	User-Name	The identification name or user name of the user.
2	User-Password	Contains the login password. The password data is encrypted using a shared secret and the nonce value from the Authenticator field of the Access-Request.
3	CHAP-Password	During CHAP, the user encrypts the challenge and returns a value. The value is forwarded from the NAS to the RADIUS server in this attribute.
4	NAS-IP-Address	The IP address of the NAS to which the RADIUS server should respond.
18	Reply Message	This sends text that can be displayed to the user to indicate some event or needed action.
26	Vendor-Specific	This attribute allows vendors to implement and communicate special features relevant only to their equipment. Interestingly, if they choose to make their vendor-specific attributes public, other vendors can support the features, forming a sort of nested standards process. Microsoft has done this for MS-CHAP.

There are many possible attributes. Some of the more common ones are listed in Table 8.1.

EAP over RADIUS

Because EAP was designed to extend authentication via dial-in modems, and given that so many modem pools use RADIUS, a method was needed to carry EAP over RADIUS. Extensions to RADIUS that accomplish this are described in RFC2869. These extensions are relevant to Wi-Fi LAN because WPA and RSN also use EAP. Several RADIUS extensions are defined in RFC2869. RFC2869 also has some updated procedures for sending accounting information, and it describes how to support Apple Computer's ARAP for dial-in support of Apple machines. We focus only on the section dealing with EAP over RADIUS.

In the early RADIUS standard, only two messages were available for sending authentication information between parties: Access-Request to send data from the NAS to the RADIUS server, and Access-Challenge to send data from the RADIUS server to the NAS. As the name suggests, Access-Challenge has a particular purpose similar to the challenge used in CHAP. However, RFC2869 uses this message in a more general way to pass information back from the RADIUS server. Thus EAP messages are sent to the authentication messages inside an Access-Request message and responses are returned inside an Access-Challenge message.

The EAP message itself is sent inside one or more special attributes that have a type value of 79. All the usual EAP messages can be sent. There are a few rules to help existing RADIUS implementations map the requests to the existing conventions. For example, the identity of the dial-in user is usually sent in an EAP-Response/Identity message. This message is forwarded to the RADIUS server in an EAP attribute, but the identity information should also be copied into a User-Name attribute (type 1) and included so that RADIUS servers, including older versions, can still understand and maybe forward the message to the right place.

Recall that EAPOL includes a message called EAPOL-Start designed to kick the authenticator into action when a new device arrives and wants to get connected. RFC2869 defines a similar message called EAP-Start, which is an EAP attribute with no data. The attribute is just two bytes—a type field of 79 indicating the EAP-Message attribute and a length byte of value 2. This can be used by the NAS to get the RADIUS server started, as shown in Figure 8.14.

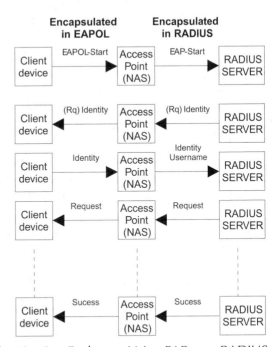

Figure 8.14 Authentication Exchange Using EAP over RADIUS

In Figure 8.14 we have shown the access point in place of the dial-up NAS, although the principles are just the same. The access point also contains an IEEE 802.1X authenticator, which talks EAP to the new client (supplicant). EAP messages that the IEEE 802.1X authenticator wants to pass back to the authentication server are packaged in RADIUS and sent to the RADIUS server. Let's step through the sequence of events.

First the new device sends an EAPOL-Start to the access point authenticator. If the access point knows that the RADIUS server supports EAP, it can go ahead and issue the EAP-Request/Identity message to the client device and send the response to the server directly. If, however, it is unsure about the server's capability, it can ask the RADIUS server to initiate the EAP exchange by sending the RADIUS server an EAP-Start message in an Access-Request message. If the server doesn't support EAP, it replays with a reject message (this is not a good idea for every exchange because the RADIUS server could be deluged with messages). If the server is EAP enabled, it sends the EAP-Request/Identity message in a RADIUS Access-Challenge message. Figure 8.14 provides an example in which the authentication method is TLS. At the end of the exchange, an EAP-Success or EAP-Fail signifies the result.

Use of RADIUS in WPA and RSN

As shown in Figure 8.14, the way RADIUS and EAP over RADIUS work fits very well with Wi-Fi WPA/RSN architecture. However, there is one important difference between the Wi-Fi and the dial-up case: For dial-up, the concern is only initial authentication, whereas WPA/RSN is concerned with establishing a lasting security context. In the dial-up case, it is only necessary to determine whether the user should be admitted to the system. Because of the nature of phone lines, an attacker is unlikely to hijack a dial-in modem once it has connected (although such an approach is theoretically possible). Therefore, once authentication is complete, there is a tendency for the NAS to sit back and assume a good guy is connected. However, as we have seen, with Wi-Fi LAN it is trivially easy to hijack an established connection just by stealing a legitimate MAC address.

Protection against session hijacking is provided by per-packet authentication and integrity protection. To provide this protection, the authentication server must pass a secret master key down to the access point. This process of generating and passing the keys is covered in great detail in Chapter 10. Earlier RADIUS servers based on RFC2865–2869 did not provide the ability to send keys from the authentication server to the NAS. The RFC assumes that the password is sent the other way for validation. However, one vendor, Microsoft, has solved this problem for another security protocol. Microsoft helped create an RFC covering their proprietary extensions to RADIUS (RFC2548: Microsoft Vendor-Specific

RADIUS Attributes). These extensions contain an attribute called MS-MPPE-Recv-Key, which is specifically intended to deliver key information to the NAS. In fact the description in the RFC says:

> The MS-MPPE-Recv-Key Attribute contains a session key for use by the Microsoft Point-to-Point Encryption Protocol (MPPE). As the name implies, this key is intended for encrypting packets received by the NAS from the remote host. This attribute is only included in Access-Accept packets.

In the IEEE 802.11i context, "MPPE" becomes "WPA" or "RSN," "NAS" becomes "access point," and "remote host" becomes "mobile device." At Microsoft's suggestion, this attribute was adopted into WPA as the recommended way to pass the master key information from the RADIUS server to the access point. It almost goes without saying that this attribute supports (and requires) encryption of the key material prior to transmission and therefore provides a more secure key delivery mechanism. Whether this attribute will make it into 802.11i is another story. The National Institute of Standards and Technology (NIST) has requested that it be deprecated in favor of a standard attribute using a key wrap algorithm.

Now we have all the pieces for using WPA/RSN in conjunction with RADIUS. The requirements are that the access point should support RADIUS, including the extensions for EAP and at least the Microsoft key delivery attribute. Also, the RADIUS server must not only support these protocols but must also understand that it is required to send the pairwise master key (PMK) to the access point (see Chapter 10). It is not mandatory under RSN to use RADIUS, although it is under WPA. Therefore, it is likely that this approach will become popular and that the RADIUS server vendors will ensure that their software provides support.

Summary

This chapter begins with a basic definition of access control. On the surface, the process of establishing the identity of the caller, checking for authorization, and opening or closing the gate is extremely simple. So simple, in fact, that the qualification requirements for a nightclub's doorman tend to be more concerned with physical mass than cranial capacity. We have seen how the three-party model of caller, security guard, and authorizer has been adopted first for dial-up modem authentication, second for LAN access authentication using IEEE 802.1X, and finally for wireless LAN authorization using IEEE 802.11 and IEEE 802.1X.

This chapter also reviewed how the messages between the three controlling parties are carefully defined using the protocols EAP and RADIUS. We observed that wireless LAN places an additional burden on the process because it is so vulnerable to session hijack. In the case of WPA and RSN, it is necessary to establish a set of secret keys between the access point and the mobile device to protect against hijack. It this way, the authorization obtained during the access control procedure becomes like an access pass that can be used over and over with each packet of data sent.

The establishment of the secret session keys and their binding to the access control procedure has been one of the challenges of developing new security protocols (see Chapter 10). In Chapter 9, we look at the upper-level authentication protocols that ensure beyond doubt that the entities that you intend to authorize really are who they say they are.

9 Chapter

Upper-Layer Authentication

This chapter reviews several of the major authentication methods. We cover in some detail the way that Transport Layer Security and Kerberos V5 work and how they can be applied to Wi-Fi network security. We also look at some newer ideas, such as ways to link together Wi-Fi LAN user authentication with cellular phone authentication.

Introduction

Chapter 7 defines three major layers of security: wireless LAN layer, the access control layer, and the authentication layer. This chapter looks at the authentication layer and, more specifically, at the protocols used to implement authentication. IEEE 802.11 lies in the wireless LAN layer, which is considered the lowest layer, and IEEE 802.1X lies in the access control layer. The authentication methods use higher-layer protocols and the term "upper-layer authentication" reflects the fact that the methods do not depend on specific LAN technology. A range of different methods can be used for authentication in RSN; some of the major ones are described here.

We look first at Transport Layer Security (TLS), the default method for WPA that can also be used with RSN. Later in the chapter we look at Kerberos V5 and some of the new methods being invented, such as Protected EAP (PEAP) and the use of cellular phone authentication for Wi-Fi LAN devices (GSM-SIM). We also examine the inner workings of the authentication process and see how the messages are mostly exchanged between the supplicant and the server, with the access point (authenticator) playing a sort of observant go between in the process.

Who Decides Which Authentication Method to Use?

Given the number of authentication methods that could be used with RSN, the question arises, which one is correct? There is no simple answer. If you are starting from scratch to implement security, you should choose the method that is most widely supported in the available products. Today a leading candidate is TLS. However, if you have an existing system such as Kerberos V5 in operation, perhaps used with your wired network, it makes sense to try to apply that existing system to RSN. RSN is intended to provide this flexibility. In the interests of interoperability, the Wi-Fi Alliance has mandated that all WPA products should, at least, support TLS.

The Wi-Fi Alliance was free to choose which upper-layer authentication methods should be supported. However, the IEEE 802 working group is more restricted in specifying such things because, by virtue of being "upper-layer," the authentication method falls outside the scope of LAN protocol standards.

As such, IEEE 802.11 cannot and does not define the upper-layer authentication method, and instead leaves it to the implementers of the systems to decide. This was an issue of much rancor during the early days of the IEEE 802.11i standards work. Some people pointed out that it would be very hard to guarantee interoperability between different vendors' systems unless all the details of the authentication methods were specified. However, other people pointed out that, because of the range of different applications for Wi-Fi LAN, a single authentication method could not be suitable in all cases. This problem has been reduced by WPA, which does specify the method (TLS). It seems very likely that the method that is deployed for WPA will also be the most popular one when the transition to IEEE 802.11i RSN occurs.

This chapter presents solutions for several choices, including TLS, Kerberos V5, Protected EAP (PEAP), and the use of cellular phone authentication for wireless LAN devices (GSM-SIM). While the use of TLS is well defined through WPA, different vendors may implement other methods differently and interoperability cannot always be guaranteed. For example, the RFCs for Kerberos as defined by the IETF do not specify how to implement over IEEE 802.1X, let alone RSN. If you are not using WPA with TLS, you need to check carefully whether a vendor supports the authentication method you want, and whether they do so in the same way as any other vendor whose products you have purchased.

Use of Keys in Upper-Layer Authentication

Authentication is part of a process of creating a security context within which communications can take place. Because the process of full authentication is costly and time consuming, it is common to do full authentication occasionally and provide some token that can be used as proof of authentication in subsequent transactions. In the case of RSN, and indeed most security protocols, the proof is provided by creating secret key values as part of the authentication process.

The upper-layer authentication method is responsible for proving beyond a doubt that each party possesses some secret knowledge connected to their identity, and for providing the tokens or keys needed to support a security context. It has to do this in a way that does not leak any useful information about the shared secrets.

Before looking in detail at individual methods, let's look at the two main classes of solution: symmetric keys and asymmetric keys, sometimes known as secret and public keys, respectively.

Symmetric Keys

The concept of the symmetric secret key is simple. Each party has a copy of some secret information. Authentication occurs when each party proves to the other that they know the secret. This is like the child's method, "You can't come in unless you tell me the password." When each party has proved itself, they can both create matching session keys for use in the security context. Such keys are derived from the secret master key but may also incorporate other information, such as the time and arbitrary numbers created for the session (called nonces). The purpose of these extra items is to ensure that the session keys are usable only in the current session and cannot be reused later.

The main limitation with the secret key approach is that you have to get the secret to both parties in the first place. Sometimes that is not a problem. To communicate with your domestic partner, for example, you could agree on your secret Wi-Fi LAN key during a private moment when no one else is listening. This scenario, or at least the key exchange part, also works in corporate environments in which there is a secure place for the two parties, such as the employee and the IT manager, to meet. However, the approach doesn't scale at all for widespread use. In a huge corporation it is hard to distribute such keys and, in the case of Internet commerce, it is impossible. When you want to make a secure exchange with another party in another country whom you have never met, and never will, there is no practical way to safely agree on secret keys by informal communication.

Asymmetric Keys

To deal with the situation in which you can't easily distribute the secret key, the idea of asymmetric key encryption was invented, leading to the use of public keys.

Public key encryption is supported by a set of components often referred to as PKI (public key infrastructure).

First, let's look at the encryption part of public key use. The very words "public key" sound like a contradiction in terms. If the key is public, what use can it be for privacy? However, this name is misleading because a person who uses public key encryption actually has two keys. One key is made public and the other must be kept private. Furthermore, these are not any two keys; the public and the private copies are a mathematically connected pair. The way public key encryption works is fascinating and almost counterintuitive.

As an analogy, suppose a wizard wants to send you a message. He writes the message on a piece of paper and puts it in a magic box. Now he closes the box and recites your name three times. The box is immediately sealed and cannot now be opened by anyone except you; not even the wizard can open it. When the box arrives, you recite a secret word three times and the box opens. The wizard knows your name and can seal the box with it; that is your public key. But only you know the secret word to open the box again; that is your private key.

How does this work with encryption? Many encryption systems are symmetric in that the same key is used to encrypt and then decrypt the message. However, public key systems use an asymmetrical method in which different keys are used for encryption and decryption. You encrypt with key E and decrypt with key D. Furthermore, you *can't* decrypt with key E, and knowing E doesn't enable you to compute D. In public key encryption, E is the spell to seal the box, or the public key. D is the spell to open the box, or the private key.

When you want to use public key encryption through programs such as PGP (Pretty Good Privacy), you first use a key-generating utility. You run this utility and usually enter some personal information to help ensure your keys are unique to you. The utility then generates two key values, a **public key** and a **private key**. The public key can be given to anyone. And the key can be used to encrypt a message using your public key and send it to you. Only you can decrypt the message because only you know the private key. It's like magic!

A subtle and important variant of this method lets you *sign* messages. Signing a message is like signing a document: It is intended to prove that the message came from a particular person. Message signing works in the reverse way from encryption. You use a private key to create a signature and a public key to check the signature. In a simple case, you take your name and encrypt it with your private key. The result is added to the end of your message. Anyone who receives the message (friend or foe) can decrypt the signature using your public key. If the signature successfully decrypts and reveals your name, it proves that you must have sent the message because no one else knows the secret key that was used to encrypt it. A forger could not have encrypted your name correctly because she wouldn't know your secret key. So this proves that you approved the message in the same way that signing a letter does—actually, much stronger.

In reality, the above scheme doesn't prevent someone from creating a new bogus message and copying your encrypted signature from a valid message (like photocopying your signature on a letter). To protect against this, you must do more than include your name in the signature; you must include other information as well. In practice, the entire contents of the message are usually included in the signature computation to protect against tampering.

Because verifying that a message really came from the sender is very important, systems like PGP do both encryption and message signing. Remember that public key encryption by itself provides privacy but does not authenticate the sender. Suppose you receive an encrypted message saying, "Sally, come quickly, I need your help. Meet me at the bar downtown, Fred." How do you know the message is real (ignoring the fact that your name probably isn't Sally)? The message is encrypted with your public key, so anyone could have forged it. A burglar may want you to leave your house, or worse. But if Fred *signed* the message with his private key, you can verify that it was really him who sent it, right?

Well, maybe … it depends. Now we are back to our original key distribution problem. How do you know that Fred's public key really belongs to Fred? In this case, it's probably because you met Fred face to face and he told you the public key. Or more likely, you have had various exchanges of e-mail with Fred using his key and you trust that it really is him. But suppose you just started using public key yesterday and you received an e-mail (unencrypted) from Fred two days ago that said, "Hi. This PGP stuff is cool—let's use it. My public key is: FREDSKEY." Can you be sure that Fred sent this message and not some (computer-literate) burglar? This is reminiscent of the sort of problem that we had with the distribution of symmetric secret keys.

Certificates and Certification Authorities

What is needed is a way to certify that public keys are legitimate. This issue of *certifying* that a public key really belongs to the expected person becomes even more important when you use the method for Internet transactions with complete strangers or corporations. Think about e-commerce. You really want to be sure that the Web site you are giving your credit card details to is who they say they are. When your order doesn't show up, and you call to inquire, you don't want to hear, "Sorry, we have no record of that transaction" because someone was impersonating the vendor. The solution comes by using a trusted third party: a certificate authority.

Essentially, a **certificate authority** is a trusted independent organization that certifies a set of public and private keys for use with PKI transactions. The authority handles this task by generating certificates in a standard format. A certificate is just a bunch of data. It has no physical form. However, when another party sends you a certificate, it contains enough information for you to validate who they are and establish a secure context. With most Web purchases, this is a one-way context that protects the consumer. The vendor gets protection through your credit card details!

Suppose you set up a Web company selling flags. You get a Web domain name such as www.myflagsarebest.com. You want this address to be certified to you so, when people come to your site and go to the secure purchase area, they are sure that no one is hijacking the connection. You can go to a certificate authority and purchase a certificate that binds your company and its Web site into your public and private key pair.

When someone visits your site and goes to the secure area, you send her your certificate. The browser on her PC looks at the certificate and evaluates who issued it. Assuming you went to a well-known certificate authority, the browser will likely accept the certificate as trusted (you can control this in the advanced options of the browser). If not, it notifies the user that an untrusted certificate has arrived and prompts her to decide whether to proceed.[1] The certificate contains the public key for your site, so now the browser can start encrypting all the messages. Your Web server is able to decrypt the messages with your private key, and so the transaction is protected. The customer can feel confident that the credit card details and order information are going to the right place and not being snooped along the way.

How does the browser know that the certificate was really issued by the certificate authority and not just made up by a crook? Because the entire certificate is signed by the certificate authority using *its* private key, and therefore it can be proved authentic because its validity can be tested by checking the signature with the authority's public key, which is also in the certificate. Neat, huh? Note that the browser may, in any case, choose to send a message to the certificate authority to check for *revocation*. If someone had compromised your Web site or somehow found out your secret key, you might want to disable the certificate. This would prevent someone else issuing copies of your certificate in the event he got your secret key. To disable the certificate, you notify the certificate authority, which marks it as revoked and informs anyone who asks that this is the case. It's the same idea as canceling a stolen credit card.

This example has been simplified for the purpose of illustrating how certificates work. Full details of Internet transactions and security are outside the scope of this book. However, the example does outline the general approach taken by

---

1. Unfortunately at this point 99% of users don't understand the message and click "proceed" anyway.

SSL (Secure Socket Layer) used by all the main browsers (and invented by Netscape). SSL is the basis of TLS, which is covered in more detail later in this chapter.

A Detailed Look at Upper-Level Authentication Methods

We have looked at an overview of two approaches: symmetric (secret) key and asymmetric (public) key. In practice the two methods are often combined. In particular, it is common for systems to use PKI to establish a security context and then exchange key values and use symmetric keys for encryption. The reason for this is that asymmetric key encryption takes more processing power than symmetric key encryption does.

However, the distinction is useful because the two major upper-level authentication methods we cover fall into both camps. Kerberos is more often based on the secret key approach, while TLS is based on a certificate approach. The following sections look at each of these methods in detail and show how they can be incorporated into the RSN model. We also consider three other methods, each of interest for a different reason:

- Cisco LEAP is important because it has already been deployed using WEP and was the first adopted method to use IEEE 802.1X and EAP.
- Protected EAP (PEAP) is a new approach that allows complete privacy in the authentication. Even the identity of the supplicant can be hidden from outside observers.
- EAP-SIM is an approach that allows cellular phone type devices to incorporate IEEE 802.11 interfaces and authenticate using IEEE 802.1X.

Transport Layer Security (TLS)

In the early years of the World Wide Web, Netscape dominated the design of browsers. In fact, most of the innovations in the area during those years came from Netscape. One of those innovations related to security. The early use of the Web was mostly technical. However, the potential for Web trading soon became apparent. A major obstacle to trading was the problem of securing the transaction information. Netscape invented a security approach that came to be known as SSL to help address this problem.

SSL was based on the use of digital certificates. Although it allows for certificates in both the server and the client, the most common model is that the server identifies itself with a certificate and the client uses a password or some other method such as credit card details. The use of a certificate on the server has the tremendous advantage that purchasers do not need to register with the site prior to making purchases. Registration is a nuisance and it may be necessary to distribute the password by a method separate from the Internet. Sometimes password distribution is done by post office mail. You would have to go to the Web site and register. Then you would be mailed a letter containing your password, which could be used to log in and make purchases. But such delays and inconvenience put people off shopping. By contrast, the use of certificates with SSL offers a way to identify and validate Internet traders immediately as well as providing a secure link so sensitive information like credit card details can be sent. No prior arrangement is necessary, enabling the all important *impulse purchase*.

SSL was built into the Netscape browser and eventually became a standard method for secure Web transactions. It provides a way to authenticate one or both parties and then to open a private communication channel with encryption and integrity checking. However, although the specifications for SSL were made available, it was still a proprietary solution controlled by a single vendor. Vendors and customers prefer technology that is built on international standards rather than proprietary solutions. Therefore, a decision was made to standardize SSL (or a related version) within the IETF.

The result is TLS, which is described in IETF RFC-2246 released in 1999. TLS is the standardized version of SSL. In fact the RFC clearly states this in its introduction:

> This document and the TLS protocol itself are based on the SSL 3.0 Protocol Specification as published by Netscape.

However, as the RFC also points out, the differences are such that the two do not interoperate directly. TLS is entirely concerned with the transport protocol layer and builds on to the TCP/IP layer. It does not concern itself with browsers, operating systems, or sockets (originally a UNIX concept but now extended to Microsoft Windows, Apple Macintosh, and other systems).

Functions of TLS

TLS provides more services than we need for WPA/RSN upper-layer authentication. Full TLS provides authentication, encryption, and, in principle, data compression functions.[2] WPA and RSN have their own built-in encryption methods such as TKIP or AES–CCMP, and neither WPA nor RSN specifies the use of data compression. However, the authentication method of TLS is very suitable and fits well into the EAP/IEEE 802.1X model.

---

2. As far as we are aware, the compression functions have never been used in practice.

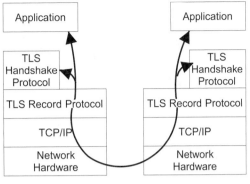

Figure 9.1 TLS Layers

We'll look at TLS overall first before focusing on the WPA/RSN capabilities. TLS is divided into two layers: the **record protocol** and the **handshake protocol**. The record protocol is responsible for shifting data between the two ends of the link using the parameters agreed via the handshake protocol.

The layers are shown diagrammatically in Figure 9.1. You can see how TLS relies on a reliable connection such as TCP/IP to send messages backward and forward. Data comes from the application to the TLS record protocol, where it gets encrypted and compressed as appropriate prior to being sent to the other end. Assuming the other end is valid, the message is then decrypted and uncompressed before delivery.

Notice how the TLS handshake protocol also uses the record protocol to send its messages during the handshake phase. This seems counterintuitive because the handshake protocol is used to negotiate the parameters of the record protocol layer over which it is communicating. TLS is design to handle this bootstrap process; in its initial state, the record protocol just forwards data without any encryption or compression. The record protocol layer operates according to a group of settings or parameters called a **connection state**. The connection state should be thought of as the configuration settings for the layer. It includes things like "which encryption algorithm is in use" and "what are the encryption keys." The record protocol layer can store four connection states: two connection states for each direction of communication. Two of the states are current and two are pending, as follows:

- Current transmit connection state
- Pending transmit connection state
- Current receive connection state
- Pending receive connection state

The difference between current and pending is quite simple. Current refers to the settings that are in effect now. Pending is a group of settings that are being prepared for use next. When the change occurs, the pending state becomes the current state and a new empty pending set is created, as shown in Figure 9.2. When the connection is first initialized, the current state is NULL: Everything just passes through. There are no keys, no encryption method, and no compression. During this time the handshake protocol can operate and build up the security parameters in the pending states. When everything is ready, the pending states become the current states and the security goes into effect.

TLS uses certificates for authentication (see the discussion of certificates earlier in the chapter). There are a number of different types of certificate, all working on similar principles. TLS is flexible enough to deal with all the cases, but it makes reading the TLS specification rather tedious. Suffice it to say, a certificate is typically delivered by the server for the client to verify. In rare applications, the server may also request a certificate from the client. Client certificates are typically used only when there is an *in-house* certificate authority—for example, when a corporation issues its own certificates for its employees.

Certificates are based on public key cryptography. It is a clever technique, but it is expensive in processing requirements. The nature of public key crypto methods means that many more computations are needed to encode and decode messages than for symmetric key operations. As a result, TLS does not use public key encryption for bulk data transfers of the record layer; instead, it uses symmetric keys that are agreed upon between the parties during the public key phase. The handshake protocol uses the certificates to perform public key cryptography during the authentication process. It also uses the public key cryptography to exchange some session keys that can be used by the record layer to encrypt data during the session. This approach greatly reduces the workload and, as it happens, fits in very nicely with the way in which WPA/RSN is organized.

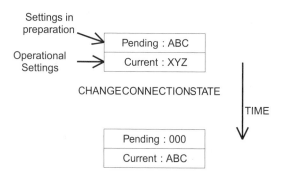

Figure 9.2 Changing Connection State

Handshake Exchange

A relationship is established between two parties in TLS by using a handshake exchange. This involves a series of messages sent between the parties in a specific order, as summarized in Figure 9.3 and explained in the following sections.

There are several options concerning which messages are sent and what information they contain, but the order is important and, before the end of the handshake, every message is checked for validity. At the start of the handshake, the two parties exchange **hello messages**, rather like people actually. Remember that TLS is not symmetrical, so one party must take the role of the server and the other the client. Ideally, the client should send the hello message first.

Client Hello (client → server)

The client hello is more than just a courtesy message; it contains a list of the ciphersuites and compression methods that the client can support. A cipher suite is a combination of cryptographic methods used together to perform security. In TLS the ciphersuite defines the type of certificates, the encryption method, and

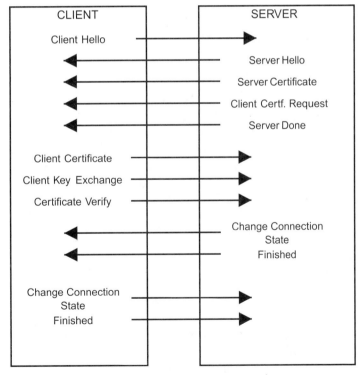

Figure 9.3 TLS Message Exchange Summary

the integrity-checking method. The TLS RFC defines some standard combinations, and the client can indicate which ones it supports, in order of preference. Importantly, the Client Hello also carries a random number called ClientHello.random, which can be any value but should be completely unpredictable to everyone (except the client). This random number is used to generate liveness.

> ### A Note on Liveness
>
> When watching sports on TV, you will often hear reference to a live broadcast. This means the broadcast is happening in real time and is not a recording made earlier. It is in this context that we refer to liveness in security. You need to know that the negotiation is live and that you are not dealing with a recording of a previous exchange. Generating and incorporating a different number with each session makes it much harder to use recorded data in an attack. A truly random number has the disadvantage that there is a small probability that the same value will occur twice. A number that is guaranteed never to be used again is called a **nonce**.

Server Hello (server → client):

When the server receives the Client Hello message, it must check that it is able to support one of the chosen ciphersuites and compression methods; then it replies with a Server Hello message. The Server Hello contains two more important items. First, it contains another random number, called ServerHello.random, which is different from the client's random value. Second, it contains a session ID that the client and server use to refer to the session from then on. One of the features of TLS is that a security session, once established, can be *resumed* multiple times by the client indicating current session ID in the Client Hello message. This is useful for browsers to quickly return to pages that have already been visited. At this stage the client and server have exchanged greetings with the result:

1. They have synchronized their states.
2. They have agreed on a session ID.
3. They have agreed on a ciphersuite.
4. They have exchanged two random numbers (nonces).

"Synchronizing their states" simply means that they both have the same understanding of what is going on. It's no good if one thinks the handshake is just starting and the other thinks it's nearly finished. Also, during the handshake both the client and the server must carefully keep copies of all the messages they have sent or received. At the end of the handshake, they will be required to prove that they have these copies to help ensure that no one has altered or inserted any messages.

Server Certificate (server → client)

The next phase involves the certificate exchanges. If the session is being resumed, this stage can be skipped. The server sends its certificate to the client. Remember that there are two important things in the certificate. First, it contains the name and public key of the server. These can be used to encrypt messages to the server and validate signed messages from the server. Second, it is signed by a certificate authority to prove that it is authentic. The client validates the certificate using the certificate authority's public key and then remembers the server's public key to encrypt further messages to the server. Although a bogus server could copy and send the valid certificate, it would not subsequently be able to decrypt the correct pre-master secret because it does not have the secret part of the public/private key pair.

Client Certificate (client → server)

The server may require the client to send a certificate. For Web browsing applications, it is unusual for the client to have a certificate—though this might change in the future as credit card use becomes more integrated with Web security. Already some services have emerged that allow members of the public to register and obtain digital certificates, which may then be used for access to subscription services. However, the financial industry is reluctant to adopt new technology too quickly, for very good reasons. The majority of transactions are still done using the traditional (and pitifully insecure) method of giving a credit card number and expiry date, albeit over a secure communications channel. For these types of transaction, the server sends a certificate but the client does not.

If a corporation is using TLS for internal network security, it might choose to give out certificates to its own employees. In this case, the IT department becomes a certificate authority and issues certificates for its own servers and all the users. If this approach is taken, the server can be configured to request a certificate from the user. The fact that the client produces a certificate proves nothing, of course, because it could easily have been copied from a previous session. However, the client can subsequently prove that it also has the certificate secret key by digitally signing a message to the server. This is done in the certificate verify stage that we explore later.

So far the client and server have exchanged hello messages. The server has sent a certificate and may have requested the client to do the same. At this point the server sends a **Server Hello Done message** and waits for the client to take the next step. If the server requested a certificate, the first thing the client should do is send it over; it will be checked later. Now comes the interesting part: The client and server establish a mutual secret key for use in further communications.

Client Key Exchange (client → server)

The goal of this phase is to create a mutual secret key between the client and the server, called the master secret. This key binds together the random numbers that were exchanged in the hello message with a secret value that is created dynamically and known only by the two parties (the client and the server). Note that the random numbers (nonces) sent during the hello phase could be seen by anybody monitoring the link; they are exchanged in the clear and not encrypted. By contrast, the random value created at this stage is known as the **pre-master secret** to reflect the fact that it is secret and will be used to generate the master key. The simplest way to generate the pre-master key and get it securely to both the server and the client is to take advantage of the server's certificate. The client simply generates a random number (48 bytes), encrypts it using the server's public key, and sends it to the server using a **client key exchange** message. The server decrypts it with its private key and, bingo, both sides have the pre-master secret.

Client Certificate Verification

If the client sent a certificate, now is the time for it to prove that it is the legal owner of that certificate. This is where those copies of all the messages come in useful. The client proves itself by hashing together all the messages up to this point (see the sidebar "A Note on Hashing"), including both the ones sent and the ones received. It then sends the result to the server and *signs the message* with the secret key of its certificate. The server receives the message and checks the signature using the client's public key as delivered in the client's certificate. If the signature checks out, the server also computes the hash of messages and checks that the result matches. If the signature or the hash check fails, the server should assume that the client is bogus. If it checks out, the server can be sure that the client knows the secret key for the certificate.

The client and server are now in a position to compute the master secret. The details of how this is done are rather complicated, but the concept is simple. Both parties have the following identical information:

- Pre-master secret
- Client random number (nonce)
- Server random number (nonce)

They both now cryptographically combine these values by hashing to produce a 48-byte (384-bit) master key. Because they both have the same values and use

A Note on Hashing

Hashing is an operation used frequently in cryptography. Its purpose is to combine two or more numbers to produce a result in such a way that it is extremely hard or impossible to reverse the process. In other words, if A and B are hashed together to produce the result C, then knowledge of C tells you nothing about A or B.

Consider normal arithmetic. The basic adding rule is $a + b = c$. If we know **a** and **b**, we can easily work out **c**. However, if we know **b** and **c**, we can, as easily, work out **a** $(a = c - b)$. Hash algorithms do not have this reversible property. So **a hash b** = **c** may be easy to compute; but given **b** and **c**, it is effectively impossible to work out **a**.

One application of hashing is to protect a master key by generating a temporary session key. Suppose **a = 128-bit master key** and **b = time of day,** then you could generate a new 128-bit key **c** by hashing together **a** and **b**. Even if the attacker knows the time of day and discovers the new key **c**, he cannot derive the original master key. In this example the new key is the same length as the original one.

Another use of hashes is to combine a large number of bits into a small number. This is used to generate messages' integrity checks. Suppose you hash a 1,000-byte message (8,000 bits) with a secret key to produce a result, which is only 64 bits long. Given the result, an attacker cannot compute the secret key or the original message. However, there is only one correct result that corresponds to the message. By sending the result with the message, the receiver can check that a message is intact and unaltered. Even if a single bit of the 1,000-byte message was altered, the resulting 64-bit hash result would be totally different.

the same algorithm, they will, of course, both compute the same key. The incorporation of the random numbers ensures liveness and guarantees that no one can use a recording of a previous exchange. The *quality* of the random number generator on both sides needs to be high. Some so-called random numbers generate a random distribution of numbers, but in an entirely predictable way. For example, the Rand() function available in many programming languages always produces the same "random" sequence after initialization. The random number used in security must *really* be unpredictable even after reinitialization.

Change Connection State

The object of the handshake has been to authenticate and create a new **pending connection state** ready to be turned on when all the keys and other required information have been obtained. Remember that there is a current state and a pending state. After initialization, the current state is "no encryption." The master key that has been created is now used to initialize the pending state according to the cipher suite in use. How this is done depends of the details of the cipher suite. For example, the cipher might not need all 384 bits of the master key or will want to derive different keys for receive and transmit, which it can do by further hashing the master key. This is done in WPA/RSN, for example. Suffice it to say that once the master key is established, both the client and the server are able to fully set up the pending connection state and then switch it to become the current state. When the switch is performed, each side sends a **change connection state message** to the other.

Finished

The handshake performs one more operation before completing—confirming that the new cipher suite is operating and that there was no tampering with any of the handshake messages. Each side sends a finished message for this purpose. Remember that the new cipher suite has now been activated, so this message will be encrypted with the new master key. The finished message contains a hash value covering the new master secret and all the handshake messages that have been exchanged from the hello message up to (but not including) the finished message. Assuming the message is received correctly, the new cipher suite is operational. The receiving party can compute the corresponding hash value from its own records and check that the result matches. If it does, everything is valid and it is safe to start passing data using the new master key.

If the TLS session was being resumed, the client and server go straight from the hello message to the finished message, computing a new master key from the new random numbers (in the hello messages) and the old master secret. This process avoids the expensive certificate operations but still prevents bogus clients or servers because knowledge of the pre-master secret is exclusively held by the original authenticated client and server.

Relationship of TLS Handshake and WPA/RSN

This TLS handshake process accomplishes three things:

- It has authenticated the server (and optionally the client).
- It has generated a secret master key for the session.
- It has initialized and put into effect a ciphersuite to protect communications.

Now we need to consider how this method can be applied to support WPA or IEEE 802.11i RSN networks. In WPA, encryption and integrity protection is provided by WEP or TKIP. RSN may support TKIP or AES–CCMP. These functions operate only between an access point and a wireless device. The TLS handshake described here is exclusively concerned with two parties: the authentication server and the client. There is no mention of the three-way model we have adopted for IEEE 802.1X with a supplicant, authenticator, and authentication server.

For WPA and RSN, all we need from TLS is the authentication function and the master key generation function. WPA/RSN deals with its own cipher suites. WPA/RSN takes the master secret generated by TLS and then derives a set of keys for use in encrypting the wireless link (see Chapter 10). In this case, although the master key is generated, the TLS record protocol connection state is not updated—that is, for WPA/RSN we don't use the TLS record protocol for encryption; we just hijack its handshake exchange to generate a secure master key.

In this way, TLS does integrate well with the IEEE 802.1X model and is specified to run over EAP. It is the default mandatory mode for WPA.

TLS over EAP

Although the designers of TLS probably thought that it would most often be used over a TCP/IP connection, they defined it in a more general way. RFC2246 simply says:

> At the lowest level, layered on top of some reliable transport protocol (e.g., TCP), is the TLS Record Protocol.

The key words are "layered on top of some reliable transport protocol." This general definition left the door open to implement parts of TLS directly over EAP—"parts" because EAP does not deal with normal data transfer; it is specifically concerned with the authentication phase. When we use TLS in conjunction with WPA/RSN, we want it to run over EAP because that allows us to tie it into the IEEE 802.1X.

RFC2716, PPP EAP TLS Authentication Protocol, defines how to perform the TLS handshake over EAP. As the name suggests, it was originally considered (like EAP itself) in the context of dial–in access authentication using PPP. But we can adapt it for use also with IEEE 802.1X and RSN.

EAP always starts and ends with a similar sequence. Usually, an identity request/response message is exchanged. Then a series of EAP requests and responses are sent that are specific to the authentication method, as identified by a Type field in each message. Finally an EAP-Success or EAP-Failure message is sent to indicate the result (see Chapter 8 for more detail on these structures). RFC2716 defines all the middle messages that we were somewhat vague about in Chapter 8. The general format of the EAP-Request/Response messages is shown in Figure 9.4.

Code	Identifier	Length	Type	Request / Response Data

Figure 9.4 Format of EAP Message

For TLS, the RFC defines the Type field for these EAP requests and responses to be the value 13. Only clients and servers that understand EAP-TLS will attempt to decode these messages. RFC2716 also defines two new fields to go after the Type field. These fields are Flags and Length, as shown in Figure 9.5.

Why does length appear twice? The first Length field refers to the length of this EAP frame. However, the second Length field refers to the length of an EAP-TLS packet. EAP-TLS packets can be quite long, exceeding the maximum size of an EAP message. In such a case, the EAP-TLS packet is fragmented—that is, broken into multiple pieces—and sent in several exchanges. The second length value, in the TLS field, refers to the overall TLS message and not the current frame. Actually this second Length field is optional and is not normally included if the EAP-TLS data fits into the current frame.

The Flags field contains three bits:

- **Length included flag**: Indicates whether the Length field is present
- **More fragments flag**: Set if more fragments are to follow in subsequent exchanges
- **Start flag**: Used to signal start of handshake

The sequence of exchanges that make up the EAP-TLS handshake are outlined in Figure 9.6. We assume that the server has become aware of the client through some method such as EAP-Start. Study the diagram for a minute before we work through it. Here is a commentary of the steps:

1. {request} This is the start of the EAP exchange. Server requests identity of client.
2. {response} Here the client sends an identity message. For corporate use, this could identify the owner of the client certificate that will be sent. If the client does not intend to send a certificate, it will effectively be anonymous and could therefore send any identity here, such as the string "anonymous".

Code	Identifier	Length	'13'	Flags	Length	EAP-TLS Data

Figure 9.5 Format of EAP-TLS Message

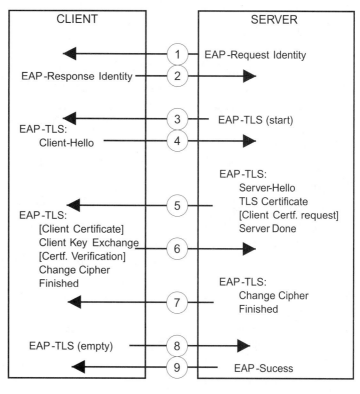

Items in square brackets: [...] are optional

Figure 9.6   EAP-TLS Handshake

3. {request} The server sends an empty EAP–TLS request with the flag bit start set. This is the only time the start bit is set.

4. {response} The client sends it Client Hello message containing the same information as for normal TLS.

5. {request} The server sends two or three TLS messages in a single request: The server hello, optionally the client certificate request, and the server finished message.

6. {response} The client now replies with several TLS messages in a single response:

- Client certificate (if requested)
- Pre-master secret in key exchange message
- Client certificate verification information

- Change cipher
- Finished

Notice how the client goes ahead, creates the pre-master secret, computes the master secret, and "puts the cipher into effect," all in one go. However, note that the entire EAP message is sent in the original ciphersuite, which is usually open (that is, no encryption). The new ciphersuite is not put into effect until after the end of the EAP messages.

7. {request} The server sends all its remaining messages in a single EAP request.

8. {response} The client has nothing more to say but must respond so it sends an empty response message.

9. Finally to complete the EAP handshake, the server sends an EAP-Success, assuming everything has gone well. If any of the steps failed, the server would have previously sent an EAP-Fail at the point the problem was detected.

The use of EAP provides the key for implementing TLS with WPA or RSN. For one thing, the use of EAP means that no IP address is needed and the wireless device can exchange EAP messages to the access point and perform the entire handshake prior to being granted access to the wired network. The access point does not need to understand TLS to complete the transaction, providing it has an authentication server on the network to which to send the EAP messages. And the access point can watch out for the EAP-Success message to learn when it should connect the IEEE 802.1X switch and allow access to the network. However, there are still two unanswered questions:

- How does the access point send EAP messages to the authentication server?
- How does the access point get a copy of the master key for use with TKIP or AES–CCMP encryption?

The answer to these questions lies in the use of RADIUS (see Chapter 8). RADIUS is a protocol that allows a device to communicate with an authentication server. It has been much extended over the years although the basic principles are unchanged. One of the key enhancements in relation to WPA/RSN was the inclusion of messages that allow the forwarding of EAP requests and responses directly to the server. The issue of how to get the master key back to the access point is not one that is currently covered by the RADIUS RFCs. Also it is not covered directly by the IEEE 802.11 standard because this is out of scope for the standard. However, WPA specifies the use of a specific Microsoft-defined attribute to ensure interoperability between vendors. This turns out to be the same attribute that is already used in a similar way to send key information to a dial-up modem pool.

Summary of TLS

This section describes how TLS works. TLS is not specifically designed for use with wireless networks. It is based on SSL, a security method used at the application level. However, the invention of a method to support TLS over EAP, combined with changes to the RADIUS protocol to support EAP over RADIUS, has opened a path whereby WPA and RSN can build on the substantial existing support for the protocol. SSL is very widely deployed in Web browsers and servers and it is highly proven. Certificate authorities are well established and provide the infrastructure needed for SSL operation. Now the adoption of TLS for WPA will take advantage of SSL's success.

The next section looks at another popular authentication approach—Kerberos V5. Although this has not been specified for WPA, it is still a viable option for RSN and may be more appropriate for customers that already have extensive Kerberos installations.

Kerberos

Kerberos can be used to provide security services for an IP network and has been around for a relatively long time. The early work was done at Massachusetts Institute of Technology during the 1980s and subsequently it went through various stages of standardization in the IETF (Neuman and Ts'o, 1994). Version 5, the current major version, was issued in RFC1510 in 1993. This RFC has stood up well to practical implementation and has needed little modification although there are several more recent extensions. By the way, no introduction to Kerberos seems to be complete without mentioning that the name "Kerberos" comes from the three-headed dog that guarded the gates to Hades in Greek mythology, although which particular hell is guarded in the case of network security is not obvious to us.

Using Tickets

The really good idea in Kerberos is that credentials can be embedded into a special document called a ticket. In much the same way that you can go to Orlando, Florida, and buy a week-long multipark ticket to mouse-related theme parks, a Kerberos ticket provides a network user access to a variety of network services for a limited period of time.[3]

Let's consider a network of separately administered servers in a large campus using password-based authentication. To access several services, you would need to log in separately to each service, such as the e-mail server, file servers, the database

---

3. Kerberos tickets are service specific, so in practice you would need a set rather than a single ticket.

server, printers, and so on. Each time you logged in, your session would be interrupted and you would have to type a password. In the worst case, you would have to know a different password for each service or, if you have a single password, the service itself would have to go back to some central authority to verify your credentials. This approach places the onus on the network servers to check you out every time you ask for access. Checking credentials can be a time-consuming task and, frankly, servers have better things to do with their time.

The situation gets worse if there are different authentication servers for different network domains. Now the server has to go to its local authentication server to check you out and that server might need to go back to your home server to complete the check. As the network grows, this process becomes an unmanageable mess.

Using tickets greatly simplifies the process, which starts with a master access ticket that your computer must get when you first join the network. Before your computer can get the first ticket, you have to prove your identity, in other words, perform master authentication. However, once you are validated, your computer gets the master ticket, establishing a security context. This ticket can now be used to get other tickets specific to the services you want. Your computer can usually handle that task without interrupting you.

Once your computer has a ticket for a particular service, it presents the ticket to that service to get access. Now the onus is on your computer to get the tickets and the load is taken off the services. All the services do is validate a ticket when it is presented, which they can usually do locally and without referring to any other authority.

This description is somewhat simplified, but all the key principles are here. Most of the rest of Kerberos is concerned with ticket management and deals with special cases like cross-domain access and ticket referral (more later). There are a couple of aspects of Kerberos that are problematic (Bellovin and Merritt, 1991).

The first issue is that Kerberos is essentially password based. There have been schemes designed that allow the use of digital certificates with Kerberos, but the predominant model is that of an actual person using the computer. People are able to enter a user password from memory when prompted. Today many network devices are machines, not people; and the password model does not work so well with machines because stored passwords are subject to attack while stored on a machine.

The second issue is that dictionary attacks were not considered a serious threat 20 years ago. In this type of attack, the enemy holds a database with hundreds of millions of passwords—the sort of passwords humans tend to make up and various combinations of them. The attack simply involves trying every password. This is a threat if it can be performed *offline*. In other words, if you can record the messages from an encrypted logon and then go home and run your attack against the recording rather than the real system. Kerberos can be vulnerable to this type of attack unless special steps are taken.

Kerberos Tickets

A ticket is just a piece of data in a special format. All Kerberos tickets have the same basic structure but, to help the explanation, we'll say that there are three types of ticket:

- Ticket-granting
- Service access
- Referral

The introduction to this chapter notes that a master ticket must be obtained before all others. In Kerberos there is nothing quite so strong as a master ticket but, instead, there is a similar concept called a **ticket-granting ticket (TGT)**. The ticket-granting ticket lets you get other tickets from a key distribution center (KDC) for the local security domain (called "realm" in Kerberos).

Obtaining the Ticket-Granting Ticket

When a computer (the client) first connects to the network, it has to contact a KDC to obtain a TGT. The KDC has two parts: an authentication service (AS) and a ticket-granting service (TGS), as shown in Figure 9.7.

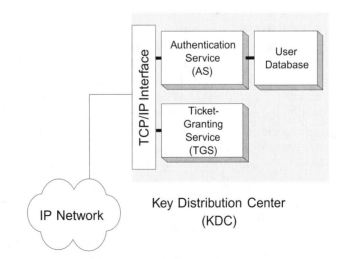

Figure 9.7 Authentication Service and Ticket-Granting Service

It is the job of the authentication server to check the client and confirm that it is allowed access to the network. Kerberos uses the approach of **shared secrets**. The client has some secret information and a copy of this information is stored in a protected user database accessible to the AS. It is expected that the secret on the client side will be stored in the user's head. In other words, there is no copy of the secret password on the computer and a person is expected to remember and enter the password during initial login. After the user enters her password, the client sends a request to the AS asking for a TGT. The request incorporates proof of the secret password. The AS verifies that the secret information matches the copy in the user database and that current security policy allows access. If so, it sends back a TGT to the client.

Once the client possesses the TGT, it can apply to the TGS for tickets to other services on the network. It presents its TGT and indicates which service it wants. The TGS creates and sends a ticket that the client can subsequently present to the service to get access.

Let's pause a moment and look at a few points here. The first question that arises is why bother with the whole TGT concept. If the KDC knows your secret password, why not just go directly to ask for a service ticket using your secret password? If it works to get a TGT, why not do the same for a service ticket? The main reason why the TGT approach is a good idea is that it helps protect the secret information. The right way to do authentication is to use the master password to establish a security context, but then to create temporary session keys for the actual operations. If one of the session keys becomes compromised or discovered, the damage lasts only until you log off or until the lifetime of the key expires. If you were to use the secret password every time you obtained a service key, you would be giving an attacker more chances to attack it. Protection of the master secret is paramount.

The other point is that the user only wants to type the password in once. To avoid the user retyping it all the time, the client computer would have to keep a copy of the password in memory for the duration of the session. If it is stored in memory, it is vulnerable to attack. If you only use the password once to obtain the TGT, you can delete the password from the memory of the client. A similar argument applies on the AS. It has to look up the user in a database to verify the password. It would not want to access the database every time the client requested a ticket so it would have to cache a copy in memory, increasing risk to the password. By generating a temporary key in the TGT, this problem is solved.

Service Tickets

A service ticket must be held by the client until it is presented to the required service. The ticket contains some information that only the service can understand.

The client cannot interpret this part of the ticket. When the ticket is sent, the service decodes its own secret part and confirms the client's identity and other credentials. The ticket contains other information, such as period of validity. Like a credit card, it has a start date and expiry date (not in months, of course).

Typically, service tickets last only for a few hours, after which the client must return to the KDC and get a new ticket or renew the existing ticket. Ticket life only affects your ability to log on to the service; once you are in, you stay in until you are logged off, regardless of whether your ticket expires in between (although you might lose critical services, like your file system).

Although we have distinguished TGT and service tickets to help the explanation, in most ways they are the same. The TGS is just a service like any other when it comes to presenting tickets. However the TGS is the only service that can create and issue new tickets. Ordinary services can't create tickets. There are a couple of special cases in which this presents a problem.

Suppose that the service you are using needs to access another service on your behalf. For example, suppose your organization has a special-purpose supercomputer for crunching billions of vector computations a second. You want to use it to process some data that is located on a file server. You can get a ticket to use the Giga-cruncher; but, to do the job, the cruncher needs a ticket to access your data on the file server. This situation can be resolved in one of two ways. The first is known as the **proxy method**. In this case you, the client, go to the KDC and request a special ticket to allow the Giga-cruncher to access the file server on your behalf. This proxy ticket is then given to the cruncher prior to the job starting. This approach is shown in Figure 9.8.

1. Client obtains ticket for service **a**.
2. Client presents ticket to service **a** and gets access.
3. Client obtains proxy ticket for service **b**.
4. Client gives ticket to service **a**, which uses it to get access to service **b**.

The second approach is to give the cruncher the right to go to the KDC directly and get tickets on your behalf. You can obtain a special TGT from the KDC, which the cruncher can use to obtain tickets on your behalf. You then give this special TGT to the cruncher. When it realizes it needs access to the file server, it can go and get a ticket just for this purpose. The sequence of events, as shown in Figure 9.9, is as follows:

1. Client obtains ticket for service **a**.
2. Client presents ticket and obtains access to service **a**.
3. Client obtains TGT for service **a** to use on its behalf.

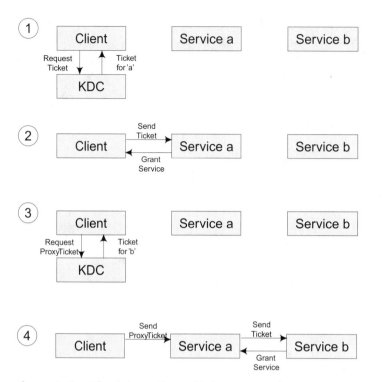

Figure 9.8 Obtaining a Proxy Ticket

4. Service **a** obtains ticket for service **b** using client TGT rights. This is called a **forwarded** ticket.

Cross-Domain Access

The discussion so far assumes that there is just one KDC in control of a single security domain called a realm. We have also assumed that the TGS is on the same physical server as the AS. This need not be the case in practice, and there could be one AS and several separate TGS servers. This type of rearrangement is basically transparent to the method. However, accessing services that are in the domain of another AS is a different story and requires special handling.

There are a number of reasons why you might have separate security domains in an organization. Different sites are one reason: An office in Los Angeles would probably be administered separately from an office in London, for example. Domains could also be used at a much lower level, as with university departments. You might be cooperating with another company and you might have decided to give certain employees in the other company access to certain servers in your company.

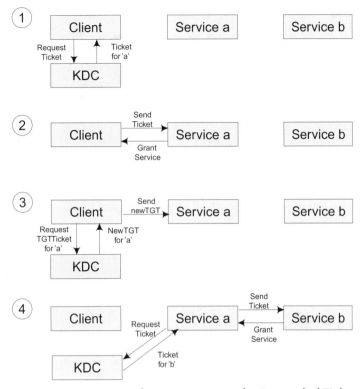

Figure 9.9 Use of a Forwarded Ticket

If an employee of Missiles Galore wants to access a server at partner company Nukes Unlimited, the Missiles employee needs a ticket for the Nukes server. Only the TGS in the Nukes domain can issue tickets for the Nukes servers, but the Missiles employee doesn't have a TGT for the Nukes TGS.

Kerberos handles this situation using referral tickets. The authentication servers at both Nukes and Missiles are configured in advance to allow some users to cross over domains; the two authentication servers share a secret between them. When the computer of the Missiles employee (the client) wants to get to the Nukes file server, it asks its own AS to give it a TGT for Nukes. The local AS cannot do this because it doesn't have the rights to issue such a ticket, but it knows that such access is allowed for this user. So instead, it issues a **referral ticket** telling the client to ask the AS in the Nukes network directly. This referral ticket is presented to the Nukes AS, which is able to confirm that it was created by its friend, the AS at Missiles. Given that they have an agreement, the Nukes AS then issues a TGT for its own network to the client. The client can use this TGT to obtain service tickets to certain servers on the Nukes network.

How Tickets Work

So far we have only described where tickets come from and what you do with them. We have said nothing about what they contain or why they are secure. A prime requirement of a ticket is that you cannot forge one; that is, make a new one or modify an existing one without permission. Also the service that is presented with a ticket has to be sure it was issued by the TGS and that the client is the valid ticket holder. Not surprisingly, these requirements are achieved by encrypting parts of the ticket with secret keys. Multiple sets of keys can be involved. Let's start from the top when the client first goes to the AS and asks for a TGT.

The client needs to send its identity and its secret to the AS. This is akin to the user name and password of a typical login. The server uses the identity information to look up its own copy of the client's master secret from the user database. To be more correct, the client only needs to prove that it possesses the master password; it doesn't need to send the actual password to the AS. The identity is not considered confidential and is sent in the clear, or unencrypted. The proof of password is achieved by using it to encrypt some value that can be checked by the server. Usually this is a timestamp with the date and time at the moment of sending. The server can decrypt the timestamp with its copy of the client's master secret, and if it produces a sensible value that matches its own clock, it accepts the request. By the way, this is where Kerberos is vulnerable to dictionary attack. An enemy monitoring the link knows, to within a few seconds, the time when the message is sent. Therefore, he can take a copy of the request away and run a dictionary attack by encrypting the known time value with millions of possible passwords until a match is found.

At this point the AS creates the TGT. It generates a new random key that the client and the TGS can use later to protect *their* communications. This is called the **session key** and it needs to be delivered securely to both the client and the TGS. The ticket also needs to contain other information for the TGS so it can confirm the identity of the client and so on. This is all accomplished by constructing the response out of two halves. One half is intended to be understood only by the client. The other half is the TGT and is intended to be understood only by the ticket-granting server (Figure 9.10).

This message is sent from the AS to the client. The data is private because both halves are separately encrypted. This is the last time the client's master secret is used until a new TGT is required. The client decrypts its part of the message and stores the session key that will be used to protect the communication with the TGS. It also saves the TGT for later use. Note that it cannot read the contents of the TGT (except the header) because it is encrypted in the TGS's secret. The client doesn't know this secret; it is shared only between the AS and the TGS. Note

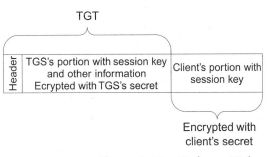

TGT

| Header | TGS's portion with session key and other information Ecrypted with TGS's secret | Client's portion with session key |

Encrypted with client's secret

Figure 9.10 Kerberos Ticket

also that this exchange has provided implicit mutual authentication. The AS confirms that the client knows the master key by checking the time stamp value. The client confirms that the AS knows the master key because otherwise the message returned would not make sense when decrypted.

Now the client is ready to go and get service tickets. It sends the TGT to the TGS with a request for some service. Suppose the client is requesting access to a printer service. The TGS is able to decrypt the ticket and hence finds out the session key for use with this client. It is also able to check that the client is valid and find out other information that was placed there originally by the AS, such as its access rights. With the request, the client also sends the current time encrypted with the session key to prevent replay attacks—that is, to stop someone recording the message and playing it back later while pretending to be the client. After the TGS has extracted the session key from the ticket, it can decrypt the timestamp value and check that the request is live and not an old one. Using a rather morbid example, this is like proving that a photograph of a hostage is recent by getting him to hold up to the camera a copy of a current newspaper.

Assuming the TGS is prepared to issue a ticket for the printer, it now repeats the same process that was done by the AS when the TGT was created. It generates a new random session key for use with the printer service and builds a new ticket. This is encrypted with the secret key that is shared between the TGS and the printer. The *new* session key is encrypted in the *current* session key and sent back along with the service ticket. Optionally, the TGS can re-encrypt the time value sent by the client so the client can confirm that the message is live and not a replay.

The granting of tickets and their use is iterative. That is, the process of getting and using a TGT is essentially repeated in subsequent service tickets. The client master key is used only at the beginning, and afterwards session keys are used that have a limited life. An attacker has few chances to get at the client master keys. However, as mentioned before, there are a few weaknesses of which to be aware.

The first problem is dictionary attacks. Because the AS reply is encrypted in the client's master key and some fields in the plaintext are known (such as the timestamp), it is possible for a recording of the reply to be taken away and tested against millions of possible passwords. If the user is allowed to choose the password for the master key, sooner or later someone will choose a weak password, such as the name of his dog or where she went on holiday last year. Such passwords will certainly be discovered by an offline dictionary attack. Protection against offline dictionary attack can be provided by mechanisms called **zero knowledge password proofs**. Examples of such protocols are EKE (Bellovin and Merritt, 1992) and SRP (Wu, 1998) (RFC2945). These protocols are not strictly part of Kerberos V5, and full explanation is beyond the scope of this book. Suffice it to say that the password is mixed up with temporary secret keys that are established for the transfer and discarded afterward. Because an attacker doesn't know the temporary key and it is different on each login, a dictionary attack doesn't give useful information. The downside is that such methods require significant computation resources and are subject to patent licensing requirements.

Another problem with Kerberos is the fact that the identity is sent unencrypted. An attacker can, at least, track which user is accessing the network. Remember that the Kerberos ticket request could be going over a wide area link and, of course, in the case of wireless, such requests will be visible to anyone. Some people think that this lack of anonymity is a problem.

Use of Kerberos in RSN

IEEE 802.11 RSN does not directly specify how to implement Kerberos. It only specifies IEEE 802.1X with its associated use of EAP. As a result, there are several ways Kerberos could be applied. What we describe here is an approach that was proposed by several vendors during IEEE 802.11 standards meetings.

The general picture we have used so far to describe how RSN authentication works has three components in three boxes: the supplicant, the authenticator, and the authentication server (see the discussion in Chapter 8 on IEEE 802.1X/EAP and Figure 9.11).

The RADIUS protocol is needed only if the authentication server is separate from the authenticator and connected by an IP network. For small networks, such as might be used at home, a simple authentication server can be built right in to the access point, eliminating the need for any communications protocol between it and the authenticator (Figure 9.12). In this case the user configures a list of users and passwords directly into the access point and the details of the EAP communications are hidden.

The Kerberos model lies somewhere between the first model (Figure 9.11) and the second (Figure 9.12). But before going on to describe the Kerberos model in detail, we need to work through a few steps.

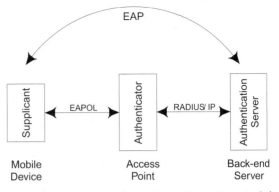

Figure 9.11   Three-Party Security Model

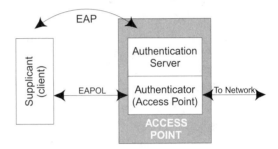

Figure 9.12   Small Network with Built-in Authentication Server

First of all, consider the situation existing *after* the client has been authenticated and connected to the network. By then, it has an IP address, and it has obtained a TGT. The client can happily send Kerberos requests to the TGS to get new service tickets. It can submit those new tickets to services and generally go about its business. At this point, Kerberos is being used exactly as it was intended. The tricky part, however, is how to get to this state from startup. How is the authentication performed and how does the access point make a decision to admit the client to the network in the first place?

Now let's look at an interesting concept. As we know, Kerberos tickets allow a client to get access to a service. Previously, we have described services in terms of file servers and printers, but network access could also be considered as a service. As an example, access to the DHCP server that allocates IP addresses could be considered a service that should be provided only to valid clients. The neat concept is to treat the *access point* itself as a service. In other words, we view the access point as a service that passes data packets to and from a wired LAN. In Kerberos terminology, we would say that, in order to be allowed to use this service, you have to present a valid ticket first. The process of getting connected to the network becomes:

1. Authenticate to the Kerberos AS and get a TGT.
2. Go to the TGS and get a valid ticket for network access (in other words, a ticket to the access point).
3. Present the ticket to the access point, which then confirms its validity and allows you to connect to the network.

This is an attractive concept because it makes the access control for the network just like any other Kerberos service. It has the superb result of simplifying roaming: When the client wants to move to a different access point, it presents the same ticket to the next access point and so on.

Attractive as this may seem, you may be thinking, "Hang on a cotton picking moment … that can't work!" This is a classic example of "which came first, the chicken or the egg?" You need a ticket to get access to the network, but you need access to the network to get a ticket!

In fact, the situation might be even worse. If the client is using DHCP, it won't have an IP address until it can get to the DHCP server. Suppose you need a ticket to get to the DHCP server as well.[4] The client is stuck: It doesn't have an IP address and, even if it did, it couldn't get to the network to authenticate with the AS anyway because it doesn't have a ticket for the access point. A method has been developed to overcome this deadlock. The solution requires the use of a **proxy Kerberos application server** residing on the access point (this is just extra firmware). The proxy is a sort of trusted friend connected to the network that can act on the client's behalf.

Imagine you go out for the evening and want to enter an exclusive nightclub. The doorman says you can't come in because you are not a member. "So how do I become a member?", you ask. The doorman tells you to apply to the club's owner Luigi. "Where is Luigi?", you ask with a sinking feeling. The doorman tells you that Luigi is at the bar inside the club! What you need in this situation is a friend who is already a member of the club to go in and ask Luigi to give you membership. In the network, the Kerberos proxy is the equivalent of that friend.

Figure 9.13 shows where the proxy resides in the scheme of things. In some ways the picture looks like Figure 9.12, in which the authentication server is in the access point. However, the proxy cannot make the access decision by itself. It

---

4. It would be unusual to require a ticket for the DHCP server, but we use this as an example because it is analogous to the problem of getting rights to use the access point.

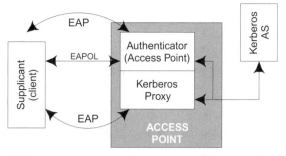

Figure 9.13 Use of a Proxy to Obtain Tickets

can only act as the client's advocate. This is what we meant when we said that the Kerberos case is somewhere between Figure 9.11 and Figure 9.12. The EAP transaction terminates at the proxy, but the authentication is done elsewhere in the network. At the time of writing, the operation of the Kerberos proxy is described in draft-ietf-cat-iakerb-08, an IETF draft titled "Initial and Pass Through Authentication Using Kerberos V5 and the GSS-API (IAKERB)."

The opening lines in the abstract of this document read:

> This document defines extensions to the Kerberos protocol specification (RFC 1510 [1]) and GSSAPI Kerberos protocol mechanism RFC 1964 [2]) that enables a client to obtain Kerberos tickets for services where the KDC is not accessible to the client, but is accessible to the application server.

This seems to be just what we need. We'll come back to GSS-API shortly, but first let's focus on what the Kerberos proxy does. When the mobile device (client) first comes within range, it connects to the access point. At this stage the IEEE 802.1X controlled port is open (disconnected) so the client cannot communicate with the network. It can, however, communicate to the IEEE 802.1X authenticator, which is closely connected to the Kerberos proxy. The client uses EAP to talk to the Kerberos proxy. In the process the proxy finds out the identity of the client and obtains its secret key information. It can then use this to make a request to the Kerberos AS on the client's behalf. If a TGT is granted by the AS, this can be passed back to the proxy and then to the client. The completion of this phase closes the IEEE 802.1X controlled port. However, in this case there is a second switch in the series that prevents the client getting to the network until it presents a ticket for the access point service, as shown in Figure 9.14.

Referring to Figure 9.14, there are two notional switches that must be closed before data can flow from the client to the network. We say "notional" because, most likely, these are not physical switches but functions buried in software (see Figure 9.14).

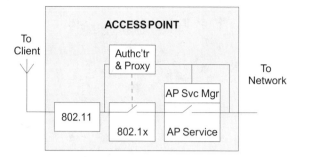

Figure 9.14 Example Access Point Supporting Kerberos

At the start, both switches are open as shown. All client data packets emerge from the IEEE 802.11 part of the access point and these go to the IEEE 802.1X authenticator and also to the AP service manager. As we know, the IEEE 802.1X authentication listens only to EAP packets; everything else is ignored. The AP service manager is only interested in Kerberos messages and waits to be presented with a valid ticket before it closes its switch.

After the EAP authentication, the IEEE 802.1X switch closes and the client will have obtained a TGT with the help of the proxy. However, it still cannot talk to the network because it has not presented a ticket to the AP service manager. And because the AP service manager is a Kerberos agent, it would also need an IP address to present such a ticket. The services of the proxy are needed several more times.

The client needs one or two more tickets. It needs one for the access point and it may need one for the DHCP server (let's assume so). First, it asks the proxy to obtain a ticket for the access point. The proxy uses the client's TGT to request the access point ticket from the KDC. The ticket is passed back to the client. Now the client asks the proxy to present its access point ticket to the AP service manager. Assuming the ticket is valid, the AP closes the switch and the client can at last talk to the network. However, the client still doesn't have an IP address so it must ask the proxy two more favors: to obtain a ticket for the DHCP server and to present this ticket to the DHCP server. Finally, the client can obtain its IP address and become a full member of the network. It thanks the proxy for the hard work (actually, it doesn't, but that's life) and does all further Kerberos requests for itself.

The IAKERB describes a proxy for use with GSS-API, and the client uses EAP to talk to the proxy. How do these two statements fit together? The approach proposed to use EAP with Kerberos takes advantage of a concept called GSS-API. **GSS-API** provides an abstract way to define security services. Imagine a team designing an operating system that has secure communications between the application and a remote server. The team has to provide an authentication method, and they have to provide privacy and integrity services linked to the authentication method. The question is, "Which method should they choose?" If they pick one, it may not meet everybody's requirements. That might mean they have to implement several different methods and allow the user to select the method. Worse still, the team knows that in the future new methods are likely to be invented and then they will be faced with upgrading the operating system.

At the risk of being controversial, we should say that if the operating system design team works for a company that owns 95% of the installed base, they may feel comfortable in defining a specific solution and setting that as the benchmark. This more pragmatic approach has been taken in WPA, which simply defines TLS and the mandatory solution. However, let's go back to our more general-minded design team.

All the methods considered by the design team are likely to have some characteristics in common. They must all implement effective authentication. They all have privacy services (in other words, encryption) and they all provide message integrity to prevent forgery. Because these characteristics are common across all methods, the idea was hatched to have a generic interface between the operating system and the security services. This would, in principle, allow the team to plug in security methods according to their needs and avoid the operating system design having to commit to a single approach (see Figure 9.15).

The interface by which the communication occurs between the operating system and the security services is called GSS-API, which (finally) we can tell you stands for Generic Security Service Application Programming Interface defined in RFC2743. There is an RFC defining how to use Kerberos with GSS-API (RFC1964) and, importantly from our perspective, there is also a draft that specifies how to use GSS-API in conjunction with EAP. By joining these together, we can now support Kerberos over EAP and hence fit Kerberos into the IEEE 802.1X model.

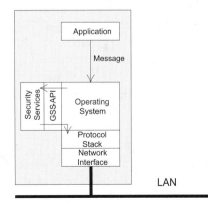

Figure 9.15 Role of GSS-API

If you think all of this looks rather complicated, you are not alone. But the complexity lies more in the number of standards and drafts involved in specifying operation rather than in the basic concepts. It is a complexity that is not transferred to the network owner, assuming you are already maintaining a Kerberos-based network.

The main security weakness in the approach comes from the fact that the access points must share a secret with the KDC. This is needed to validate the ticket that is used to gain service from the access point. Apart from being an administrative nuisance to maintain this secret in many access points, it is necessary that the same secret be shared by all the access points if the ticket is to be used for roaming. Such widespread use of a secret is generally frowned upon by security experts. In its favor Kerberos is well known and well tested, it is relatively easy to maintain, and it is the basis of access security for a number of major operating systems, including Microsoft Windows 2000.

Cisco Light EAP (LEAP)

This book avoids focusing on vendor-specific or proprietary approaches. However, we make an exception for Cisco LEAP because it has been quite widely deployed and a number of authentication server manufacturers have added support in their RADIUS servers. LEAP, sometimes called EAP-Cisco Wireless, is interesting in that it was really the first commercial use of IEEE 802.1X and EAP for wireless LAN. The basic model used in LEAP is the same as that used in WPA, although the two should not be confused. LEAP is definitely not WPA. It falls far short of the security levels provided by WPA or RSN, but its introduction was far-sighted and solved some real problems in wireless LAN deployment.

LEAP has not been standardized and the details have not been published. However, the protocol has been reverse-engineered and made public, enabling other vendors to implement compatible components. The information in this book is based on that publicly available material and a certain amount of inspired guesswork. Therefore, it cannot be guaranteed accurate. If you want the official details, you should apply to Cisco directly.

Consistent with IEEE 802.1X, LEAP divides the system into a supplicant, authenticator, and authentication server. The supplicant resides in the mobile device. At the time LEAP was introduced, workstation operating systems did not support IEEE 802.1X and special software and drivers had to be loaded for this function.

The authenticator resides in the access point. Naturally, such support was initially restricted to Cisco access points. Note that a generic IEEE 802.1X authenticator is not sufficient because of the way the encryption keys are handled. The access point must have specific support for LEAP as well as IEEE 802.1X.

The authentication server is implemented by a RADIUS server. LEAP follows the approach for EAP over RADIUS in RFC2869, although this RFC was still in draft form when LEAP was designed. It also uses proprietary RADIUS attributes to pass keys back from the server.

LEAP is a two-way challenge response protocol based on a shared secret key known to the authentication server and the mobile device (not the access point). It is based on the MS-CHAPv1 commonly used for remote dial-up authentication. Unlike conventional MS-CHAP, the authentication is mutual, with separate challenges being issued by the authentication server and the mobile device. This does not explicitly authenticate the access point itself. If a rogue access point could somehow be attached to the wired network with a connection to the authentication server, it could act as a "man in the middle" in the authentication exchange. However, the access point must have a legitimate security relationship with the authentication server to receive the session encryption key, so a rogue access point would be unable to send or receive encrypted data to the mobile device.

Once mutual authentication is completed, the session encryption key is sent to the access point in a RADIUS attribute. This attribute is encrypted using a secret shared between the access point and the server. The client also computes a copy of the session key. The key is not transmitted across the wireless link but is computed based on some nonce value. We do not know how this is done because it is a proprietary protocol, but our best guess is that is uses some combination of the challenge text exchanged during authentication. The access point signals successful authentication by sending an EAPOL-Success message to the mobile device. It then activates encryption by sending an EAPOL-Key message. The process is summarized here and shown in Figure 9.16:

1. The authentication server challenges the mobile device by sending a random string. The mobile device must prove it knows the key by sending a response derived from the challenge.

2. The mobile device sends a challenge to the authentication server, which must also respond correctly.

3. The authentication server generates and sends a session key to the access point with the EAP success notification in a RADIUS message.

4. The access point notifies the mobile device of authentication using the EAPOL-Success message. At this point the client computes the matching session key.

5. The access point sends an EAPOL-Key message to activate encryption. Note that this does not send the actual key; it is just a notification message.

6. The mobile device and access point communicate using WEP encryption.

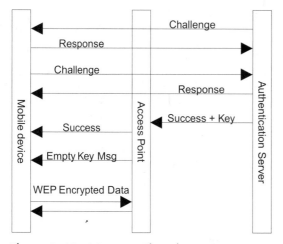

Figure 9.16   Message Flow for LEAP

On the wireless side LEAP uses IEEE 802.1X and EAPOL as described in Chapter 8 on access control. On the wired side LEAP uses EAP over RADIUS. The EAP type number for LEAP is 17.

LEAP embodies many of the base concepts that are now incorporated into WPA and RSN. However, WPA/RSN has added many more details that improve the overall security. LEAP originally ran over WEP, which has known weaknesses, although the ability of LEAP to generate temporary keys helps reduce the effectiveness of attacks. LEAP uses MS-CHAPv1, which is known to be vulnerable to some dictionary attacks. Overall, though, LEAP represented a major step forward in wireless LAN security when it was introduced, with the benefits of:

- Mutual authentication
- Temporary session keys
- Centralized key management

Protected EAP Protocol (PEAP)

PEAP, as the name suggests, provides a way to do EAP negotiation safe from prying eyes. The original motivation was to make password-based client security safe from offline dictionary attack. To achieve this, the EAP session is completely hidden from attackers. It was hard to decide whether PEAP should be in Chapter 8 in the discussion of access control or here, in the coverage of upper-layer authentication. PEAP is a sort of welding together of EAP and TLS in an attempt to maintain the flexibility of EAP while overcoming its lack of inherent security protection.

First, let's consider the security weaknesses of EAP. EAP is like a good sandwich: meaty center surrounded by two slices of thin bread (apologies to vegetarians). The meaty center is the authentication exchange between the client and the server. If a method like TLS is used, the security credentials of this part are good. The thin slices of bread are the parts of EAP that are common to all methods—the EAP-Identity phase and the EAP-Success or EAP-Fail messages at the end. This is where the security weaknesses occur:

- Because the EAP-Identity message is unprotected, it can be snooped, allowing an enemy to learn the identity of the user that is attempting to connect.
- The EAP-Success/Fail message is unprotected and could be spoofed by an attacker.

A solution to both these problems is to perform the EAP negotiation in a private encrypted "tunnel." If we have an existing secure connection between the client and the server, then we can do the EAP negotiation quite safely and the client's identity will not be revealed. All the flexibility of EAP will still be available; you can negotiate any of the upper-layer authentication methods available. This is the basic idea behind PEAP: The entire EAP negotiation is protected.

The obvious question is how to establish such a secure communication channel, given that the purpose of EAP *is* to set up a secure communication channel! To answer the question, we need to go back to one of the basic principles of security and consider the difference between privacy and authenticity. Privacy means that no unwanted party can understand the protected communications. Authenticity means that the two (or more) parties can mutually prove their identity.

It is quite possible to have privacy without authenticity and sometimes this is useful. Digressing for a slightly seedy analogy here, consider sexy chit-chat lines. People call a premium toll phone number and talk to a complete stranger with a sexy voice about any subject they care to choose (although probably not sports related). The illusion is that the woman or man who answers the phone is in some sort of private intimate setting. However, in practice these are regular call center operations with people sitting at rows of desks, each with a phone. This is a case in which the caller wants privacy, but doesn't care about (or get) authenticity.

The object of EAP is authenticity: Extensible Authentication Protocol. The object of PEAP is to do this authentication in private. To meet both objectives, we first establish privacy *without* authenticity; and then we perform the authentication using the private connection. In other words, we use a two-phase approach:

- In the first phase, EAP is used in a conventional way to establish a secure connection using TLS. Only the server is authenticated in this phase.

- In the second phase, the secure connection is used for another complete EAP negotiation in which full authentication is performed.

TLS is the chosen method to establish privacy in phase 1; but once the private channel is established, any EAP-supported method could be negotiated. It does not have to be TLS.

Notice that the first phase of PEAP does involve some level of authentication; the server is always required to prove its identity. It can do this by using a certificate, as described for regular TLS. It lets the client know that the server is legitimate and not some rogue server trying to attract unwary clients. This is especially important for wireless LAN because it is relatively easy for people to set up rogue access points and falsely advertise that they belong to a valid network. We review the two phases of EAP separately.

Phase 1

From the outside, phase 1 looks like a normal EAP negotiation. If you study how TLS over EAP works (earlier in this chapter), then you understand how the first phase of PEAP works. The difference comes at the end of the phase when, instead of sending an EAP-Success, the negotiation moves into phase 2 and starts an entirely new EAP session encrypted using the newly negotiated keys.

At the start of both phase 1 and phase 2, the server sends an EAP-Request/ Identity message. The client must reply with an identity response. However, the client is explicitly allowed to send an anonymous identity in the first EAP round. In normal EAP, the identity is often used to determine which upper-layer authentication method will be used. The same is true for PEAP so the identity sent in the first phase may enable the server to determine that PEAP will be used. However, it could be some arbitrary name like "peap@anonymous.com". The client's real identity is sent during phase 2. Sometimes the authenticator uses the name to specify which backend server will be consulted for authentication decisions. This might be the case for an access point in a reception area serving a variety of companies. In such a case, a sort of half-anonymous name can be used such as "anonymous@MyCo.com". The company name is real, but the user name is not given until later, when the secure connection to the company's server is established.

During the TLS negotiation, the server might request a client certificate. Providing such a certificate will compromise the identity of the client. In PEAP the client has the right to refuse to provide a certificate and the server should still proceed to phase 2. If the client provides a certificate and wants to use TLS anyway, there is hardly any point in going to phase 2 because mutual authentication will be achieved in phase 1.

Phase 2

Phase 2 is a conventional EAP negotiation allowing any upper-layer protocol that the authentication server supports. The only difference is that all the EAP messages are sent using the encrypted session established in phase 1. It is quite safe to send the real identity of the client. The authenticator is not allowed to compare the identity given in the second phase to that given in the first phase. It is understood that the first phase identity may be meaningless.

PEAP allows an attacker to get through phase 1 unchallenged. Because there is no authentication, any attacker can do the TLS negotiation and establish a secure connection to the authentication server. Therefore at the start of phase 2, the client must be treated as completely untrusted even though it is working in a secure link. Obviously, if the client cannot authenticate itself successfully in the second phase, it should be unceremoniously disconnected.

Status of PEAP

At the time of writing, PEAP is still in draft form.[5] However, it is essentially complete and may proceed to RFC status. An attack (described in Chapter 15) that eliminates the benefits provided by PEAP was recently identified, and it is unclear yet how that attack will affect the status of PEAP within the IETF. By the time you read this, there may or may not be an RFC number assigned.

Authentication in the Cellular Phone World: EAP-SIM

This last upper-layer authentication method reviewed in this chapter is interesting because it comes from a different industry from the others. The authentication methods that have built up around IETF and IEEE 802 have largely been associated with the data-processing industry. The model used in discussing and developing the solution revolves around the use of computers in education, industry, and the home. Over the years the ways in which computers are used have changed, and the models have been updated accordingly. However, it has always been against a backdrop of computer-based infrastructure.

New paradigms are now appearing. Over the next ten years, computer infrastructure will become important for home consumer electronics, and the computer industry, home entertainment industry, and the mobile phone industry will start to blur together. New types of cellular phones are being designed and deployed with digital communications capability. The cellular phone of the future will, in effect, be a small portable computer with capabilities exceeding laptops of today.

---

5. IETF: draft-josefsson-pppext-eap-tls-eap-05.txt.

Up to now, the mobile phone networks and infrastructure have been quite separate from the Internet technologies used by the computer industry. But as phones turn into computers, all this has to change. If a phone looks like a mobile computer, it faces all the same issues of security found in a conventional computer. Furthermore, the new cellular phones will need to connect to the Internet and other computers and servers. Therefore, a way is needed to bridge the gap between the existing mobile phone infrastructure and the Internet infrastructure.

This change is relevant to wireless LANs and IEEE 802.11 because products are now being deployed that have both cellular phone data capability and an IEEE 802.11 wireless LAN capability built in. When you are within range of an access point, you can connect to the Internet using wireless LAN and, at other times, you can use the cellular data network, albeit at a lower data rate (for more information, see Chapter 14).

Each authentication method requires a way of storing secret information at the client end. In Kerberos, for example, it is assumed that users remember passwords. In TLS the client might need to have a certificate. For a large proportion of the world's cellular phones, the secret information is held in a **smart card**, often referred to as a **SIM card**. The SIM card is a small plastic chip with an embedded microprocessor. SIM cards are used in all GSM mobile phones around the world and in many PCS phones in the United States. The idea of the SIM card is that it contains all the information about your subscription for the phone service. It contains your phone number, your address book, and, importantly, your security codes. You can pick up any compatible cellular phone and insert your SIM card, and it will immediately have your information and start receiving your phone calls. The SIM card itself is a small plastic token, as shown in Figure 9.17.

The secret information in the SIM card is not known by the subscriber. It is known only by the cellular phone company. When you subscribe to the phone service, the phone company programs a unique SIM card for you and installs the secret onto it. It can then authenticate you as a subscriber and also encrypt the data going between your phone and the network. This scenario is similar to one

Figure 9.17 SIM Card Next to a Quarter

in which a company installs client certificates on the computers of their employees so they can validate them for network access. When a mobile phone with Wi-Fi LAN capability wants to connect to an access point and authenticate to the network, it makes a lot of sense to leverage the secret stored in the SIM card. In fact, if you can link the authentication server back to the cellular phone billing system, you can provide subscriber access control as well as subscriber billing. Like it or not, this gives the phone company the ability to charge you for Wi-Fi LAN network access.

Overview of Authentication in a GSM Network

This section outlines how authentication is done in a conventional GSM network. This discussion also applies to many of the United States–based digital cellular networks that are based on GSM technology (although they may appear under a different name). The model was originally designed with voice communications in mind rather than data transfer, but it bears a striking similarity to the methods used for data security.

When a cellular phone comes within range of a base station and recognizes a compatible service, it may choose to try to register with the network—that is, to join the cell. Before the network allows the phone to connect, the phone must prove that it is a paid-up subscriber for the service. It needs to authenticate itself, and its identity needs to be verified with some subscriber database server in the network.

The basic approach to authentication is a challenge response method whereby the network sends a random value and the phone has to encrypt it[6] with its secret key and send it back for verification. In GSM three numbers are used during authentication and subsequent secure communications:

- Random challenge: RAND
- 64-bit session key, which is used to encrypt the wireless communications: Kc
- Response value called SRES that is computed by combining the secret key and the RAND value

Together, these three numbers are referred to as a **triplet** (RAND, SRES, Kc).

When a phone wants to register to a new network, it sends its identification number. This is stored in the SIM card and is called the **International Mobile Subscriber Identity** (IMSI) value. It is unique for each subscriber, rather like MAC addresses in the LAN network. The network can identify the home operator for

---

6. Technically, the current algorithms are keyed hash functions rather than encryption functions. The SRES is only 4 bytes long so the algorithm cannot be a reversible encryption.

the cellular phone from the IMSI and it requests the authentication center to create and forward a triplet for the authentication. This referral method allows phones to roam to different networks and still be authenticated by their home network provider.

When the local network receives the security triplet, it sends the RAND value to the phone, which passes it to the SIM card. Being a smart card, the SIM has it own microprocessor and is able to compute the other two components of the triplet using an encryption method and secret key hidden inside. The resulting value of SRES is returned to the network for confirmation and then the session opens using the Kc value for link encryption (see Figure 9.18 for an illustration of this process).

There are a couple of points worth noting. First, the network is not explicitly authenticated because it could accept any value of SRES without checking (although, if the network doesn't have a valid triplet, the encrypted communication would fail because Kc will not match between the network and the phone). Second, the algorithm used to generate SRES and Kc is not accessible outside the SIM card or to the network. When roaming, the network requests the authentication center associated with your home operator to provide a triplet; so the method used to generate SRES and Kc can be proprietary to the home network operator. The operator also issues the SIM card. Therefore, it is common for different network operators to use their own flavor of algorithm for security inside the SIM card—a sort of security by obscurity in addition to the usual protections.

Linking GSM Security to Wi-Fi LAN Security

Why would you want to link the existing GSM authentication system to Wi-Fi LAN operation? Well, as mentioned earlier, phones are becoming more like computers and users will want high-speed Internet access combined with mobility.

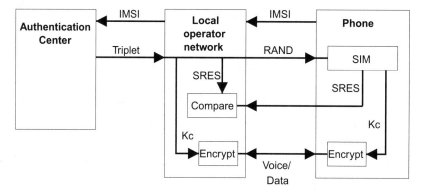

Figure 9.18 Authentication Overview for GSM Phone Connection

One way to achieve this is to build IEEE 802.11 into a cellular phone and allow the phone to choose between available connections, using Wi-Fi LAN whenever available. In fact, at least one major cellular phone vendor has introduced a plug-in PC card for laptops that does precisely this. It has both IEEE 802.11 capability and GSM-GPRS cellular data capability. In an ideal scenario, the mobile phone operator deploys access points as well as cell phone base stations and the device can automatically switch to use the best infrastructure available. It follows that a single authentication and billing infrastructure is needed and, because a SIM card is available, it makes sense to use it also for the Wi-Fi LAN authentication.

An example of handover is shown in Figure 9.19. When the subscriber is using the cell phone network, data goes to the local cellular base station and GSM authentication must be used. When the subscriber uses the Wi-Fi LAN, data goes to the access point and RSN authentication must be used. However, in both cases the authentication server must be the same.

EAP-SIM

At the time of writing, the proposal to use cellular phone SIM authentication is a draft in IETF: draft-haverinen-pppext-eap-sim-09.txt. Eventually, this draft may make the transition into an RFC. Essentially, the object of the method is to use the existing GSM style authentication unchanged so far as possible. Some things cannot be changed because they are built into the SIM card standard and method of operation.

One of the problems faced in converting cellular authentication to RSN is that the SIM card does not produce a very long master session key—only 64 bits. By

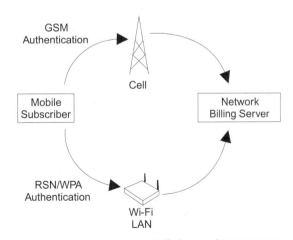

Figure 9.19 Roaming Between Cellular and Wi-Fi LAN

today's standards, we need at least 128 bits for the master key. The SIM card produces the session key as part of its triplet containing the challenge and response information. To get a larger master key, multiple triplets are used. Instead of simply sending one challenge, the server can send two, or three, challenges during the EAP process. Each time a challenge arrives, the SIM card computes a corresponding triplet containing another 64-bit session key. By joining together the 64-bit triplet keys, a session key of arbitrary length can be created.

Another concern relates to the fact that the identity of the subscriber is visible in each authentication. The identity can be determined by observing the IMSI value, which is unique to the cellular phone. To avoid the access points gathering data about the subscriber from the IMSI value, the EAP-SIM draft introduces the idea of **IMSI privacy**. Remember the IMSI is the unique identity of the mobile device. If we can hide the identity, a degree of anonymity is possible. In addition, it is more difficult to mount an attack based on observing a large number of authentications; the attacker simply wouldn't know which authentication belongs to which device. Therefore the EAP-SIM draft has a scheme whereby, during authentication, the server and mobile device agree on a new subscriber identity to use for the *next* authentication. This is called a **pseudonym**. The new value is set using encryption so the identity changes every time the device connects and only the device and server know which identity will be used each time.

The third problem with GSM authentication is that the method does not explicitly authenticate the network. If a rogue server were to accept the challenge response without really checking, the mobile device would incorrectly think it has connected to a legitimate network. This problem is resolved by having the mobile device send a nonce value at the start of the negotiation. The server has to incorporate the nonce value into an encrypted response. To do this correctly, it has to have access to legitimate triplets.

The actual message exchanges used for EAP-SIM authentication are shown in Figure 9.20 and described here:

1. It all starts with the usual EAP request-identity message. On the first operation the cellular phone sends its actual IMSI information. However, for all subsequent connects, it sends a pseudonym as agreed on with the server during the previous authentication. After this, the EAP-SIM specific messages start.

2. The server sends an EAP-Request/SIM/Start message telling the mobile that it is ready to proceed with authentication.

3. The mobile responds by sending its nonce value (this is a 16-byte unique value).

4. The server has several jobs to do at this stage:
   - **Get Triplets**: After the server receives the identity or pseudonym for the cellular phone, it asks the authentication center of the home operator to

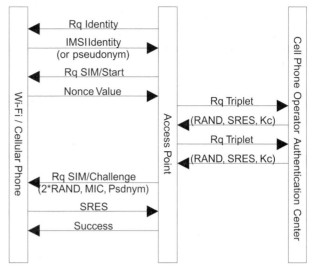

Figure 9.20   Message Flow for GSM-SIM

send several triplets; let's suppose two triplets are obtained. We write this as 2*(RAND, SRES, Kc) to indicate that each of the two triples has three pieces of information.

- **Compute Session Key**: The server computes a 128-bit session key using the two (64-bit) Kc values. Rather than just concatenating the values as described earlier, it combines the two values with the mobile's nonce value using a hashing algorithm.

- **Protect the RAND values**: The values of RAND form the challenge texts. The mobile device uses these to generate its own copies of the triplets using the SIM card. Therefore the RAND values must be sent to the mobile unencrypted and are vulnerable to tampering. To prevent this, an integrity check is computed across both values using the session key that has just been just derived

- **Compose new pseudonym**: The server creates the pseudonym that the mobile should use next time it authenticates. This is then encrypted using the new session key.

5. Now the server is ready to respond to the mobile. It sends an EAP–Request/ SIM/Challenge containing the two RAND values, the integrity check, and the encrypted new pseudonym.

6. Having received the two values of RAND, the mobile now submits each in turn to the SIM card and gets back the corresponding values of SRES and Kc.

Assuming everything is legitimate, these will match those held at the network server. The mobile then computes the session key using its copy of the nonce and verifies the integrity check word sent by the server. It is also able to decrypt and store the new pseudonym.

7. Now the mobile sends back the values of SRES that the SIM card computed. This is the way in which the network can confirm that the mobile really has a valid SIM card. In the same way as the server did for RAND, the mobile computes an integrity check over the two values of SRES and sends this back with the response.

8. Assuming that the server is able to confirm a match with its copy of SRES and verify the integrity checkword, the authentication is now complete and an EAP-Success message is sent. The mobile and network have mutually authenticated and also generated a strong session key from which link layer keys can be derived.

Status of GSM-SIM Authentication

As previously mentioned, the EAP-SIM method was a draft at the time of writing. However, the bigger issue is whether the idea of authenticating Wi-Fi LAN by cellular phone methods will catch on. There are few such systems available. However, if terminals that combine cellular phone connectivity and Wi-Fi LAN capability become widespread, cellular phone operators may install access points all over the place and a combined authentication process with the strength of RSN would then be a real requirement. The issue of public Wi-Fi LAN access and its security implications are reviewed in Chapter 14.

Summary

Wi-Fi operates at a low level in the network layer hierarchy. Protocols such as TCP/IP operate at a higher layer and depend on the lower layers to transport data from place to place. One of the problems in the original security concept for Wi-Fi was that the security system was all contained within the lower layers. This led to problems and, most of all, it made it very difficult to provide centralized management of secret keys. The solution came by the use of upper-layer authentication methods.

A number of security protocols have been developed and tested over the years and are well trusted by corporate system administrators. These systems have been developed for use in large secure networks using centralized and remote management. We call these methods upper-layer authentication methods because they work at the top of the protocol stack rather than at the bottom. This chapter describes several methods that can be used in conjunction with RSN and WPA Wi-Fi networks.

First we reviewed TLS, which is closely related to SSL. We provided an overview of certificate-based security and described the message exchange involved in TLS. For a more in-depth look at TLS, you could also refer to Eric Rescorla's book *SSL and TLS* (Rescorla, 2001). We showed how TLS could be used in conjunction with EAP and RADIUS so it could be applied to key management in WPA and RSN.

Next we looked at Kerberos v5. Kerberos is based on the concept of service tickets managed though central servers. We showed how Kerberos could be applied to RSN without using RADIUS through an interesting technique of proxy servers.

At the end of the chapter we covered Cisco LEAP, a proprietary approach introduced for use with WEP to assist in the management of keys. LEAP was the first Wi-Fi–related security approach to be based on IEEE 802.1X and has been deployed in many corporate sites. Finally, we looked at two newer methods, PEAP and GSM-SIM. GSM-SIM is interesting because it bridges the gap between the cellular phone industry and the networking industry, allowing Wi-Fi systems to be authenticated by the cellular phone infrastructure.

Chapter 10

WPA and RSN Key Hierarchy

We talked about keys in the introduction to WPA/RSN and explained how, unlike WEP, both WPA and RSN use multiple keys at different levels. In fact, there are so many keys used, it's hard enough for the designer to keep track of them all, let alone an attacker. But don't panic, although there are many keys, they are all hidden away inside the workings of WPA/RSN—the administrator needs only to define a single master key from which all these others are derived.

This chapter describes what a key hierarchy is and why so many keys are needed. We look at the key hierarchies for TKIP and AES–CCMP, the two ciphersuites described in Chapters 11 and 12. We also review what steps are involved in creating and updating the hierarchy, both when the Wi-Fi LAN is first started and during normal operation.

Pairwise and Group Keys

IEEE 802.11 Wi-Fi LANs are designed to allow multiple devices to communicate. In practice, this means a group of mobile devices must share the radio channel and communicate with a single access point. Many LANs provide shared access. For example, conventional Ethernet LAN workstations share the wiring by transmitting one at a time and trying to avoid collisions. For efficiency, most shared LANs also provide the capability for one workstation to send data simultaneously to several others. Data sent between two workstations is called **unicast** and data sent from one to multiple workstations is called **multicast**; the case in which one workstation sends to *all* the others is a special case of multicast called **broadcast**. Multicast and unicast messages have different security characteristics.

Unicast data sent between two parties needs to be private to those two parties. This is best accomplished by using a specific key for each pair of devices communicating. We call this a **pairwise** key; usually it protects communication between a mobile device and the access point. This means that each mobile device needs to store one pairwise key, and the access point needs a set of pairwise keys—one for each mobile device that is associated.

By contrast, broadcast (or multicast) data must be received by multiple parties who form a trusted group. Therefore, a key must be shared by all the members of that trusted group. This is called the **group key**. Each trusted mobile device and the access point need to know a single group key. The concept of pairwise and group keys is shown in Figure 10.1.

The methods of managing the pairwise keys and the group keys are somewhat different so we define each as a separate key hierarchy. We refer to the **pairwise key hierarchy** to describe all the keys used between a pair of devices (one of

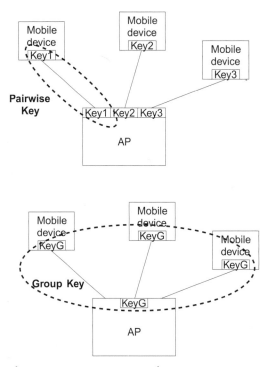

Figure 10.1 Pairwise and Group Keys

which is usually the access point) and the **group key hierarchy** to describe the various keys shared by all the devices.

The next important terms are **preshared** keys and **server-based** keys. As the name suggests, preshared keys are installed in the access point and in the mobile device by some method outside WPA/RSN. It could be that you phone up a user and tell him the password, or send him a letter that he has to eat after reading or whatever eccentric method you choose. Most WEP systems use preshared keys—it is the responsibility of the user to get the keys delivered to the two parties who want to communicate. Preshared keys bypass the concept of upper-layer authentication completely; you are assumed to be authentic simply by proving possession of the key.

The alternative, server-based keys, requires an upper-layer authentication process that allows the mobile device and an authentication server to generate matching secret keys. The authentication sever arranges for the access point to get a copy for use in session protection. It has the major advantage that the operator can keep a single key database that can be used in conjunction with many access points. When a new employee joins, for example, the administrator has to update only one database.

Preshared keys are easier to implement in small networks. Most older WEP systems *only* supported preshared group keys.

Pairwise Key Hierarchy

The pairwise key hierarchy is the most complicated, so let's review that first. The hierarchy starts at the top with a **pairwise master key (PMK)** delivered from the upper-layer authentication server or with a preshared key. Let's put preshared keys aside for the moment and look at the server-key approach. The PMK is the top of the pairwise key hierarchy. There is a different PMK for each mobile device, and from this all other pairwise keys are derived. The following paragraphs show how the PMK is created and how it is used to generate the actual keys used in encryption.

Creating and Delivering the PMK

Let's do a one-paragraph review of IEEE 802.1X. In Chapter 8 we saw that the IEEE 802.1X model has three components: a supplicant, an authenticator, and an authentication server (which we abbreviate just to *server* here). The mobile device is the supplicant and connects to an access point containing the authenticator. The supplicant uses EAP to communicate, first with the authenticator (in the access point), and then to the server. The server makes a decision to admit (or block) the supplicant and informs both the authenticator and the supplicant. By this method the authentication and authorization is done centrally (at the server).

The highest key in the whole security context is held both by the user and the server, or the user's equipment and the server. This "supreme secret" key might be in a smart card, stored on a laptop disk, or remembered in a person's head. During the EAP authentication process, the chosen authentication method proves that both parties know the supreme secret. Chapter 9 outlined several ways to do this authentication. To be useful for RSN or WPA, the authentication method must, as a by-product of the authentication process, generate random-like key material that we can use for our key hierarchies. An authentication method that does this is called **key-generating**. Methods discussed in Chapter 9, such as TLS (SSL) and Kerberos, are key-generating.

When using upper-layer authentication, you use the *key material generated during authentication* to create the PMK. If, instead of upper-layer authentication, you are using a preshared key, this preshared key is used directly as the PMK.

Authentication occurs between the supplicant and the server, and the result is that both the mobile device and the server generate matching PMKs. But in order to use the keys to protect the wireless link, we need also to provide the PMK to the access point. How do we get the PMK from the server to the access point? In corporate networks, the access point(s) are connected to the authentication server by a network connection, usually using TCP/IP protocol, and it is necessary to transfer the PMK across the network. In small systems, it might be that a simple server is actually built into the access point unit. In this case, it is easy to transfer the key material.

The IEEE 802.11i specification does not explicitly say how the PMK should be transferred from the server to the access point, although recommendations are given. By contrast, WPA specifies transfer of the PMK to the access point using the RADIUS protocol. The RADIUS attribute MS-MPPE-Recv-key (vendor_id=17) is used for this purpose. More details of RADIUS are provided in Chapter 8.

At the end of the upper-level authentication phase and after completion of the key transfer, both the mobile device and the access point will have a copy of the PMK. The process of obtaining the PMK ends with the EAP-Success message being sent by the authentication, as described in Chapter 8. In the IEEE 802.1X model of the world, the EAP-Success message results in opening of the data port and data starting to flow. However, in WPA/RSN, this is not the case. There are further hurdles to clear before data is allowed. We need to derive keys for encryption between the access point and the mobile device. We need to verify that the keys are matching and we need to distribute a group key for use in broadcasts.

If you are using preshared keys, none of the upper-layer authentication process is required and the value of the PMK is programmed directly into the mobile device and access point independently. The PMK is required to be 256 bits long— that is, 32 bytes. Because 32 bytes would be a very long password to remember, systems using preshared keys may allow users to enter a shorter password, which the system then expands to 256 bits. IEEE 802.11i has a suggested method for generating a key from a shorter pass phrase. This allows users to enter memorable text strings and have then converted into a preshared master key in a consistent manner.

Computing the Temporal Keys

In your enthusiasm to get encryption turned on, you might think at this stage that we are ready to slot the PMK into the encryption engine and get going. But we have a long way to go yet before we reach that stage. That is why it is called a hierarchy! The PMK is not used directly for any security operations. Instead it is used to derive a separate set of keys that *will* be used in protecting a link between two devices (for example, between the access point and a mobile device). Four separate keys are needed to do the job because there are two layers to protect—the EAPOL handshake and the user's data—and two cryptographic functions at each layer: encryption and integrity.[1]

- Data Encryption key (128 bits)
- Data Integrity key (128 bits)
- EAPOL-Key Encryption key (128 bits)
- EAPOL-Key Integrity key (128 bits)

These are referred to as the **temporal keys** because they are recomputed every time a mobile device associates to the access point. The collection of all four keys together is referred to as the **pairwise transient key (PTK)**. For RSN/TKIP and WPA, each of these keys must be 128 bits long so that the PTK is a total of 512 bits long.

The first two temporal keys sound familiar. They are the ones used to encrypt the data and protect it from modification. The second two we have not seen before. These are used to protect the communications between the access point and mobile device during the initial handshake.[2] For the moment, just accept that these EAPOL keys are needed; we will discuss them again shortly.

Because the temporal keys are recomputed each time a mobile device connects, there has to be something that changes when the computation is done; otherwise, you'd end up with the same temporal keys every time. This is called adding **liveness** to the keys, ensuring that old keys no longer work. Liveness is achieved

---

1. Chapter 12 explains that AES–CCMP is designed so a single key can be used for both encryption and integrity, reducing by one the number of keys needed

2. And for various notifications after the handshake.

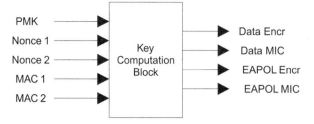

Figure 10.2 Temporal Key Computation

by including a couple of special values called **nonces** in the computation. The value of the nonce is quite arbitrary except in one respect: a nonce value is *never* used twice[3] with the same key. The word "nonce" can be thought of as "N – once"— in other words, a value (N) only used once.[4] They say lightning never strikes in the same place twice (which is not true) and similarly nonces never come up with the same value twice (which should be true by design).

The temporal keys are effectively shared between the two devices because both ends of the link compute an identical copy. It is not enough for one device to include its own nonce value. Each device must generate a nonce, pass its nonce to the other device, and then derive the temporal keys by including *both* nonces in the computation. Also, to make sure the identity of the two devices is bound into the keys, the MAC address of each is included in the computation. Figure 10.2 summarizes the process and shows the inputs to the temporal key computation and the four output keys. The inputs are the PMK, a nonce from each side, and the MAC address of each side. The outputs are four 128-bit keys. How the "key computation block" is implemented is described later.

Exchanging and Verifying Key Information

We have described how the authentication server and the mobile device mutually prove their identity and how key information must be derived by the mobile device and distributed to the access point. We have seen how the PMK is used to generate a set of temporal keys. However, one important step is missing: The

---

3. In some practical systems, "never" is compromised to mean "extremely unlikely." For example, if a very large true random number is used, the probability of getting the same value twice might be considered acceptably low.

4. The word "nonce" actually derives from medieval English. For an interesting diversion, enter the phrase "for the nonce" into an Internet search engine (include the quotation marks) and choose among the numerous definitions.

mobile device has not yet verified that the access point is legitimate. Because we were able to talk to the server through the access point, it seems reasonable to assume it is trusted. However, it could be an access point that some hacker planted in the office and hooked up to the internal network. Maybe your janitor is a master hacker! Okay, maybe not, but the principle of security is *trust no one* so the access point must prove its credentials.

This is where the requirement for a secure connection between the authentication server and the access point is important. A secure connection requires that the server and the access point share their own secret—so the janitor's AP cannot establish such a connection unless it knows the server's secret, even though it is connected inside the office. The access point can only receive the PMK from the server through the secure connection. So if the access point can prove to the mobile device that it possesses the PMK, then it proves that it is trusted by the authentication server, which is master of all security. So this defines the test: The access point and the mobile device must prove to each other that they both possess a copy of the secret PMK.

This idea of mutually proving possession of a secret key was also part of WEP but, as we saw in Chapter 6, the method used was completely broken and was easily tricked. In WPA/RSN the processes of proving key ownership is combined with the process of deriving the temporal keys using a key message exchange before the connection can be opened for business. There are four steps to the process, giving the name "four-way exchange," and the exchange is done using EAPOL-Key messages.

First we will look at the four-way exchange in overview and then drill down in more detail. The four-way exchange occurs between the access point and the mobile device. However, for consistency with IEEE 802.1X, these are referred to as the authenticator and the supplicant respectively. Remember, **A**uthenticator = **A**ccess Point.

A Note on EAPOL-Key Messages

The standard for EAP does not specify by what type of network its messages should be sent. EAP was originally designed for use with PPP, which commonly runs over ordinary dial-up connections. IEEE 802.1X defined how to use EAP over a LAN and dubbed this "EAPOL." The standard also defined a "key message" that was intended to allow the supplicant and authenticator to exchange secret key information. The format of this key message is defined and also the method of encrypting the key value contained in the message. IEEE 802.11i uses the basic format of the EAPOL-Key message but modifies it in several ways to improve security.

The first step is for both the supplicant and authenticator to generate a nonce value. There is no connection between the two values—they are independent—however, there are specific rules about how the values are generated that are covered later in this chapter. The nonce selected by the authenticator is called **ANonce** and that of the supplicant is the **SNonce**. This is followed by the exchange of four messages that we refer to as A, B, C, and D.

Message (A): Authenticator → Supplicant

The first EAPOL-Key message is sent from the authenticator to the supplicant and contains ANonce. This message is not encrypted or protected from tampering. Tampering with the value simply makes the handshake fail so there is no danger here.

Once the supplicant has received message (A), it has all the information it needs to compute the temporal keys. It already had the PMK, its own SNonce, and MAC address and now it has the ANonce and MAC address of the authenticator. So the supplicant now computes the four temporal keys using the algorithm described later in this chapter.

Message (B): Supplicant → Authenticator

The authenticator cannot compute its keys yet because it does not know the value of SNonce. This is now sent by the supplicant using message (B). This message is unencrypted but it has a feature that was not in message (A): It includes a message integrity code (MIC) to prevent tampering. This is the first use of the EAPOL-Key Integrity key, one of the four temporal keys described earlier. Computing the MIC over the whole of message (B) prevents anyone from modifying the message without detection. However, more importantly, it allows the authenticator to verify that the supplicant really does know the PMK. If the supplicant's PMK doesn't match that of the authenticator, the MIC check will fail. Of course, the authenticator has not computed the keys yet; but because the message is not encrypted, it can first extract SNonce, and then compute all the temporal keys and finally go back and check the MIC value before moving to the next phase.

At this point the first half of the four-way exchange is completed. Both sides have now derived the four temporal keys and the authenticator has verified that the supplicant must have a matching PMK. So far, neither side has started encrypting.

Message (C): Authenticator → Supplicant

This message is sent by the authenticator to tell the supplicant that it is ready to start using the new keys for encryption. It is important to synchronize this operation because, if either the access point or the mobile device turns on encryption before the other side is ready, the link will break. Message (C) includes a MIC check so the supplicant can verify that the authenticator has a matching PMK. It also contains the starting sequence number that will be used for the first encrypted frame to be sent using the key (normally, 0). Note that because the MIC is computed using a key derived from both the PMK and the supplicant's nonce, a message recorded from a previous handshake can't be successfully replayed.

The message is sent unencrypted and the authenticator does not install its temporal keys until it has received the final message (D). The authenticator waits to install the keys because, if message (C) fails to arrive at the supplicant, the authenticator must resend message (C). If the keys are installed too early, the resend would be encrypted and the supplicant would reject it.

Message (D): Supplicant → Authenticator

When the supplicant receives message (C), it replies with message (D). This acknowledges completion of the four-way handshake and indicates that the supplicant will now install the keys and start encryption. The message is sent unencrypted and then the supplicant installs its keys. Upon receipt, the authenticator also installs its keys so subsequent messages are all encrypted.

Let's review what has been accomplished by this exchange:

1. ANonce and SNonce values have been exchanged.
2. Temporal keys have been computed.
3. Supplicant has proved knowledge of the PMK.
4. Authenticator has proved knowledge of the PMK.
5. Both devices have synchronized and turned on encryption of unicast packets.

Completing the Handshake

At this point both the mobile device and the access point have obtained, computed, and installed encryption keys. They are now communicating over a secure channel using encryption in both directions. However, we are not quite finished yet. Although the pairwise key hierarchy is now installed, we still have to set up the group key hierarchy so the access point can send broadcasts and multicast messages to the newly authenticated mobile device.

Group Key Hierarchy

IEEE 802.11 supports multicast and broadcast messages. One example in which multicast is useful is video distribution. If you want to send a live broadcast to many stations, you don't want to have to send to each station individually—you want to transmit one copy on the LAN and allow all the relevant stations to receive the video frames. This is an example of group multicast. A special case of multicast is broadcast, in which the message is sent to all devices on the LAN. Broadcasts are used widely in LAN protocols.

In an infrastructure network (that is, a network using an access point), multicasts are *only* sent from the access point to the mobile devices. Mobile devices are not allowed to send broadcasts directly; however, they can initiate a broadcast by sending the message to the access point, which then broadcasts it on the station's behalf (to both the wireless devices and any attached wired LAN). On the wireless side, we want multicasts and broadcasts to be encrypted and protected from tampering.

We cannot use the pairwise keys for broadcasts. Each mobile device has a different set of pairwise keys so it would be necessary to send multiple copies of the broadcast, each encrypted differently. While this would work, it would completely defeat the advantage of the multicast message. Therefore, a separate key hierarchy is maintained specifically for use in encrypting multicasts. This is called the group key hierarchy.

Unlike pairwise keys, all the mobile devices and the access point share a single set of group keys. This allows all the stations to decrypt a multicast message sent from the access point. While this solves a problem, it also creates one: how to handle the case in which a mobile station leaves the network.

If a mobile device chooses to leave the Wi-Fi LAN, it should notify the access point by sending an IEEE 802.11 disassociate message. When it does this, the access point erases the copy of the pairwise keys for the departing mobile device and stops sending it messages. If the device wants to rejoin later, it must go through the whole key establishment phase from scratch. But what about the group key? Even though the device has left the network, it can still receive and decrypt the multicasts that are sent because it still has a valid group key available. This is not acceptable from a security standpoint; if a device leaves the network, it should no longer be allowed any access at all.

The solution to this problem is to change the group key when a device leaves the network. This is a bit like changing the locks on your house after a long-term guest leaves; you don't want anyone to have a door key who is not living in your house. So group keys have an added complication: the need to rekey.

Negotiating the pairwise keys was complicated because we had to start with no secure connection in place and we ran the risk of all sorts of attacks from simple snooping to message forgery. The situation for group keys is easier because we can wait until the pairwise keys are established and then use the secure link to send the group key value. This provides a significant simplification and means that the actual group key values can be sent directly to each station without concern about interception or modification. Group key distribution is done using EAPOL-Key messages, as for pairwise key. However, only two messages are needed, not four.

The access point performs the following steps during group key distribution:

1. Create a 256-bit group master key (GMK).
2. Derive the 256-bit **group transient key** (GTK) from which the group temporal keys are obtained.
3. After each pairwise secure connection is established:
   - Send GTK to mobile device with current sequence number.
   - Check for acknowledgment of receipt.

Because it is necessary to update the group key from time to time, a method is needed to perform the update without causing a break in the service. This would be a problem if the mobile device could store only a single group key because it takes time to go round each device and give them all the new key value. What key would you use for multicast transmissions during this update period—the old one or the new one? Whichever you chose, some of the stations would not be able to decrypt.

Fortunately, the original WEP standard made provision for multiple keys to be stored in the mobile device: Up to four keys can be installed at one time. Each transmitted frame carries a 2-bit field called KeyID that specifies which of the four keys should be used for decryption. Pairwise keys are sent with a KeyID value of 0. But we can take advantage of the other three key storage slots for group key updates.

Suppose that the current group keys are installed into KeyID 1. When we want to update, the authenticator sends the new key with instructions to put it at KeyID 2. During this key update phase, multicasts are still sent using KeyID 1 until all the attached stations have been informed of the new key. Finally, the authenticator switches over and all the multicasts from then on (until the next key change) are sent with KeyID 2.

We now know how to send the GTK, but how is the GMK generated and how is the GTK derived? In the case of pairwise keys, the PMK was produced by the upper-layer authentication method (or by using preshared keys). Clearly, this process doesn't apply for the group keys because the key is not generated per device. However, because the object of the group keys is only to protect messages and not provide authentication, there is no need to tie the key into the identity of any specific device. In fact the key can be quite arbitrarily chosen. You haven't even got the problem of ensuring that both ends of a link pick the same value because the access point simply sends its chosen value in the EAPOL-Key messages.

So the rule is as follows: The access point allocates a GMK simply by choosing a 256-bit cryptographic-quality random number. This sounds easy but there is a gotcha: the words "cryptographic-quality" are important. Many programming languages provide a function that produces a "random" number on request. Usually the numbers produced look random but actually are quite predictable. They may come from a stored table or be derived from the clock value. If an attacker knows how your "random" number is generated, he can guess your GMK. *Cryptographic quality* means that no one in the universe knows what the random value will be until the moment it is generated. Methods for generating such numbers are suggested in the IEEE 802.11i standard.

Once the GMK is selected, it is necessary to derive the group temporal keys. Two keys are required:

- Group Encryption key (128 bits)
- Group Integrity key (128 bits)

The combination of these two keys forms a 256-bit value, the GTK. This is the value that is sent by the access point to each attached station. The GTK is derived from the GMK by combining with a nonce value and the MAC address of the access point. Given that the GMK is completely random to start with, this is arguably an unnecessary step but it does provide consistency with the pairwise key case.

Summary of the Key Establishment Process

The following steps summarize the process of establishing and distributing the keys used by WPA or RSN:

- If you are using a security server, the authentication phase is completed using an upper-layer authentication. If successful, this both authenticates the supplicant and authorizes it to join the network. If you are using a preshared key, authentication is assumed and subsequently verified during the four-way key handshake.
- Once authorized, the mobile device and access point perform a four-way handshake to generate temporal keys and prove mutual knowledge of the PMK.
- Finally the access point computes and distributes group keys.

Only after all these phases have completed is user data finally allowed to flow between the authenticator and the supplicant. At last the communications link is open for business and all the keys are available to implement the encryption and protection needed.

Key Hierarchy Using AES–CCMP

Most of what has been described so far in this section applies to both AES–CCMP[5] and TKIP[6] cipher methods. The method of deriving and delivering keys applies across the board—using the four-way handshake for pairwise keys and the two-way handshake for group keys. However, there is a difference in one respect: the size and number of keys needed is different, depending on the encryption method in use.

Given that AES–CCMP provides a higher level of security, you might expect that the AES–CCMP keys would be bigger or perhaps more numerous. However, in fact, the reverse is true. Whereas a total of 768 temporal key bits are needed for TKIP, only 512 are needed for AES–CCMP. The reason is because in AES–CCMP the integrity and encryption functions are combined into a single calculation, whereas with TKIP they are two quite distinct operations, each requiring a separate key.

For AES–CCMP, the pairwise temporal keys are:

- Data Encryption/Integrity key (128 bits)
- EAPOL-Key Encryption key (128 bits)
- EAPOL-Key Integrity key (128 bits)

And the group temporal key is:

- Group Encryption/Integrity key (128 bits)

The PMK and GMK are still created in the same way but, at the temporal key computation phase, fewer key bits are generated; otherwise, there is no difference in operations. While the four-way handshake is mandated for both WPA and 802.11i, it is possible that new key hierarchy schemes will be introduced for 802.11i in the future. The four-way handshake has been criticized for being slow because it can take several seconds to complete. The slow handshake presents problems for system that need rapid handover between access points such as voice-over-IP terminals.

---

5. Details of AES–CCMP are given in Chapter 12.
6. Details of TKIP are given in Chapter 11.

Mixed Environments

In some cases an access point might have to support both TKIP and AES–CCMP devices in the same network. Suppose, for example, you have upgraded your old WEP systems to TKIP and now want to buy new mobile device using AES–CCMP. At least for a period, until the old cards are replaced, you will need to have both operating side by side. This is not a problem for the pairwise keys. If the access point is well designed it will know which device is using what method and store the keys appropriately. It will also know how to encrypt and decrypt messages from and to each device separately. However, a difficulty arises regarding group keys and multicasts. The access point has to send a broadcast to all the mobile devices; but if they are using different encryption methods, how can this be done? The answer is that they must all use the same encryption method for multicast reception; the standard requires in this case that TKIP should be used for multicasts even when AES–CCMP is being used for pairwise exchanges.

If you want to set up this mixed environment, you need to check that the AES–CCMP supporting product you purchase also supports TKIP, at least for broadcast reception. In practice, it is likely that most AES cards will have the option to operate entirely in TKIP mode for the foreseeable future, especially for cards operating in the popular IEEE 802.11b frequency band. Note that for security purposes, RSN also disallows the use of TKIP for pairwise if AES–CCMP is chosen for multicast

Summary of Key Hierarchies

Figures 10.3 through 10.6 summarize the key hierarchy, showing how the various keys are derived. These diagrams are provided as a quick reference prior to the detailed description of how the key derivation is implemented.

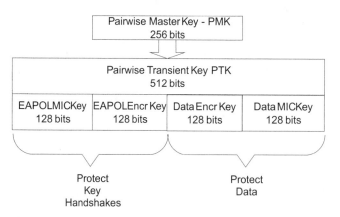

Figure 10.3 TKIP Pairwise Key Hierarchy

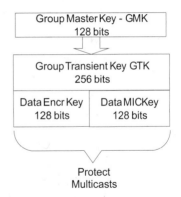

Group Master Key - GMK
128 bits

Group Transient Key GTK
256 bits

Data Encr Key 128 bits	Data MICKey 128 bits

Protect
Multicasts

Figure 10.4 TKIP Group Key Hierarchy

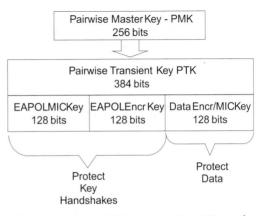

Pairwise Master Key - PMK
256 bits

Pairwise Transient Key PTK
384 bits

EAPOLMICKey 128 bits	EAPOLEncr Key 128 bits	Data Encr/MICKey 128 bits

Protect
Key
Handshakes

Protect
Data

Figure 10.5 AES Pairwise Key Hierarchy

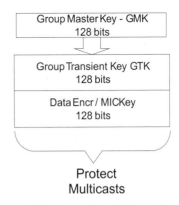

Group Master Key - GMK
128 bits

Group Transient Key GTK
128 bits

Data Encr / MICKey
128 bits

Protect
Multicasts

Figure 10.6 AES Group Key Hierarchy

Details of Key Derivation for WPA

This section describes the message formats and exchanges that are used in establishing the key hierarchies. In particular, we show the frame format used for the EAPOL-Key frames used in the four-way and two-way exchanges. The details shown here apply specifically to WPA but are basically similar for IEEE 802.11i TKIP and AES as well.

Prior to the key exchanges and temporal key derivation, several things will already have occurred. The access point will have advertised its capabilities and a mobile device will have selected a security method, associated, and initiated an authentication exchange. If upper-layer authentication is in operation, an exchange between the supplicant and authentication server will have completed, resulting in the delivery of a PMK to the access point. The access point will have intercepted an EAP-Success message and delivered it to the supplicant. Receipt of EAP-Success by the access point triggers the four-way key exchange.

In WPA, the key exchange is done using a special variant of the EAPOL-Key message, which is different from that defined in IEEE 802.1X. This variant has some extra fields and is shown in Figure 10.7.

The descriptor shown in Figure 10.7 appears in the message body section of an EAPOL frame. In practice, it would be preceded by the EAPOL header, as appropriate for IEEE 802.11. The purpose of each field is described in Table 10.1. The

Descriptor Type 1 byte	
Key Information 2 bytes	Key Length 2 bytes
Replay Counter 8 bytes	
Key Nonce 32 bytes	
EAPOL-Key IV 16 bytes	
Key Receive Sequence Counter (RSC) 8 bytes	
Key Identifier 8 bytes	
Key MIC 16 bytes	
Key Data Length 2 bytes	Key Data 0 ... n bytes

Figure 10.7   WPA Version of EAPOL-Key Descriptor

Table 10.1 Fields of the WPA EAPOL-Key Message

Descriptor Type	Unique value (254) that identifies this descriptor as the WPA variant.
Key Information	This field contains several subfields that provide information about the key type and how it should be used. It also contains various control bits to assist in the handshake procedure.
Key Length	The length of the key in bytes. Note in the pairwise key this is the length of the PTK, even though the actual PTK is not sent in a key frame; it is the *target* key.
Replay Counter	This value is incremented with every message to detect any attempts at replaying an old message. The exception is when this message is in response to an ACK request, in which case the replay value of the message being "ACKed" is inserted.
Key Nonce	Nonce value used to derive temporal pairwise keys or group keys.
EAPOL-Key IV	For group key transfer, the GTK is encrypted using the EAPOL-Key Encryption key in conjunction with this IV value. The encrypted GTK is placed in the Key Data area.
Key Sequence Start	This indicates the value of the sequence number to be expected in the first frame received after the keys are installed. The sequence number protects against replay attacks.
Key Identifier	This is not used in WPA. In the future it might be used to enable multiple keys to be set up in advance.
Key MIC	This is an integrity check value computed across the entire EAPOL-Key frame from the EAPOL Protocol version field to the end of the key material (this field is set to 0 during the computation).
Key Data Length	Defines the length number of bytes in the Key Data field (which might be different from the actual key itself).
Key Data	Material that needs to be sent in secret. For example, in the case of the group key, this is the encrypted value of the GTK. In some pairwise key messages, this carries an information element.

most complicated field is Key Information, which is divided into a number of control bits and subfields. Understanding the contents of this field is essential to understanding how the handshake works. The Key Information field is a 16-bit value divided up as shown in Figure 10.8. and described in Table 10.2. The meaning of the control bits 5 through 9 is shown in Table 10.3.

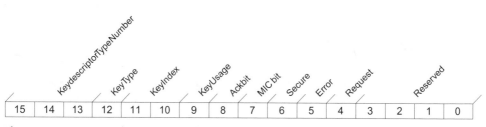

Figure 10.8 Key Information Field

Table 10.2 Key Information Field Summary

Bits 0–3	Currently unused and set to 0.
Bits 4–9	Control bits set at different stages of the handshake.
Bits 10–11	Indicate the key index in the case of group keys. This allows the keys to be updated late by installing new group keys at a different index position to the current operation group key.
Bit 12	Distinguishes between the pairwise and group key messages
Bits 13–15	Indicate the version and allow different schemes and key encryption methods to be used in the future. The value of 001 indicates that: EAPOL MIC is calculated using HMAC-MD5 EAPOL key encryption is done using RC4

Table 10.3 EAPOL-Key Message Control Bits

Request	This bit is used by the supplicant to request that the authenticator initiate a new four-way handshake to refresh the keys.
Error	In TKIP (see Chapter 11), if a MIC failure is detected by a mobile device, a key message is sent with the Error bit set to inform the access point. The Request bit will also be set to request a rekey operation.
Secure	This is set when the four-way key exchange is completed to indicate that the link is now secure.
MIC	This bit is used to indicate when a MIC has been computed for this message and inserted into the MIC field.
ACK	This is set in messages from the authenticator to indicate that it expects a response from the supplicant.
Install	For pairwise keys, this bit indicates that the new key should be installed and put into effect. For group keys, this bit is 0.

The Key Data field is used differently in pairwise and group key handshakes. You might expect that this field would be used to send the actual key to the other party encrypted using the EAPOL-Key Encryption key. This is true in the case of the GTK; however, the pairwise keys are computed independently by the supplicant and the authenticator and are not sent in the key message at all.

In the case of pairwise keys, the Key Data field is used for another purpose. It is used to send a copy of the WPA/RSN Information Element. Information elements in general are described in Chapter 5 and this element in particular is discussed further in Chapter 13. For the moment, just accept that the information element needs to be transferred and that the Key Data field is used for this purpose.

Four-Way Handshake

One of the best ways to understand use of the EAPOL-Key descriptor is to look at a practical example. In the following paragraphs, we follow a four-way handshake.

Message (A): Authenticator → Supplicant

At the starting state, no keys are known so the MIC cannot be computed. The authenticator uses this message only to send its value of ANonce to the supplicant. The contents of message (A) are shown in Table 10.4.

Table 10.4 Message (A) Contents

Descriptor type	254
Key Information	Request, Error: 0
	Secure: 0
	MIC: 0
	Ack: 1
	Install: 0
	Index: 0
	Key type: Pairwise
	Descriptor type: 1
Key Length	64
Replay Counter	<current value>
Key Nonce	ANonce
EAP-Key IV	0
RSC	0
Key Identifier	0
Key MIC	0
Key Data Length	0

- The Error bit is 0 because this is the first message.

- The Secure bit is 0 because the four-way handshake has not completed yet.

- There is no MIC so the MIC bit is 0.

- The authenticator requires the supplicant to send a reply so it sets the ACK bit. If no reply is received after a timeout, the authenticator may resend the message three times before giving up. However, the message should be resent as is, that is, with the same replay field so that, in case the supplicant did receive a previous message, it knows it is a duplicate and not a new message.

- We are not ready to install keys so Install is 0.

- The Index field is not used with pairwise keys.

- The Key Type field indicates "pairwise" and the Descriptor Type field is set to 1.

- The Replay Counter is the value of a counter that is set to 0 when the PMK is first established and is incremented between successive messages.

- The value of ANonce is passed in the Key Nonce field and all the other fields are set to 0. Note that the value of ANonce can't be any old nonce. It has to be selected in a particular way, as described later in this chapter.

- The value of EAP-Key IV is 0 because there is no key data.

- RSC is 0 because the keys are no yet ready for installation.

- Key identifier is reserved and always 0.

Message (A) is sent without any protection. It is not encrypted and there is no MIC. This is the *only* key message that is ever sent without the MIC bit set to 1—a fact that can be exploited by the supplicant, which should discard the message if any of the fixed fields are different from what has been described here. For example, if the supplicant sees the MIC bit as 0 but the Install bit set, it knows there is foul play.

Given that the supplicant checks the expected fields, an attacker is limited to modifying the Replay Counter or the ANonce fields. Changing the Replay Counter can only result in message rejection and so is pointless. Any changes to the ANonce value will be caught in message (B) because the temporal keys computed by the supplicant from the corrupted ANonce value would be invalid. In such a case message (B) would fail the MIC test and be discarded. Therefore, the fact that message (A) is unprotected does not compromise security.

Message (B): Supplicant → Authenticator

After successful delivery of the first message, the supplicant has a copy of ANonce and generates it own value of SNonce. It is then able to compute the transient

Table 10.5 Message (B) Contents

Descriptor type	254
Key Information	Request, Error: 0
	Secure: 0
	MIC: 1
	Ack: 0
	Install: 0
	Index: 0
	Key type: Pairwise
	Descriptor type: 1
Key Length	64
Replay Counter	From rcvd Key Message
Key Nonce	SNonce
EAPOL-Key IV	0
RSC	0
Key Identifier	0
Key MIC	MIC Value
Key Data Length	Length of Key Data
Key Data	Information Element

key. Next, it prepares to send message (B) to the authenticator. This message contains a MIC value and thus proves that the supplicant knows the PMK. The fields for message (B) are shown in Table 10.5.

- The Error field is 0 because there was no MIC value on the previous frame (therefore MIC failure is impossible).
- The Secure field remains 0 until the end of the four-way handshake.
- The MIC field is 1 to indicate that a MIC value has been computed and attached to this message.
- This message is in response to the ACK bit, which was set in message (A). Therefore the ACK bit in this message is clear.
- Install is set to 0 because the keys are not agreed on yet.
- Index is not used.
- Key Type indicates pairwise.
- Descriptor type is 1.

- The Replay Counter in this message should be set to the same value as the counter sent in message (A). This is because it is a response to the ACK bit in message (A). Any other value should be rejected by the authenticator.
- The value of SNonce is sent in the Key Nonce field. This value is needed by the authenticator to compute its copy of the temporal keys.
- The MIC value is placed in the Key MIC position.
- This frame contains unencrypted Key Data. This is the information element that was used to negotiate the security parameters during the association phase. Inclusion of the element here prevents a rogue mobile device from switching security parameters after the initial negotiation. More information about the information element is given in Chapter 13. The data is not encrypted because the IE was sent in the open during association and is not a secret; however, it is protected by the MIC field and cannot therefore be altered.

The fact that the descriptor type field is 1 indicates that the MIC value should be computed using an algorithm called HMAC-MD5, which produces a 16-byte MIC value. The MIC calculation is performed over more the just message (B). It includes all the bytes from the EAPOL protocol version field in the header up to and including the Key Data.

A Note on HMAC-MD5

MD5 is a *Message Digest algorithm* — it takes a message of arbitrary length and produces a 128-bit value called a **message digest**. It doesn't matter how long the input message is, the digest is always 128 bits. Different input messages could produce the same message digest. However, the algorithm is such that you cannot work in reverse: given a 128-bit digest, you cannot compute a message that would produce that value when processed. Therefore publishing the digest gives nothing away about the message. MD5 is documented in RFC 1321.

To apply MD-5 to actual messages for the purpose of a MIC, MD-5 is used with Hash Message Authentication Code. HMAC as defined in RFC 2104.

To compute the MIC, the supplicant needs to use the newly computed temporal keys. In fact this will be the first use of the keys. If the supplicant does not know the correct PMK, it cannot produce a MIC value that will correspond to the expected result. So the MIC in this message achieves two things: It prevents tampering with the message and it proves that the supplicant knows the PMK.

Message (C): Authenticator → Supplicant

When message (B) is received by the authenticator, it is able to extract the value of SNonce because the message is unencrypted. The authenticator then has all the information to compute its copy of the temporal keys. After this is done, the pairwise key distribution is effectively complete. However, the remaining message exchanges, messages (C) and (D), are used to ensure that the keys are put into effect in a synchronized way. Message (C) serves two functions. First, it verifies to the supplicant that the authenticator knows the PMK and is thus a trusted party. Second, it tells the supplicant that the authenticator is ready to install and start using the data encryption keys. The authenticator does not actually install the keys until *after* it has received message (D). Note that if a retransmission of message (C) is needed due to failure to get a response, the retransmission should be a copy of the original (unencrypted) transmission. The format of message (C) is shown in Table 10.6.

The MIC bit is set and a corresponding MIC value added. The ACK bit is set to indicate a response is required. The value of ANonce is included for reference; although this serves no purpose at this point, it can be used as a check to ensure that this is part of the same four-way handshake.

Table 10.6 Message (C) Contents

Descriptor type	254
Key Information	Request, Error: 0
	Secure: 0
	MIC: 1
	Ack: 1
	Install: 0
	Index: 0
	Key type: Pairwise
	Descriptor type: 1
Key Length	64
Replay Counter	<Current Value>
Key Nonce	ANonce
EAPOL-Key IV	0
RSC	Starting Sequence Number
Key Identifier	0
Key MIC	MIC Value
Key Data Length	Length of Key Data
Key Data	Information Element

In this message the RSC is used to inform the mobile device of the starting sequence number the access point intends to use. Normally, this would be 0. The Key Data field is used to send a copy of the IE that the access point used in negotiating security during the association phase.

Assuming no retransmit is required, this is the last unencrypted message sent by the authenticator during the life of these pairwise keys. All subsequent messages are encrypted and protected using the temporal data keys.

Message (D): Supplicant → Authenticator

This final message verifies to the authenticator that the keys are about to be installed. The settings in the message are shown in Table 10.7.

There is nothing surprising or new in the settings for this message, which is similar to message (B) but without the Key Data field. The Secure bit is not set until the four-way handshake has successfully completed and both supplicant and authenticator have installed the keys. This does not happen until message (D) has been received and decoded successfully. Once this has happened, the authenticator is in a position to deliver the group keys. Note that the **Key Sequence Start** field indicates to the authenticator the sequence number of the first frame the supplicant intends to send.

Table 10.7 Message (D) Contents

Descriptor type	254
Key Information	Request, Error: 0
	Secure: 0
	MIC: 1
	Ack: 0
	Install: 1
	Index: 0
	Key type: Pairwise
	Descriptor type: 1
Key Length	64
Replay Counter	From rcvd Key Message
Key Nonce	SNonce
EAPOL-Key IV	0
RSC	Starting Sequence Number
Key Identifier	0
Key MIC	MIC Value
Key Data Length	0

Group Key Handshake

After the complexities of the pairwise key exchange, which had to start off with no security in place and build up step by step, the group key delivery is relatively simple. Basically, there are only two messages. The first sends the key and the second acknowledges that the keys are installed. As explained earlier, there is no key synchronization message because the mobile device is able to store more than one group key at a time and the access point can select the key used on a message-by-message basis. Therefore, as long as the access point knows that a new key has been installed, it can start using it at any time in the future; typically, this is after all the other mobile devices have been updated.

The group key is sent in an EAPOL-key message, which we will call message (α). This has the same format as for pairwise keys. However, an important difference is that the Key Data field is used to send the GTK. The fields for the first group key message are shown in Table 10.8.

Table 10.8 Group Key Update

Descriptor type	254
Key Information	Request, Error: 0
	Secure: 1
	MIC: 1
	Ack: 1
	Install: 1
	Index: nn
	Key type: Group
	Descriptor type: 1
Key Length	32
Replay Counter	<Current Value>
Key Nonce	GNonce
EAPOL-Key IV	IV for encryption of Key Data
RSC	Sequence number of the last encrypted group message
Key Identifier	0
Key MIC	MIC Value
Key Data Length	32
Key Data	<encrypted GTK>

Note that the Secure bit is set because the group key exchange occurs after the pairwise keys are established. The MIC is set (and included) and the ACK bit indicates a reply is required. For the Group Key message the Install bit is set. The Index field is important in the group key message. These two bits indicate which key location should be used to store the new key. For smooth updates, the Key ID index value will not be the value currently in use.

The value of GNonce is included for reference. GNonce is a nonce value selected to derive the GTK from the GMK. The supplicant does not actually need to know this value because the key derivation is done by the access point and not by the mobile device, but it is sent anyway for reference.

Finally, the actual GTK is sent, encrypted with the EAPOL Encryption key that was created as part of the pairwise key handshake. For descriptor type 1, the key is encrypted using RC4 stream cipher[7] after discarding the first 256 bytes of the RC4 cipher stream output. No padding is added so 32 bytes of GTK produces 32 encrypted bytes, which are placed directly into the EAPOL-Key message.

When it is filled out, message (α) is sent to the mobile device, which can decrypt the GTK and install it at the appropriate Key ID index. It then replies with an acknowledge message, message (β), which has the same as for pairwise message (D) except that the Secure bit is set and the Type bit indicates Group.

As a last point, it is expected that the group keys will be updated fairly regularly. For example, they should be updated when a mobile device leaves the network. Also they should be updated if a MIC failure occurs when decoding a multicast. Key updates can occur at any time simply by the access point initiating a group key update frame by sending message (α). However, they can also be requested by a mobile device. In this case the mobile device should send message (β) to the access point with the ACK bit set. This causes the access point to create a new GTK and distribute it to every device (one at a time).

Nonce Selection

The idea of the nonce values is that they are used only once with a given key. The important thing is that this should hold true even when the mobile device or access point is restarted or even if a Wi-Fi LAN adapter card is moved from one laptop to another. The combination of key and MAC address should never use the same nonce value twice. If all equipment had a calendar/clock (and could guarantee it was correct), this problem can be easily solved. For example, the nonce value could be initialized after startup, to the value of Network Time (number of seconds since midnight, Dec 31st, 1899). Providing, on average, you don't need a

---

7. See Chapter 6 on WEP and Chapter 11 on TKIP for more information on RC4.

nonce more than once per second, you will always get a value that has not been used before (unless time starts to run backwards, which seems unlikely).

However, not all systems have a calendar clock and the accuracy can't be guaranteed anyway. Therefore, the nonce is created from a large counter that is initialized to a random value at start up. The idea is that if the counter is large enough, the probability that you will ever reuse the same range of values is so small as to be unimportant. This counter is 256 bits long.

Suppose that an access point starts up and sets its 256-bit nonce counter to a perfectly random value. Then suppose that the access point generates ten thousand nonces before the next restart (incrementing the counter each time). New nonces are needed only when the group keys are refreshed and when a mobile device joins the network. Given the size of the nonce counter, the probability that the access point will reinitialize the counter to one of the 10,000 values it has just used is an embarrassingly low 1 in 10^{-70}—probably about the same probability that time *will* start to run backwards. There is a problem, however, because this analysis relies on generation of a perfectly random number, which can also be difficult to do.

Because of the difficulty of generating perfect random numbers, RSN and WPA specify a way to generate the starting value for the nonce counter by using a pseudorandom number generator. The formula is written using the function PRF-256. This is the random number generator function that is also used for key derivation. Operation of this function is described in the following section on key computation. Here is the formula for computing the start value of the nonce counter:

Starting nonce = PRF-256(Random Number, "Init Counter", MAC || Time)

where:

- Random Number is the best random number the equipment can make.
- "Init Counter" is a literal string.
- MAC || Time is the MAC address of the device concatenated with the best guess at Network Time (if known).

If an attacker is going to base an attack on finding duplicate nonce values, he is going to have to wait a long time!

Computing the Temporal Keys

Earlier we described how the temporal keys are generated from the master keys, but we were not specific about how this is accomplished. Obviously the derivation must be done in a very specific way; any ambiguity might result in two different vendors' products deriving keys that don't match and hence failing to work together. We casually mentioned earlier that the key information needed to be expanded—getting more bits that we started with. For example, although the PMK is 256 bits, it has to be expanded into 512 bits before being divided up into the four temporal keys.

This section explains how the key generation and computation is done. In practice, both generation and expansion occur during the same process. Key expansion seems counterintuitive because it implies that additional bits are generated from "thin air." However, the object is not to increase the size of the base key (in other words, the key entropy), but to derive several keys, all of which appear unrelated to an outside observer. For example, in the case of the four pairwise temporal keys, if an attacker knows one of the four temporal keys, it should be impossible to derive any of the others. It doesn't matter how many bits you expand the master key into, the strength against brute force attacks remains the same.

The approach to key expansion is to use a pseudorandom number generator (PRNG) and keep generating random bytes until you have enough for your key expansion. The starting condition or **seed** of the PRNG is based on the known information such as your master keys. Diagrammatically, this relationship is shown in Figure 10.9, which is really an expanded version of Figure 10.2, the key computation block. An important point is that, given the same seed, the PRNG always produces the same "random" output stream so two independent devices can generate the same set of keys by starting with the same seed value.

The PRNG function is used in several places in RSN and WPA. For example, it was used to generate the starting nonce; it is used to expand the pairwise keys and also to generate the GTK. This would create a potential problem if the same PRNG were to be used in each of these different cases. If you want a random stream of data for two different purposes in a security system, you must be absolutely sure that they will not both use an identical pseudorandom stream. On the other hand, we would like to use a single PRNG function for implementation

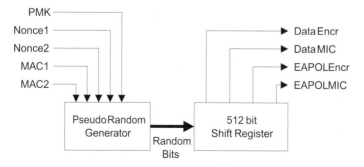

Figure 10.9   Temporal Key Computation

efficiency, so what is needed is a PRNG that is guaranteed to provide a different stream for different uses even when the seed information appears the same.

To achieve this, RSN and WPA define a set of pseudorandom functions, each incorporating a different text string into the input. There are different functions, each designed to produce a certain number of bits. These are referred to as PRF-n, where n is the number of bits required. The defined choices are:

- PRF-128
- PRF-256
- PRF-384
- PRF-512

Each function takes three parameters and produces the desired number of random bits. The three parameters are:

1. A secret key (K)
2. A text string specific to the application (e.g., nonce generation versus pairwise key expansion)
3. Some data specific to each case, such as nonces or MAC addresses

The notation used for these functions is: PRF-n(K, A, B). So, for example, when we specify that the starting value for the nonce is:

Starting nonce = PRF-256(Random Number, "Init Counter", MAC || Time)

it means that the PRF-256 function is invoked with:

K = Random number
A = The text string "Init Counter"
B = A sequence of bytes formed by the MAC address followed by a number representing time

In a similar way, the computation of the pairwise temporal keys is written:

PRF-512(PMK, "Pairwise key expansion", MAC1||MAC2||Nonce1||Nonce2)

Here MAC1 and MAC2 are the MAC addresses of the two devices where MAC1 is the smaller (numerically) and MAC2 is the larger of the two addresses. Similarly, Nonce1 is the smallest value between ANonce and SNonce, while Nonce2 is the largest of the two values.

The group temporal keys are derived as follows:

PRF-256(GMK, "Group key expansion", MAC||GNonce)

Here, MAC is the MAC address of the authenticator, that is, the access point for infrastructure networks.

We see how all the various keys can be derived by using PRF-n, so how is the PRF-n implemented? Obviously, this has to be carefully specified if we hope to have interoperability.

All the variants of PRF are implemented using the same algorithm based on HMAC-SHA-1.[8] We have seen HMAC-MD5 before; it was used to produce the MIC for EAPOL-Key messages. But we are not generating a MIC here; we want a random number generator. Like HMAC-MD5, HMAC-SHA-1 is also a hashing algorithm that can be used to generate MIC values. It is approved by the US National Institute for Science and Technology (NIST; www.nist.gov), which publishes the details of the algorithm. The method of computation is different from MD5, but the effect is the same. They both take in a stream of data and produce a message digest of fixed length. HMAC-MD5 produces 16 bytes and HMAC-SHA-1 produces 20 bytes. The message digest is quite unpredictable (except by using the algorithm) and tells you nothing about the contents of the message that was "digested." Even if you changed one single bit in input message, an entirely new digest would be produced with no apparent connection to the previous value. There's a clue to how we can make a hashing algorithm into a pseudorandom number generator.

We take a message and hash it using HMAC-SHA-1 to get a 160-bit (20-byte) result. Now change one bit in the input message and produce another 160 bits. We already know that this 160 bits appears unrelated to the first one, so if we put them together, we get 320 bits of apparently random data. By repeating this process, we can generate a pseudorandom stream of almost any number of bits. This is how HMAC-SHA-1 is used to implement the PRF-n functions. Here are the details:

1. Start with the function **PRF-n (K, A, B)** where n can be 128, 256, 384, or 512.

2. Initialize a single byte counter variable i to 0.

3. Create a block of data by concatenating the following:
   - A (the application-specific text)
   - 0 (a single 0 byte)

---

8. SHA stands for secure hash algorithm.

- B (the special data)
- i (the counter, a single byte value)

  This is written: A | 0 | B | i

4. Compute the hash of this block of data using key K:

   $r = HMAC\text{-}SHA\text{-}1(K, A \,|\, 0 \,|\, B \,|\, i)$

5. Store the value of r for later in a register called R.

6. Now repeat this calculation as many times as needed to generate the needed number of random bits (because 160 are generated each time, you may get more than you need, whereupon the extra bits are discarded). Before each iteration, increment the counter i by one and after each iteration appending the result bits r to the register R.

After the required number of iterations, you have your random stream of bytes.

Summary

One of the weaknesses of WEP was that it had a very simple concept of keys. The key was simply a data string that was loaded into both the access point and the wireless device. The key was used directly in authentication and encryption and was not changed except by manual reconfiguration. Such usage makes the keys extremely vulnerable to attack. This chapter has shown how RSN and WPA have a much more complicated system that ensures the keys used in the actual cryptographic operations never expose the master secret held between the client and the authentication server. The system also ensures that fresh keys are established every time a session is started.

A range of keys is used, derived from a pairwise master key. The PMK may itself be generated from the upper-layer authentication method in use. Two problems are discussed and solutions shown in this chapter. The first is how to derive keys in a way that ensures they are unpredictable and different each time they are generated. The second is how, safely, to ensure that all trusted parties generate the same keys while preventing an attacker joining in the key generation process or subverting it in any way.

These problems have been solved in WPA and RSN and this chapter describes how the solutions work. Once the keys have been safely generated, they must be used within a good security cipher. The next two chapters look at the choices for security protocol: TKIP and CCMP.

Chapter 11

TKIP

Chapter 11 reviews one of the new security protocols that was developed specifically for use with existing Wi-Fi equipment. We will see that the TKIP security protocol provides a huge improvement over WEP and yet is able to operate on the same type of hardware and can even be applied to many older Wi-Fi systems through firmware upgrades. We start off with an overview of what TKIP is intended to accomplish and then work through each of the functions of TKIP in detail.

What Is TKIP and Why Was It Created?

TKIP stands for Temporal Key Integrity Protocol, but that's not important right now (or probably ever). TKIP exists for one reason: *to allow WEP systems to be upgraded to be secure*. This is the reason TKIP was created and this requirement guided the design throughout the standardization process. TKIP has now been adopted as part of the WPA certification and also is included as part of RSN in IEEE 802.11i. In 2001, when WEP was blown apart, there were millions of installed Wi-Fi systems, all suddenly without a viable link layer security solution. Originally, the new security measures of the IEEE 802.11i standard were expected to come into effect gradually, starting with applications where very high security was needed. However, when WEP was broken, in an instant, all these millions of systems were rendered insecure. A solution was needed that would allow them to be upgraded and become secure again.

The requirement that TKIP should run on legacy hardware (that is, hardware already installed using WEP) was a severe restriction on the approach to be taken. In the case of AES (see Chapter 12), the solution was designed from scratch; the designers could focus on the best solution possible within the general constraints that it should be practical and cost-effective to implement. In some ways, this ability to start from scratch mode made the AES approach a simpler problem to solve. But TKIP had the requirement to be secure *and* available as an upgrade to WEP systems.

To help understand why upgrading existing WEP systems is a significant problem, we need to take a look at the internals of Wi-Fi LAN systems and how they are built. We start with a Wi-Fi adapter card. There are not too many manufacturers of silicon chips for Wi-Fi LAN. In fact, the majority of existing WEP-based Wi-Fi LAN systems are based on the chips of only two or three companies. There are essentially four parts to a Wi-Fi LAN card:

- Radio Frequency (RF) section
- Modem section
- MAC (Medium Access Control) section
- Host interface to connect to your computer—PC card or USB, for example

Roughly speaking, the RF section deals with receiving and transmitting through the antenna; the modem deals with extracting data from the received signals; and the MAC deals with protocol issues, including WEP encryption. The four components are shown in Figure 11.1.

The RF section requires very special design and the use of exotic semiconductor materials. However, the remaining parts can be implemented in standard run-of-the-mill integrated circuit (IC) technology. The key to reducing cost in electronics is to cram everything you can into a minimum number of integrated circuits and then produce a huge quantity of them. Therefore, successive generations of Wi-Fi LAN designs used fewer and fewer components. In the latest systems, Host Interface, MAC, and modem blocks are combined into a single IC. Eventually, we might expect that the RF section will also be included, to produce a single IC solution.

The part we want to look at is the MAC section of the IC. This is the part that implements most of the IEEE 802.11 protocol. On one side (the Host Interface side), it receives, from the computer, packets of data for transmission and instructions for activities such as "look for a new AP" or "issue a request connection to that AP." It also delivers *to* the computer packets of data that have been received. On the other side (by the modem), it delivers a stream of bits containing all the various IEEE 802.11 control and data frames, including special functions like sleep

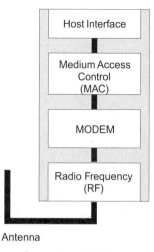

To Computer

Figure 11.1   Components of a Wi-Fi LAN Adapter

modes, data acknowledgment, and retransmission of lost data. Importantly (for us), it also encrypts and decrypts the data frames.

Because the MAC operations are rather complex, all the implementations are built around a small microprocessor embedded inside the IC. The microprocessor is programmed to handle all the formatting and timing operations to control the protocol. Typically, however, this processor is not very powerful and certain operations are just too fast for it to handle. Therefore, the MAC is implemented as a combination of firmware and hardware, as shown in Figure 11.2.

Figure 11.2 shows a block called Hardware Assist. If you want to go to the store for a loaf of bread, you can walk. But if you want to go at 70 mph, you need hardware assistance (in other words, your automobile). So it is with the MAC.

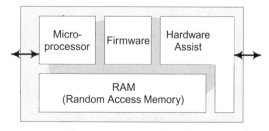

Figure 11.2   Inside the MAC Chip

The small microprocessors in the Wi-Fi cards shipped from 1997 to 2003 need help to go at 11Mbps, and that comes in the form of custom hardware in the IC.

If all the MAC functions were done only by the microprocessor, it would be possible to change the security system just by downloading new firmware. However, because encryption and decryption requires a fair bit of computation, the implementation of WEP almost always depends on the hardware assist functions and, of course, these functions cannot be changed after manufacture.

You can see now why TKIP is necessary. The hardware assist functions in these earlier systems cannot support AES–CCMP. They can support only RC4 (WEP). Therefore, the designers set out to find a way to implement real security using the existing RC4 implementation, and in a way that can be done through firmware upgrades. This is TKIP.

TKIP Overview

WEP has some serious shortcomings, as listed in Table 11.1.

TKIP introduces a set of measures that address each one of these weaknesses. In some ways, it's like the way in which the Hubble telescope problem was repaired. The Hubble telescope is a huge optical telescope placed in space and orbiting the earth. Because it is in orbit, where there is just a clear vacuum to look through and no gravity to distort the lenses, the results were expected to be spectacular. Excitement turned to despair as the telescope was tested and it was found that the main mirror had been manufactured with a defect and was not perfectly shaped. The solution was not to replace the main mirror, which was not possible in space; it was to add some corrective lenses in the light path to the optical receiver after the main mirror.

TKIP solves the problems of WEP in a similar way. It cannot change the major items such as the way RC4 is implemented in hardware, but it can add a series of corrective tools around the existing hardware. The changes applied to WEP to

Table 11.1 Weaknesses of WEP

1	The IV value is too short and not protected from reuse.
2	The way keys are constructed from the IV makes it susceptible to weak key attacks (FMS attack).
3	There is no effective detection of message tampering (message integrity).
4	It directly uses the master key and has no built-in provision to update the keys.
5	There is no protection against message replay.

IVs and Nonces

The terms "IV" and "nonce" can be confused because they seem to refer to the same concept. The initialization vector is a term for data that is introduced into the cryptographic process to provide liveness. Often a nonce value is used for the IV value so the terms IV and nonce appear to refer to the same thing. However, the IV could be generated by other means, such as a random number rather than a true nonce. In WEP, the method for generating the IV was unspecified, which was a significant problem.

Table 11.2 Changes from WEP to TKIP

Purpose	Change	Weakness Addressed
Message Integrity	Add a message integrity protocol to prevent tampering that can be implemented in software on a low-power microprocessor.	(3)
IV selection and use	Change the rules for how IV values are selected and reuse the IV as a replay counter.	(1) (3)
Per-Packet Key Mixing	Change the encryption key for every frame.	(1)(2)(4)
IV Size	Increase the size of the IV to avoid ever reusing the same IV.	(1)(4)
Key Management	Add a mechanism to distribute and change the broadcast keys (see Chapter 10).	(4)

make TKIP are summarized in Table 11.2. The numbers in parentheses indicate which weaknesses in Table 11.1 are addressed by each change.

Message Integrity

Message integrity is an essential part of security. If an attacker is able to modify a message, there are many ways in which your system can be compromised. WEP had a method for detecting modification called the integrity check value (ICV), but the ICV offers no real protection at all. The ICV is not considered part of TKIP security (although its value is still checked).

If you want to detect tampering, one simple method would be to add together all the bytes in the message together to create a "checksum" value and then send

The standard term used in security for the check value is message authentication code (MAC). Unfortunately MAC is already used in LAN standards to mean medium access control. To avoid confusion, the term **MIC** is used in the 802.11 standard.

this along with the message. The receiving party can perform the same computation and verify that it gets the same result. If a bit changes, the sum won't get the same result.

Such a simple approach is of no use for security because the attacker can simply recompute the checksum to match any changes he makes to the message. However, the general idea is similar: Combine together all the bytes in the message to produce a check value called the MIC (message integrity code) and then send the MIC along with the message. The MIC is computed using a special non-reversible process and combining a secret key. As a result, an attacker cannot recompute the MIC value unless he knows the secret key. Only the intended receiver can recompute and check the result.

There are several well-known secure methods for computing the MIC. Such methods have been well tried and tested in other protocols and security applications. However, for TKIP there was a problem. All the well-known methods require introduction of a new cryptographic algorithm or require computations using fast multiply operations. The ones that use multiply operations were considered, but they generally need at least one multiply operation for each group of four bytes. That would mean, for a typical 1514-byte data packet, at least 379 multiply operations. The microprocessor inside the MAC chip of most Wi-Fi cards is not very powerful; typically, it doesn't have any sort of fast multiplication hardware. In a small microprocessor a 32-bit multiply might take 50μs to complete. That would mean that it would take nearly 20ms to compute the MIC, reducing the data throughput from 11Mbps down to less than 1Mbps.

One proposal was to move the computation of the MIC up to the software driver level. After all, if you are using a laptop with a modern PC processor, such computations can be done in almost no time. But what about the poor old access point? Most access points do not have such a high-power processor and are already hard pressed to keep up with a multitude of connected stations.

What was needed was a method that was as secure as the well-known approaches but that could be done without either multiplication or new cryptographic algorithms. This was a tough goal. It was like saying, "I want a car as fast as a Porsche but with a 500cc engine"—not practical. However, a good compromise solution came from cryptographer Niels Ferguson using a method that he called Michael. Michael is a method of computing the MIC that uses no multiplications, just shift and add operations, and is limited to a fairly short checkword. Michael can be implemented on existing access points without ruining their performance. However, the cost of the simplicity is that Michael is vulnerable to brute force attacks during which an attacker is able to make many attacks rapidly one after the other. Michael makes up for this vulnerability by introducing the concept of **countermeasures**.

The concept of countermeasures is straightforward: Have a reliable method to detect when an attack is being made and take action to slam the door in the attacker's face. The simplest countermeasure is just to shut the whole network down when an attack is detected, thus preventing the attacker from making repeated attempts.

We will look at the details of Michael later; but for now, it is enough to know that the method allows the computation of a MIC value that is added to the message prior to encryption and checked by the receiver after decryption. This value provides the message integrity missing in WEP.

Michael operates on MSDUs; the computation to produce the MIC is done on the MSDU rather than on each MPDU. This has two advantages. First, for the

Technical Note: MSDUs Versus MPDUs

In the standard, and in this book, you will see references to MSDUs and MPDUs. To understand TKIP and AES–CCMP, you must understand the difference between the two. Both refer to a single packet of data, with a destination and source address (and potentially other stuff). The MSDU is the packet of data going between the host computer's software and the wireless LAN MAC. MPDUs are packets of data going between the MAC and the antenna. For transmissions, MSDUs are sent by the operating system (OS) to the MAC layer and are converted to MPDUs ready to be sent over the radio. For receptions, MPDUs arrive via the antenna and are converted to MSDUs prior to being delivered to the OS.

There is one very important point to mention: One MSDU can be broken into multiple parts to produce several MPDUs in a process called fragmentation. The multiple MPDUs are then reassembled into a single MSDU at the other end. This is done so that, if a transmission is lost due to noise, only the MPDU needs be resent, rather than the whole MSDU.

When talking about encryption, you must be clear whether you are talking about MSDU or MPDU. To help remember which is which, think of "S" as squadron and "P" as plane—it takes a group of planes to make a squadron. These acronyms stand for MAC Service Data Unit and MAC Protocol Data Unit.

mobile device, it allows the implementer to perform the computation in the device driver running on the host computer prior to forwarding the MSDU to the Wi-Fi LAN adapter card. Second, it reduces the overhead because it is not necessary to add a MIC value to every fragment (MPDU) of the message. By contrast, TKIP *encryption* is done at the MPDU level.

Michael requires its own secret key, which must be different from the secret key used for encryption. Creating such a key is easily accomplished when you are generating temporal keys from a master key, as described in Chapter 10.

IV Selection and Use

Chapter 6 explained the purpose of the IV (initialization vector) and how it is prepended to the secret key to generate the encryption key for each packet. We also noted that there are three fundamental weaknesses with the way IVs are used in WEP:

- The IV is too short so IV values are reused regularly in a busy network.
- The IV is not specific to the station so the same IV can be used with the same secret key on multiple wireless devices.
- The way the IV is prepended to the key makes it susceptible to Fluhrer-Mantin-Shamir attack (FMS) attack (this is discussed in more detail later).

For a further explanation of why IV reuse is a problem, see Chapter 6.

In the WEP standard, there were no requirements to avoid IV reuse. In fact, it was not mandatory to change the value of IV at all! Many vendors picked a random value for IV for each packet, which seems intuitively to be a good idea. However, at the end of the day, if you want to avoid IV reuse for the longest time possible, the simple approach is to start with a value of one and count up by one for each packet. In TKIP, this behavior has been mandated as part of the standard.

Incrementing the IV delays IV reuse, but it doesn't get you out of the problem of "too short" IV. Even counting up, all the values will be used after about 16 million frames, which happens surprisingly fast in a busy network. Like the odometer on a car, when a binary counter reaches its maximum value, the next increment returns it all to 0—this is called rollover. TKIP introduces several new rules for using the IV. Essentially, there are three differences in how IVs are used compared to WEP:

- IV size is increased from 24 bits to 48 bits.
- IV has a secondary role as a sequence counter to avoid replay attacks.
- IV is constructed to avoid certain "weak keys."

IV Length

The WEP IV, at 24 bits, allowed only 16,777,216 values before a duplicate IV would be used. This is unacceptable in practice when this number of frames could be sent in a few hours. Chapter 6 discussed the FMS attack, the most effective attack against WEP, and showed how WEP is very susceptible because its IV appears first in the frame and advertises when a *weak key* is being used. Some vendors try to reduce the potency of this attack by skipping IV values that would produce weak keys. However, this strategy just reduces the number of possible IV values still further, making one problem better but another one worse!

In designing TKIP, the security experts recommended that the IV *must* be increased in size to provide a robust solution. There was some debate about how to do this; but in the end, the IEEE 802.11 task group (i) decided to insert 32 extra bits in between the existing WEP IV and the start of the encrypted data. This was a contentious decision because not all vendors can upgrade their legacy systems to meet this requirement. However, most can.

Potentially, the extra 32 bits added to the original 24 gives a new IV of 56 bits; however, in practice only 48 bits is used because 1 byte must be "thrown away" to avoid weak keys. The advantages of going to a 48-bit IV are startling. Suppose you have a device sending 10,000 packets per second. This is feasible using 64-byte packets at 11Mbps. for example. The 24-bit IV would roll over in less than half and hour, while the 48-bit IV would not roll over for over 900 hundred years! Moving to a 48-bit IV effectively eliminates the IV rollover problem, although you still have to be careful to avoid two devices separately using the same IV value with the same key.

Increasing the IV length sounds straightforward, but it introduces some real problems for practical implementation. Remember that the original WEP IV is joined on the front of the secret key to create the RC4 encryption key. Thus, a 40-bit[1] secret key is joined to the 24-bit IV to produce a 64-bit RC4 key. The hardware in legacy systems assumes this type of key structure and can't be upgraded to suddenly deal with a 88-bit RC4 key created by joining the new 48-bit IV to the old 40-bit secret key. In TKIP this problem is solved in an interesting way. Instead of simply forming a new RC4 key by joining the secret key and the IV, the IV is split into two pieces. The first 16 bits of the new IV are padded out to 24 bits in a way that avoids known weak keys. This 24-bit value is used in the same way as for WEP systems. However, rather than joining this value to the ordinary secret key, a new *mixed key* is generated by merging together the secret key and the remaining 32 bits of the IV (and some other stuff, too). The way in which the long IV is

---

1. Or 104 bits when using the Wi-Fi 128-bit WEP mode.

incorporated into the key, called per-packet key mixing, is described in more detail later in this chapter and is shown in Figure 11.3. The important thing to note here is that this approach allows us to achieve two objectives:

- The value of the key used for RC4 encryption is different for every IV value.
- The structure of the RC4 key is a 24-bit "old IV" field and a 104-bit secret key field.

These objectives have been achieved with the advantage of a 48-bit IV value.

IV as a Sequence Counter—the TSC

WEP had no protection against replay attack. An enemy could record a valid packet and play it back again later, in the expectation that, if it decrypted correctly the first time, it probably would do so again. In a replay attack, the enemy doesn't attempt to decode your messages, but she does try to guess what you are doing. In an extreme example, by recording messages while you delete a file and replaying them later, she could cause a file of the same name to be deleted without ever breaking the encryption. Replay prevention is designed to block old messages used in this way. TKIP has a mechanism to enforce this called the TKIP sequence counter (TSC).

In reality, the TSC and the IV value are the same thing. This value always starts with 0 and increments by 1 for each packet sent. Because the IV is guaranteed not to repeat for a given key, we can prevent reply by ignoring any messages with a TSC that we have already received. These rules mean that it is not possible to mount a *replay* attack by recording earlier messages and sending them again.

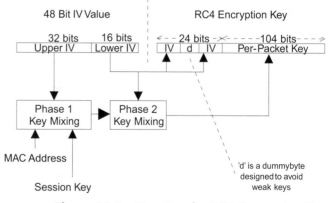

Figure 11.3 Creating the RC4 Encryption Key

The simplest way to prevent replay attacks is to throw out any received messages in which the TSC has not increased by 1 compared to the last message. However, there are a number of reasons why this simple approach would not work in practice. First, it is possible for frames to be lost in transmission due to interference and noise. If a frame with TSC 1234 is received and then the next frame (1235) is lost, the subsequent arriving frame would have a TSC of 1236, a value that is 2 greater than the last TSC seen. Because of the lost frame, all subsequent frames would get rejected on the basis that the TSC did not increase by 1.

So let's revise the rule: *throw out any messages that have a TSC less than or equal to the last message*. But what about retransmission? According to the standard, frames must be acknowledged by the receiver with a short ACK message. If they are not acknowledged, the message should be retransmitted with a bit set to indicate that it is a duplicate. Being a repeat message, these will have the same TSC as the original attempt. In practice, this works okay because only one valid copy is needed at the receiving end so it is no problem to throw out the duplicates when checking the TSC at the receiver. The possibility of retransmissions illustrates that duplicate TSCs should not always be treated as evidence of an attack.

A more difficult problem arises due to a new concept called **burst-ack**. In the original IEEE 802.11 standard, each data frame sent must be acknowledged separately. While this requirement is effective, it is somewhat inefficient because the transmitter has to keep stopping and waiting for the ACK message to be received before proceeding. The idea of burst-ack is to send up to 16 frames in quick succession and then allow the receiver to acknowledge all 16 in one message. If some of the messages were not received successfully, the receiver can specify which ones need to be resent. Burst-ack has not yet been added to the standard, but it is likely to be included in the future.

Can you see the problem from the perspective of the TSC? Suppose 16 frames are sent, each with a TSC greater than the last, and the receiver fails to get the first one. It then requests that the first frame be resent, which would happen *with its original TSC value*. This value would be 15 less than the last frame received and would thus be rejected, according to the rule of "TSC must be greater."

To accommodate this burst-ack, TKIP uses the concept of a **replay window**. The receiver keeps track of the highest TSC received and also the last 16 TSC values received. When a new frame is received, it categorizes the frame as one of three types:

- ACCEPT: TSC is larger than the largest seen so far.
- REJECT: TSC is less than the value of the largest—16.
- WINDOW: TSC is less than the largest, but more than the lower limit (largest—16).

For the WINDOW category, it checks to see whether a frame with that TSC has been received before. If so, it rejects it. The receiver must keep a record of the last 16 TSC values and check them off as they are received.

This set of rules is more complicated than the simple test we started with, but it effectively prevents replay attacks while allowing the protocol to run efficiently.

Countering the FMS Attack

The most devastating attack against WEP was described in a paper by Scott Fluhrer, Itsik Mantin, and Adi Shamirand and is usually referred to as the FMS attack. This weakness allows script tools to deduce the secret key by monitoring the link. Let's take a (very) quick look at the attack.

The RC4 cipher generates a pseudorandom stream of bytes that can be combined with the data to be encrypted so the whole stream of data looks like random noise. To generate the random sequence, RC4 uses a 256-byte array of values that is reorganized into a different pattern between each byte of random output. The 256-byte array is initialized using the secret encryption key.

Certain key values, called weak keys, create a situation in which the first few bytes of pseudorandom output are not all that random. In other words, if a weak key were being used, there would be a higher probability of certain values coming out in the first few bytes. This fact is exploitable: If you know a weak key is being used, you can work backwards to guess the entire encryption key value just by looking at the first few bytes from a collection of packets. WEP has this particular weakness because it uses the IV value as the first bytes of the key, and the IV value is visible to everyone. As a result, a weak key will eventually be used, thereby giving an enemy the basis for an attack.

Ron Rivest, the designer of RC4, recommended a simple solution to this problem. You simply generate, and throw away, 256 bytes of the random stream before you start encrypting. This approach denies the attacker a chance to get hold of the dangerous first few bytes and ensures that the whole 256-byte array is fully churned up and no longer contains any accessible key information. Well, this would be a simple answer except that, for most of the Wi-Fi cards shipped with WEP, the hardware assist in the MAC chip does not support this solution. It is programmed to start using the first random bytes as soon as they are ready.

Given this severe known weakness, and denied the opportunity to resolve it in the recommended way, the designers of TKIP decided on a two-pronged defense:

- Try to avoid weak keys.
- Try to further obscure the secret key.

The FMS attack depends on the ability of the attacker to collect multiple samples of frames with weak keys. Only about 60 frames are needed before the first bits of information emerge and complete decoding of the key can occur after a few million packets. So how to defeat the attack? The approach adopted in TKIP is to change the secret key with every packet.[2] If you take this approach, the attacker can never get enough samples to attack any given key. This sounds impractical, but in the next section you will see how you can make this change even on older adapter cards.

Another defense against FMS attack is to avoid using weak keys at all. The problem is that no one knows for sure what all the weak keys are. Cryptographers can say that a certain type of key is weak—but they can't say that all the others are strong. However, the following section on key mixing shows that two bits in the IV are always fixed to a specific value to avoid a well-known class of weak keys.

Some vendors have modified their WEP implementations to avoid IVs that produce weak keys. However, there is another problem with this approach. We already know that there are not enough IV values available when the IV is 24 bits long. If we now reduce the IV space still further, we reduce one problem but make another one worse! This problem is removed in TKIP simply by doubling the length of the IV.

This section focuses on the changes to the use of the IV in TKIP. There are three significant changes: The length is increased to 48 bits, the IV doubles up as a sequence counter (the TSC), and the IV is combined with the secret key in a more complicated way than WEP. The last feature achieves two results: It enables the 48-bit IV to be incorporated without changing the implementation hardware and it avoids the use of a known class of weak keys. The changes to the IV provide a significant amount of extra security over WEP.

Per-Packet Key Mixing

The previous section explains that the basis of an FMS attack is an enemy trying to guess the key based on observing the first few bytes of the encrypted data. The attacker needs to analyze quite a few frames to make a reasonable guess. To defeat this attack (in its current known form), the encryption key is changed for every packet sent. After all, an enemy can't attack the key if it keeps changing.

This issue of "keys" is a little confusing. In the WEP scenario, it was simple. There was a WEP key and it was used for everything. If it was compromised, then all was lost. Such a simple approach is not good enough for TKIP, so there are multiple levels of keys derived from a single master key. Session keys are derived from the master key. These keys are then split into pieces for various uses, one of

---

2. With WEP the encryption key did change with each packet because it contained the IV. However, the *secret* part of the key (excluding the IV) was constant.

which is encryption (for more detail, see Chapter 10). What per-packet key mixing does is to further derive a key specifically for each and every packet sent. In other words, at the level of RC4, every packet uses a different, and apparently unrelated, key. The session keys and master key do not, of course, change every packet! In addition to making it harder to mount attacks, the generation of a key per packet allows the extended-length IV value to be incorporated.

The process of key derivation involves mixing together various bits of information in a hash function. The result produced bears no obvious relationship to the values you start with; however, if both ends of a link start off with the same information and use the same hash method, they will produce the same result—in other words, matching keys.

The problem is that the computation to derive the key can be processing intensive. There is not a lot of computing power in the MAC chip of most WEP-based Wi-Fi cards. So, on the face of it, deriving a new key for every packet might seem infeasible. But there was another trick up the sleeve of Doug Whiting and Russ Housley, the inventors of the key-mixing scheme. The calculation was divided into two phases. Phase 1 involves all the data that is relatively static, such as the secret session key, the high order 32 bits of the IV, and the MAC address. Phase 2 is a quicker computation and includes the only item that changes every packet—the low order 16 bits of the IV. Even in this case, the next IV value is known so the processor can go off and compute one or more mixed keys in advance, anticipating that a frame will arrive shortly and need decrypting.

We briefly mentioned that the MAC address is included in the computation of the mixed key. There is an excellent reason for this inclusion. Two devices are communicating using a shared session key, which means that the same session is used for messages in both directions. A uses the same session key to send messages to B as B does when sending to A. But if both A and B start with an IV of 0 and then increment the IV by 1 for each packet sent, you immediately get IV collisions. They both are using the same IV value with the same key. One way to avoid this problem is for A to use only even IV values and B to use only odd values, for example. However, this further reduces our IV number space and doesn't help for broadcasts and multicasts.

We do know that for A and B to work in the LAN, they must have different MAC addresses. So by mixing the MAC address into the per-packet key, we guarantee that even if both devices use the same IV and the same session key, the mixed key used by A in encrypting the packet will be different from that used by B. Problem solved.

The process of combining the MAC address session key and IV is shown in Figure 11.3. Notice how the lower bits of the IV are only incorporated into the phase 2 computation so the phase 1 computation only needs to be redone every 2^{16} (that is, 65,536) packets. Only 16 bits of the new, long IV go into the old WEP IV position. The middle byte of the old IV d is computed by copying the first byte and setting certain bits to fixed values to avoid creating a class of weak keys.

Details of the mixing algorithm for the two phases of the key mixing are given later. However, at this point we have seen the essentials of all the mechanisms that have been added to TKIP to make it both secure and compatible with old WEP systems.

All the problems with WEP have been solved in TKIP. The list of weaknesses is completely covered. The solutions used allow backwards implementation on WEP hardware—an example of excellent engineering: not just finding a good solution, but finding one within severe and sometimes perverse constraints. The following section revisits the concepts described so far in this chapter and looks at the details at implementation issues.

TKIP Implementation Details

This section gets into the details of how the TKIP algorithm is implemented. This may be of interest only if you yourself are a designer. If you don't need to know these details but still want to read on, we admire your dedication!

The first assumption we make is that master keys have been distributed and session keys derived on both sides of the communications link. The master keys could have been obtained using an upper layer authentication method based on EAP, or preshared master keys could be in use. The latter case is analogous to the WEP approach, in which keys are distributed out of band and programmed, or simply typed, into the devices. This approach could be used for smaller networks or ad-hoc mode (IBSS) operation.

Chapter 10 describes the way in which the keys are derived. As noted in that chapter, three types of key are derived for TKIP:

- Key to protect the EAPOL-Key exchange messages
- Pairwise key to be used for actual message protection using TKIP
- Group key to protect broadcasts using TKIP

It is the second two types of key information that we are interested in here. From the pairwise key information are derived temporal keys:

- Temporal Encryption key (128 bit): This is used as an input to the key mixing stage prior to actual RC4 encryption.

- Temporal Authenticator TX MIC key: This is used with the Michael authentication method to create the MIC on frames transmitted by the authenticator (access point in ESS network).
- Temporal Authenticator RX MIC key: This is used with Michael to create the MIC on frames transmitted by the supplicant (typically the mobile device).

For the group keys, only the first two types of key need be derived because broadcasts (and multicasts) are sent out only by the authenticator and never by the supplicant.

TKIP's task is to provide a security service for validating the integrity of received data and to obscure transmitted data beyond recognition. To accomplish this, TKIP employs a set of tools:

- IV generation and checking
- MIC generation and checking
- Encryption and decryption

For the transmit side, the position of these components relative to other MAC activities is shown in Figure 11.4. The four processes of TKIP are shown as follows:

- Michael
- Key derivation
- IV/TSC
- RC4

Note that the integrity check value is computed over, and appended to, the MSDU prior to fragmentation. As a result, the check value bytes are present only in the last MPDU and are within the encrypted payload. The original (WEP) checkword, the ICV, is still computed and appended to each MPDU, although it is not included as part of TKIP packet integrity checking.

Because the MIC is computed at the MSDU level, it is not possible to include the IV value in the MIC computation for two reasons. First, because the MSDU might be fragmented, there might be multiple values of IV used to send the fragments of the MSDU, so which value of IV would you choose? Second, the value for the IV must not be selected until after the fragment is removed from the transmission queues. In future to support multimedia, IEEE 802.11e could have up to eight priority queues for outbound frames and the order in which fragments are selected for transmission depends on many factors related to priority and real-time constraints. Therefore, MSDUs of higher priority can overtake a previous MSDU

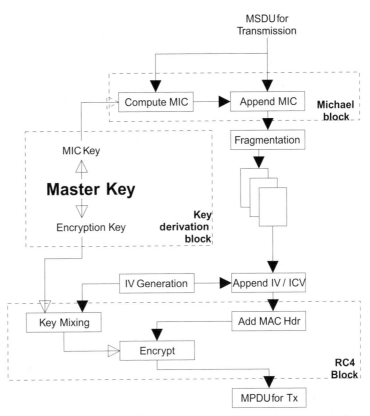

Figure 11.4 TKIP Role in Transmission

or even interrupt it between fragments. In TKIP, we have only one IV counter for the whole link (and not one per queue), and so the assignment of the IV value has to wait until the last moment, when a fragment is selected for transmission. As a result, the value cannot be known when the MIC is calculated

Computing the MIC at the MSDU level, and not protecting the IV, allows an attacker to block a station by replaying old frames with a new IV value. The problem arises because the IV doubles up as the TKIP sequence counter (TSC) used to avoid replay attacks. Such forged frames will, of course, fail to decrypt correctly and be discarded. They do not threaten the integrity of the protocol. However, the effect is to make subsequent valid frames look like a replay attack. When a valid frame arrives, it might be rejected because the TSC value has been "used up" by the attacking station. This is a class of **denial-of-service** attack. In wireless, there are many simple ways to deny service that cannot be prevented and do present a potential nuisance.

The Encryption box shown in Figure 11.4 is assumed to be the same RC4 encryption used in WEP. Most manufacturers implemented this box in a way that can't be changed by firmware upgrades. Existing WEP equipment often includes hardware initialization of the RC4 S-Box. The fact that this unit could not be changed was the biggest problem for the design of TKIP.

Before looking at each of the TKIP elements in detail, let's look at the corresponding receive chain, as shown in Figure 11.5.

The receive chain is not quite the reverse of the transmit chain. For one thing, decryption is not the first operation. Instead, the TSC (derived from the IV) is checked as a replay defense. Note that the ICV value is checked and used to reject the packet. This is not technically an integrity check, but it is a quick indication of whether the decryption has been successful: Decrypting a packet with the wrong key or IV values is almost certain to produce a bad ICV value.

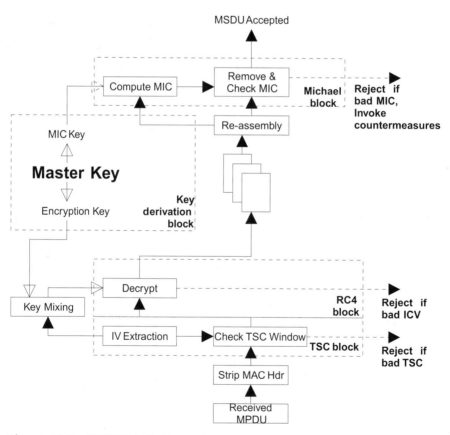

Figure 11.5 TKIP Role in Reception

The MIC is checked after all the fragments have been received and reassembled into an MSDU. Note that if the MIC fails, not only will the MSDU be discarded but countermeasures may be invoked. Although possible, it is extremely unlikely that random errors in transmission would be such that the frame would pass the CRC check and then decrypt to produce an acceptable ICV. If we receive a MIC failure, we can be very sure that it is due to intentional tampering and not just random interference or transmission errors.

Message Integrity—Michael

Michael works by computing an 8-byte check value called the message integrity code (MIC) and appending this to the MSDU prior to transmission. The MIC is computed over the entire (unencrypted) data in the frame and also the source and destination MAC addresses. Michael was invented by Neils Ferguson (2002) and was designed specifically to address the special needs of TKIP, in particular the need to be implemented using a relatively low power processor and without high-speed hardware multiply.

The adoption of Michael by the standards group was somewhat controversial. The algorithm is new, and *"new"* is considered a bad word by cryptographers. Cryptographers like well-studied algorithms. Furthermore, the security level, measured by the equivalent key bit size, is low—the design goal is only 20 bits of security, so a randomly chosen MIC value has about a one in a million chance of being accepted as valid. One in a million is not considered to be very rare by cryptographic standards. As a result of this weakness, mandatory countermeasures were added to stop an attacker from making rapidly repeating attempts with random MIC value.

There are several well-known ways to implement a MIC with very high levels of security; the problem is that these methods are just too processing intensive to be run by older equipment already in the field. Because the whole point of TKIP was to allow upgrade of that equipment, these attractive methods were simply not viable. The weaknesses of Michael are in no way criticisms. The IEEE 802.11 task group (i) could have chosen to design an approach as strong as any known. The weaknesses come from the need to design an approach that could be used with existing WEP hardware. In the end, the standards group felt that this was the best solution within these constraints and that the countermeasures overcome any risk from attacks on the basic method.

Countermeasures

Let's elaborate on what is meant by **countermeasures**. Suppose you are an attacker and you want to get a forged message past the MIC check. The most likely scenario is that you have captured a previous message and modified it in some way. You want the modification to go unnoticed. It is already going to be hard to get the message accepted to the point at which the MIC value is even checked—you have to get past the IV replay protection and the ICV decryption check first. But let's suppose you have figured out how to do that. The 8-byte MIC value is encrypted in the frame along with the data so you won't know what the original value is. However, you do know *where* it is because RC4 encrypts each byte separately and therefore you are able to substitute random values into the field where you know the MIC bytes will be. When the message is decrypted, your inserted random bytes will certainly be changed to another value. However, because they are random, you don't really care about that. You just think about that one in a million chance that the inserted bytes will happen to be right.

In most cases your replacement MIC bytes will not match the message contents and the message will be thrown away. However, there is a small chance that the bytes *will* match the message and, bingo, you've succeeded in your attack. The message is delivered as valid despite having been altered.

A chance of one in a million doesn't sound too good; but remember, people do actually win the lottery, although it will never (statistically) be you. If an attacker is able to try this trick a million times, all the odds change. Sooner or later, the attack will succeed if it is not detected. The purpose of countermeasures is to detect such an attack and stop the attacker having too many plays at the game.

The purpose of countermeasures with Michael is to reliably detect an attack and close down communication to the attacked station for a period of one minute. This simple action limits the attacker to one try per minute, meaning that on average it would take one year of continuous trying to get a random packet through. Unless you have a particularly bad network administration department, someone will notice the network going up and down once per minute all year long ("ours wouldn't," I hear some cynics say).

The actual countermeasures used with Michael are a little more sophisticated. The object is to prevent the attacker from making repeated attacks, but also to try to keep the network going as long as possible. We don't want to tear everything down on the first detected problem.

The approach is to disable the keys for a link as soon as the attack is detected. The compromised devices are then unable to communicate until new keys are generated. Typically the new keys are generated immediately and the network can recover quickly. However, Michael has a 60-second "blackout" rule that says that, if there has been any MIC attack within the last 60 seconds, generation of new keys must be delayed until the 60-second period has expired. This limits the attacker to one try per minute for the entire network.

MIC Failure at Mobile Device

There are two cases in which the supplicant (in the mobile device) can detect a MIC failure. The first is received multicasts (broadcasts) that indicate an attack on the group keys. The other is received unicast messages in which a failure indicates an attack on the pairwise keys. The required behavior is similar in both cases:

For a MIC failure on a multicast message:

1. Delete the local copy of the group key.
2. Request a new copy of the group key from the authenticator using an EAPOL message (indicates MIC failure).
3. Log the event and inform system manager if possible.

For a MIC failure on a unicast message:

1. Drop any received frames and block any transmitted frames *except for* IEEE 802.1X messages (to allow new key exchange).
2. Request new pairwise keys by sending EAPOL message to the authenticator.
3. Log the event and notify the operator if possible.

MIC Failure at Access Point

Although the access point does not receive multicast messages (and hence can't discover a MIC failure for the group key), there are still two cases to consider. The first is a MIC failure detected in a received unicast message, and the second is notification of a group key MIC failure due to receiving an EAPOL key message from a mobile device. The actions to take in each case are as follows:

For a MIC failure related to the group key:

1. Delete the existing group key and stop sending multicast messages.
2. Log the event and notify the operator.
3. If there has been another MIC failure within the last 60 seconds, wait until the 60-second blackout period expires.
4. Create a new group key and distribute to all stations.

For a MIC failure related to pairwise keys:

1. Log the event and notify the system operator.
2. Drop any received frames and block any transmitted frames except IEEE 802.1X messages (to allow new key exchange).
3. If there has been another MIC failure within the last 60 seconds, wait until the 60-second blackout period expires.
4. Initiate a four-way key exchange to establish new pairwise keys.

On first encountering these countermeasures, many people express a concern that an attacker could cause untold disruption to the network. On the face of it, if an attacker sends a forged multicast message every 59 seconds, the network would be permanently in blackout period and unable to operate. In principle, this is true and is another class of denial-of-service attack. However, it is important to note that, in practice, it is extremely difficult to forge a frame to do this. The frame must first pass the TSC check and must decrypt correctly before the MIC is even looked at. Consider these issues:

1. You have to forge a frame where the TSC (TKIP sequence counter) is correct so the frame is not immediately dropped as "out of sequence."
2. The TSC is also part of the IV, and the IV is mixed into the per-packet encryption key. So if you change the TSC, the frame will not decrypt correctly; the ICV will not give a good value and the frame will be deleted.

So to mount the denial-of-service attack, you have to capture a valid frame during transmission, prevent it being delivered to its intended destination, modify the MIC (to make it invalid), recompute the ICV so that it matches the changed MIC value, and finally deliver the message so as to trigger the MIC failure.

Frankly there are many ways to the mount denial-of-service attacks, and most of them are much simpler than trying to trigger the Michael countermeasures. The simplest way to mount a DoS attack is just to send disassociate messages for each of the connected stations. By its very nature, wireless communications is subject to DoS attack. Look at the way the Soviet Union successfully denied its population access to western TV stations by jamming. DoS is a service attack rather than a security attack; and while the countermeasures give one more mechanism, triggering countermeasures is by no means the easiest approach for the enemy.

Computation of the MIC

The computation of the MIC in Michael uses only substitutions, rotations, and exclusive OR operations. There are no multiplies. The units of data that are handled are based on 32-bit words. These characteristics make the method suitable for implementation on lower-power processors. Many of the access points shipped between 1998 and 2002 were based on low-cost 32-bit CISC processors such as the Intel I486. Consistent with this, operations that are endian dependent are defined to be little endian (as for Intel processors).

The data to be protected by the MIC includes the actual payload and the source and destination address fields. These are ordered as shown in Figure 11.6.

DA	SA	User Data

Figure 11.6 Data for MIC Computation

The first part of the algorithm is to organize the data into 32-bit words. This is done for both the key and the data. The 64-bit key is divided into two 32-bit words called K0 and K1. This task must be done in the right order and is designed to be easy for Intel x86 processors. The conversion to two 32-bit words is shown in Figure 11.7 where the 64-bit key is treated as 8 bytes, stored sequentially in memory.

The least significant byte of the information is always stored in the lowest memory address and K0 is stored lower than K1. After splitting the key, the data must also be split into 32-bit words. To guarantee this, the data must be padded to a multiple of 4 bytes. First, a single byte value of 0x5a is added to the end of the data. Finally, extra pad bytes with a value of 0 are added. At least four 0 bytes must be added and the total length of the data must be a multiple of 4 bytes. Thus, between four and seven zeros are always added.

As an example, if the original user data was 1 byte:

- MSDU data is 13 bytes (two 6-byte addresses plus 1 user data byte).
- Value 0x5a is added to give 14 bytes.
- Six 0 bytes are added, giving a total of 20 bytes (5 x 32-bit words) to be processed by Michael.

Note that these extra bytes are not really added to the data or ever sent over the link. They are just added for the purpose of computing the MIC and are then discarded. Now we have two 32-bit key words K0, K1, and a set of data words M0, M1... Mn. The last word Mn is always 0 and the second to last word is always non zero (because of the 0x5a that was added). Our object is to compute a 64-bit

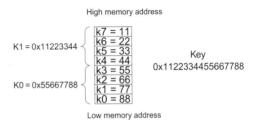

Figure 11.7 Little Endian Key Splitting

MIC value comprising two 32-bit words, V0 and V1, which will be appended to the data prior to encryption.

The algorithm works as follows:

1. Make a copy of the key: $l = K_0$ and $r = K_1$.

2. Exclusive OR the first data word M_0 with l.

3. Call the Michael block function with the values of l and r; new values are returned.

4. Repeat steps 2 and 3 for all the remaining data blocks.

The final values of l and r form the MIC result V_0 and V_1, respectively. In programming language style, this sequence can be represented as follows::

```
(l, r) ← (K₀, K₁)
for i=0 to N-1 do
    l ← l ⊕ Mᵢ
    (l, r) ← FnMichael(l, r)
V₀ = l
V₁ = r
```

The Michael block function FnMichael takes two words (l, r), processes them together, and produces two new values of (l, r). The details of the computations are provided in programming language style here:

```
(l, r) ← FnMichael (l, r)
r ← r ⊕ (l <<< 17)
l ← (l + r) mod 2³²
r ← r ⊕ XSWAP(l)
l ← (l + r) mod 2³²
r ← r ⊕ (l <<< 3)
l ← (l + r) mod 2³²
r ← r ⊕ (l >>> 2)
l ← (l + r) mod 2³²
return (l, r)
```

The key to the operations here is:

$\oplus$: Exclusive OR

$+$: twos compliment addition

$<<<$: rotate left

$>>>$: rotate right

$\text{mod}(2^n)$: discard any bits of higher significance than n

XSWAP: given a 32-bit word, swap the lower 16 bits and the upper 16 bits (hexadecimal 12345678 becomes 56781234)

The resulting two words can now be appended onto the actual MSDU data (non-padded) as 8 bytes of extra data. Notice that, because this process occurs at the MSDU level, it is completely transparent to the rest of the 802.11 MAC and encryption.

Per-Packet Key Mixing

The key-mixing function creates a new key for every packet transmitted. It was introduced for two reasons:

- As a way to protect against RC4 weak key attacks. The recommended defense (discard the first 256 bytes of key stream) was not possible in existing deployed hardware.
- As a way to incorporate the extra bits of the extended IV.

The approach is to combine the session key, the IV and the source MAC address together with a hash function to produce a **mixed key**. Including the source MAC address provides added protection against forgery and also separates out the key space of the two communicating devices that share the session key.

Performing a hash operation for every packet to be encrypted or decrypted is a major overhead and hard work for the low-power MAC processor typical in earlier Wi-Fi LAN systems. To ease the burden, the mixing has been divided into two phases. During phase 1, the session key and source address are hashed. The result remains constant during the session. In phase 2, performed for every packet, the IV is mixed with the result of the first phase to produce an encryption key. This key is then used to initialize the RC4 encryption hardware.

Note that even the second part of the key-mixing computation can be performed in advance because the IV increases monotonically. Therefore, a station knows which values of IV will be coming up shortly and could precompute a number of keys in advance. This step avoids the need for a real-time computation when a packet is received. The two phases of key mixing are shown in Figure 11.3. As you can see in this figure, 104 bits of mixed key material are needed to form the total RC4 key of 128 bits when the IV is added.

There is nothing very glamorous about the computations for the key mixing but let's quickly look at the algorithm.

The inputs to the computation are abbreviated:

TSC = TKIP Sequence Counter (48 bits)

TSCU = Upper 32 bits of TSC (32 bits)

TSCL = Lower 16 bits of TSC (16 bits)

TA = Transmitter address, the MAC address of the encrypting station (48 bits)

TK = The temporal session key (128 bits)

P1K = Output of the first phase (80 bits)

P2K = Output of the second phase (128 bits); this becomes the RC4Key.

The two phases can be written as the following functions:

$$P1K \leftarrow Phase1(TA, TSCU, TK)$$

$$P2K \leftarrow Phase2(P1K, TSCL, TK)$$

When the system starts up or a new key exchange occurs, the TSC is reset to 0. The system typically computes the value of P1K right away and stores it for use in generating P2K. P1K needs to be recomputed every time TSCU changes, which is every 65536 packets. There is no reason why the next value of P1K can't be computed in advance so there will be no delay when TCSU actually changes.

Substitution Table or S-Box

Both phase 1 and phase 2 require a byte substitution table or S-box. The substitution table is to the computer what logarithm tables used to be to schoolchildren before calculators.[3] You take a value and look up a corresponding value in a table. The calculations have been done in advance to determine the correct values in the table. A typical substitution table for a byte value is 256 bytes long so there is one entry for each value of the byte.

However, key mixing uses 16-bit word values. A full substitution table for a 16-bit value would be 2^{16} or 65,336 words long—a total of 128Kbytes! However, this full table is needed only if you want to be able to have a reversible function and create a second table that will "undo" the substitution and get you back where you started. You do not need such a table for hashing functions; in fact, this type of reversal is something you want to prevent. Therefore, the key-mixing algorithm uses a partial substitution table with 512 word entries, which you can think of as two tables, each with 256 words. To make the substitution for a 16-bit word X, we use the upper byte of X as an index into the first table and the lower byte of X as an index into the second table. Then we exclusive OR the two words

---

3. This is true for the S-box of RC-4, which is generated by computation. However, unlike log-tables, S-boxes for other algorithms may contain values that are not mathematically generated.

from the tables to produce a final 16-bit word substitution. This is denoted in the algorithm by the function:

```
i = S[j]
```

where *i* is the result of substituting for *j*.

The 512 values for the substitution table are listed in the standard. The same substation tables must be used by everyone for this approach to work.

Phase 1 Computation

The output of phase 1 is only 80 bits long (not 128), but it uses all 128 bits of the temporal key in the computation. The result is computed in an array of five 16-bit words called $P1K_0$, $P1K_1$, $P1K_2$, $P1K_3$, and $P1K_4$. The following terminology is used in the algorithm:

TSC_1 = bits 16–31 of the TSC (the middle 16 bits)

TSC_2 = bits 32–47 of the TSC (the upper 16 bits)

TA_n = n^{th} byte of the encrypting station's MAC address

(TA_0 = lowest byte, TA_5 = highest byte)

TK_n = n^{th} byte of the temporal key

(TK_0 = lowest byte, TK_5 = highest byte)

the expression $X \cap Y$ is used to denote combining two bytes into a 16-bit word so that:

$$X \cap Y = 256*X + Y$$

S[ ] denotes the result from the 16-bit substitution table:

```
PHASE1_STEP1
    P1K₀ = TSC₁
    P1K₁ = TSC₂
    P1K₂ = TA₁ ∩ TA₀
    P1K₃ = TA₃ ∩ TA₂
    P1K₄ = TA₅ ∩ TA₄

PHASE1_STEP2:
    FOR i = 0 to 3
    BEGIN
        P1K₀ = P1K₀ + S[ P1K₄ ⊕  (TK₁ ∩ TK₀) ]
        P1K₁ = P1K₁ + S[ P1K₀ ⊕  (TK₅ ∩ TK₄) ]
        P1K₂ = P1K₂ + S[ P1K₁ ⊕  (TK₉ ∩ TK₈) ]
        P1K₃ = P1K₃ + S[ P1K₂ ⊕  (TK₁₃ ∩ TK₁₂) ]
        P1K₄ = P1K₄ + S[ P1K₃ ⊕  (TK₁ ∩ TK₀) ]  + i
```

```
        P1K₀ = P1K₀ + S[ P1K₄ ⊕  (TK₃ ∩ TK₂) ]
        P1K₁ = P1K₁ + S[ P1K₀ ⊕  (TK₇ ∩ TK₆) ]
        P1K₂ = P1K₂ + S[ P1K₁ ⊕  (TK₁₁ ∩ TK₁₀) ]
        P1K₃ = P1K₃ + S[ P1K₂ ⊕  (TK₁₅ ∩ TK₁₄) ]
        P1K₄ = P1K₄ + S[ P1K₃ ⊕  (TK₃ ∩ TK₂) ]  +  2*i  +  1
    END
```

Although this is quite a bit of computation—certainly more than in phase 2—the arithmetic comprises entirely shifts, adds, and exclusive OR operations.

Phase 2 Computation

On the face of it, phase 2 looks more complicated than phase 1. However, although there are more steps, there is no repeating loop in the computation. The result is computed in an array of six 16-bits words called: PPK_0, PPK_1, PPK_2, PPK_3, and PPK_4. The following terminology is used in the algorithm:

$P1K_n$ = output words from phase 1

TSC_0 = bits 0 - 15 of the TSC (the lower 16 bits)

TK_n = n^{th} byte of the temporal key

(TK_0 = lowest byte, TK_5 = highest byte)

The expression $X \cap Y$ is used to denote combining two bytes into a 16-bit word so that:

$$X \cap Y = 256*X + Y$$

The expression >>>(word) means that the 16-bit word is rotated one place right.

The expression → (word) means that the 16-bit word is shifted one place right.

S[ ] denotes the result from the 16-bit substitution table.

$RC4Key_n$ means the nth byte of the RC4 key used for encryption.

```
PHASE2,STEP1:
        PPK₀ = P1K₀
        PPK₁ = P1K₁
        PPK₂ = P1K₂
        PPK₃ = P1K₃
        PPK₄ = P1K₄
        PPK₅ = P1K₅ + TSC₀

PHASE2,STEP2:
        PPK₀ = PPK₀ + S[ PPK₅ ⊕  (TK₁ ∩ TK₀) ]
        PPK₁ = PPK₁ + S[ PPK₀ ⊕  (TK₃ ∩ TK₂) ]
        PPK₂ = PPK₂ + S[ PPK₁ ⊕  (TK₅ ∩ TK₄) ]
        PPK₃ = PPK₃ + S[ PPK₂ ⊕  (TK₇ ∩ TK₆) ]
        PPK₄ = PPK₄ + S[ PPK₃ ⊕  (TK₉ ∩ TK₈) ]
```

```
        PPK₅ = PPK₅ +  S[ PPK₄ ⊕  (TK₁₁ ∩ TK₁₀) ]
        PPK₀ = PPK₀ +  >>>(PPK₅ ⊕  (TK₁₃ ∩ TK₁₂))
        PPK₁ = PPK₁ +  >>>(PPK₀ ⊕  (TK₁₅ ∩ TK₁₄))
        PPK₂ = PPK₂ +  >>>(PPK₁)
        PPK₃ = PPK₃ +  >>>(PPK₂)
        PPK₄ = PPK₄ +  >>>(PPK₃)
        PPK₅ = PPK₅ +  >>>(PPK₄)
PHASE2,STEP3:
        RC4Key₀  =  UpperByte(TSC₀)
        RC4Key₁  =  (UpperByte (TSC₀) | 0x20) & 0x7F
        RC4Key₂  =  LowerByte(TSC₀)
        RC4Key₃  =  LowerByte ((PPK₅ ⊕   → (TK₁ ∩ TK₀))
        RC4Key₄  =  LowerByte (PPK₀)
        RC4Key₅  =  UpperByte (PPK₀)
        RC4Key₆  =  LowerByte (PPK₁)
        RC4Key₇  =  UpperByte (PPK₁)
        RC4Key₈  =  LowerByte (PPK₂)
        RC4Key₉  =  UpperByte (PPK₂)
        RC4Key₁₀ =  LowerByte (PPK₃)
        RC4Key₁₁ =  UpperByte (PPK₃)
        RC4Key₁₂ =  LowerByte (PPK₄)
        RC4Key₁₃ =  UpperByte (PPK₄)
        RC4Key₁₄ =  LowerByte (PPK₅)
        RC4Key₁₅ =  UpperByte (PPK₅)
```

The final output of phase 2 is an array of 16 bytes containing the RC4 key to be used in encryption. This can be loaded into the legacy WEP encryption engine prior to processing the MPDU for transmission. The first 3 bytes of this key are transmitted as the WEP IV field (24 bits) and contain the lower 16 bits of the TKIP IV value and the TSC. The second byte of the WEP IV is a repeat of the first byte, except that bit 5 is forced to 1 and bit 4 is forced to 0. Forcing these bits prevents generation of the major class of weak keys. This byte is ignored on receipt.

Summary

This chapter describes how the designers started with the limitations of existing WEP systems and devised a whole new security protocol to fit. TKIP is a masterpiece of retro-engineering and provides real security in a way that WEP never could. All the major weaknesses of WEP have been addressed, including weak key attacks, lack of tamper detection, lack of replay protection, and others. Furthermore, TKIP has been designed by some of the most eminent experts in the field and confidence in the integrity of the solution is high.

Still, there is no doubt that TKIP is a compromise. The necessary simplicity of the Michael integrity protection means that network disruptive countermeasures are necessary. Also, although the weak key vulnerability has been mitigated by the key-mixing approach, the fundamental weakness in the first bytes of the RC4 key stream is still there and might in future be compromised in some way. It seems unlikely now, but it could happen.   •

Assuming no cracks show up, it seems likely that TKIP will be around for a long time and that new systems will also provide support, not just old WEP systems. However, there are a number of reasons why completely new users might want to consider the use of AES-based security, as described in the next chapter.

12 Chapter

AES–CCMP

AES–CCMP is the strongest security in development for IEEE 802.11i. This chapter looks at why AES was chosen and at its credentials as an encryption algorithm. Security systems use AES in conjunction with an operating mode; some of the simpler and more common modes are covered here. We then introduce CCMP, the protocol used with IEEE 802.11, and explain how it is implemented in practice. This chapter shows how CCMP fits into the IEEE 802.11 framework and provides state-of-the-art security for the most demanding users.

Introduction

Chapter 11 looked in detail at TKIP, one of the options for implementing encryption and message authentication under RSN. TKIP, which is mandatory to implement for WPA, will be widely used for Wi-Fi LAN security due to its ability to be used on older WEP cards. However, it is not the default mode for IEEE 802.11i. The default mode is based on a block ciphersuite called the Advanced Encryption Standard or **AES**. AES-based security can generally be considered as stronger than TKIP-based security. This is not to say that TKIP is inadequate. In reality, TKIP is extremely strong and quite suitable for commercial applications. So why was an AES-based solution defined? And what does it mean to say that it is more secure? The answers to these questions and a detailed look at how AES–CCMP works are provided in this chapter.

First, let's clarify what we mean when we talk about RSN using AES. AES is not a security protocol; it is a block cipher. In RSN the security protocol built around AES is called Counter Mode–CBC MAC Protocol, or CCMP. CCMP defines a set of rules that use the AES block cipher to enable the encryption and protection of IEEE 802.11 frames of data. AES is to CCMP what RC4 is to TKIP.

One reason that CCMP is considered stronger than TKIP is that it was designed from the ground up to provide security for IEEE 802.11. The designers took a clean sheet of paper and created CCMP using the best-known techniques. By contrast, TKIP is a compromise, designed to accommodate existing WEP hardware and some aspects of TKIP, notably the Michael integrity protocol, are known to be vulnerable.

Why AES?

When the IEEE 802.11 security task group started work in 2000, its goal was to create a solution that was really secure in all the ways discussed in the first section of this book. It was known at that time that WEP was not very secure, although the really devastating attacks on WEP were only discovered later.

One of the important tasks of the group was to select an encryption algorithm for the new security standard. The encryption algorithm is the root of security. It takes known data and converts it into random-looking ciphertext. By itself, an encryption algorithm is by no means sufficient for implementing secure communications: An entire security protocol must be defined for that purpose. However, the encryption algorithm is at the heart of all the operations. If your encryption algorithm requires too much processing power, too much memory, or, in the worst scenario, can be compromised, all the other complexity you built into the security protocol will not produce a useful solution.

The timing of the task group on this decision was good because another agency had been considering the same question for a while. No less than the U.S. National Institute for Science and Technology (NIST) had been looking for an encryption method for the U.S. government and other agencies in a range of security applications. NIST's approach was to hold a sort of competition in which the best experts from around the world submitted a proposal and methods. Eventually, this process resulted in the selection of a method and the approval of a standard, FIPS 197 specifying AES (NIST, 2002). NIST's own announcement is so well written that I include the first part here so you can read the details for yourself:

DEPARTMENT OF COMMERCE
National Institute of Standards and Technology
[Docket No. 000929280–1201–01]
RIN 0693–ZA42
Announcing Approval of Federal Information Processing Standard
(FIPS) 197, Advanced Encryption Standard (AES)

AGENCY: National Institute of Standards and Technology (NIST), Commerce.

ACTION: Notice.

The Secretary of Commerce approves FIPS 197, Advanced Encryption Standard (AES), and makes it compulsory and binding on Federal agencies for the protection of sensitive, unclassified information. A new robust encryption algorithm was needed to replace the aging Data Encryption Standard (FIPS 46–3), which had been developed in the 1970s. In September 1997, NIST issued a Federal Register notice soliciting an unclassified, publicly disclosed encryption algorithm that would be available royalty-free worldwide. Following the submission of 15 candidate algorithms and three publicly held conferences to discuss and analyze the candidates, the field was narrowed to five candidates. NIST continued to study all available information and analyses about the candidate algorithms, and selected one of the algorithms, the Rijndael algorithm, to propose for the AES.

EFFECTIVE DATE: This standard is effective May 26, 2002.

FOR FURTHER INFORMATION CONTACT: Ms. Elaine Barker, (301) 975–2911, National Institute of Standards and Technology, 10 Bureau Drive, STOP 8930, Gaithersburg, MD 20899–8930.

A copy of FIPS 197 is available electronically from the NIST web site at: *<http://csrc.nist.gov/encryption/aes/index.html/>*.

The IEEE 802.11 task group decided to adopt AES as its core encryption protocol. One benefit of the choice was high confidence that the method is secure, given the amount of review it has received in the NIST selection process. However, there were other less obvious benefits, too. Encryption technology is subject to export control in the United States and other countries. By using a method that is well understood by government agencies, applications for export licenses are more easily processed.

The selection of AES for IEEE 802.11i was made before all the trouble with WEP became well known. The expectation was that AES-based solutions would gradually replace WEP as the new standard became deployed. It was not expected that existing Wi-Fi LAN adapters would be upgraded to AES. In most cases, this would not be practical because the hardware needed to implement AES is different from that needed for RC4. However, when the flaws of WEP became known, there was a sudden need to upgrade all the existing hardware and this led to the creation and deployment of TKIP. As a result, we now have three potential solutions: WEP, TKIP, and CCMP. There is a lot in common between WPA/TKIP and RSN/CCMP–based systems. Key management, for example, is almost entirely the same. The biggest differences occur at the low layers where the data is encrypted and decrypted. We start by looking at the cipher AES, and how it can be applied to real data.

AES Overview

AES is a block cipher. Using mathematical and logical operations, the method combines a key and a 128-bit block of data (unencrypted) to produce a block of different data (encrypted). For all practical purposes, it is impossible perform this transform if you don't know the key. AES is reversible (that is, you can convert back to the original data using decryption), which is useful, but not essential to all security protocols. The encrypted and unencrypted blocks are exactly the same size. The conversion of a single block of 128 bits of data is all that AES does—but it does it quite efficiently and is extremely secure. It is very unlikely that any fundamental weakness will be discovered in future.

AES is based on the Rijndael algorithm, invented by Joan Daeman and Vincent Rijmen. This algorithm is very well documented, including the algorithm and implementation details (Daeman and Rijmen, 2000, 2001). The overview in this book provides a flavor of the method and does not attempt to provide any mathematical justification, although it is necessary to look at some of the quirky arithmetic involved.

The Rijndael algorithm allows for a selection of block sizes and key sizes. The choices are 128, 192, or 256 bits for each. When NIST adopted Rijndael for AES, it specified only one block size, 128 bits, but retained the choice of three key lengths. IEEE 802.11i goes one step further and restricts both the key size and the block length to 128 bits. This simplifies implementation and relieves the users of having to make yet another choice during installation.

Modes of Operation

You can use AES to encrypt and decrypt a single fixed length block of data. However, in practice real messages do not occur as fixed-length blocks. Wi-Fi LAN data, for example, is transmitted in frames of various different lengths, typically between 512 to 12,000 bits in each frame. Therefore, to make use of a block cipher like AES, you need to define a way of converting an arbitrary-length message into a sequence of fixed-length blocks prior to encryption. Similarly, the method has to enable you to reassemble messages from blocks during decryption. The method used to convert between messages and blocks is referred to as the block cipher's **mode of operation**.

There are quite a few different modes that can be used in conjunction with AES. NIST, for example, has a list of 16 different approaches on its Web site and is open for more proposals. The choice of the mode is very important because it has implications both for the complexity of implementation and also for security. Bad modes can create security loopholes even though the underlying AES encryption is so strong.

CCMP uses a mode called CCM, which itself is based on counter mode. Before looking at these modes, let's consider the issue of message authenticity.

AES provides a method for encrypting data, obscuring the content so it cannot be read by an attacker. However, and just as important, the receiver needs to know that the message is authentic—that it has not been modified. This is usually accomplished by adding a message integrity code (MIC).[1] For efficiency, we want this MIC to be computed using the AES encryption algorithm so it makes sense that the operating mode should define how to provide both encryption *and* authenticity.

To understand modes of operation, we start by reviewing one of the most simple and intuitive modes: Electronic Code Book (ECB). The mode is generally indicated by being placed after the letters "AES" so a system using Electronic Code Book described as AES/ECB.

Electronic Code Book (ECB)

ECB mode (Menezes et al., 1996; Schneier, 1996) simply takes a piece off the input message one block at a time and encrypts each block sequentially using the same key until no more pieces are left. This process is shown in Figure 12.1, which displays the computation for both serial (one block at a time) and parallel encryption.

This approach sounds simple, but it has a couple of problems. The most obvious is that the message may not be an exact multiple of the block size so you have to pad out any partial block at the end and remember the real length. However, there is also a security problem: If two blocks have the same data, the encrypted result of the two blocks will also be the same, giving information to any onlooker.

Consider a message composed of a string of the same letter repeated 64 times, for example, "AAAAAAA…". If the AES block size is 128 bits (16 bytes), then using ECB would break down the message to four blocks, each with a string of 16 A's. After encryption, the four blocks would each produce identical ciphertext, informing an onlooker that this message has a repeating pattern. Because of this weakness (and others), practical systems do not use ECB. It is not, for example, on the list of NIST-recommended modes. Even the strongest block cipher cannot protect against weaknesses in the mode.

Counter Mode

Counter mode is more complicated that ECB and operates in quite a different way. It does not use the AES block cipher directly to encrypt the data. Instead, it encrypts the value of an arbitrary value called the **counter** and then XORs the

---

1. The term "MAC" is widely used in cryptography, but IEEE 802.11i (and other chapters in this book) use the term MIC instead because the acronym MAC is already used.

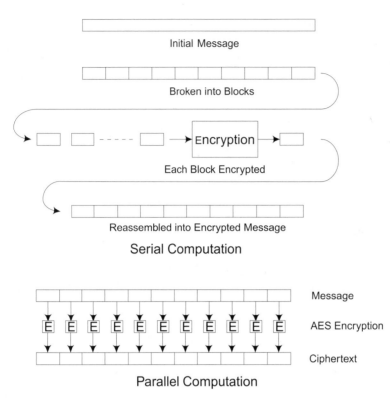

Serial Computation

AES Encryption

Parallel Computation

Figure 12.1   ECB Operating Mode

result with the data to produce ciphertext. The counter is generally incremented by 1 for each successive block processed—hence the name. This process is shown in Figure 12.2.

In this example the message is divided into blocks, and each block is XORed, with the result of encrypting the counter value using AES. In Figure 12.2 the

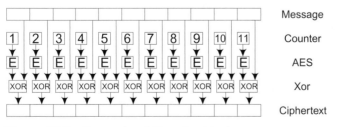

Figure 12.2   Example of Counter Mode

counter starts at 1 and increments up to 11. In practice, the counter might start at an arbitrary value and might increment by some other value or pattern. The important thing is that the receiving party who wants to decrypt the message must know the starting value of the counter and the rules for advancing it.

Because the counter changes value for each block, the problem seen in ECB with repeating blocks is avoided. Even if two blocks of data were identical, they would be combined with a different counter value to produce different ciphertext. However, as presented, this method would still encrypt two identical, but separate, messages to the same result. This is why, in practice, the counter does not start at 1. Typically, it is initialized from a nonce value that changes for each successive message.

Counter mode has some interesting properties. Decryption is exactly the same process as encryption because XORing the same value twice takes you back to the original value.[2] This means that implementations only need to implement the AES encryption block (and not the decryption block). The other useful feature, for some applications, is that the encryption can be done completely in parallel. Because all the counter values are known at the start, you could have a bank of AES encryption devices and encrypt an entire message in a single parallel operation. This is not the case for many of the other modes. The last useful property is that there is no problem if the message doesn't break into an exact number of blocks. You simply take the last (short) block and XOR it with the encrypted counter output using only the number of bits you need. Therefore, the length of the ciphertext can be exactly the same as the length of the input message. Because each block operation depends on the state of the counter from the previous block, counter mode is essentially stream cipher.

Counter mode has been used for more than twenty years and is well known and trusted by the cryptographic community. Its simplicity and maturity make it an attractive option for RSN. However, basic counter mode does not provide any message authentication, only encryption. Therefore, for RSN, additional capability must be added.

Counter Mode + CBC MAC : CCM

CCM mode was created especially for use in IEEE 802.11i RSN, but it is applicable to other systems as well and has been submitted to NIST as a general mode for use with AES. It has also been submitted to the IETF for use in IP security. CCM was invented by three of the cryptographers participating in the IEEE 802.11i standards group: Doug Whiting, Russ Housley, and Niels Ferguson. It builds on top of counter mode.

---

2. This is an example in which the underlying cipher does not need to be reversible.

CCM uses counter mode in conjunction with a message authentication method called cipher block chaining (CBC). CBC is used to produce a message integrity code (MIC). The MIC is called a message authentication code by the cryptographic community, leading to the name CBC-MAC.

CBC-MAC is another technique that has been used for many years and has been standardized internationally. For more information, see Bellare et al. (2000). It is really simple in concept:

1. Take the first block in the message and encrypt it using AES (or any block cipher).

2. XOR the result with the second block and then encrypt the result.

3. XOR the result with the next block and encrypt that…and so on.

The result is a single block (128 bits in our case) that combines all the data in the message. If one or more bits were to change in the message, the result would be completely different (okay, so there is a 2^{-128} chance it will be the same). CBC-MAC is simple but cannot be parallelized; the encryption operations must be done sequentially. Furthermore, it should be noted that, by itself, CBC-MAC can only be used on messages that are an exact number of blocks. CCMP provides a solution based on padding, as described later; however, the padding method has raised concerns among some cryptographers.

CCM mode pulls together two well-known approaches, counter mode and CBC-MAC. It adds some features that are very useful for certain applications such as RSN. The features it adds are:

- Specification of a nonce so successive messages are separated cryptographically.
- Linking together the encryption and authentication (message integrity) under a single key.
- Extension of the authentication to cover data that is not to be encrypted.

The last item needs further explanation and is important for RSN. In most existing methods that perform both encryption and authentication, an assumption is made that the entire message will be encrypted. However, in IEEE 802.11, only part of the message needs to be encrypted. The header portion of the IEEE 802.11 frame contains the MAC addresses used to deliver the frame as well as other information relevant to operation of the Wi-Fi LAN. These fields must be sent "in the clear" so other wireless devices can operate. Therefore, only the data portion of the frame is encrypted. However, although the header is not encrypted, the receiver would still like assurance that it has not been modified. For example, you don't want an attacker to change the source address so you accidentally reply to him instead of to the original sender. To achieve this, CCM mode allows the encryption to be performed on a subpart of the message that is authenticated by CBC–MAC.

As a general rule, using the same key for two separate cryptographic functions is not wise. This rule appears to be broken here because the same key is used for both encryption and authentication. However, although the same key is used, it is in each case used in conjunction with an initialization vector (IV). The construction of the IV is different for the counter mode and CBC–MAC portions, thus leading, in effect, to two separate keys. The effectiveness of this separation has been shown by cryptographers (Jonsson, 2002).

Offset Codebook Mode (OCB)

OCB mode was invented by Phil Rogaway of the University of California, Davis, following on from work done at IBM Research Labs. It is an **authenticated encryption scheme,** which means it achieves both message encryption and authentication in a single computation. OCB has some advantages:

- OCB is parallelizable so it can be done faster using multiple hardware blocks.
- OCB is very efficient, taking only slightly more than the theoretical minimum encryption operations possible.
- OCB is provably secure, which means it can be "proved" that it is as secure as the underlying block cipher (AES).

Because of its advantages, OCB was the first mode selected by the IEEE 802.11i working group and was given the name WRAP. However, concern was raised over intellectual property rights. The standards group was concerned about mandating a method that might, in the future, result in the need to make license payments. Therefore, CCMP was adopted as mandatory and OCB was eventually dropped. It is mentioned here because a few vendors have implemented WRAP, and it is possible you might encounter it as a proprietary mode in some early implementations.

If you want more details of OCB, visit Rogaway's Web site www.cs.ucdavis.edu/ ~rogaway or read the conference paper (Rogaway et al., 2001).

How CCMP Is Used in RSN

This section describes how Wi-Fi LAN packets are encrypted using CCMP. The first important point is that CCMP encrypts data at the MPDU level. The difference between MPDU and MSDU is discussed in Chapter 11; but to recap, the MPDU corresponds to the frames that actually get transmitted over the radio link.

There is one MPDU for each frame transmitted, and the MPDU itself might be the result of fragmenting larger packets passed from a higher layer, called MSDUs.

Steps in Encrypting a Transmission

Figure 12.3 shows the flow of data from MSDU to MPDU and eventually out to the radio link.

The data arrives as an MSDU and may be broken into fragments. Each fragment is formed into an MPDU and assigned its own IEEE 802.11 header containing source and destination addresses and other information. At this point, each MPDU is processed by the CCMP algorithm to generate a new encrypted MPDU. Only the data part is encrypted, not the header. However, CCMP does more than just encrypt portions of the MPDU. It also inserts extra fields, causing the resulting encrypted MPDU to be 16 bytes longer than the original.

An overview of the steps in encrypting an MPDU are shown in Figure 12.4 and described below:

1. We start with an unencrypted MPDU, complete with IEEE 802.11 MAC header. The header includes the source and destination address, but the values of some fields will not be known until later and are set to 0 for now.

2. The MAC header is separated from the MPDU and put aside. Information from the header is extracted and used while creating the 8-byte MIC value. At this stage the 8-byte CCMP header is constructed for later inclusion into the MPDU

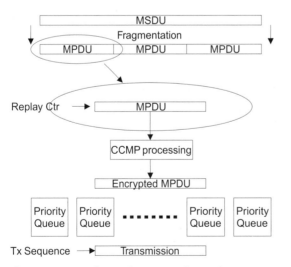

Figure 12.3 Flow of Frames Through CCMP

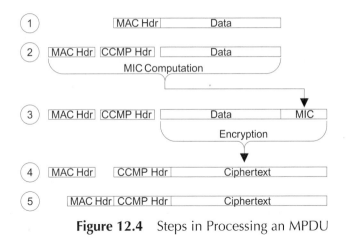

Figure 12.4 Steps in Processing an MPDU

3. The MIC value is now computed so as to protect the CCMP header, the data, and parts of the IEEE 802.11 header. Liveness is ensured by the inclusion of a nonce value. The MIC is appended to the data.

4. The combination of data and MIC is encrypted. After encryption the CCMP header is prepended.

5. Finally the MAC header is restored onto the front of the new MPDU and the MPDU is ready to the queued for transmission. The transmission logic need have no knowledge of the CCMP header. From here until transmission, only the MAC header will be updated.

The encrypted MPDUs are placed on a queue prior to transmission. There might be several queues waiting their turn based on some priority policy. This allows for later extension to accommodate different traffic classes under IEEE 802.11e. Immediately prior to transmission, some of the fields of the IEEE 802.11 header are updated to meet transmission rules. Those fields that are subject to such changes are called **mutable fields** and are excluded from the MIC computation.

CCMP Header

The CCMP header must be prepended to the encrypted data and transmitted in the clear (that is unencrypted). The CCMP header has two purposes. First, it provides the 48-bit packet number (PN) that provides replay protection and enables the receiver to derive the value of the nonce that was used in the encryption. Second, in the case of multicasts, it tells the receiver which group key has been used (see Chapter 10). The format of the CCMP header is very similar to that used for the TKIP header. This is intentional to simplify implementation for access points

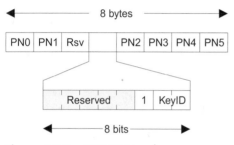

Figure 12.5 CCMP Header

that need to receive transmissions from a mixed group of TKIP and CCMP mobile devices. The format is shown in Figure 12.5.

Six bytes are used for the 48-bit PN value, 1 byte is reserved, and the remaining byte contains the KeyID bits, the function of which is described in Chapter 10. Note that the bit next to the KeyID bits is set to a value of 1, corresponding to the Extended IV bit in TKIP. This value indicates that the frame format is RSN rather than the earlier WEP format.

Overview of Implementation

Implementation of the CCMP block can be viewed as a single process with inputs and outputs, as shown in Figure 12.6.

Note that the decryption phase has the same inputs as the encryption phase (except that the input MPDU is encrypted). This is because the header information, including the CCMP header, is transmitted across the link in the clear and can therefore be extracted by the receiver prior to decryption.

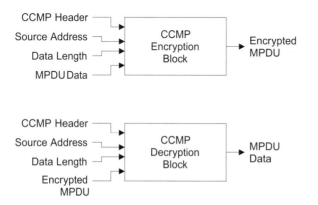

Figure 12.6 Encryption and Decryption with CCMP

The implementation of CCMP (shown in Figure 12.4 as a "block") must keep a sequence counter called the packet number (PN), which it increments for each packet processed. This prevents an attacker trying to reuse a packet that has previously been sent. The PN is 48 bits long, large enough to ensure it never overflows. There will never be two packets sent with the same sequence value. Of course if you power down the device and restart, the PN will be reset, but this will be with a different key value and hence does not create a threat.

Implementation of the CCMP encryption block is shown in Figure 12.7.

Note how the computation occurs in two stages: first, the MIC is calculated and appended to the MPDU, and then the entire MPDU (including MIC) is encrypted to produce the result. Let's look in more detail at each step.

An encrypted MPDU contains two more fields than an unencrypted MPDU. It has the CCMP header and the MIC value. The MIC field is 8 octets (64 bits). Note that the MIC is only half the size of the AES block but is still long enough to reduce the chance of a successful MIC forgery to less than 1 in 10^{19}.

The order of fields in the encrypted MPDU is shown in Figure 12.8.

Steps in Encrypting an MPDU

Before starting the encryption process, it is useful to prepare all the pieces of the MPDU in the order they will eventually appear. We start off with three pieces: the MAC header, the CCMP header, and the plaintext data, as shown in Figure 12.8a. The mutable fields of the MAC header are masked out by setting them to

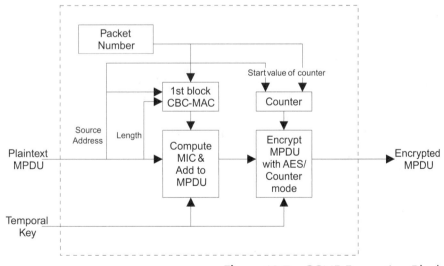

Figure 12.7 CCMP Encryption Block

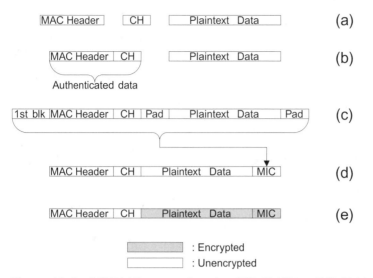

MAC Header   CH   Plaintext Data   (a)

MAC Header   CH   Plaintext Data   (b)
Authenticated data

1st blk MAC Header   CH   Pad   Plaintext Data   Pad   (c)

MAC Header   CH   Plaintext Data   MIC   (d)

MAC Header   CH   Plaintext Data   MIC   (e)

☐ : Encrypted
☐ : Unencrypted

Figure 12.8   MPDU Encrypted under CCMP (CH = CCMP Header)

0. The CCMP header is filled in with the PN and KeyID bits. Note that the PN is incremented by one for each MPDU *prior* to being used. The data portion can be filled in with plaintext data.

The MAC header and CCMP headers will not be encrypted but need to be protected by the MIC. These two items are grouped together to form the **authenticated data,** as shown in Figure 12.8b. The first job after assembling the pieces is to compute the MIC.

Computing the MIC

Computation of the MIC is done using CBC-MAC, which encrypts a starting block and then successively XORs subsequent blocks and encrypts the result. The final MIC is one 128-bit block, but we only need a 64-bit MIC so, for CCMP, we discard the lower 64 bits of the result.

In CCMP the *first* block of the CBC-MAC computation is not taken directly from our MPDU but is formed in a special way using a nonce value. The format of the first block is shown in Figure 12.9 comprising a nonce and two other fields: **Flag** and **DLen**.

The nonce guarantees freshness by ensuring that each encryption uses data that has never been used before (under a given key). You might think that we could just use the packet number (PN) for the nonce because it increments for each MPDU and hence never repeats. However, remember that the key is shared between at least two communicating parties (more for the group key) and these

Byte Number

| 0 | 1 | 2 | 3 | 4 | 5 | 6 | 7 | 8 | 9 | 10 | 11 | 12 | 13 | 14 | 15 |

| Flag | Nonce | | | | | | | | | | | | DLen | | |

Figure 12.9 Format of the First Block for CBC-MAC

parties may, each at some point, use a PN that has already been used by another party, violating the "use once per key" rule. To avoid this problem, the nonce is formed by combining the PN with the MAC address of the sender.

The third field included in the nonce is the **Priority** field. The Priority field is a placeholder for future capability when there are different traffic streams with different characteristics (audio, video, and so on). In such a case, it might be useful to have a separate PN for each type of data. The three fields combine to create the 104-bit nonce, as shown in Figure 12.10.

The other two fields that, with the nonce, create the first block for CBC-MAC are also shown in Figure 12.10. The flag field has a fixed value of 01011001 and indicates, among other things, that the MIC is 64 bits. In other (non-RSN) applications of CCM, the Flags field might be different, but this does not concern us here. The last field, DLen, indicates the length of the plaintext data.

Once the first block has been prepared, the MIC is computed one block at a time by incorporating the authenticated data and then incorporating the plaintext data. One of the characteristics of CBC-MAC is that it works only for an exact number of blocks. If the data doesn't divide into an exact number, it must be padded. For the purposes of the MIC computation, CCMP requires that *both* the authenticated data *and* the plaintext data be padded to an exact number of blocks. In IEEE 802.11, it is likely that neither the authenticated data nor the plaintext data will be a suitable length, so each is padded with zeros to meet this requirement, as shown in Figure 12.8C. The MIC is computed across the combination of the special first block, the authenticated data, and the plaintext data, including the

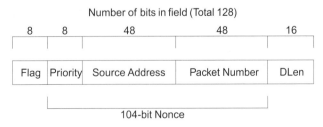

Figure 12.10 Constructing the First Block for CBC-MAC

zero pad bytes. Note that the pad bytes are only inserted for the MIC computation and are not actually inserted in the MPDU, as illustrated by Figure 12.8d.

Encrypting the MPDU

Once the MIC has been computed and appended to the plaintext data, we are ready to start encrypting the MPDU. The encryption occurs using counter mode and starting with the data immediately following the CCMP header in the template. Note that because of the padding during the MIC computation, we are guaranteed that the blocks to be encrypted will be aligned with the blocks included in the MIC computation. The encrypted data replaces the original data for the entire data portion and the MIC value, resulting in a complete encrypted MPDU ready to be queued for transmission, as shown in Figure 12.8E. It is not necessary to use padding for the encryption stage because counter mode allows any excess bits in the last block to be discarded.

An essential step in counter mode is to initialize the counter in a way that avoids ever using the same start value twice. Therefore the counter is constructed from a nonce in an almost identical way to that for the MIC. In fact the nonce value used *is* identical to that of the MIC and includes the sequence counter, source MAC address, and priority fields. This value is then joined with two fields: Flag and Counter ("Ctr"), as shown in Figure 12.11.

The ctr value starts at 1 and counts up as counter mode proceeds. Because the nonce is a unique value and the ctr field is 16 bits long, you are guaranteed to have unique counter values for any message with fewer than 65536 blocks. This easily accommodates the largest MPDUs allowed in IEEE 802.11.

Well, almost ready. First we need to put back all the fields in the MAC header that were masked out for the MIC computation. Although these fields are not used for the MIC, they may still be important.

Once the counter is initialized, encryption can proceed as described in the previous section "Counter Mode" in this chapter. Each successive value of the

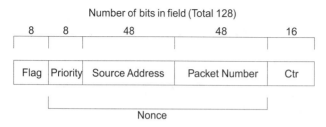

Number of bits in field (Total 128)

8	8	48	48	16
Flag	Priority	Source Address	Packet Number	Ctr

Nonce

Figure 12.11   Constructing the Counter for CCMP AES Counter Mode

counter is encrypted using the secret key and XORed with the template data to produce the encrypted data.

Decrypting MPDUs

When the encrypted MPDU is delivered to the receiver, the first job is to get the right key for decryption. The correct pairwise keys are selected based on the source MAC address in the MAC header. There are a number of steps the receiver must take to extract and check the validity of the received data. Decryption is only one step and this process is more generally called **decapsulation**.

The packet number (PN) is sent unencrypted in the CCMP header. The first thing the receiver does is to read the PN and compare to the last frame received. If the sequence number is lower or equal to the last one, it should be discarded as a replay of an old message. In this case the receiver goes no further with the MPDU.

Assuming the PN matches, the next step is to prepare for decryption using AES/counter mode. This requires the computation of the starting value for the counter, which must match that value used in encryption. All the information is available in the received frame. The sequence number can be combined with the source MAC address and priority to create the nonce. This is then combined with the known flag value and the start ctr value (also 1) to create the initial counter. Note there is no secret here: Any attacker can compute the same value. However, it is of no use unless the secret key is also known. Decryption proceeds as for encryption. Successive values of the counter are encrypted and XORed with the received MPDU to restore the unencrypted data and the MIC value.

The next stage is to verify that the MIC value is correct. The MIC value is recalculated across the same data (and padding) as the original MPDU at the sender. The mutable fields in the header are masked out and the computation performed over the whole MPDU, excluding the MIC. Of course, if the data is unaltered from when it was sent, and we have the right secret key, the same result will be obtained. This can be compared to the MIC value sent with the frame: A match means the frame is valid. A mismatch is most likely evidence of an attack and the frame will be discarded.

Interestingly, with CCMP the process of decryption is almost identical to that for encryption, leading to a nice simplification for implementation. Once the MPDU is decoded, the MIC and CCMP header can be removed, and is the remaining data is passed up for reassembly with other received fragments to reform the MSDU. You can see how the CCMP process gives protection against forgery, eavesdropping, and copy/replay attacks. It is very strong.

As we said at the start of the chapter, the most advanced security protocol is of no use if the underlying cipher mechanism (in this case, AES) has a flaw. AES has no known flaws that might compromise security. If you are interested, Appendix A describes how AES works. This appendix includes some mathematics, which may be unfamiliar. If you are prepared to accept AES as a "black box" that encrypts blocks of data, then feel free to skip the appendix!

Summary

A large number of Wi-Fi systems have been deployed based on the RC4 encryption algorithm. This was part of the IEEE 802.11 WEP implementation and has been included in the WPA TKIP specification to allow firmware upgrades possibly in combination with a driver upgrade. However, when the IEEE 802.11 committee started looking for a new security solution to be built from scratch, they chose instead the cipher AES on which to build. This chapter has explained why that decision was made and how it has been incorporated into the RSN solution.

AES is a cipher that can be used in many ways to create security protocols. This chapter has looked at the various modes that have been designed to use AES in practical situations—in particular, a new mode called CCM that was invented to support IEEE 802.11 TGi RSN and that is now likely to be adopted by NIST as one of the standard modes for AES. This mode forms the basis of CCMP, the AES-based protocol for IEEE 802.11i. We have now covered, in this book, all the core protocols needed to implement WPA and RSN security. The next chapter looks at how the techniques are applied to IBSS networks and covers additional mechanisms that enable Wi-Fi systems to identify and safely select other Wi-Fi systems that support the new security provisions.

13 Chapter

Wi-Fi LAN Coordination: ESS and IBSS

Chapter 13 covers a range of topics. We look at the process by which a mobile device is able to find an access point and join the network. This leads to a discussion on how the mobile device and access point ensure they have compatible security properties and how a mobile device might be able to roam from one access point to another which incurring a large delay due to the authentication process.

In the second half of the chapter, we revisit the IBSS or ad-hoc style of network. Such networks do not use access points and present extra problems for security implementation. In this chapter we look at the solution proposed by the IEEE 802.11i standards group.

Network Coordination

A Wi-Fi LAN needs to be coordinated at many levels. At the lowest levels the IEEE 802.11 standard specifies procedures to synchronize timing and avoid multiple devices transmitting at the same time. At higher levels there are procedures to enable smooth joining and exiting from the network. We are interested in these higher-level procedures because they impact on the security operations.

ESS Versus IBSS

Most Wi-Fi LAN systems are organized with one or more access points and a number of clients. A typical home installation has one access point and two or three clients. A large corporate network might have hundreds of access points and thousands of clients. In IEEE 802.11, networks of this type are called **infrastructure mode** or ESS networks. IEEE 802.11 also supports a mode called **ad-hoc** or IBSS network. The significant difference is that in IBSS mode, there is no access point and any mobile device can talk to any other directly. On the face of it, IBSS is simpler and more efficient for small networks but creates management problems because no one device is in control.

As we described in Chapter 5, both types of networks are controlled using management messages that are independent of the actual data being passed from device to device. The management and control messages allow the network to share the available transmission time efficiently and also enable the access point to exercise control of the network. For a review of the types of messages used, look again at Chapter 5.

From an architectural point of view, IBSS presents quite a few problems for security. If you have an access point, you can give that access point the responsibility for checking the credentials of new devices and, because all the data must pass through, it can effectively block unwelcome devices. However, in the IBSS case you cannot enforce effective controls because any device can talk to any other. We come back to this issue later in the chapter. For now, though, let's review the procedures and messages that allow the access point to maintain control in an ESS network.

Joining an ESS Network

The original IEEE 802.11 required that a new mobile device (an aspirant device) must pass two phases before being allowed to join the network. The first phase is an authentication exchange whereby the aspirant device is supposed to prove its credentials to the access point. We now know that the original method was very insecure, but the basic idea was to block any unwanted devices by rejecting them at an early stage. If an aspirant device passes the authentication phase it is then required to associate to the access point. The process of association is intended to check that the capabilities of the device and the access point are compatible and negotiate some of the variable parameters such as data rate. Once a device is associated, it must send all its data frames to the access point, which will then be responsible for forwarding the data on to its destination.

If the device decides to move to another access point, perhaps for better signal strength, it is required to dissociate from the current access point before associating with the new one. No device can be associated with two access points at the same time. By contrast, in the original IEEE 802.11 standard, it is acceptable to authenticate with another access point in advance, to reduce time during the handover.

In RSN/WPA we cannot use so simple a system. RSN/WPA is based on IEEE 802.1X and EAP. From the point of view of IEEE 802.11, EAP messages are not management or control frames. They do not belong to IEEE 802.11 and are therefore treated like ordinary data frames. Before we can even start the IEEE 802.1X process, an aspirant device must already be connected (in other words, associated) with the access point. This turns the process of joining on its head because it means that association must be done before authentication! The network is protected by blocking data until the IEEE 802.1X and key handshakes have occurred.

For WPA/RSN the management messages that are used for authentication in the older systems are still used, but they play no part in security. However, the management messages for association still have an important role and are used in negotiating the security method to be used. To see how this is done, let's quickly review the message sequences.

The access point sends out beacon messages, usually about ten times a second. The beacons include information about the capabilities of the access point and also serve as a timing reference for some of the protocol operations such as power saving modes. Here we are concerned with the ability of the beacons to advertise capabilities. The items to be advertised include things like the network name or SSID, the supported data rates, and so on.

When a mobile device is looking for an access point with which to connect, it can listen on each radio channel for beacons or it can speed things up by issuing a probe request that basically says, "Is anybody there?" An access point receiving the request can reply immediately with a probe response, essentially with the same information as a beacon. This process allows a new mobile device to scan around quickly and find the access points available. It also allows a connected device to keep one eye open for other access points with better signal strength that might be candidates for roaming.

Once a device has identified a target access point, it attempts to pass the two stages of authentication and association. For WPA/RSN, the access point allows **open authentication**. This simply means that the authentication exchange is two messages:

- The mobile device asks to be authenticated.
- The access point says "OK."

No actual authentication is performed; it is just a null process.

The second part is more important. The device sends an association request to the access point. This tells the access point about the capabilities of the device and also specifies which capabilities of the access point the device wants to use. Assuming the access point finds these acceptable, it generally sends an association response, allowing the device to join the network. In the case of RSN and WPA, the device must then complete the IEEE 802.1X procedure and the pairwise key handshake before sending data.

WPA/RSN Information Element

The messages that pass capabilities information include **capability bits** and **Information Elements,** as described in Chapter 5. RSN/WPA systems have a specific Information Element that is used to negotiate the type of security that will be used. This works as follows. If an access point supports either RSN or WPA (or both), it includes in its beacon and probe response an Information Element with the following information:

- Whether the access point is using preshared key or authentication server (key management)
- What group security mechanism is operating
- A list of one or more pairwise key security mechanisms that are supported

For example, a company that is transitioning from WEP to WPA might use WEP for broadcast (group) security and allow either WEP or TKIP on a device-by-device basis. The Information Element would inform WPA devices and they would select to use WEP/TKIP. The older WEP stations would not understand the new Information Element and would continue to use WEP/WEP, which is acceptable in this case. Later, the company might discontinue the use of WEP and the Information Element would indicate TKIP for broadcasts and only TKIP for pairwise connections.

If that same company then migrated to RSN, it might start advertising TKIP for broadcast and a choice of AES or TKIP for pairwise connections. The Information Element for RSN is not quite the same as for WPA and may contain more information. RSN is indicated by a capability bit and, if this bit is set, the default is to use AES–CCMP for both group and pairwise connections. The Information Element would be needed only if, as in the example above, a choice was offered.

The Information Element (IE) described so far is sent by the access point in beacons and probe responses. The mobile device must also include an Information Element in its association request if it wants to use the security capabilities. Although the IE sent by the access point might have a list of protocols to choose, the one sent with the association request must indicate only a single choice. This is the selection made by the mobile device and defines the protocol that will be used from that point on.

Validating the Information Elements

If the access point advertises a choice of TKIP or WEP, the mobile device may legitimately select to use WEP. This would be pretty strange, though. If the mobile device understands the Information Element, it must support WPA or RSN, so why would it choose an inferior security system like WEP? The simple answer is that it would not—unless there had been foul play. This example leads us to a potential weakness that must be prevented.

Suppose an attacker watches an access point and makes a note of what information is sent in probe responses. Remember that these messages are not encrypted; they are open for all to see. Suppose the access point is offering both TKIP and WEP. Now a new mobile device arrives and issues a probe request. The access point responds, but the attacker goes into action and blocks the response by transmitting some well-timed garbage. The attacker now forges a message that looks exactly like the valid response except that it *offers only WEP as a choice*. The mobile device thinks the access point only supports WEP and associates with this choice. The access point might think this is strange, but it appears quite valid. What the attacker has achieved is to force the mobile device to use a weaker security method; he has successfully weakened the target system.

To prevent this type of attack, both the access point and the mobile device send another copy of the valid Information Element during the pairwise four-way handshake. The four-way handshake is protected against any sort of tampering so, although the attacker can substitute the modified Information Element in the original response, he can't substitute it in the four-way handshake. Therefore, by keeping a copy of the original message, both the mobile device and the access point can detect the attack and drop the connection.

In this example, protection of the Information Element sent by the mobile device seems less important. Suppose the mobile device selects TKIP and indicates this in its association request. There wouldn't be much point in an attacker changing the selection to WEP because, even if accepted by the access point, not much will happen when the mobile device sends TKIP-encrypted frames to an access point that is expecting WEP! However, there is another reason for protecting the mobile device's selection. This is a more subtle reason and is associated with the process of preauthentication described in the next section.

Preauthentication Using IEEE 802.1X

If you have a mobile device and move around a reasonably sized network, you need to roam. Or, to be more specific, your mobile device has to switch from one access point to another due to the limited coverage area of each access point. Ideally, you would like this to happen so fast that you, the user, don't notice it happening. You don't want your laptop to freeze up for a few seconds each time it happens and, worse still, you don't want it to come back with a "network failure" message in the middle of a file transfer.

To achieve this type of seamless handover, you need the switchover to be very fast, preferably milliseconds. This has two implications. First, you need the switchover to occur before you get outside the coverage area of the access point you are currently using. Second, you want the new access point to accept you as quickly as possible so you can continue operation. Security presents a problem for the second objective.

If you wait until the switchover before starting the authentication process, it could take a few seconds before the access point lets you back onto the network. This is especially true if you are using upper-layer authentication needing the services of some remote authentication server. One way to get around this problem is to do the authentication in advance so the access point is ready to let you join as soon as you are ready. The process is called **preauthentication**.

The original IEEE 802.11 WEP system allowed preauthentication using the simple authenticate messages. However, these messages are not relevant to RSN or WPA. We need to perform full authentication using IEEE 802.1X, including upper-layer authentication if required. The superficial difficulty is that we can't talk to the new access point until after we have associated with it—or can we? Remember, we do have an existing connection with the old access point, which, if we are doing things right, is still connecting us to the wired network. Clearly the new access point must be on the same wired network if the roaming operation is to make any sense. Therefore, we should be able to talk to the new access point *via its wired connection*. Although we may detect the new access point from the radio signal, we preauthenticate using the wired infrastructure. This is shown in Figure 13.1.

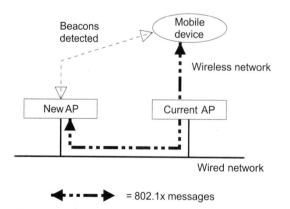

Figure 13.1 Preauthentication Communications

In principle, communicating via the wired network allows the mobile device to perform all the same EAP operations that would typically be performed wirelessly after association. This includes the conversation with a remote authentication server as well as the four-way pairwise key exchange and the group key exchange. Because all the messages are sent in EAPOL messages, they can travel equally well over a wired or wireless LAN. We say "in principle" because, although it is practical, this approach does drive a dump truck through the underlying architecture assumptions in IEEE 802.1X and causes sleepless nights among the standards purists. The problem is that technically the IEEE 802.1X authenticator controls a data port that is created when the station associates. But with preauthentication, no such port exists yet. You can think of ways to deal with this problem by creating a temporary port that get connected later, but it is a bit messy.

If preauthentication is done, the mobile can have an entire set of keys already in place at the point where it roams and associates with the new access point. If the new access point can map the mobile device onto the temporary IEEE 802.1X port that was authorized earlier, it can resume communication immediately. This is where we make further use of the copies of the Information Element that are included with the four-way handshake. When the mobile device preauthenticates, it needs to inform the authenticator which type of cipher it is going to use. This information is provided in the Information Element sent with the handshake. When the mobile device finally roams, the new access point needs to check that it has selected the same cipher in the association request that it selected during the handshake.

IBSS Ad-Hoc Networks

Several times we have mentioned IBSS networks, also called ad-hoc networks, and deferred discussion on the security issues. This section finally looks at these issues in detail and discusses a solution that may be available. At the time of writing, WPA does not provide a security solution for IBSS.

Chapter 7 discusses the **security context**. Security operations take place within a limited context that has a clear start and end. In other words, the context is created by some actions and closed by some other actions. This approach maps quite well into networks with an access point because the access point has master control of the local network. It is a place where the authenticator can reside and all the mobile devices can establish and break a security context with that authenticator.

The major advantage of an IBSS network is that there is no master device. All devices have equal status and any device can talk to any other device. This is also the major problem with IBSS networks from a security standpoint.

First, let's quickly review how an IBSS network operates. Suppose a group of people get together in a conference room for a meeting and they want to share information among their laptop computers. They agree on an SSID or network name that they will use for their meeting and configure it into their laptops, specifying IBSS operation. When the first laptop is enabled, it starts looking for beacons containing the target SSID. It ignores beacons from access points and looks only for beacons from other devices in IBSS mode. If it doesn't see any beacons, it realizes that it is the first arrival and starts sending beacons itself.

The next laptop to turn on sees the beacon from the first laptop, with the correct SSID, and synchronizes its timing. Now the two devices may share the process of sending beacons according to an algorithm defined in the IEEE 802.11 standard. If the first station goes away, the second one sends all the beacons by itself. If any device has a broadcast message to send, it just transmits and all the others listen. If any device wants to send a frame to another device, it just transmits with the target device's MAC address as the destination. Note that there is no process of association and devices can come and go as they please without any hellos or goodbyes.

In our simple example, this works very nicely. All the people in the conference room are within range of each other and all the laptops can communicate. If somebody goes out of range, they are cut off; there is no concept of roaming. Now we come to the security problem.

The conference participants might realize that their session is incredibly insecure. Not only can outsiders see their data, but anyone can join in the network just by observing the SSID over the air. What they would like is to agree on a password at the start of the meeting, limit access only to those who know the password, and encrypt the data. On the face of it, this seems straightforward, but what does it mean to "limit access to those who know the password"? Because there is no coordinator, every mobile device has to block the unwelcome newcomer and because there is no association, how do you set up encryption that needs things like sequence numbers and exchanges of nonces?

This is the problem with IBSS. Intuitively, it seems simple to share a password around the table and just encrypt the data with it. But good security is never simple. It's easy to say things like, "Oh well, it's good enough for this application; after all, meetings only last an hour or so." But this is the path that leads to problems, as we saw with WEP. Eventually people use the technology in areas in which it is "no longer good enough" and then security breaches occur. Consider that some people have proposed to use IBSS mode to implement ad-hoc neighborhood mesh networks for broadband connection to the home. A simple solution that might be good enough for short meetings will certainly fail in such an application.

There are solutions that can work and are secure. Unfortunately, they are not simple. The current proposal for IEEE 802.11i works as follows. First, let's assume that every mobile device has two personalities. When it wants to talk to another device, it assumes the role of a supplicant. When someone else wants to talk to it, it assumes the role of an authenticator. Think of a football team playing at home or away; the mobile device is either visiting (as a supplicant) or hosting (as an authenticator). This is shown is Figure 13.2, in which the role played by the device depends on the direction of communications.

Now that we have established the roles of supplicant and authenticator, we can apply the principles of IEEE 802.1X. Of course we can't use upper-layer authentication because there is no way to attach to a common authentication server. However, we can use a preshared key, which is quite appropriate for the meeting case in which the master key is distributed verbally. Once we have the preshared key and IEEE 802.1X in place, we can almost use the same approach for IBSS as we did for ESS. We can use the four-way handshake to establish pairwise keys, including the exchange of nonces. We can also use the Information Element to establish the starting value of the sequence counter. "Almost" is the operative word here because there are a couple of problems yet to solve.

The first issue is that, if we follow this model to the letter, we have to establish separate pairwise keys for each direction of communication. There are two supplicants and two authenticators, which is inefficient and unnecessary. Therefore, the

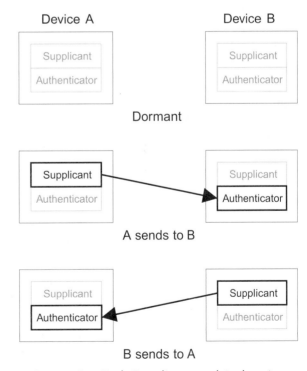

Figure 13.2 Mobile Device Supporting Both Supplicant and Authenticator

device with the lowest MAC address goes first and establishes the temporal keys, and then the authenticator in the other direction uses the same set without further ado.

The second issue is more difficult. What do we do about the group keys? Intuitively, you would think that the group keys would be shared by all the devices in the IBSS. However, there are a number of problems with this approach. Who would be responsible for creating the group key given that there is no master? And how does the group key get distributed to everyone when you don't know who else is out there? To solve this problem, we need to go back to first principles and remind ourselves of the purpose for the group key. It is to protect multicasts and broadcasts, not to allow "any to any" communication. Multicasts are *one to many* communications, not *many to many*.

In the case of an ESS network, the "one" is always the access point. In the case of an IBSS network, the "one" is the device currently transmitting the multicast. It follows that there can be a separate group key for each mobile device that is used only when that particular device is sending a multicast. Providing all the intended recipients (the "many") know the sender's group key, they can receive the message. The sender is now responsible for maintaining its own group key and for delivering it to all the other devices with which it has a pairwise key relationship.

So now we have the IBSS security solution. It is complicated. Ironically, the fact that ad-hoc networks are so simple to set up makes them more complicated to secure. In summary, the process is as follows:

1. The first device starts up and begins beaconing.
2. The second device starts up, detects the beacons, and synchronizes.
3. Whichever device has the lower MAC address now acts as a supplicant and authenticates to the other device using IEEE 802.1X. It then performs the four-way pairwise handshake to establish temporal keys derived from a shared master secret.
4. Both devices now send the other their group key.

At this point the two devices can communicate privately. Now a third device arrives and wants to join the network. It must first synchronize and then perform separate pairwise key handshakes with each of the two existing devices. It must then share its group key with both the other stations and receive a group key from each of them. It has to remember five sets of keys (including its own group key).

At this point you start to see the complexity. In general, if there are N devices in the ad-hoc network, each must keep track of 2*N−1 keys. So for 16 devices, you need to track 31 sets of keys to remain connected. This is the problem: The solution does not scale to large numbers of devices. However, given that all the devices have to be in a single wireless cell so they can all hear each other, maybe that is not too much of a price to pay. At least it's secure.

Summary

This brief chapter collects together the loose ends left over after the substantial chapters describing the security protocol. We started by reviewing the process by which mobile devices join to an access point. We then explained the use of the WPA/RSN Information Element that is employed in the negotiation of security capabilities between the mobile device and the access point.

After considering the process for joining a network, we looked at the issue of roaming from one access point to another. A problem is created if a full authentication handshake is needed every time such a roam occurs because the authentication exchange could take a second or even more. At the time of writing, there are a number of proposals for "fast roaming" using preauthentication or cached keys. We looked at one example of a preauthentication scheme.

Finally we returned to the difficult issue of security in IBSS (ad-hoc) networks. In this case the lack of a central coordinating device such as the access point creates a problem. We reviewed the approach for IBSS security as defined for IEEE 802.11i.

Part III

Wi-Fi Security in the Real World

14 Chapter

Public Wireless Hotspots

This chapter reviews an area that has seen substantial deployment and interest over the past few years—that of public Wi-Fi LAN access. The first part of the chapter discusses the motivations for creating such wireless LANs and the different types of businesses involved in deployment. The second half of the chapter looks at the security implications for users of hot spots and shows that the motivations of the network operator and the user are often quite different.

Development of Hotspots

If you're like most people, you love to have access to the Internet when traveling. It is a great way to keep your office work going when on the road, and apart from anything else, getting e-mails at your hotel in Outer Mongolia makes you feel a lot closer to home. As it happened, wireless LAN technology was developing about the same time that Internet use was expanding rapidly, and it is not surprising that the two have become linked. Today there are an increasing number of places where you can power up your laptop with a Wi-Fi wireless LAN adapter and connect to the Internet. Locations such as airports, hotels, coffee shops, and even private homes are becoming hosts for the service. This chapter reviews the types of systems and different approaches to security you might encounter. We also point out some security risks if you are a user of such networks and what you can do to protect yourself.

Public Wireless Access Defined

What is public wireless access? This is not as straightforward a question as it might sound. Some countries such as the United Kingdom regulate the use of IEEE 802.11 for providing a public service. This has caused much discussion about what constitutes "public." For example, if your company allows visitors in the lobby to get access to the Internet via Wi-Fi LAN, is it providing a public service?

In its broadest sense, "public wireless access" simply means that any person who has purchased equipment with IEEE 802.11 capability can legitimately connect to an access point and get service from an open location such as a coffee shop. The only restriction on who may connect is that they might have to pay the required fees for the privilege. If there are enough access points installed in public places, IEEE 802.11 could eventually provide almost universal wireless broadband access in cities. In principle, it means that IEEE 802.11 could compete with the existing cellular phone infrastructure in the future—a prospect that rattles the huge telecommunications providers and makes venture capitalists drool with excitement.

Barriers to Growth

It sounds rather simple to set up a Wi-Fi LAN hotspot, but several early players who launched into large-scale deployments in hotels found little financial success, and some went broke. So what went wrong?

There are two barriers to the growth of public Wi-Fi LAN. The first is what we will call the "fax machine problem," and the second is the multiparty nature of the business.

Fax Machine Problem

Facsimile machines have been around for almost a century, but sales didn't pick up until the 1980s, when they grew explosively. The barrier here was that it was no good being the only person with a fax machine—there had to be someone to send faxes to. It was only when a critical mass of fax machine owners was reached that ownership had real benefits, causing rapid acceptance. The situation is similar with Wi-Fi LAN hotspots. People won't buy an IEEE 802.11 card for public access until most hotels provide service. However, hotels won't install the required access points and network because customers don't have Wi-Fi LAN cards. This problem is being overcome now because so many people are using IEEE 802.11 in their homes and businesses; not only do they have the equipment, but it is installed on their laptops.

Multiparty Barrier

The multiparty barrier is only just being solved now, and different approaches are being tried. The issue is that, in each wireless hotspot, you have several players providing one piece of the solution and all hoping to make money out of it. For example, in a hotel you have:

1. The proprietor (hotel management)
2. The installer and operator of the local Wi-Fi access points
3. The provider of the connection to the Internet
4. The company that manages the access control and billing of the system
5. The company that sells subscriptions and provides customer service

The early entrants to the market tried to take on roles (2), (4), and (5) and negotiate directly with each hotel for installation rights. However, this meant that each location was limited to supporting a single supplier's service. People soon realized that it would make more sense if the location could support a range of different service providers and route the authentication and billing to the appropriate company when a user logs in.

Today, there are essentially three business models being deployed around these parties. We look at each briefly because the type of approach affects the security problem.

Model 1: Wireless Internet Service Provider   In this model a single company takes on the entire service provision. Often it focuses on one type of facility, such as hotels or airports. It may also provide regular wired Ethernet jacks in hotel rooms, with wireless used only in conference facilities or where wiring is difficult. To use the service, you must subscribe, which can be done on a monthly basis or on a daily basis when you are staying in a hotel. The subscription is only good for one service provider; so if the hotel where you are staying has access points from a competing service provider, you may have to subscribe to more than one service.

Model 2: Brand-Based Service Provider   In this approach, the subscription process is separated from the network provision. When you sign on, your customer service and billing are handled by a company that does not actually own a wireless network but promotes a brand.

For instance, say the service provider promotes a brand called GetItHere. GetItHere has negotiated access with other companies that own and install wireless hotspots. This separation has several benefits. The "brand" company deals with marketing and customer service. It advertises the service and explains the benefits. Potential customers are told that they can get wireless access at any location showing the GetItHere logo.

The actual network can be provided by specialist companies, individual enterprises like coffee shops, or even private individuals. These providers can focus on running the network; they get paid based on how many GetItHere customers connect. Furthermore, this approach allows the network providers to support more than one brand-based service. For example, they could support both Get-ItHere customers and ConnectItUp customers. This model makes efficient use of available wireless hotspots and provides a wider choice of locations for customers.

Model 3: Cellular Operator Extension Service   Cellular phone operators have huge existing billing and customer service organizations. They also have a massive customer base. It makes a lot of sense for them to extend their service to cover Wi-Fi LAN access. Many people would like the idea of a combined bill for cell phone and mobile Internet access. The problem for the cellular phone operators is that their existing network architecture is not compatible with Wi-Fi LAN hotspots. While access points and cell phone base-stations perform an analogous role, the approach to installation and maintenance is quite different. Therefore, although they seem natural candidates, the cellular phone operators are moving cautiously into this area. If they succeed, they have a huge advantage from a business operations point of view.

Security Issues in Public Hotspots

The security issues in public Wi-Fi LANs are different from those in corporate Wi-Fi LANs. The same goals are there: privacy, integrity, and so on. But because of the public nature of the network, there are some real additional threats. One of the underlying assumptions of corporate LANs is that there are only two groups of people using the network: those who are *trusted* and those who are *untrusted*. At the local level, most companies make no attempt to prevent one trusted person from attacking another. In other words, once you let two employees join the network, say George and Sue, you assume that they are both good citizens and will go about their legitimate business. You might have separate passwords for file access and so on, but you are not expecting George to impersonate Sue or Sue to try to hack into George's hard disk. If they were to do so, you would probably fire the offending party, who would then become part of the *untrusted* group.

The situation is quite different in a public hotspot. There are still two groups: those who can join and those who cannot. But the criterion for entry has nothing to do with trust; it just depends on whether you have paid your subscription fee. Unlike the corporate case, in this case you have to assume that one connected member may try to attack another.

Another difference between corporate and hotspot security goals is the motivation of the various participants. In a corporate LAN, it is generally assumed that the employees and employer share similar goals. The employer wants to protect the employees from attack and the employees (usually) have the interests of the company at heart. This is not the case in a wireless hotspot. The service provider just wants to get paid and doesn't really care whether you get hacked (except that it causes bad publicity for the business). The motivation of the service provider is to prevent fraud. The motivation of the users is to protect themselves, and they may not be concerned if a loophole allows them to let all their friends get access using the same account.

The third, and critical, difference between corporate and public access is that the network infrastructure behind the Wi-Fi LAN is not secure. In a corporate environment, the Wi-Fi LAN acts as a gateway between an insecure wireless world and a secure wired world. Behind the access points, the network is protected by locked wiring closets and server rooms (or in the case of smaller companies, the fact that the hub is on the boss's desk). In the public environment the backend network may be accessible to anyone, rather like an unprotected wireless network.

This difference in motivation places a greater responsibility on hotspot users to protect themselves. The rest of this chapter looks at the different ways in which hotspots are deployed and organized, but in most cases the differences are business related and do not help the security of the user. With this in mind, we look at some actions users should take before joining hotspot networks.

How Hotspots Are Organized

Although the details vary between installations, all hotspots have essentially the same architecture. The components are:

- Subscribers
- Access points to provide the wireless coverage
- Hotspot controllers to provide access control
- Authentication server to verify legitimate users
- Local content intranet services
- Public Internet services

Figure 14.1 shows how these components relate to each other. It is interesting that the use of the hotspot controller and authentication server is similar to the concept of the authenticator and authentication server in IEEE 802.1X. But note that most deployed hotspots *do not* use IEEE 802.1X today. In fact, most use *no* security measures at the Wi-Fi LAN level.

The following sections describe each of these components. The actual physical location of the various functions varies from system to system, as do the methods used to authenticate the user. However, the basic functions and requirements are more or less the same in each case.

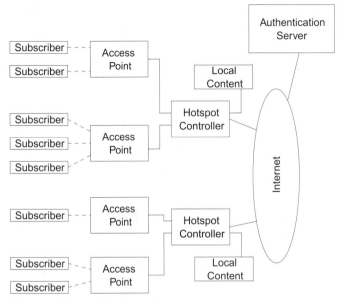

Figure 14.1 Hot Spot Components

Subscribers

In Figure 14.1, the subscriber and access point equipment are often completely standard IEEE 802.11 components—the same type you might buy to install in your office or even at home. The use of standard components is especially useful at the subscriber end. Ideally, you don't want customers to have to add any new software or hardware to their system to connect. For instance, they may want to subscribe to several services and they may use Wi-Fi LAN at the office. They will not want to have to purchase and carry around a special Wi-Fi LAN card for each hotspot they plan to use. In addition, people are very concerned about installing new software, especially drivers. They are understandably worried that, after they install the software for the hotspot, their Wi-Fi LAN will no longer work back at the office.

Requiring special hardware and software on the user's laptop computer also blocks the impulse purchase effect that is so powerful in this business. A classic example is when you are at an airport and your plane is delayed. You have several hours to kill, and you see a booth offering Internet access for $5 per hour. You sign up there and then. Hotspots can get lots of new customers this way, but many potential customers won't join if they first have to load special software.

The down side of the "no new hardware/software" approach is that it is very difficult to provide a seamless service. *Seamless* means that the system connects and registers automatically whenever the user moves into a hotspot. This is the sort of behavior you expect from a cellular phone, for example. By contrast, most hotspots require you to go through a login phase using a Web browser prior to getting access—not a great hassle until you forget your password, but an extra step nonetheless.

Currently, if you want to provide automatic registration to the network, you need to install special components onto the laptop. One interesting approach introduced by the mobile phone industry is to have a Wi-Fi LAN adapter with a slot to insert a GSM SIM card, which is the same type of smart card used in GSM cellular phones. In this case the system really can operate seamlessly and automatically identify and connect to hotspots without user intervention. One major vendor, Nokia, has introduced a combined cellular data/Wi-Fi LAN adapter so the system can switch back and forth between hotspot and cellular coverage, giving constant network access. However, approaches like this clearly need to be preconfigured and installed before you go on the road.

When IEEE 802.11i is deployed, there will be a new opportunity to provide seamless access through IEEE 802.1X. Popular operating systems will probably have built-in support for IEEE 802.1X, including operation over IEEE 802.11i. In the future, you can expect all the authentication software to be built into laptops at the factory. All you will need to do, when subscribing to a Wi-Fi LAN service, is to purchase a digital certificate for the service. After that, connection will be automatic.

Access Points

For the most part, the access points used in wireless hotspots have the same features as those used at home or in the office. Typically, WEP encryption is not used and authentication is the responsibility of the hotspot controller. While conventional access points can be used "off the shelf," vendors have started to introduce access points customized for use in hotspots. The mechanical design of the unit needs to be more robust and more tamperproof if located in a public area. You don't want screw-in antennas sticking out, for example, or you are likely to find that some curious child will screw them out and wander off. Also, you don't want the unit festooned with flashing colored LEDs because this just attracts unwanted attention. Many sites solve these problems by mounting the access points in a closet or a locked box, but new streamlined access points with integrated antennas are now available for direct mounting on a wall. The radiation pattern of the antenna might be different from an access point designed for the home, radiating mostly in one direction, for example, so the access point can be mounted at the end of a room.

One area often overlooked by system designers is how the access point shares information between users. In a conventional Wi-Fi LAN, a broadcast message sent by one mobile device is transmitted by the access point to all the other mobile devices. This is the meaning of *broadcast*. But in a wireless hotspot, you may not want this to happen. For example, upper-layer networking protocols such as Microsoft's Network Neighborhood use multicasts to advertise network file systems to other devices on the same LAN. However, in an airport you don't want your file system to be advertised to a bunch of strangers sitting in the gate area. Of course, you can disable network sharing in your laptop, but most people forget or don't know how. Therefore, it is helpful if the access point in the hotspot is smart enough to block the redistribution of such broadcasts to the whole hotspot.

The access points must be connected to the hotspot controller. Usually, this is done using wired Ethernet. If there are multiple access points, they will typically be connected together on a shared LAN using a hub. These wired connections are a source of weakness from a security standpoint. Physical security of the wires and hubs connecting the access points might be low. It could be easy for an attacker to find the hub in a closet and connect a laptop to it using a spare port. Assuming it is a shared LAN hub, it would then be easy for them to intercept all the data flowing into the hotspot. Even if WEP or RSN were used to protect the transmission on the wireless side, it would not protect against this type of interception because it occurs after the access point has decrypted the data. The attacker could also record authentication transactions for later analysis or even forge messages from a subscriber who is authenticated. This weakness in wiring plant security is a major headache for hotspot security in general.

Hotspot Controllers

The hotspot controller is the key component that makes the hotspot possible. There are many functions it has to perform, including:

- User authentication
- Collection of billing information
- Tracking usage time where subscription is time limited
- Providing local IP addresses
- Filtering requests to allow free access to certain servers and Web sites
- Emulating e-mail services to allow mail forwarding
- Emulating DNS name resolution

We have shown the hotspot controllers as independent boxes in Figure 14.1. However, while companies *do* sell self-contained hotspot controller units, hotspot controller functions can be implemented in other ways. For example, a small site may have only one access point, and the controller functions would be at a remote location connected by a frame relay link. In the case of such a small site, the access point itself could incorporate the controller functions as well. There are also solutions that make use of an ordinary PC to act as a controller. This section focuses on the functions rather than where they reside.

If the operator is charging for access, user authentication is obviously a key feature. The most common approach so far is to require login via a Web page. The idea is that when the subscriber connects and brings up a Web browser, she will always get the login screen presented, regardless of what URL she actually requested. For example, if she enters www.favoritefish.com in the browser, she will be diverted to the hotspot login screen. The controller has to do a bit of trickery to accomplish this redirect.

The access points are run in open mode without WEP encryption or authentication. Therefore, with a suitable wireless card, anybody can connect to the hotspot network. The controller will give any connected device an IP address upon request so the newly connected device can start sending packets to the Internet. However, all the packets go through the controller. And it will not forward them to the real Internet until you have logged in. The controller inspects your packets, looking for Web requests; and when it sees one, it diverts it to its own internal Web server, which presents the login screen instead. Your browser is unaware that this has happened and presents the login screen as if it came from the real Web site.

After you have entered your user name and password, or whatever is required, the controller stops intercepting your packets and forwards them to the Internet. Some controllers may store your original request and then forward it after the login so you get your requested Web site automatically after the login screen.

The use of Web login also allows security features in the browser to be used so the information for the login is protected. This results in the browser displaying "https://" in the URL address and gives you some guarantee that the hotspot is legitimate and not itself a bogus operation.

In many cases the controller will allow access to certain Web sites without having to log in. These are known as **white-list sites**. For example, an airport might allow access to the airlines' Web sites or a supermarket might allow access to their advertising sites.

In some circumstances, login via the browser might be a nuisance or a problem. If you are moving from one hotspot to another, you might be forced to log in each time because each has a separate controller. Worse, if your PC is configured to use virtual private networking (VPN), you might not be able to log in at all because the controller would be unable to decode your Web site requests. In such a case, you must turn off the VPN feature, log in, and then reenable VPN before proceeding. There are various proprietary schemes that allow the authentication process to occur automatically, avoiding the need to log in via the browser. As previously mentioned, these schemes generally need to be configured in advance or use some special hardware. The availability of RSN and IEEE 802.1X provides the opportunity for automatic authentication without using the browser. Imagine that your laptop has built-in support for IEEE 802.11i (RSN), IEEE 802.1X, and EAP/TLS authentication. If you were to purchase and install a client digital certificate for your laptop, you would be able to go to any hotspot and log in transparently. You could probably purchase the digital certificate over the Internet from a Web site that, naturally, would be on the controller's white list. This, of course, assumes that the hotspot has support for RSN, but it does show how hotspots in the future can become easier to access.

Authentication Server

The credentials of each subscriber have to be stored in a central database for verification. As outlined in Chapter 8, EAP and IEEE 802.1X allow the subscriber to negotiate access directly with the central authentication server. However, in most existing hotspots the credentials are first collected by the hotspot controller and then verified in a separate transaction between the controller and the authentication server. From an architectural standpoint, those hotspots that require subscribers to log in with a user name and password look very similar to a dial-up modem pool. When you connect to the Internet via a dial-up modem, you (or you computer) transfer your user name and password to the modem pool controller, which then uses RADIUS to verify your access rights. In is natural, therefore, that the hotspot controller will also use RADIUS for this purpose. In fact, this is one advantage of the user name/password scenario for hotspots: Existing authentication server databases can be used. In principle, the same authentication server could support both dial-up and hotspot sites.

An interesting situation exists for the hotspots based on cellular phone authentication. When cell phones were first introduced, the cellular phone industry had the same problem to resolve for user authentication and billing of mobile users. It needed a system that would allow you to roam in and out of cell sites and be identified and connected automatically. The industry now has a huge installed network that, quite clearly, works well. The idea of using a GSM SIM card or U.S. cellular equivalent in the Wi-Fi LAN adapter is that you can tap into that huge existing customer authentication and billing system. In this case the hotspot controller needs to be able to interface with and talk to the cellular phone authentication server. These servers use their own protocols designed for the cellular industry and are not based on Internet protocols. To implement such a system, therefore, a special type of authentication gateway server is needed to bridge between the Internet network and the cellular network. The hotspot controllers may still use RADIUS to communicate with this gateway, and it will convert the RADIUS requests into the appropriate form for the cellular system. The cellular authentication server will see the Wi-Fi LAN user as if it were another cell phone.

Different Types of Hotspots

Eventually hotspots might become so widespread that you could sit down almost anywhere and seamlessly connect to the Internet, much in the same way that we expect from a cell phone today. For the moment, though, hotspots are few and far between. This section looks at four types of hotspots:

- Airports
- Hotels
- Coffee shops
- Homes

Airports

Airports are huge enterprises, like small cities in their own right. Management of such a large-scale organization depends heavily on contracted services. It follows that hotspots in airports are likely to be installed and run by a specialist contractor. In some cases, individual airlines have decided to install hotspots in their executive lounges. However, the use of wireless really needs some central coordination to avoid polluting the air with many overlapping systems. Ideally, a single contractor would manage hotspots; this contractor would install coverage in suitable areas and then obtain a cut of revenues from subscribers. This approach fits the brand model discussed earlier. Naturally, the airport authority would want to be paid as well. In the case of cell phone base stations, payment is often in the form of a fixed annual fee.

Hotspots in the airport are likely to use dedicated hotspot controller units that are placed in locked equipment closets. They may even have a local authentication server capable of storing a copy of the central authentication server's entries.

Hotels

Hotels are much smaller than airports but are still unlikely to want to get involved with the installation and operation of the wireless network. Features such as network access are becoming an important differentiator for hotels attracting business customers, and many hotel chains have signed exclusive deals with hotspot companies to install equipment on their premises. Often this includes both wired and wireless network access. In these cases, there is probably a dedicated hotspot controller installed in the hotel.

Coffee Shops

Coffee shops or so-called cyber cafés use hotspots to attract business customers or even private customers who don't have high-speed Internet access at home. These enterprises are too small to need a dedicated hotspot controller. Fortunately, there are several alternatives available.

The first is to forward all the data from the access point back to some central location where a single controller can support many coffee shop–type operations. The connection could be done using a dedicated lease line connection or a frame relay connection. The problem is that the cost of such connections is quite high. The second approach is to have a special access point with built-in hotspot controller functions. Finally you can have a special access point with the ability to tunnel data across the Internet to a central site with a hotspot controller. This is the same as the first option (leased line) except that it uses a regular Internet connection to reduce cost.

Homes

The idea of a hotspot in the home is novel but contentious. Many people have broadband Internet connections to their homes. Some people share them with their neighbors, using wireless links between the houses. Here is the contentious part: Such sharing may be in violation of the contract customers have with the broadband service supplier. The legality of setting up home-based hotspots is something that a person should confirm before starting. Anyway, back to the point: If you share your Internet connection with neighbors, why not with anyone else within range? Maybe you are next door to a convenience store or in a multiunit dwelling. There could be many people who would like to use your broadband connection. If you have not turned on wireless security, there might be people using it already without your knowledge!

Some companies have had the idea to turn this into a sort of cottage industry. They market and sell hotspot wireless access to subscribers and then sign up private homes to be hotspots. We call these companies "cottage hotspot" companies. The idea goes something like this. At your home you have a computer, a Wi-Fi LAN, and a broadband Internet connection. You are prepared to let others join your Wi-Fi LAN and get Internet access for a small fee, but you have no way to collect the money. You contact the cottage hotspot company and sign up to allow your Wi-Fi LAN to be accessed. They provide you with some special software to load on your PC. This special software runs in the background and performs authentication of would-be customers. It also communicates (via your Internet connection) to a central server owned by the cottage hotspot company, and reports how many people are using your network.

At the end of the month, the cottage hotspot company sends you a check with a payment based on how successful your hotspot has been. The company, of course, is billing its subscribers and keeping a good share of the proceeds as well. Subscribers can find out where participating hotspots are from the company's Web site. The hope of the cottage hotspot companies is that, if enough homes subscribe, wireless access will be available on every street.

Home hotspots are a neat idea. It costs a person nothing to set up because he already has the equipment. The big threat to the idea comes from the reaction by the broadband Internet providers. Obviously, they would like to sell access to everybody on the street separately rather than having them all share one connection. Today, some broadband providers' contracts even limit the connection to one computer in the home, although many people have a network of computers at home. The providers generally turn a blind eye to sharing for your family use, but they are unlikely to do so if you start turning it into a business.

How to Protect Yourself When Using a Hotspot

There is no doubt that, as a user of a hotspot, you are vulnerable to many types of attack. At minimum, your data can be intercepted and read. In the worst scenario, people can get into your computer and copy, delete, or modify files or even plant a virus. The wireless traffic in a hotspot is generally not encrypted. However, even if it were, the link between the access point and the hotspot controller is unprotected and then the data is probably going on to the public Internet anyway. Given that the data is going over the Internet, you may accept that it is not private; however, the prospect of someone accessing your computer should be taken very seriously.

The biggest danger comes from shared file systems. Many popular operating systems allow your files to appear as a shared directory to other computers on the network. This is the most popular method of networking for small businesses and home users. However, if you have a shared directory and forget to "unshare" it before entering the hotspot, there is a real danger that it will be noticed by a stranger and investigated. A level of protection can be gained by always using a password for shared directories. All but the most motivated attackers will probably give up and move on.

A second danger comes from **Trojan viruses**. Like the mythical Trojan horse, a Trojan virus is carried into your computer on an infected executable file. Once there, it quietly sends out messages while connected to the network, notifying an enemy where you are and opening a portal for them to connect to your computer. Good virus protection should always be used to avoid such viruses, and personal firewall software, covered in the next section, usually blocks the port that Trojan viruses use.

Personal Firewall Software

If you need real protection, you are advised to install personal firewall software. This will not provide privacy for your data but will also protect against attacks on your computer. Such software is available from a number of companies and is now built into some operating systems. The software monitors all data going in or out of your computer. It blocks any suspicious attempts to access your computer and generally provides a single simple software switch that blocks all network sharing in one go.

When you are operating in a hotspot, you should allow only TCP/IP packets to come in and go out of your computer. This protocol is all that is needed for Internet access. Other protocols are sometimes used for computer-to-computer communication on a local network, which is just what you want to prevent. The firewall can block all non–TCP/IP traffic. Most TCP/IP data is connection oriented. For example, when you want to access a Web site or an e-mail server, your computer establishes a connection to the server and then sends and receives data. Once the connection is established, data can pass both ways. You want the firewall to allow connections that you initiate but to reject connections coming in from somewhere else. This stops other people from connecting to your computer.

Unfortunately, if you block all incoming connections, some functions won't work. For example, an FTP file transfer may require that the sending server is able to make a connection to your computer. Good firewall software has the ability to allow certain incoming connections based on knowledge of what you are trying to do. Some applications do not use connection-oriented TCP but use an IP datagram service (UDP). The use of such applications will be limited if firewall protections are in place. However, such applications—videoconferencing or voice-over IP, for example—are usually quite specialized. If you are using such applications, you may want to consider the further protection of a virtual private network (VPN).

Virtual Private Network (VPN)

VPN is a much used and often misunderstood term. It tends to be used to describe some sort of general security system operating at the TCP/IP layer. The concept of VPN is to superimpose a private network on top of a public network so you can get the advantages of a dedicated network and the low cost of a shared network. Security is a key component of implementing a VPN. Most VPNs create point-to-point connections between two users or a user and a server. If two people want to talk to each other across a crowded room, they know that anyone in the middle can hear their conversation. In the days before telephones, people used devices called speaking tubes: By putting their ears to one end, they could hear the person speaking into the other end. These were used to communicate between the bridge of a ship and the engine room, for example. In a similar way, a VPN creates a tunnel through the shared network medium so only the two parties at each end of the tunnel can read messages sent at the other end. Various security techniques are used to wrap the data being sent across the network so it is quite impenetrable to anyone in the middle. These tunnels are like independent virtual connections, hence the name VPN.

A typical use for a VPN tunnel is to connect an employee to their company's intranet. This type of connection is particularly useful when the employee is out of the office and using the Internet. One end of the tunnel resides on the employee's laptop computer and the other end in a server at the company's premises. Once such a connection is established, the employee's communication is as secure as if she were in the office, regardless of the fact that the tunnel passes over the Internet or Wi-Fi LANs or any other type of insecure network.

The concept of the tunnel is both a strength and a weakness. It is ideal if you want to communicate to only one other destination. However, it is a problem if you want to communicate with several locations at once. If you want to communicate with two or three servers, you would have to have multiple tunnels in operation. And if you want to browse Web sites, you need to turn VPN off because public Web sites do not support VPN attachment. Some companies solve this problem by requiring that *all* communications from a company laptop go to the company VPN server. If you want to browse the Internet, your data must first go to the company VPN server, then to the company intranet, and finally back out onto the Internet via the company firewall. This requirement ensures ultimate control and security, but it can hardly be considered efficient. Typically, it is available only to larger corporate users.

VPN Details

The technical details of VPN are extensive and books that focus on VPN are available. Here we just mention a few points. VPN operates at quite a high level in the protocol stack, well above the layers where RSN security operates. You need to install special client software onto your computer before you can operate a VPN. In the future, client software will probably be built into the operating system, thus simplifying management. The most popular VPN system is based on IPsec, which is defined by the IETF. There are other approaches, including some that are proprietary; but it seems likely that IPsec will eventually become universal for use with TCP/IP–based systems.

IPsec provides for two parties to negotiate and authenticate the information needed to encrypt data into a tunnel. The original IP frames are encrypted and encapsulated inside new IP frames that are then sent to the other end of the pipe. This can create problems if the original IP address is not valid at the destination network, such as when address translation is being used along the route because the encapsulated (and hidden) addresses will not be translated. This was a major problem in the early days, although many servers now have the ability to correct for the problem.

The computational overhead of encryption usually falls on the processor in the PC rather than on special hardware. This overhead can limit transfer rates, although the high speed of modern processors greatly reduces the effect of this overhead.

Regardless of the security offered by the hotspot, VPN is the most secure way to operate in a wireless hotspot. VPN eliminates all the problems of security that have been mentioned, including the weakness of the wiring plant connecting APs and the danger of network sharing with other users in the area.

If you do not have access to a VPN server, you should certainly consider the installation of a personal firewall. There are also "anonymity services" that can provide a VPN-like function for a monthly fee. These services act as a sort of *forwarding* device. All your Web accesses get sent to a server on the Internet and then are forwarded on to the Internet again by the server. Typically, the data between your computer and the server can be encrypted; it is decrypted by the server and then forwarded on to the Internet. This is ideal for use in a hotspot because it means that your data sent over the wireless link is encrypted. If you are interested in such services, type "anonymity" into a Web search engines and you will find various links to companies that can do this. For example, www.anonymizer.com.

Summary

In this chapter we have looked at the way in which Wi-Fi LANs are being used to provide public hotspots. The ideal situation is that, eventually, there will be hotspots all over the place and you will be able to sit down with your laptop or other wireless terminal and get a connection to the Internet without any special configuration or login required. In fact, it should work like cellular phones today; just turn on and use. Today, most hotspots do not work in this way; typically, a special connection procedure is required via a Web browser login screen. However, some cellular phone manufacturers have started to integrate the same type of authentication as seen in phones and this can provide more seamless access.

In the future the use of IEEE 802.1X provides a path to more seamless hotspot access. IEEE 802.1X will allow the user's computer to specify the types of authentication it can support and to negotiate access using embedded security tokens such as digital certificates and smart cards. The use of IEEE 802.1X makes IEEE 802.11i (RSN) security a logical choice for hotspots in the future. However, it must be remembered that the primary motivation of the hotspot operator is to avoid fraudulent use rather than to protect the privacy of the customer.

There are many security issues related to the use of hotspots. Most provide no security on the wireless link so your data can easily be observed by an attacker in the hotspot. Furthermore, most treat the local Wi-Fi LAN as a shared medium, allowing data for one wireless station to be broadcast to other users. This creates all sorts of risks of privacy as well as a danger of direct attacks on disk drives that you might have inadvertently left open. On top of all these issues, the data ultimately passes over a public Internet connection that must be considered totally insecure. Therefore, although you may use a personal firewall, and in the future there might be wireless encryption, it is likely that the use of VPN will continue as the most secure way to protect corporate users when they are accessing hotspots.

15 Chapter

Known Attacks: Technical Review

Earlier in the book, we explained the basics of Wi-Fi LAN technology and provided an intuitive notion of what security is all about. In this chapter, we jump into the details of the various known attacks against the security standards used in building wireless LANs, including IEEE 802.11. Some of the material may appear complex, and at least one of the attacks requires a reasonable background in cryptography for full understanding. We present the information as simply as possible; but if you're not interested in the details, skip to the next chapter, which discusses how attackers can use techniques such as described in this chapter to break into a poorly protected wireless network.

In Chapter 4, we classified attacks into four broad categories: **snooping**, **modification**, **masquerading**, and **denial of service.** In this chapter, we cover the material somewhat differently by classifying the various attacks by the security mechanism that it breaks. We also categorize the attacks so you'll understand what a successful attack provides to the bad guys.

Review of Basic Security Mechanisms

There are numerous ways to classify something as complex as security. Chapter 4 focuses on the goals of the attacker, that is, what the attacker gains if he is successful. This section introduces another method of classifying attacks based on the security mechanism targeted by the attacker.

Every effective security architecture uses one or more security mechanisms to implement the goals of the architecture. These basic security mechanisms are confidentiality, integrity, and availability.

Confidentiality

Confidentiality protects against the inadvertent or malicious disclosure of sensitive information, that is, it conceals information. Usually, confidentiality is provided by cryptographic or access control mechanisms. Let's review the definitions of these mechanisms.

Cryptography

Encryption is the process of making information indiscernible to an adversary, and **cryptography** is the study of making and breaking encryption algorithms. There are two widely used forms of encryption: symmetric and asymmetric. With symmetric encryption, the communicating parties share a secret—a key—that is used for both encryption and decryption. With asymmetric encryption, the communicating parties usually have two keys, a private key for decryption and a public key for encryption. The inverse is also true. The private key can be used to encrypt some data. In this case, the result is essentially a signature that can be verified by anyone having knowledge of the corresponding public key, if he knew or could compute the value of the encrypted data. Now, let's discuss symmetric and asymmetric encryption in more detail.

Asymmetric Encryption   Asymmetric encryption, also known as public key cryptography, uses a different key for decryption than the key used for encryption, as follows:

$$M = D(private\_key, E(public\_key, M)),$$

where M is the message, D is the decryption function, and E is the encryption function.

Usually, the two keys used in the process are referred to as a **key pair**, with one key called the private key and the other key called the public key. The public key is shared with anyone for communications purposes, and the private key remains known only to the holder, or principal, of the key pair. The public key is usually shared in the form of a certificate that includes information that uniquely identifies the holder of the key pair as well as the signature of the issuer—a trusted entity that vouches that the identity bound to the public key in the certificate is correct. The process that issues and revokes public-key certificates is called a **public key infrastructure**, or PKI.

An example of an asymmetric encryption algorithm is the widely used RSA public key algorithm designed by Rivest, Shamir, and Adleman (Rivest et al., 1979).

Symmetric Encryption   Symmetric encryption uses the same secret key, k, for both encryption and decryption, in other words:

$$M = D(k, E(k, M)).$$

Examples of popular symmetric encryption algorithms include the RC4 (Ron's Cipher 4) by Ron Rivest and AES (Advanced Encryption Standard) ciphers, both of which have already been covered in some detail (RC4 in Chapter 6, and AES in Chapter 12). Symmetric ciphers operate in one of two fashions—stream or block. In a stream cipher, such as RC4, each byte of the plaintext or ciphertext is processed individually—that is, a byte is the basic unit. In a block cipher such as AES, the plaintext or ciphertext is grouped together into blocks of a predetermined and fixed size and then processed as a single unit.

When two parties wish to communicate securely using a symmetric cipher, they first must agree upon the shared secret, k, in a secure fashion. This is usually accomplished via key distribution or key agreement, both of which are forms of key management, which we discuss next.

Key Management   Key management systems provide the means for implementing cryptographic **periods** via the secure distribution of new keys on a regular basis. An important point is that disclosure of the secret key during distribution would cause *any* cryptographic system to fail, and failing to regularly change keys would weaken most cryptographic systems. Therefore, every security architecture should use a robust key management system.

Of the two approaches to key management, manual and automatic (electronic) systems, manual systems are more prone to risk because they significantly depend on human assistance, which has historically been the weakest link in any security architecture. Automatic systems, while more difficult to design, are significantly more robust when correctly designed, implemented, and operated.

Access Control

Access control is another mechanism that supports confidentiality. We previously followed the analogy of the much-valued doorman who allows only those who live in an apartment building to enter it. Essentially, the purpose of access control is to allow only those who are authorized to use or view system resources. Typically, this is accomplished through an access control list (ACL), which in its simplest form is a look-up table based on some identity criteria. Access control mechanisms work very closely with authentication as they rely on a valid identity (proven by authentication) to make decisions concerning access. Remember we first introduced access control in Chapter 8 and authentication in Chapter 6.

Integrity

There are two aspects to integrity. With **source integrity**—also known as authentication—the information's originator is known and credible. With **data integrity**, we seek to prevent inadvertent or malicious modification of the data.

Source Integrity

Source integrity (authentication) is the process of proving either a principal's identity or a trusted source of data/system resources. Strong authentication requires two elements. The first is a common trust element—something or someone whom the object doing the authentication trusts and who can vouch for the subject or person being authenticated. The second element is a unique identity for the subject being authenticated. For example, when you use a check to pay for goods, the cashier usually asks to see your driver's license to ensure that it matches the name on the check. In other words, the clerk is authenticating your identity by trusting the Department of Motor Vehicles to have verified your identity before issuing you a driver's license. Although not foolproof, the difficulty of forging drivers' licenses encourages merchants to use them as verification when accepting checks.

Authentication works closely with access control mechanisms, which require a verified identity to make access decisions.

Data Integrity

Ensuring data integrity requires the detection and, ideally, the prevention of unauthorized modifications. Whereas cryptography detects integrity violations, access control prevents integrity violations.

Access control for data integrity is similar to using access control for confidentiality; the mechanism prevents attackers from accessing and thus modifying the data. The cryptographic approach is somewhat different in that it uses a cryptographic hash function to create a unique hash value or fingerprint of the data. To be considered a cryptographic hash function, an algorithm must meet four requirements:

- The hash value must be easy to compute.
- Creating data that results in a specific hash value must be computationally difficult so that it is difficult for adversaries to replicate that hash value and make undetected alterations to data.

- The hash function must be one way, making it difficult to recreate the data based solely on the hash value.
- Collisions—that is, identical hash values for two random data sets—must be difficult to find.

Given a cryptographic hash function, detecting integrity violations is straightforward. First, we compute the hash value for a given data set. Then, we compute a new hash value over the same data at a later time and compare it to the previous value. If the two values are not equal, the data was modified. We do this using message authentication codes and digital signatures.

Message Authentication Codes   Message authentication codes (MAC[1]) use a keyed one-way function to provide message authenticity proving that the contents have not been altered in route.

A keyed cryptographic hash is the most common way to build a MAC, requiring a shared secret, k, between the communicating parties and an agreed-upon cryptographic hash function, H. To send a message, M, along with another MAC, the sender computes the MAC using *MAC = H(k M, k),* and sends <M, MAC> to the recipient.

Upon receipt, the receiver computes a MAC value over M and compares the computed value to the received MAC. If the two values are the same, the message authenticity is valid.

While the simple MAC shown previously provides message authenticity, it should not be used in practice because a much stronger MAC exists. The HMAC MAC has a formal basis for its security properties (Krawczyk, 2003).

Digital Signatures   Digital signatures use a cryptographic hash function such as MD5 or SHA1 along with public key cryptography to ensure message authenticity and data integrity. To compute a digital signature, the sender first computes a hash value h of the message M and then encrypts this hash value using an asymmetric algorithm, typically RSA, with the sender's private key. This process of computing a digital signature is shown below:

$$h = H(M)$$
$$S = E_{RSA}(private\_key, h)$$

---

1. The cryptographic and security community use the acronym MAC while the IEEE uses MIC (message integrity check). The reason the IEEE uses MIC is that the acronym MAC was already in use. In this chapter, we use MAC.

The sender now sends the message M and the signature S to the recipient. To verify the authenticity of the message, the receiver calculates the hash value of the message, h', and decrypts the signature S using the sender's public key to obtain the original hash value h. The receiver now compares the two hash values: If they are equal, the message is authentic; if they are not, the message was either tampered (data integrity attack) or not tampered while in route from the expected sender (source integrity). The process of generating the two hash values is shown below:

$$h' = H(M)$$
$$h = D_{RSA}(public\_key, S)$$

Some people wrongly believe that cryptography provides a complete security solution. It does not. Cryptography is an extremely important tool in providing security, but it is not the complete solution to our security problems.

Review of Previous IEEE 802.11 Security Mechanisms

The original (1999) version of the IEEE 802.11 specification defines several security mechanisms. The first is the wired equivalent privacy (WEP) protocol, which was designed to provide users with the same level of confidentiality protection as that of a wired network. The standard also includes a shared key authentication mechanism and integrity protection against inadvertent errors. While access control is not specifically addressed in the standard, most vendors have implemented an access control list mechanism based on MAC addresses.

Confidentiality

In the 1999 version of the standard, confidentiality is implemented through the WEP protocol, which uses RC4 for encryption (Menezes et al, 1996; Schneier, 1996). RC4 is a proprietary stream cipher designed by Ron Rivest in 1987. The algorithm was reverse-engineered and made public anonymously in 1994. While the algorithm has received a great deal of public attention, RSA Labs still claims the algorithm is a trade secret.

RC4 and WEP

RC4 is a remarkably simple cipher. As a result, the performance of the algorithm is high. It also makes describing the algorithm easy. There are two major phases in RC4. The first phase is the key setup algorithm (KSA), which establishes a 256-byte array with a permutation of the numbers 0–255. The permutation in the array, or S-box, is established by first initializing the array with the numbers 0–255 in order. The elements in the S-box are then permuted through the following process. First, a second 256-byte array, or K-box, is filled with the key that repeats as needed to fill the array. Next, the bytes in the S-box are swapped according to the pseudocode in Equation 15-1.

Equation 15-1   RC4 Key Schedule Algorithm
```
i = j = 0;
For i = 0 to 255 do
   J = (j + S_i + K_i) mod 256;
   Swap S_i and S_j;
End;
```

The next phase in RC4 is the pseudorandom generation phase. In this phase, the algorithm in Equation 15-2 generates a pseudorandom byte R.

Equation 15-2   RC4 Pseudorandom Generation Algorithm
```
i = (i + 1) mod 256
j = (j + S_i) mod 256
Swap S_i and S_j
K = (S_i + S_j) mod 256
R = S_K
```

To produce n pseudorandom bytes, the algorithm executes Equation 15-2 n times. To encrypt plaintext, the stream of generated pseudorandom bytes is combined with the plaintext bytes using the XOR function as a combining function, as shown in Equation 15-3:

Equation 15-3   RC4 Encryption
$$C_i = P_i + R_i$$

where C_i is the ith ciphertext byte, P_i is the ith plaintext byte, and R_i is the ith pseudorandom byte. The decryption process is just the inverse encryption shown in Equation 15-3 and is shown in Equation 15-4.

Equation 15-4   RC4 Decryption
$$P_i = C_i + R_i$$

The equations shown in Equations 15-3 and 15-4 are a Vernam cipher (Vernam, 1926). The Vernam cipher, designed by Gilbert Vernam during World War I while working for AT&T, is the only completely secure encryption system provided that R_i is a true random byte. In this case, Equations 15-3 and 15-4 are known as a

one-time pad. To be completely secure R_i must be truly random, and a random sequence must never be used more than once. Because the former Soviet Union made this serious mistake following World War II, the American National Security Agency was able to decrypt a number of one-time pad enciphered messages sent by Soviet agents in a project code named VENONA (U.S. NSA, 1999).

RC4, however, is not a completely secure encryption system because it generates pseudorandom bytes, not truly random bytes. WEP uses RC4 along with an initialization vector (IV) to ensure that each message encrypts differently along with a 32-bit cyclic redundancy check to protect data integrity during the transmission of encrypted 802.11 packets.

Initialization Vector   WEP uses a 24-bit IV in an attempt to ensure that RC4's pseudorandom byte stream is not reused because reusing the same pseudorandom byte stream creates depth, which can make the attacker's job easier. The sender uses a unique key with every packet that is derived by appending the shared secret key, k, to the publicly known IV. This process is shown in Figure 15.1.

Integrity Check Value   WEP uses a 32-bit cyclic redundancy check (CRC) as an integrity check value (ICV). The ICV detects any changes (malicious or inadvertent) in the transmitted message's underlying plaintext. Unfortunately, while a CRC easily detects most inadvertent changes, it does not provide integrity or message authenticity capabilities against malicious changes. Thus, an attacker can easily modify messages protected by a CRC.

A CRC uses the mathematics of finite fields, more specifically, GF(2). Fortunately, the mechanics (not the mathematics) of how a CRC works are easily explained. A message M that is $n + 1$ bits long can be represented as an nth-degree polynomial, $M(x)$. For instance, consider a message consisting of only the single ASCII letter "O," which is represented in binary as *01001111*. The polynomial corresponding to this message is $0^7 + x^6 + 0^5 + 0^4 + x^3 + x^2 + x + 1$, or $x^6 + x^3 + x^2 + x + 1$.

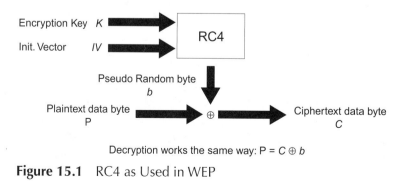

Decryption works the same way: $P = C \oplus b$

Figure 15.1   RC4 as Used in WEP

For a CRC to work, both the sender and the recipient must agree upon a polynomial $G(x)$ of degree m that will be used to calculate the CRC.[2] This polynomial will be used as a divisor for the message.

The WEP CRC polynomial is $G(x) = x^{32} + x^{26} + x^{23} + x^{22} + x^{16} + x^{12} + x^{11} + x^{10} + x^8 + x^7 + x^5 + x^4 + x^2 + x + 1$, with $m = 32$ (IEEE, 1997). Transmitting an $n + 1$-bit message, M also transmits an additional m bits, for a total message length of $n + m + 1$ bits. We'll call the message and the additional m bits the polynomial $P(x)$. The $m + 1$ bits added to the original message make $P(x)$ divisible by $G(x)$ with a remainder of 0. The $m + 1$ bits are determined by increasing the degree of $M(x)$ by m, then by multiplying $M(x)$ by x^m to obtain $M'(x)$, and then dividing $M'(x)$ by $G(x)$. The remainder, if any, is then subtracted from $M'(x)$, resulting in $P(x)$—the transmitted value of $n + m + 1$ bits.

Verification of the CRC by the recipient involves a similar process. The recipient divides $P(x)$ by $G(x)$, and if the remainder is 0, the message does not contain unintentional errors. The key word here is *unintentional* because CRCs do not prevent the introduction of intentional errors when the attacker knows $G(x)$. The attacker only needs to modify $M(x)$ and calculate new $m + 1$ bits, just as the sender did. An example of how to calculate a CRC is provided in Appendix B.

WEP Datagram Format   Figure 15.2 shows the WEP datagram format. The preamble of the datagram is a four-octet value that includes the 24-bit IV in plaintext, a 6-bit pad, and a 2-bit keyID value.

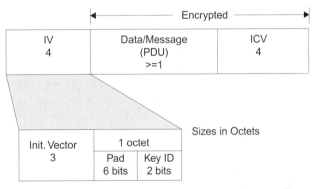

Figure 15.2   WEP Datagram Format

---

2. How this polynomial is selected is beyond the scope of this book.

The WEP datagram format can be represented by $C = RC4(IV, k) \oplus <M,$ $CRC(M)>$, which shows that RC4 encrypts both the message and the results of the CRC calculation (ICV).

An important point to remember about WEP is that the plaintext and the pseudorandom bytes produced by RC4 are *combined* with a linear function, XOR. This fact causes significant problems for WEP that are discussed later in this chapter.

Key Management

The 802.11 standard neither addresses link-layer key management nor does it provide recommendations for upper-layer key management. The standard, instead, relies only on manual key management, which is difficult to perform in a timely manner when the number of hosts is large.

As a result, only a few major vendors initially implemented any form of key management or key agreement in their high-end products, and all of these products use upper-layer methods. Unfortunately, the vendors do not provide sufficient information to determine the level of assurance their products provide. Worse, in some cases, available details indicate that vendors' "solutions'" worsen the problem by using protocols with well-known vulnerabilities—for example, an unauthenticated Diffie-Hellman key agreement.

The 802.11 standard offers two methods for using WEP keys. The first provides a window of four keys. A station or access point (AP) can decrypt packets enciphered with any one of the four keys; transmission, however, is limited to one of the four manually entered keys—the *default key*. The second method is called a **key mappings table**. In this method, each unique MAC address can have a separate key. According to the 802.11 specification, a key mappings table should have at least ten entries. The maximum size, however, is likely chip-set dependent. Having a separate key for each user makes the cryptographic attacks found by others slightly more difficult because the traffic per key will be reduced, but enforcing a reasonable key period remains a problem as the keys can only be changed manually.

Access Control

Access control is a major component of any secure architecture. The previous 802.11 standard does not define any means for access control. As a result, most vendors implement access control lists using the client's MAC address as its identity, and one major vendor implements a proprietary access control using a shared secret.

Each access point can limit network access to clients using a listed MAC address. If the client's address is not listed, access to the network is prevented.

A major wireless vendor has defined Closed Network, a proprietary access control mechanism. With this mechanism, a network manager can use either an open or a closed network. Anyone is permitted to join an open network, but only clients with knowledge of the network name, or SSID, can join a closed network. In essence, the network name acts as a shared secret. Unfortunately, because the SSID is sent over the air unencrypted, it is not a well-protected secret.

Integrity and Authentication

The current IEEE 802.11 standard does not have a robust mechanism designed specifically for integrity purposes. Some claim that the 32-bit CRC ICV function provides integrity; but, as we have seen, this is not the case in practice.

The 1999 specification has only two forms of standardized authentication in 802.11—open system and shared-key authentication.

Open System Authentication

Open system authentication is the default authentication protocol for 802.11. As the name implies, this method authenticates anyone who requests it; in essence, it provides a NULL authentication process. This method was likely included in the standard to permit the use of a single-state machine that supports authenticated and unauthenticated operation.

Shared-Key Authentication

Shared-key authentication uses a standard challenge and response along with a shared secret key to provide authentication. The station wishing to authenticate, the initiator, sends an authentication request management frame indicating that it wants to use shared-key authentication. The recipient of the authentication request, the responder, responds by sending an authentication management frame containing 128 octets of challenge text to the initiator.

The responder generates the challenge text by using the WEP pseudorandom number generator (PRNG) with the shared secret and a random IV. The IV is always sent in the clear as part of a WEP-protected frame. Once the initiator receives the management frame from the responder, it copies the contents of the challenge text into a new management frame body and then encrypts it with WEP, using the shared secret along with a new IV selected by the initiator. The initiator then sends the encrypted management frame to the responder. The responder decrypts the received frame and verifies that the 32-bit CRC integrity check value (ICV) is valid and that the challenge text matches that sent in the first message. The entire process is shown in Figure 15.3.

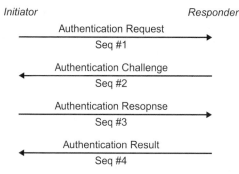

Figure 15.3 Authentication Sequence

Attacks Against the Previous IEEE 802.11 Security Mechanisms

Unfortunately, *all* of the security mechanisms defined in the 1999 version of the IEEE 802.11 standard have been proven ineffective. The problems range from issues with the lowest primitives up to the high-level protocols used.

Confidentiality

There are numerous flaws in both RC4 as used in WEP and in WEP itself that indicate that WEP provides no effective protection at this point.

RC4 Problems

Since 1994, researchers have identified a series of small flaws in RC4, none of which resulted in a practical attack. More recently, however, Itsik Mantin and Adi Shamir described a reliable distinguisher[3] for RC4 ciphertext. While this flaw was not a break, it identified a statistical bias in the second output word of RC4's pseudorandom generator. Shortly thereafter, Scott Fluhrer joined Mantin and Shamir in authoring a paper that did result in a practical and complete break (key recovery) of RC4 as used in WEP, and their attack has subsequently been implemented and released in several open source projects.

Mantin and Shamir Bias Flaw   In a paper presented at the Fast Software Encryption (FSE) 2001 conference, Mantin and Shamir (2001) described a bias in the

---

3. Given ciphertext produced by an unknown system, a cryptanalyst uses a distinguisher to identify the cryptologic, or algorithm, that produced the given ciphertext.

second word of the pseudorandom stream produced by RC4: Zero occurs as the second word with twice the expected probability (1/128 instead of 1/256) in what should be a pseudorandom sequence with all values equally likely. While this may seem a minor problem, it allows ciphertext produced by RC4 to be easily distinguished from ciphertext produced with random cipher systems and it lays the groundwork for a much larger result described below.

Fluhrer, Mantin, and Shamir Key Schedule Attack   Several months later, Scott Fluhrer and colleagues found a devastating attack against a class of keys used in RC4 that leak information about the secret key. Unfortunately for WEP, the class of weak keys found by Fluhrer, Mantin, and Shamir were exactly those used by WEP (Fluhrer et al., 2001).

Fluhrer and his colleagues found that when RC4 is used with an initialization vector appended or prepended to the secret key, certain values of the IV produce a weak key. An adversary who collects enough of these weak keys passively through eavesdropping can recover the secret key in linear time with respect to the key size; in other words, an attack against 104-bit WEP is only slightly more difficult than an attack against 40-bit WEP. Furthermore, the attack relies only on the first byte of output from the RC4 pseudorandom generator, as determined by the equation: $S[S[1] + S[S[1]]]$, where S is the S-box used in the implementation of RC4.

In most cases, determining the first pseudorandom byte would be difficult because of the variability of the underlying plaintext. But because WEP is used in an IP data-networking environment, the first byte of the vast majority of packets is 0xAA, a value in the LLC header. Thus, we have known plaintext and can easily recover the first pseudorandom byte.

Recovering the secret key now involves passively collecting enough packets of the form *<keybyteindex+3, 0xFF, N>*, where *keybyteindex* is the index of the secret key we are trying to recover and N is any byte value. This form of packet lets us guess the true key byte with an accuracy of 5%, and the trick is to collect enough such packets to ensure a correct guess. Fluhrer et al. estimate that approximately 60 such packets are required, and Stubblefield et al. (2002) found that 256 packets always selected the correct key byte. This process is iterated until all key bytes are determined.

Fluhrer et al. estimated they would need approximately four million packets to recover a 104-bit key. However, Stubblefield et al. implemented the attack and found they needed between four and six million packets to recover each key byte in an unoptimized attack. Stubblefield also optimized the attack so as to reduce the number of required packets to one million. Recovering this quantity of packets depends on the network load and can range from less than one hour in a moderately to heavily used network (300 or more packets per second) to several hours in a lightly used network.

Other WEP Problems

In addition to the problems with RC4, WEP itself has a number of flaws running the entire range of field elements in the protocol.

IV Space   WEP uses a pitifully small 24-bit IV space (2^{24} or 16,777,216).[4] Assuming a moderate to heavy network load, this space is exhausted within a few hours and creates an IV collision—that is, the same $<IV,K>$ pair is used to encrypt two different plaintexts. When multiple hosts share the same encryption key in a network, the time between collisions is obviously much shorter.

The consequence of an IV collision is significant with a stream cipher. Because of the linearity of the XOR combining function, deriving the underlying plaintext is much easier.

Given two ciphertexts produced with the same $<IV, K>$ pair:

$$C_1 = RC4(IV,K) \oplus P_1$$
$$C_2 = RC4(IV,K) \oplus P_2$$

XORing the two ciphertexts together removes the pseudorandom stream generated by RC4 and produces the XOR of the two plaintexts (Borisov et al., 2001).

$$C_1 \oplus C_2 = (RC4(IV,K) \oplus P_1) \oplus (RC4(IV,K) \oplus P_2)$$
$$C_1 \oplus C_2 = P_1 \oplus P_2$$

The XOR of two plaintexts makes it significantly easier to recover the two plaintexts because of their well-known structure.

Replay Attacks   The WEP protocol provides no form of message authentication; thus, it allows intercepted messages to be replayed or sent again without modification (Borisov et al., 2001). While replaying packets will not permit an adversary to become a peer on the network, it can result in a significant denial-of-service attack and can also be used to reduce the cost of other attacks. This lack of message authentication also permits attackers to create man-in-the-middle attacks.

WEP Message Modification   WEP uses a 32-bit CRC that is a linear function of the plaintext. Although WEP's RC4 encryption covers the ICV, the stream

---

4. An interesting side note is that the attack by Fluhrer, Mantin, and Shamir would have been easier if the IV space were larger—solving one problem makes another worse. This is a good example of why security is difficult.

encryption also uses a linear combiner, XOR. As a result, we can manipulate an intercepted packet by flipping bits in the data and CRC portions of the packet to create a new—but still valid—packet with a different plaintext than the original (Walker, 2000; Borisov et al, 2001).

Recall how WEP produces ciphertext C by XORing the plaintext with the key stream. The attacker's goal in this attack is to produce a new ciphertext C' that decrypts to a new valid message with a valid ICV. Unfortunately, the attacker can accomplish this without knowing the value of the secret encryption key. Because both the RC4 encryption and the ICV are linear in nature, the attacker can modify an intercepted message by XORing the appropriate bits in the message portion of the ciphertext, and then calculating a new CRC of the changes and XORing this new CRC with the CRC portion of the datagram. The following equations, taken from Borisov et al. (2001), show this process mathematically.

$$C' = C \oplus \, < \Delta, CRC(\Delta) >$$
$$C' = RC4(IV,K) \oplus \, < M, CRC(M) > \oplus < \Delta, CRC(\Delta) >$$
$$C' = RC4(IV,K) \oplus \, < M \oplus \Delta, CRC(M) \oplus CRC(\Delta) >$$
$$C' = RC4(IV,K) \oplus \, < M', CRC(M \oplus \Delta) >$$
$$C' = RC4(IV,K) \oplus \, < M', CRC(M') >$$

The above derivation works because the WEP CRC is linear—that is, $CRC(M) \oplus CRC(\Delta) = CRC(M \oplus \Delta)$. An example message modification is shown in Appendix B.

An Active Implementation of Fluhrer, Mantin, and Shamir

The research literature has not discussed the possibility of using active measures to speed the process of obtaining enough packets for a successful Fluhrer, Mantin, and Shamir attack. Obviously, active measures only make sense on lightly loaded networks.

The two possible approaches are simple. In the first and easiest approach, traffic analysis identifies an address resolution protocol (ARP) request packet. The ARP request is replayed continuously (remember WEP has no replay protection) until it collects enough packets from the ARP responses to determine the RC4 key. The second approach involves slightly more work. Here, we wait until we see an ARP request message and build upon it until it provides enough known plaintext to recover an adequate pseudorandom stream to forge Internet Control Message Protocol (ICMP) ping packets (Petroni, 2003). Ping packets are forged and the responses collected until the RC4 key can be collected.

Experimentation indicates that approximately 450 ping packets and replies can be sent per second between a station (STA) and an AP, and thus we can collect the required one million packets in approximately thirty-seven minutes. Of course, this attack fully loads the network, but if done during off-hours, it would likely remain unnoticed.

Several vendors, however, are now filtering most of the Fluhrer weak IVs in their firmware. This prevents the attacker from collecting enough weak IVs to recover the WEP secret key, but it reduces the cost of a previous attack against WEP, as described next.

An Inductive Chosen Plaintext Attack

This attack leverages several poor design aspects of WEP. The first is the lack of replay protection, the second is the nature of the CRC used, and the third is the fact that WEP is a stream cipher rather than a block cipher. The attack involves two steps (Arbaugh, 2001 and Petroni, 2003). The first step, or base phase, involves recovery of an initial amount of pseudorandom stream from traffic analysis (eavesdropping). The second step, the inductive phase, then forges messages with the recovered pseudorandom until a dictionary of all IVs is created.

Base Phase During the base phase, we need to collect enough pseudorandom stream for a given IV so that we can begin to forge packets. The commonly used Dynamic Host Control Protocol (DHCP) makes this easy. We simply wait until we see a DHCP discover or request message that provides us with a base of known plaintext. This base is 38 bytes in length, composed of the following known elements:

- LLC header: 6 bytes
- IP header: 20 bytes
- UDP header[5]:   8 bytes
- DHCP header: 4 bytes

This provides us with a total of 38 bytes of pseudorandom stream, which is sufficient to forge ICMP echo request packets, also known as ping packets. We use a ping packet because it elicits a response from the targeted host, and it permits an arbitrary amount of data to be appended to the echo request.

Inductive Phase Once we've recovered enough pseudorandom stream, we can begin the inductive phase. The inductive phase has two parts: recovery of the maximum transmission unit (MTU) and building the dictionary.

---

5. The 2 bytes of the UDP checksum are usually set to all zeros in most DHCP implementations. Thus, we do not need to calculate that field.

MTU Recovery

We need to recover a full MTU of the pseudorandom byte stream so we can recover a full MTU of the pseudorandom byte stream for every ping packet transmitted. The method that we use is the most complicated aspect of this attack, and it leverages the fact that the CRC provides redundant information about the underlying plaintext and the fact that WEP is a stream cipher rather than a block cipher. Our goal is to recover the MTU 1 byte at a time by guessing the next byte, and waiting for confirmation that we guessed correctly.

We begin by crafting a ping packet in a very specific fashion. We start with the 38 bytes recovered in the inductive phase, and we set $n = 38$. A proper ping packet without any additional payload is 34 bytes (38 bytes when the CRC or ICV is added), but we want to send a packet of 39, or $n + 1$ bytes. We do this by guessing the 39th byte and constructing the ping packet as shown in Figure 15.4.

We create a packet of $n - 3$ bytes (or 35 bytes—ping packet plus 1 payload byte). This is the data portion in Figure 15.4. We next calculate the CRC/ICV over this data portion, but we append only the first 3 bytes of the result. Now, we XOR this data with the n bytes of the pseudorandom stream, and prepend the IEEE 802.11 header and the appropriate IV, which results in a packet of n bytes. Finally, we guess the $n + 1$ byte and append it to the packet. Now, we have the specially crafted ping packet. We transmit it, and wait a small amount of time for a response. If we get a response, we know we guessed the correct $n + 1$ byte and we can proceed to recover the corresponding pseudorandom byte. If we don't get a

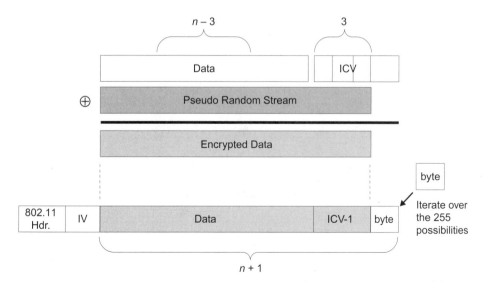

Figure 15.4 MTU Recovery Process

response, then we guessed incorrectly and we continue to try the remaining 255 byte possibilities. Once we get a response, we need to recover the $n + 1$ pseudo-random byte, as shown in Figure 15.5.

Because the host we pinged responded with an ICMP echo response packet, we know that the byte we guessed was the correct ciphertext byte for our packet. We also know the corresponding plaintext byte—the fourth byte of the ICV that we didn't use in creating the packet. We now XOR these 2 bytes together (known plaintext with corresponding ciphertext), and we recover the $n + 1$ pseudorandom byte.

Now because we recovered the $n + 1$ pseudorandom byte, we continue this process (increasing n by one to recover the $n + 2$ pseudorandom byte) until we recover a full MTU—usually 1,500 bytes for Ethernet.

Building the Dictionary

Once we've recovered the full MTU, we need to build a dictionary of all of the 2^{24} (16,777,216) possible IVs used. This dictionary (assuming an indexed flat file) will be approximately 23.5 gigabytes—well within range of today's laptop computers.

The actual recovery of the pseudorandom stream for each IV leverages the fact that the ICMP echo response returns exactly the same data that was appended to the ICMP echo request. Thus, if we send a ping equal in size to the MTU, we'll get a response of exactly the same size. But, it will be encrypted with a different IV than the one in which we transmitted the IV. Therefore, we once again have known plaintext (the data we appended to the ping request) along with the corresponding

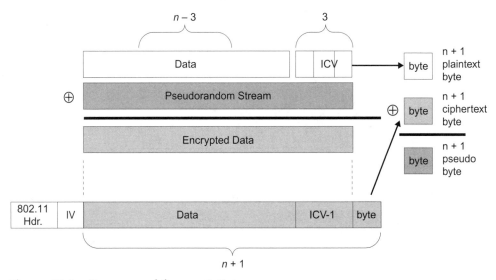

Figure 15.5 Recovery of the n + 1 Byte

plaintext. This permits the recovery of a full MTU's worth of pseudorandom for the returned IV. To build the full dictionary, we continue the above process until we have every IV.

Cost of the Attack

The cost of the inductive chosen plaintext attack depends on how aggressive the attacker wants to be. We'll assume a moderately aggressive attacker in our calculations so we can approximate worst case for the defender.

In an implementation of the attack, the average time of recovery for a single byte in the inductive phase was 1.7 seconds/byte, and the average time to recover a full MTU (1,500 bytes) was 42.8 minutes. Once a full MTU is recovered, we need to build the dictionary. A current implementation of the attack recovers IVs at a rate of 11.5 msec/IV, or 53.7 hours to recover all 2^{24} IVs with a single host—a fairly significant amount of time. However, building the dictionary is embarrassingly parallel and the total time to build the dictionary can be found by dividing 53.7 hours by the number of attacking hosts. Thus, an attacker using eight different hosts in the attack can reduce the time to around six hours—something to worry about, especially because the time required is completely independent of the key size. In other words, it takes approximately six hours to build the dictionary (or seven hours total) for both 40- and 104-bit WEP keys.

Effects of Filtering IVs

A number of vendors are now filtering IVs to protect against the multiple open source implementations of the Fluhrer et al. attack (see Chapter 16). The most aggressive filtering reduces the IV space by 6 bits to 2^{18} (262,144)—a significant reduction in IV space, and a significant reduction in the overall time of the inductive chosen plaintext attack. The reduction in time occurs only with building the dictionary so we still must take 42.8 minutes to recover a full MTU. But now instead of taking over 53 hours to build the dictionary with one attacking host, we can build the dictionary in 50.3 minutes—a serious reduction in time and the size of the dictionary shrinks considerably as well.

Ironically, the countermeasure to one attack makes another attack significantly better—better in some respects than the attack the countermeasure was designed to prevent.

Access Control

While the 1999 version of the IEEE 802.11 standard does not define a mechanism for access control, most implementations use MAC address-based access control lists. In addition, a major vendor has implemented a proprietary access control mechanism entitled Closed Network. This section describes the significant flaws found in each.

Problems with MAC-Based Access Control Lists

In theory, ACLs provide a reasonable level of security when we use a strong form of identity. Unfortunately, MAC addresses do not provide strong identity for two reasons. First, an attacker can easily observe MAC addresses because they must appear in the clear even when WEP is enabled. Second, some wireless cards allow their MAC address to be changed via software. As a result, an attacker can easily eavesdrop to determine valid MAC addresses and program the desired address into the wireless card, bypassing access control and gaining access to the network.

Problems with Proprietary Closed Network Access Control

In most IEEE 802.11 wireless networks, the access point broadcasts the network identity using a text string called SSID. This allows a mobile device to search for specific networks by listening to broadcasts called beacons. The idea of the closed network is to treat the network name or SSID as a secret so the mobile device must have prior knowledge of the SSID before connecting. In practice, security mechanisms based on a shared secret are robust, provided the secrets are well protected when in use and when distributed. Unfortunately, although the SSID can be hidden in the beacon, there are several other management messages in IEEE 802.11 that contain the network name in the clear. (The actual messages containing the SSID depend on the vendor of the access point.) As a result, an attacker can easily sniff the network name to determine the shared secret and gain access to the network. This flaw exists even with WEP-enabled networks because management frames are not protected.

Authentication

As previously discussed, the 1999 version of IEEE 802.11 provides only two forms of authentication. Obviously, the open method of authentication provides no security as all stations are permitted to associate. Unfortunately, although the shared-key authentication method was designed with security in mind, it is not secure.

Shared-Key Authentication

An attacker can easily exploit the original IEEE 802.11 shared-key authentication through a passive attack by eavesdropping on one leg of a mutual authentication. The attack works because of the protocol's fixed structure, wherein the only difference between authentication messages is the random challenge, and the weaknesses in WEP (Arbaugh et al., 2001; Arbaugh et al., 2002). The attacker first captures the second and third management messages from the authentication exchange. The second message contains the random challenge in the clear, while the third message contains the challenge encrypted with the shared authentication key. Because the attacker now knows the random challenge P, the encrypted challenge ciphertext C, and the public IV, the attacker can derive the pseudorandom stream produced using $\mathrm{WEP^{K,\,IV}_{PR}}$, with the shared key K and the public initialization variable, IV, as shown below:

$$\mathrm{WEP^{K,\,IV}_{PR}} = C \oplus P$$

The recovered pseudorandom stream, $\mathrm{WEP^{K,\,IV}_{PR}}$, is the same size as the authentication frame because all the frame's elements are known: algorithm number, sequence number, status code, element ID, length, and the challenge text. Furthermore, all but the challenge text will remain the same for *all* authentication responses. The attacker now has all of the elements to successfully authenticate to the target network without ever knowing the shared secret K. The attacker requests authentication of the AP it wishes to associate/join. The AP responds with an authentication challenge in the clear. The attacker uses the random challenge text R and the pseudorandom stream—$\mathrm{WEP^{K,\,IV}_{PR}}$—to compute a valid authentication response frame body by XORing the two values together. The attacker then computes a new ICV, as described by Borisov et al. (2001). Finally, the attacker responds with a valid authentication response message and associates with the AP to join the network.

Man-in-the-Middle Attacks

The basic concept of man-in-the-middle (MiM) attacks was introduced in Chapter 4. In this section, we discuss the details of how exactly an attacker could establish a man-in-the-middle attack against your wireless network. There are two different methods to establish a man-in-the-middle attack in a wireless network. The first is using management frames and is specific to wireless networking, and the second is ARP spoofing, which is also a problem for wired networks.

Management Frames

Because the management frames lack any integrity protection, establishing a man in the middle with IEEE 802.11 based networks is easy (there's even a hacker tool that will do it for you, described in Chapter 16). MiMs can be established regardless of any protections (WPA, RSN, VPN, and so on) that you might be using but do not necessarily pose a threat if the security protocol is strong. MiM attacks are possible because there are no integrity guarantees provided at the link layer (layer 2), and MAC addresses are easily forged.

The attack begins (assuming that the target STA is already associated to an AP) by the attacker issuing a Deauthentication message to the target STA. This causes the STA to drop its association with its current AP and look to reassociate with

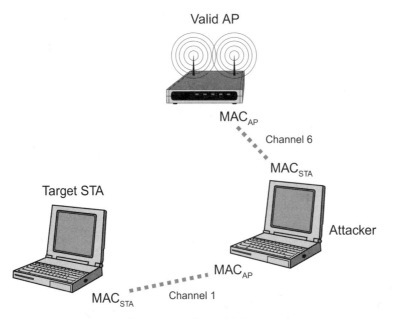

Figure 15.6 Example Man-in-the-Middle Attack

another (possibly the old) AP. At the same time, the attacker establishes a malicious AP with the same ESSID and MAC address as an AP within range of the attacker but on a different channel than the valid AP. The target STA associates with the attacker's fake AP because it is denied service at the valid AP by the attacker's forged Deauthentication messages. Once the STA has associated with the bogus AP, the bogus AP immediately associates with the valid AP and begins forwarding all traffic so authentication (if used as in WPA or RSN) completes. This process is shown in Figure 15.6. The attacker now has complete control over the traffic stream between the STA and its valid AP. If encryption is not used, then the attacker can modify packets before forwarding. If encryption is used, packets can be denied or delayed. They can also be modified to assist in other attacks, as we'll see later in this chapter.

ARP Spoofing

ARP spoofing has been a plague on wired networks for some time; and while there are some limited countermeasures available to prevent and identify ARP attacks, an ARP attack can still succeed more often than not. ARP identifies the MAC address for a given IP address. A client or STA wanting to communicate with a specific IP address issues an ARP-Request as a broadcast packet on the LAN asking to learn the MAC address of the given IP address. Because ARP packets do not have any integrity protection, anyone (even attackers with access to LAN) can respond with incorrect or malicious information, effectively poisoning the ARP cache of the requestor. Thus, from that point until the cache entry times out, the client uses an improper MAC address for the given IP address, causing all traffic to go to the attacker rather than the real recipient.

There is an important distinction between using management frames (as described in the previous section) and using ARP spoofing for establishing MiM attacks. With ARP spoofing, the attacker must have access to the link layer, whereas using management frames does not have this requirement. If encryption is being used, the attacker must first break the encryption (or be able to forge packets) before he can perform a successful ARP spoofing attack. With WEP-based networks, breaking the encryption, as we have seen, is a small problem. But with WPA- or RSN-based networks, this is a significant (and hopefully impossible) hurdle.

Problems Created by Man-in-the-Middle Attacks

Because the attacker can inject himself between communicating parties (the STA and AP) in a man-in-the-middle attack, the attacker has the ability to completely control the content of the communications (if encryption and message authenticity are not used); and even if encryption and/or message authenticity is used, the attacker can still deny or delay communications.

This section examines two different problems that occur because of MiM attacks. In the first case, the attacker can hijack, or take over, a session; even when robust authentication and access control are used without encryption. In the second case, an MiM attack eliminates the protection afforded by the use of an encrypted tunnel.

802.1x and EAP

Shortly after the IEEE 802.1x protocol was defined, a large number of users were considering using it for authenticating users at hotspots without using WEP. While in theory this is a good idea, using 802.1x this way didn't solve any problems (Mishra and Arbaugh, 2002). Essentially, the attacker simply waits until the STA is completely authenticated and then sends a forged Disassociate or Deauthentication management frame to the STA. At this point, the STA believes it no longer has a session and attempts to reconnect (the attacker can continue to send forged management frames to the STA, keeping it from establishing a session). The AP, on the other hand, believes there is still a session, and the attacker can now use that session, masquerading as the STA up until a reauthentication event takes place—usually in five minutes.

Finally, we earlier discussed in Chapter 9 the problems with EAP and so we won't duplicate that discussion here.

PEAP

PEAP was designed to protect the EAP exchange from eavesdroppers (see Chapter 9). There were two reasons for this. The first was to provide privacy and allow users to remain anonymous to eavesdroppers because traffic analysis can be a significant threat in some cases, and the second was to provide protection for the EAP control messages EAP-Success and EAP-Failure. Unfortunately, an easy MiM attack eliminates all of the protection provided by PEAP when anonymous connections are supported.

In the first phase of PEAP, an anonymous tunnel is established between the STA and the AP, with the STA sending an anonymous identity if it likes. If the STA sends an anonymous identity, then it cannot be authenticated. A TLS tunnel is created nonetheless with the anonymous credentials, and phase 2 is started, which is a normal EAP session.

The attack against PEAP works by establishing the MiM prior to phase 1 of PEAP. The attacker establishes two different anonymous tunnels. The first (PEAP phase 1) is with the AP, and second (PEAP phase 1) is with the STA. In the first tunnel with the AP, the attacker masquerades as the STA, and in the second tunnel the attacker masquerades as the AP. The STA now begins phase 2 and the attacker sees the true identity information of the STA as well as having the ability to forge EAP control messages—just as if PEAP were not being used (Asokan et al., 2003).

Denial-of-Service Attacks

We've made denial-of-service attacks into a separate section for several reasons. First, denial-of-service attacks are extremely difficult to protect against, and especially so with wireless. Any attacker with a bigger amplifier, antenna, or using more power, can deny service to an individual or group at the RF level. As a result, RF attacks are difficult but not impossible to prevent. The military, for instance, uses spread spectrum, frequency hopping, and probably ultrawide-band systems to mitigate the possibility of an attacker jamming important frequencies. We don't have that luxury because our equipment is readily available to our attackers. Therefore, RF-based denial-of-service attacks against IEEE 802.11-based networks (and actually any consumer wireless standard) are nearly impossible to prevent. An attacker with the know-how and access to the right equipment can mount a denial-of-service attack against your wireless network.

Another class of denial-of-service attack against the network and cryptographic protocols, specifically layer 2 or the MAC layer, is preventable. Unfortunately, neither the old nor the new Wi-Fi standards opted to protect against this form of attack—TGi debated the cost of protecting against layer 2 denial-of-service attacks, but opted for downward compatibility with the old standard rather than protection against denial-of-service attacks.

Layer 2 Denial-of-Service Attacks Against All Wi-Fi-Based Standards

You may have noticed that the management frames, for example, Associate-request, don't have any integrity protection. That is, these frames can easily be forged by an attacker. An attacker can deny service to a station/client or to an entire access point, and in some cases across a LAN.

The attack is trivial with the right software (see Chapter 16). If the attacker wishes to prevent a station from using the Wi-Fi LAN, he has several choices. First, when the attacker can see the AP to which the station is associated, he simply forges a Disassociation or Deauthentication frame and sends it to either the AP or STA. The AP/STA, thinking that the station wishes to leave (or the AP no longer can service the STA), grants the request and closes the association. Unfortunately, both of these management frames (Disassociation and Deauthentication) permit the attacker to use the broadcast MAC address as the target. This results in all stations associated with the targeted AP being knocked off the AP.

Second, the attacker can deny service to a station when he can see an AP on the same wired LAN as the AP to which the target station is associated. In this case, the attacker sends a forged Association-request message with the target station's MAC address to an AP on the same wired LAN. The AP that receives the association request approves (because we don't authenticate until after association) it and sends out a layer 2 update frame to the wired LAN. The router or switch now begins forwarding traffic to the AP that just sent the layer 2 update, and the actual station no longer receives any traffic. Obviously, both of these attacks need to be constantly run to prevent service to a particular station, and this is one of the reasons why TGi opted not to protect against it.

Another method of denying service to a group is similar and involves loading up an AP with bogus stations such that the resources on the AP are exhausted and the AP either reboots or no longer permits new stations to associate to it.

TGi decided not to protect against these attacks because the majority of the participants felt that a determined attacker can always resort to an RF-based attack. The majority of the members of TGi also were concerned with potential problems with backward compatibility if integrity protection were added to management frames. Unfortunately, these attacks have been implemented in an open source tool (see Chapter 16).

WPA Cryptographic Denial-of-Service Attack

Michael is a lightweight message authenticity algorithm (see Chapter 11). Because Michael provides only 20 bits of protection against message modification attacks, countermeasures were designed to prevent active attacks. These countermeasures are effective at preventing the creation of a forged message. However, they also introduce the potential for a denial-of-service attack against the entire AP.

A capable attacker can accomplish the WPA denial-of-service attack. The attack isn't trivial to accomplish, but it doesn't require rocket science either. Essentially, the attacker must accomplish three tasks. The first is to stop a valid packet from reaching the AP, and then, second, to modify the packet such that the ICV remains valid. The third and final task is to send the modified packet before a packet with a higher TSC is received by the AP.

Accomplishing all three tasks is easy once a man-in-the-middle attack is established between the AP and an STA. Because the attacker controls the connection between to the STA and AP, he can easily perform the first and third tasks. Performing the second task requires applying what we discussed earlier in this chapter and is shown in Appendix A to modify the message.

Once the attacker sends two such modified packets to the AP within a minute, the AP shuts down for exactly one minute, preventing traffic from all stations associated with the AP from communicating. The AP must also rekey stations immediately upon beginning service after the one-minute delay.

While this is a particularly brutal DoS attack, the same results are obtained by using a much easier attack—the management frame DoS described earlier.

Summary

Unfortunately, none of the original security mechanisms in IEEE 802.11 wireless local networks were robust. Adversaries easily bypass both the access control mechanisms and the shared-key authentication mechanism. Serious flaws in the WEP encapsulation process allow recovery of the secret encryption key and the malicious modification and replay of WEP-protected datagrams. Each of these problems alone poses a significant threat to deployed wireless networks—together, they make exploiting wireless networks easy.

Fortunately, both WPA and RSN prevent the confidentiality, integrity, and access control attacks (see Chapter 7). Unfortunately, however, neither WPA nor RSN prevents denial-of-service attacks using forged management frames. The topic was hotly debated during several TGi meetings, and the consensus of the task group, not necessarily the authors, was that DoS attacks are a fact of life in wireless networking and that protecting the management frames would create downward compatibility problems.

16 Chapter

Actual Attack Tools

Therefore, against those skilled in attack, an enemy does not know where to defend; against the experts in defense, the enemy does not know where to attack.

Therefore I say: 'Know the enemy but know yourself; in a hundred battles you will never be in peril.'

—Sun Tzu, *The Art of War*

This chapter looks in detail at several tools, available on the Internet, that hackers can use to attack Wi-Fi networks. Most are UNIX based and require the ability to compile (and sometimes tweak) the tool. However, more are becoming available for Microsoft Windows all the time. We explain where to get the tools, what they do, and how to use them. Some people might feel uncomfortable about our publicizing these tools and explaining their use. However, it is our goal to remove any doubt you may have about their potency. By getting in the driver's seat, you will get a better understanding of how weak the older Wi-Fi systems are. The good news is that the tools are of very limited use against WPA or RSN. Certainly, you would not be able to use them to gather any information about secret keys or encrypted data. So view this chapter as a cautionary tale and feel glad that you at least "know the enemy."

By understanding how the bad guys operate, and the tools they use, you can better design, install, and operate your defenses (in other words, better understand the threat against your system). Understanding today's threat does not necessarily make you immune. The computer security process is very much like the Borg in

Star Trek: The Next Generation. That is, the bad guys will adapt based on what you do. You must stay vigilant, react to the changes that the attackers make, and plan your responses.

Before describing the attack tools, we review the attacker's process in a generic sense to give you some insight into how you might be attacked. Not all of the bad guys operate exactly as we describe, but their process is similar.

Attacker Goals

One of the main issues to understand is, "What is the goal and/or goals of the attacker?" Different attackers have different goals. For instance, the disgruntled employee may only want to "to turn the lights out" with a denial-of-service (DoS) attack, which is an availability attack. Another attacker may want to steal personal information to facilitate identity theft, which is a confidentiality attack.

Fortunately, the goals of the attacker align with the three main security properties: availability, confidentiality, and integrity. Which one is most important to a specific attacker depends on their motivation and the underlying value of your information.

You now have an idea what the attackers want to achieve. Let's take a look at how they're going to try and do it.

Process

The process an attacker follows is very similar to the process that the military uses when planning an operation. In essence, you have to first find out where you want to go (reconnaissance). Then, you have to figure out how to get there and what you will do when you arrive (planning and collection). Finally, you need to review your collection and then execute the operation.

While it might be a bit of a stretch to say that an attacker plans and executes with military-like precision, even the most undisciplined attackers follow (unknowingly) some aspects of this process, as shown in Figure 16.1.

The process is cyclic because, at any point, additional information may be required that forces a return to an earlier phase to obtain the information.

Reconnaissance

One of the most important aspects of any attack is reconnaissance; the target must be identified. In the wireless LAN case, there are two ways that an attacker can identify a target, and the motive of an attacker plays an important part here. If the attacker is just looking for network access, then he will seek until he finds an easy victim. By contrast, in a targeted attack, the attacker focuses on finding access associated with his target, which is slightly more difficult for the attacker and significantly more difficult for the defender to defend against.

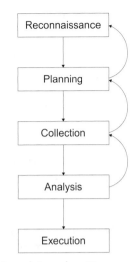

Figure 16.1 High-Level Attacker Process

If the attacker is only looking for network access, his reconnaissance could be limited to looking at any of the many publicly available databases or maps of access points. These maps and databases can be found on many Internet sites, such as www.nodedb.com, and an attacker need only find one near his current location. The process, however, is slightly more difficult for the attacker if he has to find a specific target.

Finding a wireless LAN target requires war driving, which is a process named after the term *war dialing*.[1] War driving, or wilding, seeks to find access points accessible outside the bounds of their deployment—in the street, for example.

The tools required for war driving are simple and widely available: a notebook computer, a Wi-Fi PC card, a special software program, and, optionally, a directional antenna and GPS receiver. Simple war driving can be done with a completely standard setup because both Microsoft Windows XP and Apple's MacOS X have a means to identify Wi-Fi equipment built in. They lack, however, the ability to trace; that is, to record the time and location of identified access points.

The next two sections discuss two of the most popular war driving software programs available at the time of this writing.

---

1. War dialing describes how attackers find computer systems on the plain old telephone system (POTS) network. Several tools, most notably toneloc, were written to assist attackers in finding computers attached to telephones by "brute forcing" telephone numbers—trying every possible telephone number (9999) in a given exchange. In war driving, rather than brute force telephone numbers, people drive or walk around looking for access points.

NetStumbler

One of the most popular software programs for war driving is the NetStumbler program (www.stumbler.net). This program, which only works under Microsoft Windows, provides an intuitive user interface along with the ability to connect with several types of GPS receivers. The result, when combined with a laptop and GPS, is an easily installed and operated tool for war driving.

One of the main reasons for the popularity of NetStumbler, besides the fact that it runs on the most popular operating system family, is that it is easy to install and operate. Just download, plug in a supported Wireless LAN card, and double-click!

NetStumbler displays most of the information needed in one screen, broken down into two panes (see Figure 16.2). The left pane provides shortcuts for displaying the networks in just about any fashion. By default, the main pane on the right displays all the networks. However, you can easily choose to view only those networks on a specific channel, specific SSIDs or those with encryption, and so on. In fact, the interface is so intuitive and easy to use, we won't waste any more time explaining it.

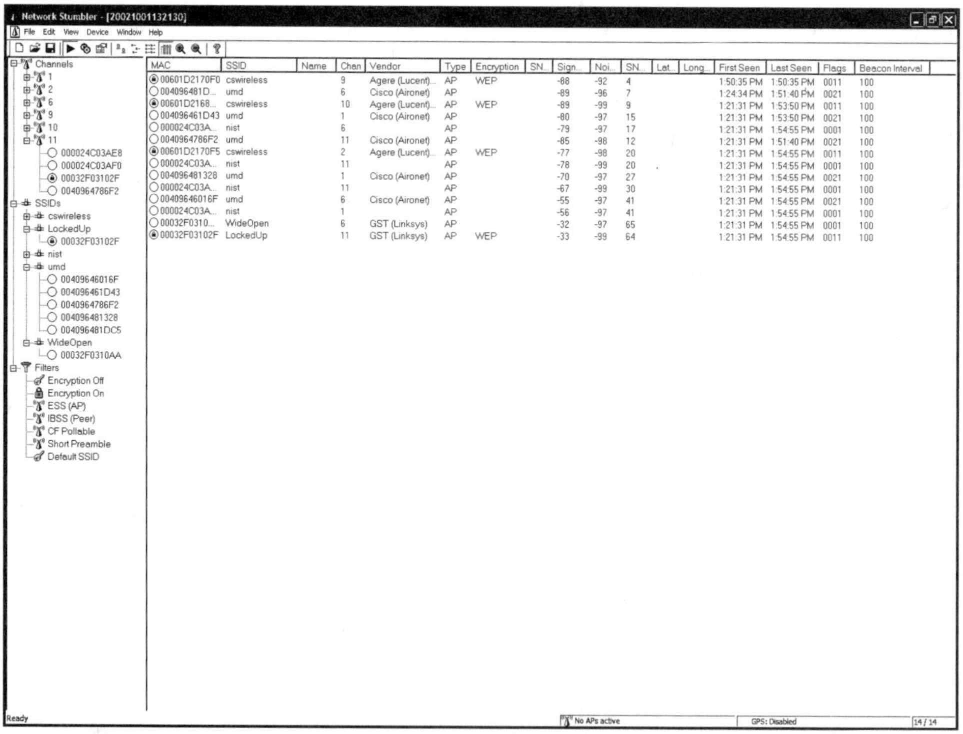

Figure 16.2 NetStumbler Main Screen

Figure 16.3   PocketStumbler

The maker of NetStumbler, Marius Milner, even has a tool worthy of James Bond: MiniStumbler, which runs on a Pocket PC (see Figure 16.3). Now, attackers can walk around the interiors of office buildings, without attracting attention, with a PDA hidden in their inner suit pocket. With this program, any wireless LANs located in publicly accessible buildings are at risk of detection, and potential compromise, if they lack basic security protection.

While NetStumbler is easy to operate, it lacks the sophistication of the next tool that we're going to describe: Kismet. From an attacker's point of view, one of the major problems with NetStumbler is that it operates in an active mode—that is, it transmits probe requests as part of the process of finding access points. Using probe requests creates an additional problem for the attacker because the attacker won't be able to identify any of the closed or cloaked networks; these networks will not respond to a probe request without the correct network name (SSID).

Kismet

Another popular tool for war driving is Kismet (www.kismetwireless.net). Kismet is a completely passive tool (does not transmit probe requests) that runs under the Linux and OpenBSD operating systems. Kismet includes all of the functionality of NetStumbler as well as basic traffic analysis functionality. An attacker running Kismet easily determines the network configuration for those networks running without basic WEP protection, and it displays character strings it sees in the traffic. This is good for finding passwords and so on. Kismet does this by examining and displaying the traffic on the targeted network such as IP headers and ARP requests. This process provides essential information to the attacker so that they may use (or should we say abuse) the targeted network.

Kismet saves the information it collects in a series of files that can be viewed later. These files contain lists of all of the information about a network, raw packet dumps, and captured WEP traffic so that it can be fed into one of the open source WEP crackers available (more on that later in this chapter).

The main window of Kismet is shown in Figure 16.4. On the right side, there is a short informational panel displaying the number of networks found (Ntwrks), the number of packets (Pckets) seen, the number of encrypted packets (Cryptd), the number of encrypted packets with a weak IV (Weak), packets interpreted as noise (Noise), the number of packets discarded due to bad CRC (ICV) values (Discrd), the packet rate (Pkts/s), and the total elapsed time in seconds (Elapsd). The lower panel lists status messages as they occur. The largest and main panel of Kismet provides a network list of all of the networks found since Kismet was started as well as information about each of the networks. The exact information shown for the networks is configurable. Figure 16.4 shows the default configuration.

The first column lists the name, or SSID, of the network found. An exclamation point (!) before the name indicates activity was seen in the last three seconds, while a period (.) indicates activity was seen in the last six seconds. The next column, headed by "T", indicates the type of network identified. An "A" indicates an access point in infrastructure mode, a "D" indicates a data-only host or station, and an "H" indicates an ad-hoc network master.

The third column, headed by "W", indicates whether WEP is used by the network. "Y" indicates yes, and "N" indicates no. One of the interesting things about Kismet is what the developer calls "fuzzy encryption detection." Some access points don't properly indicate when WEP is used by setting the appropriate bit in

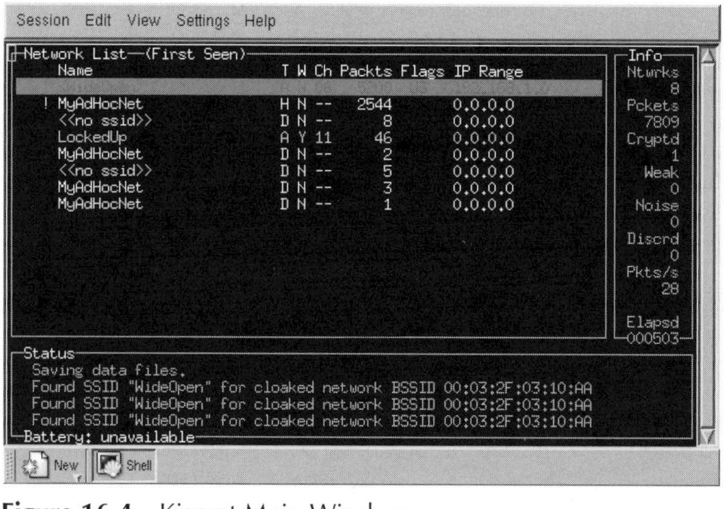

Figure 16.4 Kismet Main Window

the IEEE 802.11 header of the packet. As a result, relying solely on that bit results in misidentifying some networks as not using WEP when they really do. Kismet looks at the first few bytes of the LLC header to see whether they are the same. If they are, WEP is not used. If they aren't, encryption is being used.

The fourth column, "Ch", shows the channel that the network is using. This is followed by the number of packets seen, Packts. The sixth column, Flags, provides information about the network. Specifically, it indicates how the IP Range in the next column was determined. An "A" indicates that the IP block was found by an ARP packet, and a "U" indicates that the block was found with a UDP packet. Both indicators ("A" and "U") can be followed by a positive integer value that indicates the number of octets that match within the address block. Finally, a "D" indicates that the block was found with a DHCP packet, and a "C" indicates that Kismet identified Cisco discovery packets on the network, and thus Cisco equipment.

In addition to the main window, Kismet provides several other popup displays that provide additional information about a specific network. When Kismet starts up, it is in Auto fit mode. In this mode, the network names change position automatically based on the last network seen. In this mode, you're unable to scroll among the networks and select one to learn more information. So, the first thing you want to do is select the Sort window by pressing "s". You are presented with a number of different ways to sort the network information in the main pane. When you make a choice, the window redisplays.

You are now able to scroll among the displayed networks with the up and down arrows. In Figure 16.4, the first network, WideOpen, is selected. By pressing the "i" key, a popup window appears with all of the information Kismet knows about the selected network. An example is shown in Figure 16.5.

As you can see in Figure 16.5, Kismet provides a great deal more information about the selected network than NetStumbler. Kismet can even provide a real-time dump of the ASCII strings that it sees on the selected network. To get that information, click the "d" key in the main window (see Figure 16.6). The strings from the intercepted traffic are displayed, indicating in the example in the figure, the download of a Web page from www.ieee802.org, which we initiated as part of a test. This window continues to show the intercepted strings until you exit by clicking the "x" key.

Note that one potential issue with the use of Kismet, and specifically this function, is that it may *violate state and/or federal law* by intercepting communications. We certainly do not advocate such use and, if you are tempted to try the tool, we highly recommend that you discuss this issue with your own legal counsel before proceeding.

Kismet provides two other informational popup windows. The first provides statistics about channel and encryption usage (Figure 16.7). Open it by clicking "a" from the main window. Open the second window (Figure 16.8) by clicking "r" to show the packet reception rate.

Figure 16.5 Kismet Network Information Display

Figure 16.6 Kismet Strings Dump

We've covered only part of Kismet's capability. We haven't covered the files that Kismet generates as archival information, or the integration of Kismet with a global positioning system (GPS). Learning and using these capabilities are straightforward; but as with any powerful tool, Kismet takes a little bit of time to get the most out of it. Once you've learned the basics, however, Kismet becomes a potent tool.

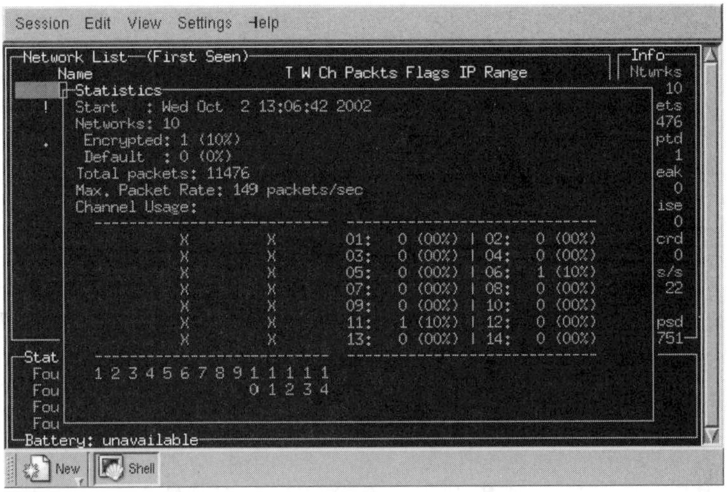

Figure 16.7   Kismet Channel Usage

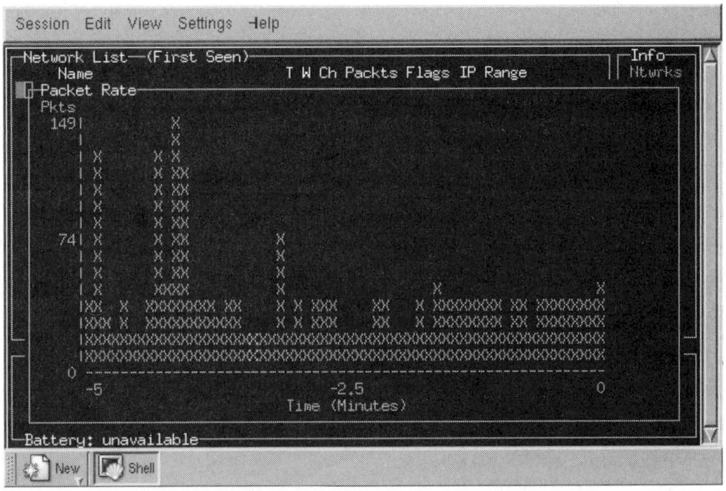

Figure 16.8   Kismet Packet Reception Rate

Example Scenarios

The remainder of this chapter describes two example scenarios. The first is a network that does not provide any security; we'll call it WideOpen. The second, which uses the original basic Wi-Fi protections, we'll call LockedUp. Both the WideOpen and the LockedUp network are shown in Figure 16.4 so you can see the initial identification of the network.

We will now pretend to be an attacker with the goal, in each case, of becoming a fully functional peer on the network.

Planning

This section explains the steps we need to follow to meet our goal of becoming a fully functional peer on each of the example, or target, networks.

WideOpen

The WideOpen network is running without WEP, and as such Kismet was able to determine the IP network address range (refer back to Figure 16.4). Kismet also creates a file of all of the captured packets (usually named *Kismet-<date>.dump*, where *<date>* is the date when the packets were captured), which you can review with a tool such as Ethereal (www.ethereal.com), as shown in Figure 16.9. Using Ethereal, you can determine the MAC address of valid clients as well as determine whether the wireless network is using shared-key authentication. In Figure 16.9, a packet trace is shown of the WideOpen network using Ethereal. A probe request from a client is shown prior to the client joining the network.

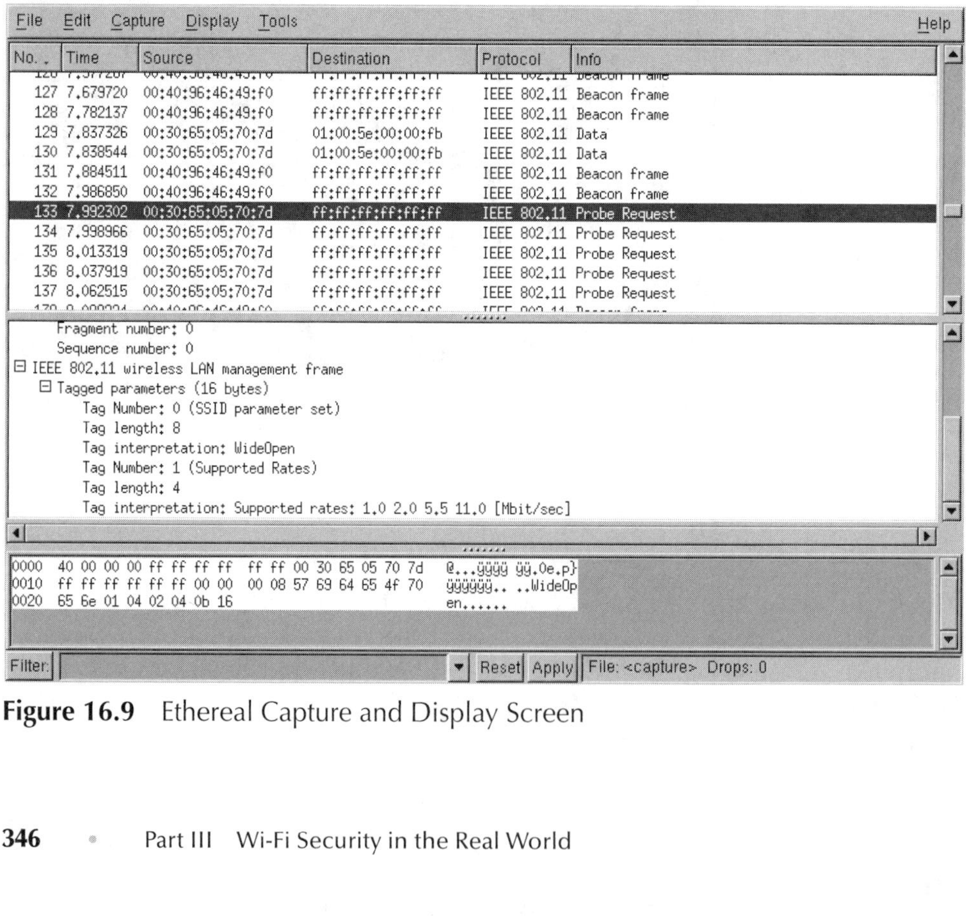

Figure 16.9 Ethereal Capture and Display Screen

At this point, we probably don't need any collection beyond that already done by Kismet. Therefore, we're ready to execute and become a peer on the network once we've successfully identified a valid client and determined whether shared-key authentication is being used. We don't expect that shared-key authentication is being used because, although shared key is specified by IEEE 802.11, shared key is not allowed in Wi-Fi certified equipment.

LockedUp

Things are much different with the LockedUp network (see Figure 16.10). In this case, we can't see any of the network parameters we see in Kismet. Therefore, we must first crack the WEP key with one of the many WEP-cracking utilities that are available on the Internet. One of the more effective programs, bsd-airtools by David Hulton (www.dachb0den.com/projects/bsd-airtools.html), comes with a set of utilities for scanning and cracking WEP networks. This example covers two of those tools, dwepdump and dwepcrack. Dwepdump collects WEP-encrypted packets and stores them in a file for later use by dwepcrack, which attempts to recover the corresponding WEP key. Both tools are explained in more detail later in this chapter.

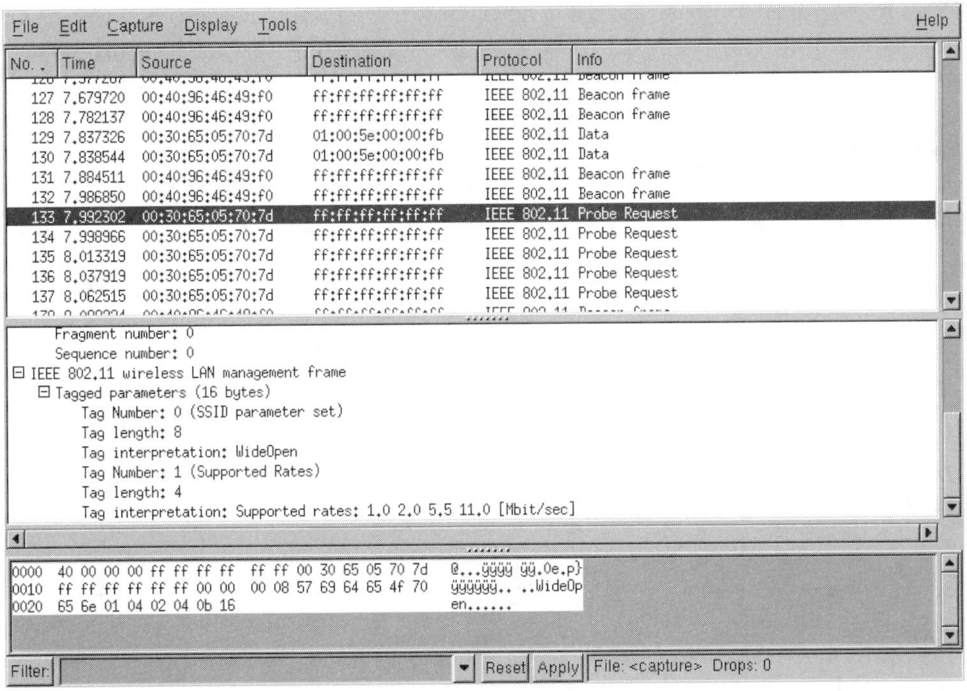

Figure 16.10   Ethereal Display of the WEP-Protected LockedUp Network

So our plan now is to move on to collection, when we'll use dwepdump to collect enough traffic to successfully break the WEP key.

Collection

The process of using dwepdump to collect enough packets to recover a WEP key is simple; the most difficult part is determining what key size (40 bits or 104 bits) the network is using. As a rule of thumb, you're probably best starting with 40 bits unless you suspect the target network is particularly concerned about security.

A sample invocation and screenshot of dwepdump collecting traffic for 40-bit WEP is shown in Figure 16.11. The screen shows six columns. The first three indicate the number (in hexadecimal) of weak IVs found for the first three key bytes. The first column is the one described by Scott Fluhrer et al. (2002) and the second and third columns are those described by the developer of bsd-airtools, who extended the FMS beyond the first key byte. The fourth column displays the total number of packets with a weak IV, the fifth column lists the total number of packets seen, and the last column displays the actual weak IV found of the first class only. We made this modification to help show what weak IVs look like; you won't see this column in the tool you download. You'll also note that the IV is printed backward.

Dwepdump must run until you collect at least 60 (0x3c in hexadecimal) weak IVs for the first byte (first column displaying 0x3c). You may also require more than 60 weak IVs for the first key byte in practice because this attack is probabilistic—in other words, each weak IV for the first byte provides a hint as to the first key byte with a 5% probability. In our experience, having around 80 weak IVs guarantees success, while 60 works most (but not all) of the time.

The length of time required to recover these packets depends on the load and number of clients visible to the collection client. It also depends on the type of

Figure 16.11 Dwepdump Screen Capture

equipment being used by the target. If *all* of the equipment being used by the target filters out weak IVs (as most of the major vendors' latest firmware does), dwepdump may never collect enough of the important first class of IVs. If, however, the equipment is not filtering weak IVs, the length of time will vary from 20 minutes to several days, depending on the network load.

Analysis

At this point in the process, we've collected enough data to begin analyzing it. In some scenarios, however, more data may be required. In such scenarios, we could just go back to collection or planning when we need to revise our plan.

Recovery of WEP Key

Once enough packets have been collected, recovering the WEP key is straightforward using dwepcrack. An example of starting dwepcrack is shown in Figure 16.12. In this case, however, the key is not correctly identified. When this happens, you have two choices. You can go back and try and collect more packets to add to those you've already collected, or you can use a fudge factor to identify the key. Dwepcrack works by calculating the probability for all 256 potential byte values for each position within the key. Thus, a 40-bit key would have an array of probabilities of [5 × 256]. The fudge factor tells the cracking program how far down the list of probabilities to try for each position. Thus, a fudge value of 2 would try the top two likely key values in each position until it found the correct match or finished trying each value. A brute-force of the entire key space would, therefore, be a fudge value of 256. It's not worth using a fudge value of 256 because it probably won't finish. Instead, you could use a value under six when you have more than 60 of the first class of weak IVs.

```
* Copyright (c) DachbOden Labs 2002 [http://dachbOden.com] *

bash-2.05# dwepcrack -w /usr/local/demo/book.cap

* dwepcrack v0.4 by h1kari <h1kari@dachbOden.com> *
* Copyright (c) DachbOden Labs 2002 [http://dachbOden.com] *

reading in captured ivs, snap headers, and samples... done
total packets: 51375

calculating ksa probabilities...
 0: 69/768 keys
 1: 16352/131328 keys
 2: 24348/197376 keys
 3: 24299/197120 keys
 4: 40827/328703 keys

warming up the grinder...
 packet length: 44
 init vector: 77:8a:6a
 default tx key: 0

progress: .
```

Figure 16.12 Dwepcrack Failing to Find the Correct Key

```
* dwepcrack v0.4 by h1kari <h1kari@dachb0den.com> *
* Copyright (c) Dachb0den Labs 2002 [http://dachb0den.com] *

reading in captured ivs, snap headers, and samples... done
total packets: 51375

calculating ksa probabilities...
  0: 69/768 keys
  1: 16352/131328 keys
  2: 24348/197376 keys
  3: 24299/197120 keys
  4: 40827/328703 keys

warming up the grinder...
  packet length: 44
  init vector: 77:8a:6a
  default tx key: 0

progress: .

wep keys successfully cracked!
  0: 70:68:78:61:7a *
done.
```

Figure 16.13 Dwepcrack Finding the Correct WEP Key

Figure 16.13 shows a run of dwepcrack using a fudge factor under six on the same set of data analyzed in Figure 16.12. In this case, however, the WEP key is found quickly after all of the data is read into memory from the file system. You'll find that the reading of the data into memory is usually the most time-consuming process and that, once that data is in memory, the amount of time spent analyzing the data is less than a minute.

Dwepcrack is an incredibly powerful tool, and it doesn't take a significant effort to learn how to use all of its power. Current versions of dwepcrack run on both FreeBSD and OpenBSD.

Passive Identification of Network Parameters

At this point, you've recovered the WEP key. But you know nothing of the network configuration. You basically have two choices. The first is to write a custom program (none currently exists for downloading) that decrypts the data you've already collected and formats it for display in Ethereal. The second is to use the WEP key and collect more traffic with your wireless LAN card set to decrypt the traffic and display it in Ethereal. Alternatively, you can set the encryption key in the Kismet configuration file and Kismet will identify the network parameters for you.

In either case, you must examine the raw packet traces to determine the IP space and other network parameters used by the target network. While this process may sound daunting, it in fact is rather trivial to accomplish.

Once you've completed this step, you have all of the information you need to become a peer on the LockedUp network.

Execution

At this point, you have obtained all of the information needed to become a fully functional peer on both the LockedUp and WideOpen networks. You cracked the

WEP key for the LockedUp network, and WideOpen does not use encryption. Next, you simply pick the time to join the network and set the parameters on your computer just as you do for any other network. The only possible curve ball is if MAC address filtering is being used. In this case, you'll immediately realize that you can't use the network, so you need to go back to the data you collected and identify a MAC address that was using the network. Now, just listen first to make sure that the address isn't still being used, and if it isn't, use the driver interface to set the MAC address to the address you've identified as valid. This works only with certain types of Wi-Fi cards on certain operating systems, for example, FreeBSD, OpenBSD, and Linux.

Other Tools of Interest

This section describes some other tools that can be used against your wireless network. The first tool is Airsnort, one of the original tools to implement the FMS attack against WEP. The second tool is Airjack, which implements wireless DoS attacks as well as establishes man-in-the-middle attacks.

Airsnort

Airsnort (http://airsnort.shmoo.com), compared to the bsdairtools described earlier in this chapter, is easy to use. It has an X-windows–based interface and an MS-Windows version in alpha testing, shown in Figure 16.14.

Figure 16.14 shows Airsnort running against our LockedUp network. Airsnort offers several features over the bsdairtools family that make the tool much easier to use. One of these features is the parallel cracking. The program is constantly working in the background to break the WEP key. When it does, it displays it in both hexidecimal and ASCII in the right columns (PW Hex and PW ASCII). Airsnort also allows you to capture on multiple networks or access points by scanning across the channels. This design causes you to miss packets sometimes, yet it remains a powerful feature.

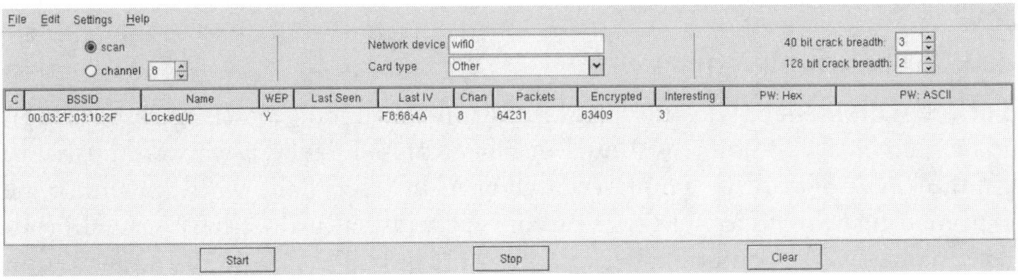

Figure 16.14 Airsnort Capture Window

Airsnort doesn't have the performance that bsdairtools has. In head-to-head tests we've run, bsdairtools seriously outperforms Airsnort. In one case, bsdairtools cracked the key in approximately 20 minutes, whereas Airsnort ran for six hours without recovering the key. The user forum for Airsnort located at http://airsnort.sourceforge.net indicates that others have had approximately the same performance from Airsnort.

Airjack

Airjack is a series of tools written by Abaddon. The tools were first described at the Black Hat Conference in 2002, and were available on the Internet for a short while at http://802.11ninja.net and run under the GNU/Linux operating system only. The tools provide an attacker with the ability to perform a DoS attack against an access point, actively determine the ESSID for a closed network, establish a man in the middle, and set the MAC address of the wireless card.

DoS Attack

The program wlan_jack continuously sends a Deauthentication message to the LAN broadcast address masquerading as an AP by using the same MAC address as the AP. This causes all of the stations/clients associated to that AP to drop their connections to the AP (disassociate); and because the attacker is continuously sending the Deauthentication message, the stations/clients can never associate to the AP for long, thereby creating a DoS attack (see Chapter 15).

ESSID Determination

The program essid_jack actively determines the ESSID for a closed network. Recall that some equipment uses the ESSID as a shared secret for access control (see Chapter 15). The ESSID can be determined passively by being patient and waiting until a station sends a Probe-Request message. If you're in a hurry, however, you can use essid_jack, which works similarly to wlan_jack in that it sends a forged Deauthentication message. It differs in that it only sends it to a single client, and then listens for the client to reassociate with the AP, during which step the ESSID is broadcast in the clear for essid_jack to sniff it and display it for you!

Man-in-the-Middle Attack

The program monkey_jack performs a man-in-the-middle attack against a station and a specific access point, as shown in Figure 15.6. However, we were unable to get the code to work by simply compiling it. In discussions with the author, he explained that the code is a proof of concept and that it does have several problems, such as a race condition, because the same card that knocks the target station off the AP (using a DoS) is also the card that is acting as the fake AP. Additionally, monkey_jack requires some changes to a wireless card driver that the author has not released.

While monkey_jack doesn't work as originally packaged, the author hobbled the code on purpose. The point of releasing the code, and of giving a talk at Black Hat 2002 (Abaddon, 2002), is to show that man-in-the-middle attacks *can* be accomplished, not to provide another tool to potential attackers.

Summary

This chapter focuses on the tools that are readily available on the Internet for anyone with the skills to compile a program under UNIX. The very existence of these tools dramatically increases the number of people who can crack your network if you are not using proper security. Our hopes in providing you with this information are twofold. First, it is essential to understand what attackers can accomplish against your defenses; this is the only way that you can have any hope of designing an effective defense. Second, you can use some of this material to test the security of your own network (with the proper approvals first) to ensure that your organization is using effective security as well.

The good news is that WPA and RSN provide the tools you need to respond to these threats. It is likely that attempts will be made to crack WPA in the future. If a crack is found, more tools will be produced. However, WPA and RSN are in a different class than WEP when it comes to the approach taken in their design, and confidence in their ability to hold up to attack is much higher.

Chapter 17

Open Source Implementation Example

Designing security architectures is not an easy job. It takes great care, experience, and knowledge. Unfortunately, this book can't give you care and experience, but it can at least provide the requisite knowledge you need to secure your wireless network. This chapter does not provide a step-by-step guide to installing specific vendors' products. Vendors change their product lines and their user interfaces far too often to make that information relevant for more than a few months. Instead of providing a single secure configuration, we'd rather teach you how to put one together yourself. For those who like to tinker or build everything yourself, we will, however, explain how to use several open and free software projects to build your own secure wireless network. The details on these projects are still very new and will probably change, but we wanted to show a "nuts and bolts" approach to help you learn.

We start with general architecture guidance for some common situations, and then we explain how to use the open and free source projects.

General Architecture Design Guidelines

We've touched on the many design issues needed for security, but now we boil these down to three key design principles for security architectures:

1. Isolate potentially hostile traffic from sensitive traffic.

2. Canalize[1] potentially hostile traffic through a small set of fixed entry points that are well protected and monitored.

3. Use a layered defense whenever possible.

Many of you will recognize these as the guidelines that apply to Internet connections. The **firewall** is an instantiation of these principles. It isolates and canalizes traffic through a fixed entry point, and it can apply additional layers of security through the use of a virtual private network or additional authentication requirements.

Wireless networks are somewhat more difficult to deal with than an Internet connection, however. Whereas an Internet connection enters the enterprise in only a few fixed locations, wireless access points must be located throughout the enterprise to provide reasonable coverage areas.

So what are our choices in providing isolation and canalization? Well, we could make each access point a firewall. While this certainly meets our goals, it also introduces a horrendous management burden in large enterprises and may not be the best approach in all situations. Certainly in small office/home office (SOHO) scenarios, this might make some sense because there is only one access point, however.

You can now recognize some of the tradeoffs you must make when designing security architectures. A good security architect must balance the threat, information value, and costs (both monetary and management) in designing the architecture. While the solution of making every access point a firewall-like device meets some of the design criteria, it introduces a potentially difficult management problem in some environments. As a result, you must select your equipment carefully.

You would be well served by working closely with your vendor or value-added reseller when choosing equipment. Don't blindly accept statements by either the vendor or their integrator that the equipment is secure. Ask them to define what they mean—for example, "Secure against what type of threat?" Be especially diligent if the vendor uses a proprietary solution. Ask who has reviewed the solution, and ask to see the details so you or someone within your organization can review it. These days, there are few reasons to use a proprietary solution because both WPA and RSN provide protection robust enough for almost all organizations. If you are extremely paranoid, you can add security using upper-layer protection, such as VPN.

Finally, remember, that WPA is an *interim* solution until IEEE 802.11i RSN is complete. It may be that the full RSN will become WPA2 in the future. The

---

1. Canalize means forcing the data down a well-defined route, like water in a canal.

cryptographic primitives used in WPA are believed to be robust, but it takes time to ensure that an algorithm is secure. For instance, RC4 was known publicly for some time before the problems were found that decimated WEP. As such, you should (if security is important to you) plan on upgrading your infrastructure to the AES-based solution (RSN) as soon as you can.

Protecting a Deployed Network

If you already have a wireless local area network deployed in your organization, you need to take several steps (if you haven't already) to ensure that it is protected. First, apply the design principles discussed in the previous section: Isolate and canalize the traffic. Second, upgrade your equipment's firmware to WPA. Let's look at each of these in turn.

Isolate and Canalize

Isolating the traffic from access points may be the most difficult aspect of trying to improve the security of your network, unless you already have your access points on the same LAN segment.

Assuming that you haven't already isolated the traffic, you essentially have two choices. The first is to run new cables to your access points, placing them on the same LAN segment without additional enterprise traffic. The second is to use your current switches to create a VLAN (IEEE 802.10) to isolate your wireless equipment. The first choice is not optimal in terms of time and cost, as it requires a great deal of work and expense. The second approach is relatively painless if your equipment already supports VLANs. If it doesn't, you must balance the purchase of new switches with the cost of running new cable (remember our discussion on tradeoffs). A VLAN provides a moderate degree of isolation. However, the isolation is not complete when the switches are attacked via ARP spoofing and other means; see http://ettercap.sourceforge.net. But the protection provided by a VLAN is better than allowing the traffic from access points to co-mingle with traffic from the rest of the organization.

Once your traffic is isolated, it is easy to canalize it (see Figure 17.1). And depending on your threat model, you can use a network address translation box, a router, or a firewall on one or multiple entry points into the organization's network.

Upgrade Equipment's Firmware to WPA

Hopefully, your installed base of access points and client cards can all be upgraded to WPA by simply reflashing the firmware on each device and by making some small configuration changes. If that's the case, you should perform that upgrade as soon as possible to support WPA.

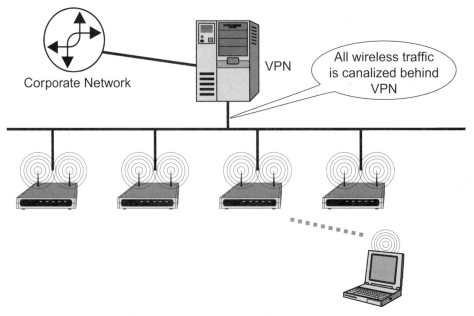

Figure 17.1 Network Architecture with Traffic Canalized

Once you've upgraded to WPA, you can use WPA in one of two modes: pre-shared key (PSK) and server-based infrastructure. In PSK mode, you enter a password at each client and each access point and you're done, though you must also update client software from your vendor. While this approach is simple, it doesn't scale well beyond the home or small office. In those cases, you need to deploy an authentication server. Later in this chapter, we discuss what you'll need to do to deploy the infrastructure for supporting both WPA and RSN.

Of course, you must check with your equipment vendor for details on upgrading the firmware and client software.

What to Do If You Can't Do Anything

The steps we've outlined involve a great deal of work and probably require you to spend money to improve things. What do you do if you can't make any of these suggested changes? The first and most important question you must answer is, "What is the utility of using wireless versus not using it?" Does it add value to your business? In addition, you have to consider the value of the information on your network. What can someone do (or get) if they break into your network? Finally, you have to consider the threat against your network. Is there a reason for someone to try and break into your network?

If you do that analysis, and you decide (and only you can make that decision) to keep using your wireless network, here are some steps that you can follow to mitigate the risks to your network. Our goals in providing this information are to help you protect yourself as best you can. Remember, however, that your network and all of the information on it *will be vulnerable*, and our recommendation is that you make the investment in time and equipment to get it right rather than relying solely on these pointers.

The whole idea is to make it as difficult as possible for someone to break into your network.

1. Use *all* available security measures provided by your equipment. That means use WEP, MAC address filtering, and shared key authentication. Yes. All of these can be broken, but not by everyone. Thus, you're reducing the threat. But, *you do remain vulnerable*. (Sorry, our lawyers made us shout that.)

2. Change your WEP key as often as possible.

3. Turn off the wireless network when it is not in use. This is probably only practical in a home or small office. But the point is to reduce the risk as much as possible.

4. Upgrade your equipment to at least WPA or, better yet, to RSN as soon as possible.

Planning to Deploy a WPA Network

If you haven't yet installed a wireless network, life is a little simpler. You don't have to worry about retrofitting; you can start out the right way from the beginning.

Consider isolating and canalizing your wireless equipment. You must also evaluate the equipment you'll be purchasing from the vendor. For instance, if IEEE 8802.11i RSN (based on AES) isn't out yet, can you upgrade the equipment you purchase later? Is the upgrade via software or hardware? (Most likely, it will be a hardware upgrade.) Also, look very carefully at proprietary vendor solutions. Ask to see the details of the proprietary solution, and who has evaluated it besides the vendor. If the vendor won't share the details with you or can't answer the question, think carefully before using that solution. Finally, if RSN is available, there is very little reason to use a proprietary solution unless you have a very specific need that RSN does not directly meet.

If you have a medium to large deployment, install an authentication server infrastructure to centralize user management and accounting, which we describe next. Finally, the biggest single thing that you *must* do is to turn off support for WEP. As long as WEP is enabled, you are susceptible to a **down-grade attack**, in other words, an attacker can associate using WEP and crack the key (see Chapter 15).

Deploying the Infrastructure

A significant amount of infrastructure is required to support WPA when you are not using preshared keys. The effort required to set up the infrastructure is, unfortunately, nontrivial. However, it is only a one-time cost, and setting it up properly will save you time in the long run.

As with everything in security, the devil is in the details, and setting up your infrastructure is no exception. Because vendor products change, it is difficult to provide a step-by-step cookbook for you. So instead, we describe in general what you must do and provide pointers to more detailed guidance, usually on the Web.

Add a RADIUS Server for IEEE 802.1X Support

The central arbiter for all access and authentication decisions in WPA is the organization's RADIUS server. It's likely that this is exactly how your Internet service provider (ISP) makes access decisions when you dial up the service. You can obtain a RADIUS server in many ways. For example, the software package Microsoft Windows 2000 Server includes a RADIUS server, and several vendors sell RADIUS servers for various operating systems. There is also an open source RADIUS server available known as FreeRADIUS, which we describe later in this chapter.

Managing a RADIUS server is an extremely important task because the server makes all of the security-relevant decisions. As a result, improper configuration can lead to breaches in your security. Fortunately, an excellent text has been recently written that describes how to install and configure FreeRADIUS (Hassell, 2003).

Use a Public Key Infrastructure for Client Certificates

To use WPA to its fullest, you need to use EAP/TLS as an authentication mechanism, and this requires using public key certificates based on the X.509 standard. Issuing and managing these certificates requires that a public key infrastructure (PKI) be established within your organization, if it hasn't been already.

Setting up a PKI has been the subject of several books, and we can't cover all of the nuances involved. We will, however, show how to use an open source cryptographic package to make certificates suitable for testing purposes or for use at home or in very small offices later in this chapter.

Install Client IEEE 802.1X Supplicant Software

To gain the full benefit of WPA, you need to upgrade your clients to use the IEEE 802.1X protocol for authentication and access control. At the time of this writing Microsoft Windows XP is the only operating system to include the client portion, the supplicant, as part of the operating system. However, your vendor will probably provide software to support older versions of Windows and the Apple Macintosh.

For UNIX, you can use supplicant software developed at the University of Maryland and released under both the GPL and BSD style licenses. The software is located at www.open1x.org and runs under FreeBSD, OpenBSD, and Linux.

To install the software, you have to review the documentation for the clients you use, and you have to generate and add public key certificates to each client. This is mandatory to support the EAP/TLS protocol.

Practical Example Based on Open Source Projects

This section walks you through some of the steps of building open source applications that you can use for setting up and evaluating a WPA or RSN network. "There is no such thing as a free lunch" and the hidden cost of using the open source projects is that you need substantial system knowledge and, to some extent, an understanding of computer programming. The vast majority of people choose instead to purchase commercial solutions and obtain professional support for installation. However, we'll take the time here to show how you can set up a test environment and even create a real operating network from tools that can be downloaded over the Internet, and we're also going to show you how to build an access point yourself using UNIX.

Our goals are to help anyone who likes to tinker and is somewhat familiar with UNIX. If that does not describe you, consider skipping this section.

We cover two versions of UNIX in this section. For the open source access point, we use the OpenBSD operating system (www.openbsd.org), and for the infrastructure, we use Red Hat Linux. For more information please see our Web site (www.wpa-security.org).

Server Infrastucture

This section shows how to use open source projects to create your own infrastructure. There are two reasons for this step. First, you may find that the open source project actually provides what you need to protect your network. Second, even if you eventually plan to use a commercial server, the exercise of seeing how the open source project is structured should be informative.

There are two specific projects that we're going to discuss: OpenSSL and FreeRADIUS:

- OpenSSL provides cryptographic primitives as well as some command line tools for creating and manipulating public key certificates. We use OpenSSL to help build a limited PKI.

- We use FreeRADIUS to provide the authentication server using the RADIUS protocol as the central point of our infrastructure.

OpenSSL Instead of a PKI

If you're going to be using WPA with server-based keys in a medium to large organization, you'll need a public key infrastructure. There are several commercial products available, but fortunately, there are also a few open source projects. The most significant is the OpenCA effort found at www.openca.org/, but it is somewhat wanting, unfortunately. Rather than focus on the details of establishing an entire certificate authority, we're going to show you how to build self-signed certificates using OpenSSL. This approach is sufficient for testing, or for a small-to-medium-sized network. The point is to show you what is involved without having to get lost in the details of a PKI.

Downloading OpenSSL   You can download the latest version of the OpenSSL from www.openssl.org. At the time of this writing, the most recent version was 0.9.7a. This is the version we'll use in our examples, but you should be able to use later versions when they are released. Before using a newer version, check with the FreeRADIUS site to see whether an older version of OpenSSL is required; the two projects are not well synchronized at the moment. You also only need the base OpenSSL distribution; you don't need the OpenSSL-engine file unless you plan on using specialized cryptographic support. In that case, you probably don't need these instructions anyway.

Once you download the file, you need to change your working directory to the location where you place source code, in other words, /usr/local/src, and check the digital signature on the following file and untar it.

```
cd /usr/local/src
tar xvfz openssl-0.9.7a.tar.gz
```

Compiling OpenSSL   The OpenSSL development team has made the compilation of OpenSSL easy and straightforward, as shown in the following syntax. This syntax works using Red Hat 7.3 and 8.0. But, you must use a different method for OpenBSD; see www.cs.umd.edu/~arunesh/bsd/openssl.html. Also, you need to be careful not to overwrite the current installation of OpenSSL when using Red Hat because that will break some of the precompiled programs in your operating system distribution. The following commands install OpenSSL in the /usr/local directory so you don't overwrite the previous installed version.

```
cd openssl-0.9.7a
./config shared --prefix=/usr/local/openssl
make
make install
```

All of the previous commands should complete without error messages.

Configuring OpenSSL Once OpenSSL is installed, you need to make some minor changes to the configuration files to make it easier to make certificates (see the next section). The file that requires editing is /usr/local/openssl/ssl/ openssl.cnf. The changes only involve modifying the default values for some of the options in certificate requests. If you're going to generate only one or two certificates, you don't really have to make these changes. If you're going to generate more certificates than that, you definitely should make these changes. You may also want to consider increasing the length of time a certificate is valid as well. The changes you want to make are all in the lines that have "default" as a portion of the identifier in the first column. An excerpt from the openssl.cnf file follows, with the changes we made in bold.

```
# req_extensions = v3_req # The extensions to add to a certificate
request

[ req_distinguished_name ]
countryName         = Country Name (2 letter code)
countryName_default= US
countryName_min     = 2
countryName_max     = 2

stateOrProvinceName= State or Province Name (full name)
stateOrProvinceName_default= Maryland

localityName      = Locality Name (eg, city)
localityName_default = College Park

0.organizationName = Organization Name (eg, company)
0.organizationName_default= University of Maryland

# we can do this but it is not needed normally :-)
#1.organizationName= Second Organization Name (eg, company)
#1.organizationName_default= World Wide Web Pty Ltd

organizationalUnitName= Organizational Unit Name (eg, section)
organizationalUnitName_default= Department of Computer Science

commonName        = Common Name (eg, YOUR name)
commonName_max      = 64

emailAddress      = Email Address
emailAddress_max = 64

# SET-ex3       = SET extension number 3

[ req_attributes ]
challengePassword   = A challenge password
challengePassword_min= 4
```

```
challengePassword_max= 20
challengePassword_default= ChangeMe!
```

```
unstructuredName = An optional company name
```

Making the Public Key Certificates

There are several steps involved in created certificates that you can use with 802.1X. First, you need to create a certificate authority certificate. This is self-signed; in other words, the certificate authority attests to the validity of itself. While this might surprise you, it is the commonly accepted method for creating a root certificate. Once the certificate authority, or root, is created, you need to create a server certificate for your RADIUS server. Then, you create certificates for all of your clients.

Creating the Certificate Authority   Several people, most recently Raymond McKay (www.impossiblereflex.com/8021x/eap-tls-HOWTO.htm), have created scripts to automate the commands needed to create a certificate authority using OpenSSL. The following script creates the self-signed root certificate.

CA.root file

```
#!/bin/sh
SSL=/usr/local/openssl
export PATH=${SSL}/bin/:${SSL}/ssl/misc:${PATH}
export LD_LIBRARY_PATH=${SSL}/lib
# private key into the CA directories
rm -rf demoCA
echo "****************************************************************"
echo "Creating self-signed private key and certificate"
echo "When prompted change the default value for the Common Name field"
echo "****************************************************************"
echo
# Generate a new self-signed certificate.
# After invocation, newreq.pem will contain a private key and certificate
# newreq.pem will be used in the next step
openssl req -new -x509 -keyout newreq.pem -out newreq.pem -passin \
pass:whatever -passout pass:whatever
echo "****************************************************************"
echo "Creating a new CA hierarchy (used later by the "ca" command)"
echo "and private key created in the last step"
echo "****************************************************************"
echo
echo "newreq.pem" | CA.pl -newca >/dev/null
echo "****************************************************************"
echo "Creating ROOT CA"
echo "****************************************************************"
echo
```

```
# Create a PKCS#12 file, using the previously created CA certificate/key
# The certificate in demoCA/cacert.pem is the same as in newreq.pem.
# Instead of using "-in demoCA/cacert.pem" we could have
# used "-in newreq.pem" and then omitted
# the "-inkey newreq.pem" because newreq.pem contains both the
# private key and certificate
openssl pkcs12 -export -in demoCA/cacert.pem -inkey newreq.pem -out\
 root.p12 -cacerts -passin pass:whatever -passout pass:whatever
# parse the PKCS#12 file just created and produce a PEM format
# certificate and key in root.pem
openssl pkcs12 -in root.p12 -out root.pem -passin pass:whatever \
-passout pass:whatever
# Convert root certificate from PEM format to DER format
openssl x509 -inform PEM -outform DER -in root.pem -out root.der
#Clean Up
rm -rf newreq.pem
```

You create the self-signed root certificate now by executing:

```
/bin/bash CA.root
```

and answering all of the questions.

Creating a Server Certificate   To perform a mutual authentication between the RADIUS server and the supplicant, you must have a public key certificate for the server. This section provides the set of commands that you must execute to request a certificate and then have it signed by your root certificate.

An important part of creating the server certificate, and the client certificate that you create in a few moments, is ensuring that the certificate has the appropriate OIDs to support Microsoft Windows XP. Now, you're probably asking, "What is an OID?" Well, don't worry, all you really need to know about them is that they're essentially a capability, indicating what type of service the holder of the certificate may use.

The OIDS needed for certificates for use with Windows XP follow. The script creating both the client and server certificates assumes that the OIDs are included in a file named xpextensions located in the same directory as you run the script.

xpextensions file
```
[ xpclient_ext]
extendedKeyUsage = 1.3.6.1.5.5.7.3.2
[ xpserver_ext ]
extendedKeyUsage = 1.3.6.1.5.5.7.3.1
```

CA.server file
```
#!/bin/sh
```

```
SSL=/usr/local/openssl
export PATH=${SSL}/bin/:${SSL}/ssl/misc:${PATH}
export LD_LIBRARY_PATH=${SSL}/lib
echo "************************************************************************"
echo "Creating server private key and certificate"
echo "When prompted enter the server name in the Common Name field."
echo "************************************************************************"
echo
# Request a new PKCS#10 certificate.
# First, newreq.pem will be overwritten with the new certificate request
openssl req -new -keyout newreq.pem -out newreq.pem -passin \
 pass:whatever -passout pass:whatever
# Sign the certificate request. The policy is defined in the
# openssl.cnf file.
# The request generated in the previous step is specified with the
# -infiles option and
# the output is in newcert.pem
# The -extensions option is necessary to add the OID for the extended
# key for server authentication
openssl ca -policy policy_anything -out newcert.pem -passin \
 pass:whatever -key whatever -extensions xpserver_ext -extfile \
 xpextensions -infiles newreq.pem
# Create a PKCS#12 file from the new certificate and its private
# key found in newreq.pem
# and place in file specified on the command line
openssl pkcs12 -export -in newcert.pem -inkey newreq.pem -out $1.p12 \
 -clcerts -passin pass:whatever -passout pass:whatever
# parse the PKCS#12 file just created and produce a PEM format
# certificate and key in certsrv.pem
openssl pkcs12 -in $1.p12 -out $1.pem -passin pass:whatever -passout \
 pass:whatever
# Convert certificate from PEM format to DER format
openssl x509 -inform PEM -outform DER -in $1.pem -out $1.der
# Clean Up
rm -rf newcert.pem newreq.pem
```

Save the script above to the file CA.server, and then create the server certificate by invoking the script with the name of the server (without spaces or special characters) as follows.

```
/bin/bash CA.server <servername>
```

When you are asked to enter the common name, you must enter the same name as you used in executing the script, for example, <servername>.

Creating a Client Certificate Now that you've created the certificate for the RADIUS server, you can create your client certificates (we'll discuss installing them on clients shortly). The following script shows the commands necessary to request and sign individual client certificates. Remember to have the proper OID file so you can use the resultant certificate with a Windows XP client as well.

CA.client file

```
#!/bin/sh
SSL=/usr/local/openssl
export PATH=${SSL}/bin/:${SSL}/ssl/misc:${PATH}
export LD_LIBRARY_PATH=${SSL}/lib
echo "**************************************************************"
echo "Creating client private key and certificate"
echo "When prompted enter the client name in the Common Name field."
echo " This is the same name used as the Username in FreeRADIUS"
echo "**************************************************************"
echo
# Request a new PKCS#10 certificate.
# First, newreq.pem will be overwritten with the new certificate request
openssl req -new -keyout newreq.pem -out newreq.pem -passin \
pass:whatever -passout pass:whatever
# Sign the certificate request. The policy is defined in the
# openssl.cnf file.
# The request generated in the previous step is specified with
# the -infiles option and
# the output is in newcert.pem
# The -extensions option is necessary to add the OID for the
# extended key for client authentication
openssl ca -policy policy_anything -out newcert.pem -passin \
 pass:whatever -key whatever -extensions xpclient_ext -extfile \
 xpextensions -infiles newreq.pem
# Create a PKCS#12 file from the new certificate and its private
# key found in newreq.pem
# and place in file specified on the command line
openssl pkcs12 -export -in newcert.pem -inkey newreq.pem -out $1.p12 \
 -clcerts -passin pass:whatever -passout pass:whatever
# parse the PKCS#12 file just created and produce a PEM format
# certificate and key in certclt.pem
openssl pkcs12 -in $1.p12 -out $1.pem -passin pass:whatever -passout \
 pass:whatever
# Convert certificate from PEM format to DER format
openssl x509 -inform PEM -outform DER -in $1.pem -out $1.der
# clean up
rm -rf newcert.pem newreq.pem
```

You use the previous script, saved to the file `ca.client`, to generate your client certificates by invoking the script with the following command without spaces or special characters in <username>.

```
/bin/bash ca.client <username>
```

Be sure to use the <username> as the common name when you create the certificate. You'll also use the same name when you create the RADIUS files.

Make a copy of the files created by executing the previous scripts, root.pem and <servername>.pem, and copy them to the directory /usr/local/1x/etc/. You'll probably have to make that directory first. You also need to save the files root.der and <username>.p12 for installation on the client machine. We describe that process a bit later in this chapter when we describe how to set up the client.

RADIUS Software

FreeRADIUS is the most widely used open source RADIUS server found at www.freeradius.org. RADIUS is a complicated protocol that can be configured in a large number of different ways. In this section, we discuss only a very basic configuration. If you're planning on using FreeRADIUS as part of your infrastructure, you definitely want to obtain a more detailed guide such as the O'Reilly book *RADIUS* by Jonathan Hassell (2003).

Downloading FreeRADIUS You can download the most recent version of FreeRADIUS from the Web site www.freeradius.org/getting.html. The most recent version at the time of writing is 0.8.1. This version has complete support for both authentication and dynamic keys. Make sure you download the signature of FreeRADIUS as well. The developers of FreeRADIUS used a detached signature (file ending in .sig) rather than an ASCII armored signature (file ending in .asc). Verifying this signature is very similar to the approach shown in Appendix B. The only difference is that you will be asked to enter the name of the file you want verified.

Now, change your working directory to your source directory and untar the FreeRADIUS source.

```
cd /usr/local/src
tar xvfz freeradius-0.8.1.tar.gz
```

Compiling FreeRADIUS Compiling FreeRADIUS is similar to compiling OpenSSL except that you have to make a few changes to the files to support EAP-TLS. First, you configure the source code by using the configure program.

```
cd freeradius-0.8.1
./configure --prefix=/usr/local/radius
```

Once the source is configured, you must make one small change to a makefile included with the source to ensure that FreeRADIUS can find your version of OpenSSL and compile EAP-TLS properly. The file that you must modify is the subdirectory src/modules/rlm_eap/types/rlm_eap_tls/ under your main FreeRADIUS directory. The changes you need to make are to ensure that the header and library files from OpenSSL can be found. A modified makefile follows.

```
# Generated automatically from Makefile.in by configure.
TARGET        = rlm_eap_tls
SRCS          = rlm_eap_tls.c eap_tls.c cb.c tls.c
RLM_CFLAGS    = $(INCLTDL) -I../.. -I/usr/local/openssl/include
HEADERS       = eap_tls.h
RLM_INSTALL =
# NOTE: You may have to switch the order of -lssl and -lcrypto below
RLM_LIBS     += -lssl -lcrypto
RLM_LDFLAGS += -L/usr/local/openssl/lib

$(STATIC_OBJS): $(HEADERS)

$(DYNAMIC_OBJS): $(HEADERS)

RLM_DIR=../../
include ${RLM_DIR}../rules.mak
```

You'll end up adding "-I/usr/local/openssl/include" to the line beginning with RLM_CFLAGS, and an entirely new line beginning with RLM_LDFLAGS, and you may have to switch the order of *-lssl* and *-lcrypto*.

Now, you can compile the FreeRADIUS source just like we did OpenSSL with the following two commands from the main FreeRADIUS directory.

```
make
make install
```

The compile and install should complete without errors.

Configuring FreeRADIUS   Now, you're ready to make the changes to the various FreeRADIUS configuration files. There are three files that you must modify (remember you're only doing a basic setup here), and they are all located in the directory /usr/local/radius/etc/raddb. The files are clients.conf, radiusd.conf, and users.

clients.conf – The clients.conf file is responsible for determining who/what can connect to the RADIUS server to authenticate users. In your case, you want the access points to be able to connect. There are two ways to enter the access point information. First, list each access point individually. Second, list a subnet. A key point for security here is that if you decide to use the subnet approach, all of the access points will use the same password—not the best idea from the standpoint of security; however, if you have hundreds of access points, a separate password for each becomes a management nightmare. The choice is yours.

You can specify an access point at a time by using the following template.

```
client <ipaddress> {
  secret = <password>
  shortname = <descriptive_name_for_accounting_purposes>
}
```

You would create a copy of the template, above, for each access point, entering the IP address, password, and name for each into your clients.conf file.

The second approach is to use a single entry for an entire local area network of access points. You do this using the following template.

```
client <subnet>/<mask> {
  secret = <password>
  shortname = LAN
}
```

You enter the subnet and mask along with the globally shared password into the previous template and place it in the clients.conf file. Remember, you need to use only one of the approaches we outlined.

radiusd.conf – You need to change only a few parts of this file. But, you need to create two new files, /usr/local/radius/etc/raddb/DH and /usr/local/radius/etc/raddb/random, as part of the changes. The contents of both of these files need to be random so you use the Linux random device to create files with the following commands.

```
dd if=/dev/random of=/usr/local/radius/etc/raddb/random count=1 bs=128
dd if=/dev/random of=/usr/local/radius/etc/raddb/DH count=1 bs=128
```

This creates two files with 128 random bytes each. The device /dev/random may block if there is insufficient entropy (randomness) available. If one of these commands hang, you can do one of two things. First, you can wait a while until the entropy pool is refreshed, or second, you can use the /dev/urandom device instead, which will not block (at the cost of the bytes being generated by a pseudorandom function).

Once you've created these two files, you need to make your changes to radiusd.conf. The first set of changes is to the following Extensible Authentication Protocol section. The items in bold were changed from the original file.

```
# Extensible Authentication Protocol
#
# For all EAP related authentications
eap {
```

```
# Invoke the default supported EAP type when
# EAP-Identity response is received
default_eap_type = tls

# Default expiry time to clean the EAP list,
# It is maintained to co-relate the
# EAP-response for each EAP-request sent.
timer_expire = 60

# Supported EAP-types
# md5 {
# }

## FIXME: EAP-TLS is highly experimental EAP-Type at the moment.
# Please give feedback.
tls {
private_key_password = whatever# CHANGE THIS TO YOUR PASSWORD
private_key_file = /usr/local/1x/etc/<servername>.pem

# Sometimes Private key & Certificate are located
# in the same file, then private_key_file & certificate_file
# must contain the same file name.
certificate_file = /usr/local/1x/etc/<servername>.pem

# Trusted Root CA list
CA_file = /usr/local/1x/etc/root.pem

dh_file = /usr/local/1x/etc/DH
random_file = /usr/local/1x/etc/random
#
# This can never exceed MAX_RADIUS_LEN (4096)
# preferably half the MAX_RADIUS_LEN, to
# accomodate other attributes in RADIUS packet.
# On most APs the MAX packet length is configured
# between 1500 - 1600. In these cases, fragment
# size should be <= 1024.
fragment_size = 1024
# include_length is a flag which is by default set to yes
# If set to yes, Total Length of the message is included
# in EVERY packet we send.
# If set to no, Total Length of the message is included
# ONLY in the First packet of a fragment series.
include_length = yes
}
}
```

Change your EAP section to match the previous script, being sure to change the private_key_password and the names of the private_key_file and certificate_file attributes to your file names. You also need to ensure that the paths are set to where you've placed the files you generated using OpenSSL.

Now, you need to make changes to the authorization section and uncomment the eap line so the section looks like the one that follows. The important part is that eap must be added as supported.

```
# Authorization. First preprocess (hints and huntgroups files),
# then realms, and finally look in the "users" file.
# The order of the realm modules will determine the order that
# we try to find a matching realm.
# Make *sure* that 'preprocess' comes before any realm if you
# need to setup hints for the remote radius server
authorize {
#
# The preprocess module takes care of sanitizing some bizarre
# attributes in the request, and turning them into attributes
# which are more standard.
#
# It takes care of processing the 'raddb/hints' and the
# 'raddb/huntgroups' files.
#
# It also adds a Client-IP-Address attribute to the request.
#
preprocess

#
# The chap module will set 'Auth-Type := CHAP' if we are
# handling a CHAP request and Auth-Type has not already been set
#
# chap

# counter
# attr_filter
eap
suffix
files
# etc_smbpasswd
}
```

Now, you make your last change to the Authentication section, uncommenting the reference to EAP. Again, the important part is that EAP (eap in bold above) be uncommented.

```
# Authentication.
#
# This section lists which modules are available for authentication.
# Note that it does NOT mean 'try each module in order'. It means
# that you have to have a module from the 'authorize' section add
# a configuration attribute 'Auth-Type := FOO'. That authentication type
# is then used to pick the appropriate module from the list below.
```

```
#
# The default Auth-Type is Local. That is, whatever is not included
# inside
# an authtype section will be called only if Auth-Type is set to Local
#
# So you should do the following:
# Set Auth-Type to an appropriate value in the authorize section. For
# example chap
# will set Auth-Type to CHAP, ldap to LDAP etc
# After that create corresponding authtype sections in the authenticate
# section below
# and call the appropriate modules (chap for CHAP etc)
authenticate {
# pam
unix

# Uncomment it if you want to use ldap for authentication
# authtype LDAP {
# ldap
# }
# mschap
eap

# Uncomment it if you want to support CHAP
# authtype CHAP {
# chap
# }

# Uncomment the following if you want to support PAP and you
# extract user passwords from the user database (LDAP,SQL, etc).
# You should use the 'files'module to set 'Auth-Type := PAP' for
# this to work.
# authtype PAP {
# pap
# }
#
}
```

users – Open the users file in your favorite editor and search for the string "John Doe". Now, enter a line for each of your client certificates using their full name, as follows:

```
"<clientsfullname>" Auth-Type := EAP
```

You can also add the following line for testing purposes, but make sure to remove it after your testing is completed.

```
"test" Auth-Type := Local, User-Password == "test"
```

Now, you're ready to test your installation. Because FreeRADIUS may be using a different version of OpenSSL than the one installed on your system, you need to build a custom shell to start the FreeRADIUS daemon in a way that it can find the OpenSSL libraries. Use the run-radiusd script created by Adam Sulmicki, as follows.

```
#!/bin/bash -x

export LD_LIBRARY_PATH=/usr/local/openssl/lib
export LD_PRELOAD=/usr/local/openssl/lib/libcrypto.so

/usr/local/radius/sbin/radiusd $@
```

Testing FreeRADIUS   Now, start FreeRADIUS in debug mode from a shell, as follows:

```
run-radiusd -X -A
```

You'll see a great deal of output, and eventually the last line should read "Ready to process requests." You can now test the installation with the following command:

```
/usr/local/radius/bin/radtest test test localhost 0 testing123
```

If you get Access-Accept, everything is configured properly and you can delete the test line from the users file. You may also want to delete the entry for localhost in the clients.conf file. If, however, you get no response or Access-Reject, you need to review the configuration files. You may also have to either disable your packet filtering firewall (in other words, iptables), with the command service iptables stop or add a rule to permit the RADIUS requests to work on port 1812.

Building an Open Source Access Point

In this section, we're going to show you how to build an access point yourself using UNIX. The access point you'll build won't have WPA support (it wasn't completed at the time this book was written), but we'll provide links and how-to's on our Web page, www.wpa-security.org, once the work is finished.

AP Hardware

If you are building your own access point, there's a limited amount of hardware you can use. The easiest, and most expensive, is to use a laptop. An alternative is to use a low-cost single-board computer running an Intel-compatible CPU such as those available at www.soekris.com.

In the next section, we're going to assume that you're using a laptop.

AP Software

Linux, FreeBSD, and OpenBSD all have the capability of running as an access point using a WLAN card based on the Intersil Prism2 chipset. These cards are the most common cards available, with manufacturers such as Samsung, Compaq, and others shipping PCMCIA WLAN cards based on the Prism2 or Prism2.5 chipsets. At the time of writing, a list of companies using the Intersil Prism 2 chipset was available at: www.intersil.com/design/prism/prismuser/index.asp

We cover how to use both OpenBSD and Linux as access points.

OpenBSD For the first step, you need to install the latest version of the Open-BSD operating system. The installation files and instructions can be found at www.openbsd.org. Once the operating system is installed, you can begin setting the system up as an access point. You're going to be amazed at how easy it is to turn a laptop into an access point, albeit an expensive one.

The first step is to set up your wired network connection, assuming that you'll be using your access point to connect to a wired network and not as a stand–alone server. Details on how to do this can be found at the OpenBSD Web site.

The second step is to insert your Prism2 WLAN card into the laptop. The console window should display several lines of information about wi0. This is the operating system kernel recognizing the card you just inserted. One of the lines should start with "wi0: PRISM 2". If not, the card you are using may not be a PRISM2-based card, and these instructions will not work for you.

At this point, it would probably help if you familiarized yourself with the manual page for the wicontrol command by typing:

man wicontrol

The command wicontrol configures Prism2-based wireless cards. As you could see from the manual entry, you are able to select normal station mode, ad-hoc mode, or hostap mode. The last mode, hostap, is what we're discussing here. wicontrol also allows you to set the channel, MAC address (remember earlier when we said it was easy to clone MAC addresses? You use wicontrol.), WEP, and the WEP keys. Unfortunately, right now the default distribution of OpenBSD (and the other open source UNIX-based projects) supports only vanilla WEP. The University of Maryland MISSL group, however, is working on incorporating WPA into OpenBSD. While it is too early to describe this work in this book, we'll have more details on the MISSL Web page (www.missl.cs.umd.edu), and on the Web page for this book (www.wpa-security.org).

Okay. Now that you're familiar with wicontrol, we can configure and turn on our home brew access point using the following commands as root.

```
wicontrol wi0 -e 1 -k "Hello" -p 6 -f 11 -n myap
# Make sure the IP_address is on the same subnet as your wired device
ifconfig wi0 inet <IP_address> netmask <Net_mask>
# Or you can use DHCP to configure the IP address
brconfig bridge0 add <wired_device> add wi0 up
```

The first command enables WEP encryption using the key "Hello" as well as hostap mode on channel 11, and the command assigns the network name of "myap". In the second command, we're manually configuring the IP address for the machine. You could also use DHCP for this as well. The third and final command enables bridging between the wireless interface (our AP) and the wired interface just like the commercial access points.

That's it. We're done. If you set up the wired device with routing and so on, and you have a DHCP server running, you can start up a client and associate and start using your new AP!

You should, however, add additional security to the AP by using the built-in IPsec implementation. You can start learning about this from the OpenBSD documentation, and several how-to's that you'll find linked to our Web site.

Linux   You can also use Linux as your base operating system, and we've used Linux Red Hat 8.0 and the hostap software by Jouni Malinen at www.hostap.epitest.fi/. The hostap software is another implementation of a prism2/2.5/3 driver for UNIX. Hostap, however, includes support for MAC access control lists, IEEE 802.1x, dynamic WEP rekeying, RADIUS, and minimal support for interaccess point protocol support (IAPP).

The hostap software has a large number of capabilities, and covering them all here would be difficult. Therefore for the sake of brevity, we won't cover much about hostap here. But, we will post more information on our Web site (www.wpa-security.org).

Making It All Work

Now that your server infrastructure is built, we can talk about configuring your access points to use your servers. Given the large number of access points available on the market today, we can't present configuration information for all of them. Therefore, we've picked one of the more common access points. While we're not covering many access points, we will include links to sources of information about other access points on our Web site.

We're also only going to describe configuring Microsoft Windows XP for the very same reasons, but again we will provide links to a how-to for configuring an open source supplicant, Xsupplicant, at the end of this chapter and on our Web site.

Configuring Cisco Access Points to Use 802.1X

Currently, not all of the commercial access points support IEEE 802.1X. That will change as WPA becomes more widely available. Until then, IEEE 802.1X is currently only supported by the major wireless vendors such as Cisco, Agere, and a few others. If you're going to buy a new access point, you must be certain that it supports IEEE 802.1X if you want to use the best security available.

The following sections give some practical examples of configuring the Cisco products via their Web interface. Note that we cannot guarantee the accuracy of this information because products change, and you should consult the documentation provided with the product for definitive information.

Configuring a Cisco AP to use IEEE 802.1X is straightforward and involves only a few changes to the AP configuration. This section uses the Web management interface, but you can do this configuration via the console as well.

First make sure that you're running at least firmware version 11.08T to ensure that IEEE 802.1X support is available.

Setting the RADIUS Server Properties – From the home page of the Web-based interface, select Setup to open the menu shown in Figure 17.2.

Select Security at the bottom of the screen to open the screen shown in Figure 17.3.

Select the fifth item from this screen, Authentication Server, to set up the server, as shown in Figure 17.4.

This screen is the first of the two screens in which you do all of your work. In the first column, enter the IP address for your FreeRADIUS server. Now select RADIUS from the Server Type dropdown menu. Enter the port number, 1812, into the Port column, followed by the shared secret that you used when you set up the file clients.conf as part of the FreeRADIUS configuration earlier. Finally, set the timeout to the default 20 seconds. Click OK, and return to the Security Setup screen. Now select Radio Data Encryption (WEP) (Figure 17.5).

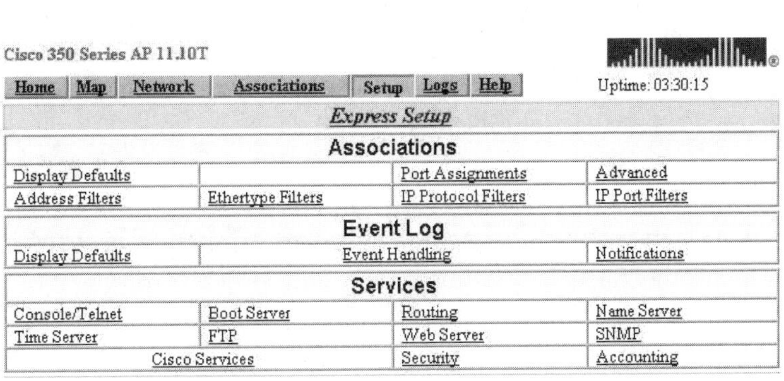

Cisco 350 Series AP 11.10T

| Home | Map | Network | Associations | Setup | Logs | Help | Uptime: 03:30:15 |

Express Setup

Associations

| Display Defaults | | Port Assignments | Advanced |
| Address Filters | Ethertype Filters | IP Protocol Filters | IP Port Filters |

Event Log

| Display Defaults | | Event Handling | Notifications |

Services

Console/Telnet	Boot Server	Routing	Name Server
Time Server	FTP	Web Server	SNMP
	Cisco Services	Security	Accounting

Figure 17.2 Setup Screen for Cisco 350 Series AP

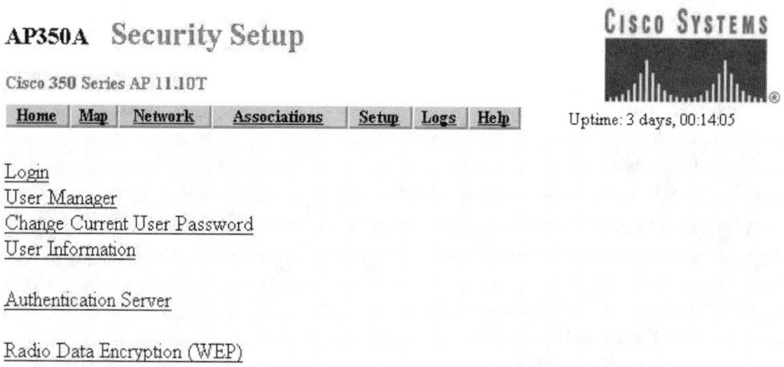

AP350A Security Setup

Cisco 350 Series AP 11.10T

| Home | Map | Network | Associations | Setup | Logs | Help |

CISCO SYSTEMS

Uptime: 3 days, 00:14:05

Login
User Manager
Change Current User Password
User Information

Authentication Server

Radio Data Encryption (WEP)

Figure 17.3 Security Setup Screen

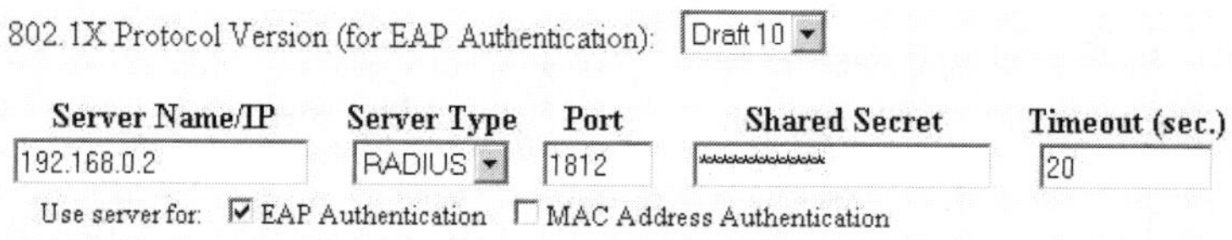

802.1X Protocol Version (for EAP Authentication): Draft 10 ▾

Server Name/IP	Server Type	Port	Shared Secret	Timeout (sec.)
192.168.0.2	RADIUS ▾	1812	************	20

Use server for: ☑ EAP Authentication ☐ MAC Address Authentication

Figure 17.4 Authentication Server Setup

Use of Data Encryption by Stations is: Not Available
Must set an Encryption Key or enable Broadcast Key Rotation first

	Open	Shared	Network-EAP
Accept Authentication Type:	☑	☐	☐
Require EAP:	☑	☐	

	Transmit With Key	Encryption Key	Key Size
WEP Key 1:	-		not set ▾
WEP Key 2:	-		not set ▾

Figure 17.5 WEP Setup Screen

Select Open for both Accept Authentication Type and Require EAP. Now, go back to the Security Setup screen, and select Radio Data Encryption (WEP) again. You should see the screen shown in Figure 17.6.

In the first dropdown menu, make sure you select Full Encryption; if you do not make this selection, Windows XP will not associate with your access point.

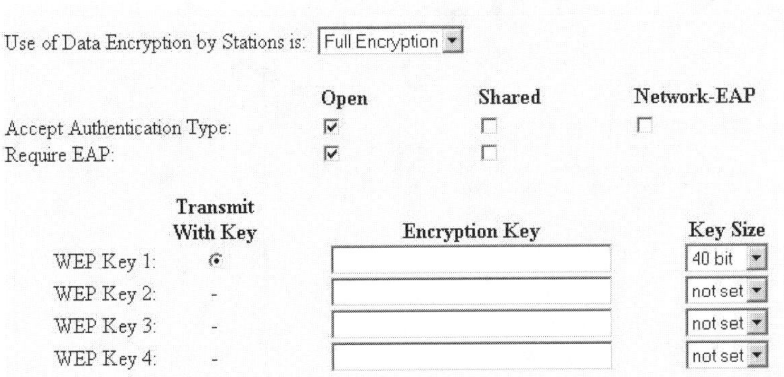

Figure 17.6 WEP Screen

Now, you need to select the first WEP key and enter a value for the key. This key is the multicast key only, and will be used only when the AP transmits multicast data. Clients will still negotiate pairwise keys.

Client Software – 802.1X supplicant (or client) support is currently only built into Windows XP. However, several vendors are now supporting previous versions of Windows, and an open source implementation is available for most open source UNIX-based operating systems.

Windows XP – There are two steps in configuring Windows XP SP1. The configuration for XP SP1 is slightly different from that for XP, but you should be able to work through those differences. The how-to's listed at the end of this chapter cover XP configuration, so XP SP1 configuration is covered here to show you how to use 802.1X with your infrastructure. In the first step, the certificates you generated earlier are installed on the client. The second step involves configuring the wireless device on Windows XP.

You should update your version of Windows XP to Service Pack 1. SP1 contains an important security patch that can prevent a man-in-the-middle attack due to a malformed packet. Therefore, the remaining instructions assume a SP1 installation.

Installing Public Key Certificates – For this step, we need the root.der and <clientusename>.p12 files you created earlier. Copy both files to the Windows XP client. Now, double-click the root.der file to display the popup window shown in Figure 17.7.

Click the Install Certificate button to open the Certificate Import Wizard. Click the Next button to open the window shown in Figure 17.8.

Select the option Place all certificates in the following store and click Browse to open a browser, as shown in Figure 17.9.

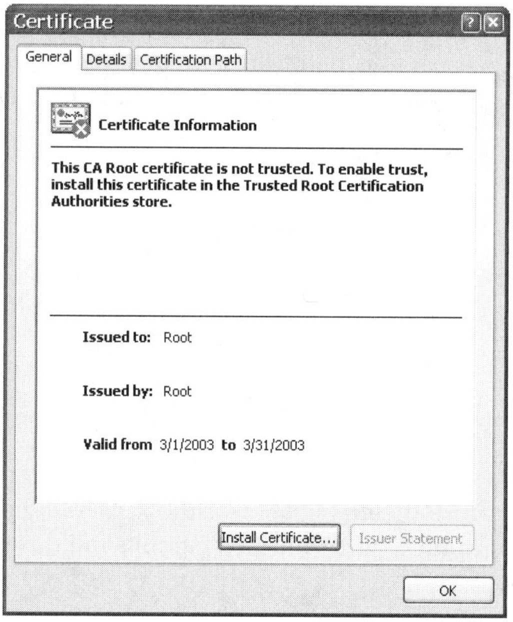

Figure 17.7   Certificate Information Popup

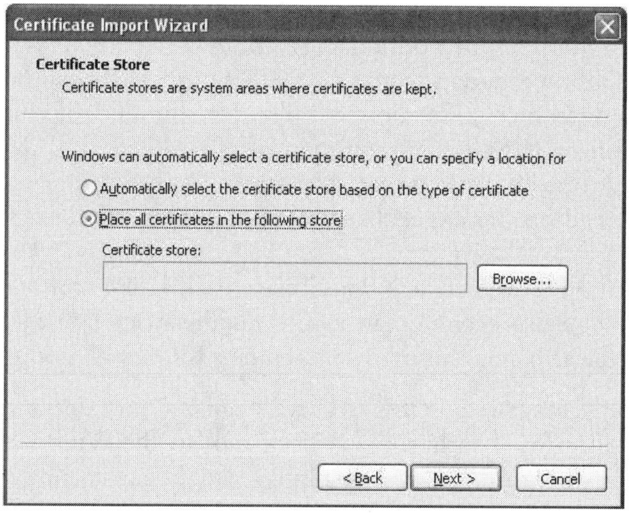

Figure 17.8   Certificate Import Wizard

Figure 17.9   Certificate Store Browser

Select Trusted Root Certificate Authorities and click OK and then Next and Finish. Answer Yes when you're asked if you want to import the certificate. Now, you should see a message that the certificate was imported successfully.

Now, double-click the <clientusername>.p12 file. The Certificate Import Wizard appears once again. Click Next and leave the filename alone and click Next again. Now, you are asked to enter the challenge password you used when generating the certificate. Click Next. Select the option "Automatically select the certificate store based on type of certificate" and click Next. Wait for a message indicating that the certificate was imported successfully, and then click Finish. A popup window will tell you that you imported the certificate correctly.

Now you can set up the wireless device.

Wireless Device Configuration – Open the Wireless Configuration Panel by double-clicking on one of the terminals icon in the lower-right corner of your screen. You can find the correct icon by moving your mouse over the icons until one says "Wireless Network". That is the icon you need to double-click (see Figure 17.10).

Select your network, and check the Advanced tab to open the panel shown in Figure 17.11.

Select your network and click the Authentication tab to open the window shown in Figure 17.12.

Now select the Enable network access control using IEEE 802.1X radio button and ensure that the EAP type is listed as Smart Card or other Certificate. Click the Properties button to open the Smart Card or Other Certificate Properties window shown in Figure 17.13.

Select the options Use a certificate on this computer and Validate server certificate, and ensure that the Trusted root certificate authority option is set to the root certificate you imported earlier.

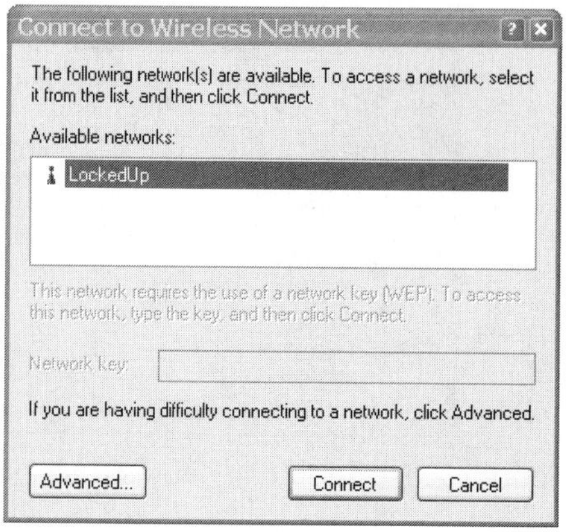

Figure 17.10   Wireless Configuration Panel

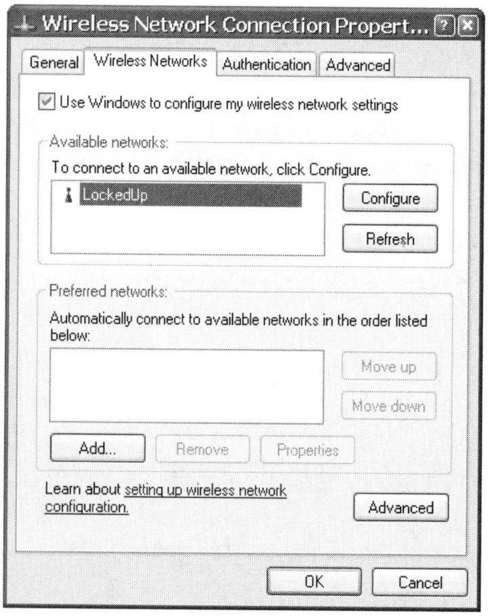

Figure 17.11   Wireless Networks Configuration Panel

If everything works (which we know always is the case), you'll be connected to your network using WPA.

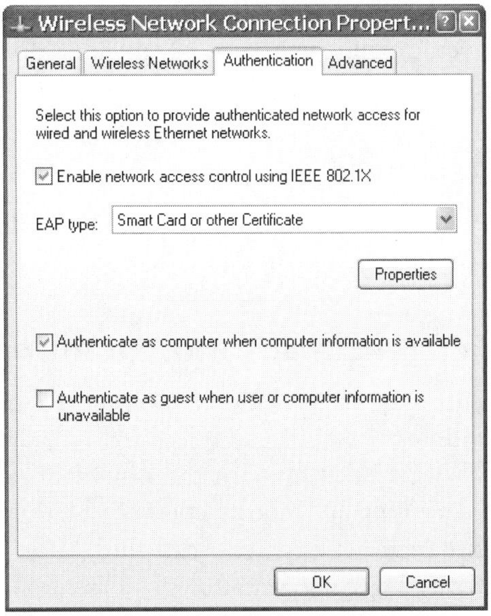

Figure 17.12 Wireless Network Authentication Configuration Panel

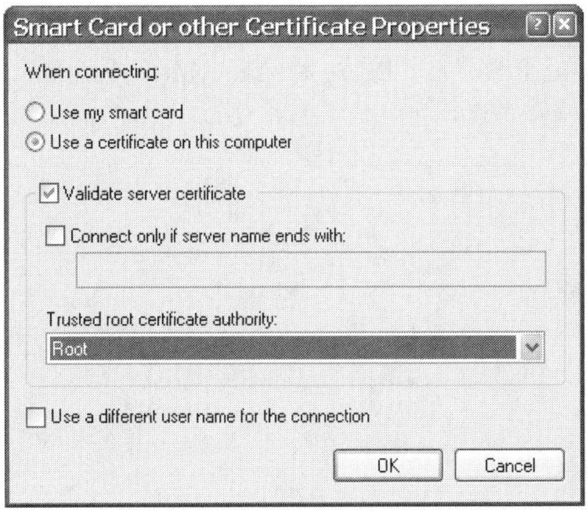

Figure 17.13 Smart Card or Other Certificate Properties Window

Summary

This chapter explained how to build your own small enterprise or test network using open source software as well as some commercial products. We should stress, at this point, that the point of this exercise was to make you familiar with how to build a working wireless network that uses WPA. If you plan to use this setup operationally, you should consider doing many other tasks beyond the scope of this book.

Acknowledgments

Portions of this chapter are based on the how-to's from Adam Sulmicki, Mike van Opstal, and Raymond McKay.

References and More Information

This section provides a pointer to using a Windows Server instead of Open Source.

Mike Van Opstal of the University of Maryland has written an excellent how-to on using a Windows 2000 as a RADIUS and DHCP server. Rather than duplicate that material here, you can find Mike's how-to at www.cs.umd.edu/~mvanopst/8021x/howto/server.html and a link to it at our site www.wpa-security.org/Windows/server.html.

Adam Sulmicki's how-to can be found at www.missl.cs.umd.edu/wireless/eaptls/ and Raymond McKay's how-to can be found at www.impossiblereflex.com/8021x/eap-tls-HOWTO.htm. Finally, you can find more information about using OpenSSL at the following URL: www.pseudonym.org/ssl/ssl_cook.htm, and in the book by John Viega, Matt Messier, and Pravir Chandra (2002) entitled *Network Security with OpenSSL*.

Appendixes

Overview of the AES Block Cipher

The AES block cipher is the same as the Rijndael algorithm but with a fixed block size of 128 bits (see Chapter 12). In IEEE 802.11i RSN, a further simplification is made by restricting the key size as well as the block size to 128 bits. The following description relates only to the RSN version.

You can think of the encryption of the block of data as a sort of production process in which various operations are applied repeatedly until the finished product, the ciphertext, is produced. A medieval blacksmith made a sword by starting with a strip of iron and repeatedly heating it, hammering it, adding impurities, folding it, and quenching it in cold water. By folding the metal ten times, the sword ended up with a thousand fine layers. In AES the data is the raw material loaded into a state array. The state array is processed through ten rounds of manipulation, after which it is unloaded to form the resulting encrypted block of data. At each stage of the process, the state is combined with a different **round key**, each of which is created and derived from the cipher key.

Although this sounds like a lot of work, one of the key advantages of the Rijndael algorithm is that it uses only simple operations such as shift, exclusive OR, and table substitution. Many encryption approaches require multiplication operations that are very expensive to implement. Rijndael uses **finite field** byte multiplication, a special operation that can be simplified down to a few logical operations or lookups in a 256-byte table. This appendix begins with an overview of finite field arithmetic. If you are just interested in the encryption steps for AES, skip to the next section.

Finite Field Arithmetic

When you were six years old, you probably spent quite a bit of time reciting multiplication tables and doing long additions and multiplications. You might have found it hard to remember to pass the carry from one column of digits to the next in an addition, but you did it because the teacher said, "This is the way the world works." Now you encounter finite field arithmetic, which has a different set of rules and, on first inspection, sounds like it came from outer space. Finite field arithmetic is important in cryptography and is the basis of the familiar cyclic redundancy check (CRC) used to detect errors in data packets.

Conventional arithmetic operates on an infinite range of values, even if you limit it to positive integers. However, if your entire universe is defined by a single byte, you have only 256 values to deal with. What often happens is that normal arithmetic is applied to byte values and any overflows or underflows during the conventional arithmetic are discarded. This works for many types of calculations, but in some sense discarding the carry violates the rules of conventional arithmetic. Your primary school teacher didn't talk about number universes that had only 256 values. Finite field arithmetic is defined specifically to handle such finite number universes. The rules apply to cases like single byte arithmetic so, in some sense, it is more valid than the familiar arithmetic. But let's not get too philosophical here; this type of arithmetic enables some good tricks and allows some neat shortcuts in the computations. This section is not intended to be a rigorous description of finite field mathematics; and if you are a pure mathematician, you probably won't like it. However, we do introduce the basics and explain why some of the computations used in cryptography look a little weird.

For our application, we are interested only in finite fields that can be represented by binary numbers. For purposes of finite field arithmetic, we can represent a binary number by polynomials of the form:

$$a_{(n-1)}x^{(n-1)} + a_{(n-2)}x^{(n-2)} + \ldots\ldots + a_2x^2 + a_1x + a_0 \tag{A.1}$$

The value of x is not important as it is only the coefficients $a_{(n)}$ that we are interested in. However if the coefficients have the value 0 or 1 and x represents the value 2, then the value of the polynomial, computed using conventional arithmetic, corresponds to the binary value.

Each of the coefficients corresponds to one bit of a binary number. So, for example, the 8-bit value 10010111 would be written as:

$$x^7 + 0 + 0 + x^4 + 0 + x^2 + x + 1 \tag{A.2}$$

or more simply:

$$\mathbf{x}^7 + \mathbf{x}^4 + \mathbf{x}^2 + \mathbf{x} + 1 \qquad\qquad (A.3)$$

Treating the numbers as polynomials leads to some interesting and different behavior when you are performing arithmetic operations. This is okay, providing such treatment still follows some basic rules such as:

if $A + B = C$ then $A = B - C$
and if $A \times B = C$ then $A = C \div B$

In the following sections we look at the main operations in turn.

Addition

When you add two polynomials, each term is added independently; there is no concept of a carry from one term to another. For example, in conventional arithmetic

$$(\mathbf{x}^3 + \mathbf{x}^2 + 1) \ + \ (\mathbf{x}^2 + x) \ = \ (\mathbf{x}^3 + 2\mathbf{x}^2 + \mathbf{x} + 1) \qquad (A.4)$$

In our binary representation, the coefficients can be only 0 or 1. The value 2 is not possible. Therefore, we have the rule that, when adding the coefficients, the following addition rule applies:

- $0 + 0 = 0$
- $0 + 1 = 1$
- $1 + 0 = 1$
- $1 + 1 = 0$ (there is no carry)

By a useful coincidence, this is the same result as what you get when you perform an exclusive OR operation, which is easier for digital logic than a binary addition.

Using our binary rules, the addition of the two polynomials in equation A.4 is:

$$(\mathbf{x}^3 + \mathbf{x}^2 + 1) \ + \ (\mathbf{x}^2 + x) \ = \ (\mathbf{x}^3 + 0 + \mathbf{x} + 1) = (\mathbf{x}^3 + \mathbf{x} + 1) \qquad (A.5)$$

This corresponds to the binary computation:

```
   1101      (x³ + x² + 1)
   0110 +    (x² + x)
  ------
   1011      (x³ + x + 1)
```
$$(A.6)$$

Notice how the addition has now been entirely replaced by the exclusive OR operation. Addition of 2 bytes under these rules is really an XOR operation, and addition *cannot* have a result bigger than 1 byte, which is consistent with our 1-byte universe.

Subtraction

The same logic that made addition become XOR also applies to subtraction. Suppose we want to subtract the two polynomials in (A.4). In conventional arithmetic the result would be:

$$(x^3 + x^2 + 1) \ - \ (x^2 + x) \ = \ (x^3 + 0^2 - x + 1) \tag{A.7}$$

The coefficient of the x term is -1. There is no -1 value in a single binary digit. The subtraction table for two binary digits is:

- $1 - 1 = 0$
- $1 - 0 = 1$
- $0 - 1 = 1$ (there is no borrow)
- $0 - 0 = 0$

Once again this is the same as the XOR operation so that the binary subtraction takes the form:

```
  1101      (x³ + x² + 1)
  0110 -    (x² + x)
  ------
  1011      (x³ + x + 1)
```

Surprising but true—in this byte arithmetic universe addition and subtraction become the same operation and are replaced by the exclusive OR operation. Notice also how this new arithmetic also obeys the rule that if $A + B = C$, then $A = B - C$.

Multiplication

Multiplication deviates even more from conventional arithmetic because of the way polynomials multiply together. The basic rule for multiplying two polynomials is to multiply all the terms together and then add terms of similar order (in other words, the same power of x). Here is a simple example in normal mathematics:

$$(x^3 + x^2 + 1)(x^2 + x) = (x^5 + x^4 + x^2 + x^4 + x^3 + x) =$$
$$(x^5 + 2x^4 + x^3 + x^2 + x) \tag{A.7}$$

By now you might guess that in our binary universe the x^4 term will disappear, leading to the result:

```
  1101        (x³ + x² + 1)
  0110 ×      (x² + x)
---------
  101110      (x⁵ + x³ + x² + x)
```

$$\begin{array}{ll} 1101 & (\mathbf{x}^3 + \mathbf{x}^2 + 1) \\ 0110 \ \times & (\mathbf{x}^2 + \mathbf{x}) \\ \hline 101110 & (\mathbf{x}^5 + \mathbf{x}^3 + \mathbf{x}^2 + \mathbf{x}) \end{array} \qquad (\text{A.8})$$

So far this looks straightforward enough and, by following the good old school long multiplication rules, we can work out the multiplications using only shift and XOR operations:

$$(\mathbf{x}^3 + \mathbf{x}^2 + 1)\,(\mathbf{x}^2 + \mathbf{x}) = (\mathbf{x}^3 + \mathbf{x}^2 + 1)\,\mathbf{x}^2 \ ^+\ (\mathbf{x}^3 + \mathbf{x}^2 + 1)\,\mathbf{x} \qquad (\text{A.9})$$

Multiplying by x^2 is the same as shifting left by two places because:

$$(\mathbf{x}^3 + \mathbf{x}^2 + 1)\,\mathbf{x}^2 = \mathbf{x}^5 + \mathbf{x}^3 + \mathbf{x}^2 \qquad (\text{A.10})$$

This means that the long multiplication can be done using the accumulate row method as follows:

```
   1101
   0110 ×
 ------
   0000
  11010
 110100
0000000
 -------
 0101110
```

$$\qquad (\text{A.11})$$

Notice how the intermediate rows are just the first value shifted and the result is just the XOR of the rows. Great! Now we have a really efficient way to do addition, subtraction, and multiplication by using this polynomial-based arithmetic. However, there is a snag that we discuss after looking at division.

Division

Division works by the shift and subtract method familiar under the name long division. Of course, in our case the subtraction is done using an XOR operation. An example is shown here and should be fairly self-explanatory:

```
          1101
       --------
0110)0101110
       0110000        (shift divisor to match most significant bit)
       -------
       0011110        (result of subtraction)
       011000
       ------
       0000110
         0110                                                    (A.12)
```

This is the reverse of the multiplication shown in the previous section. Gratifyingly, we get back to the result before the multiplication, showing that our arithmetic satisfies the rules that if A × B = C, then B = C ÷ A.

Galois Field GF()

Now comes the hard part. Not hard to implement but hard to understand. When we did addition and subtraction, it was not possible for the result to overflow. The result always fitted into a byte. However, based on our long multiplication approach, it is clearly possible that the result of multiplying two 8-bit numbers could be more than 8 bits long. Such an overflow is not allowed to exist in our finite field of 256 values, so what has gone wrong?

Let's go back to ordinary numbers instead of polynomials for a moment. Let's define a finite field that comprises seven digits {0, 1, 2, 3, 4, 5, 6}. We will define addition and multiplication to be the conventional operations except that the result "rolls over" from 6 back to 0. So if we add 1 to 6, we get 0. If we multiply 2 by 4, we get 1 (2 * 4 = 4 + 4 = 6 + 2 = 1—work it out). We can make an addition table, as shown in Table A.1. Taking any two numbers from the top row and left column, the sum is found in the intersection of the row and columns.

Table A.1 Addition Table

	0	1	2	3	4	5	6
0	0	1	2	3	4	5	6
1	1	2	3	4	5	6	0
2	2	3	4	5	6	0	1
3	3	4	5	6	0	1	2
4	4	5	6	0	1	2	3
5	5	6	0	1	2	3	4
6	6	0	1	2	3	4	5

	0	1	2	3	4	5	6
0	0	0	0	0	0	0	0
1	0	1	2	3	4	5	6
2	0	2	4	6	1	3	5
3	0	3	6	2	5	1	4
4	0	4	1	5	2	6	3
5	0	5	3	1	6	4	2
6	0	6	5	4	3	2	1

In a similar way we can define a multiplication table, as shown in Table A.2. Here the product value is in the intersection of each row and column. These tables can be used for subtraction and division as well. To work out the value of m/n, you go to the nth column, find the entry m in the column, and the answer is the row number. For example, to compute 6/3, go to the third column and find the value 6, then look to the left to see the answer 6/3 = 2. Note that this rule does not work if you try to divide by 0; try it and you'll see the problem. As with conventional arithmetic, dividing by 0 is undefined.

These tables show that it is possible to define a finite number universe with familiar and useful arithmetic operations that really work. However, this approach does not work in all cases. Suppose we want a universe with six numbers: {0, 1, 2, 3, 4, 5}. Applying the "roll over rule" whereby 5 + 1 = 0, the addition and multiplication tables come out as shown in Tables A.3 and A.4.

Look at column 2 of the multiplication table. 0 appears twice. Numbers 1, 3, 5 don't appear at all! Column 3 only has the values 0 and 3. What this means is that

Table A.3 Addition Table

	0	1	2	3	4	5
0	0	1	2	3	4	5
1	1	2	3	4	5	0
2	2	3	4	5	0	1
3	3	4	5	0	1	2
4	4	5	0	1	2	3
5	5	0	1	2	3	4

Table A.4 Multiplication Table

	0	1	2	3	4	5
0	0	0	0	0	0	0
1	0	1	2	3	4	5
2	0	2	4	0	2	4
3	0	3	0	3	0	3
4	0	4	2	0	4	2
5	0	5	4	3	2	1

it is impossible to do meaningful division in this number universe. The problem is that there are six numbers and both 2 and 3 are factors of 6. This means that 2 * 3 = 0 and also 2 * 0 = 0.

Because of this factoring problem, this type of finite number universe can only have all four arithmetic operations $(+, -, *, \div)$ if the number of values in the universe is a prime number. It works when there are seven values because seven is a prime number. It doesn't work with eight, nine, or ten values, but it works with eleven values and so on.

If we return to our polynomial representation, a similar rule applies. The finite field should be bounded by a polynomial that is irreducible. A polynomial is reducible if it can be factored. For example $(x^2 + 1)$ is reducible because:

$$(\mathbf{x}^2 + 1) \;=\; (\mathbf{x} + 1)\,(\mathbf{x} + 1) \qquad \text{(using finite field arithmetic)} \qquad \text{(A.13)}$$

To make our finite field arithmetic work, we need a finite field that is bounded by an irreducible polynomial and has 256 elements. Such a field can be created and is called a **Galois Field**, denoted by GF(256). We will not present the theory behind how a Galois Field is created. However, it has the property that it has 2^n entries and the entries are derived from, and bounded by, an irreducible polynomial. For GF(256), that polynomial is:

$$\mathbf{x}^8 + \mathbf{x}^4 + \mathbf{x}^3 + \mathbf{x}^1 + 1 \qquad \text{(A.14)}$$

This corresponds to the binary value 100011011 or hexadecimal 11B.

Let's remind ourselves of why we digressed to discuss the Galois Field. The problem was that multiplication according to the rules we had defined caused undefined results due to overflows. The question was how these should be handled and avoided? The answer lies in treating the possible 256 values as members of the GF(256) field. This field is limited by the irreducible polynomial that defines our GF(256). We can think of the rules of multiplication in the same way as shown in Table A.2. In that case the result wraps around the prime number that defines the number of elements in the field; in Table A.2 this prime number is 7. In conventional arithmetic, we would say that the result is the remainder after dividing by 7 or that the result is computed modulo 7.

In Table A.2, a multiplication can be computed as follows:

Result = (A x B) mod 7.

or

Result = Remainder((A x B) / 7)

Example: 6 * 6 = 36 mod 7 = Remainder(36/7) = 1

The same rule is now applied to our byte computations in the GF(256) field:

Result = (A x B) mod x8 + x4 + x3 + x1 + 1   (the irreducible polynomial)

or

Result = Remainder((A x B) / (x8 + x4 + x3 + x1 + 1))

Lets see how this works in practice. We saw in (A.11) the result of a multiplication that did not overflow outside the byte value. Let's take an example that clearly does want to overflow:

```
01101001 * 00101001
```

Using the accumulate row approach:

```
0110100100000          (corresponds to 00101001)
0001101001000          (corresponds to 00101001)
0000001101001          (corresponds to 00101001)
-------------
0111000000001          (XOR rows)                        (A.15)
```

The intermediate result in (A.15) is 12 bits long—we need to reduce it by wrapping around the irreducible polynomial. To do this, we need to divide by our irreducible polynomial and take the remainder:

```
                    1110
          -------------
100011011)0111000000001     (Result (A.15) ÷ irreducible polynomial)
          100011011000
          -------------
           011011011001
           10001101100
           -----------
            01010110101
            1000110110
            ----------
            0010000011                                            (A.16)
```

So the remainder after removing the overflow is 10000011. In other words, in our finite field:

```
01101001 * 00101001  =  10000011
```

All values are within our single byte space. Hooray! However, although it still uses only shift and XOR, the computation now seems rather complicated and long-winded. We had to do both long multiplication and long division to get the result. There is a good trick we can use to simplify the computation, however. If we look at the accumulate row approach to multiplication, each intermediate row represents the first multiplier shifted left to correspond to a bit in the second multiplier. After this, all the rows are added together and the result is taken modulus our field polynomial 100011011. However, rather than waiting until all the rows are accumulated before adding together, you can shift and add 1 bit at a time as the computation proceeds. Let's look at the previous multiplication, 01101001 * 00101001, done in this way. The sequence of events is shown in Figure A.1. The process for computing A x B is as follows:

- Start with an accumulator value of 0.
- Take each bit of B in turn, starting with the most significant bit.

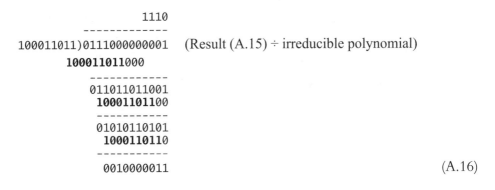

Figure A.1 Multiply by Shift and Add

- For each bit, first multiply the accumulator by 2 (shift left).
- If the bit is 1, add the value of A to the accumulator.

The final value of the accumulator is the answer.

Figure A.1 shows the computation for the same example we used earlier (A.15) and you can see that the result is the same—this is good. In the previous example we reduced the result of (A.15) to be within range by dividing by the value 100011101 and taking the remainder. This gave the result shown in (A.16). However, if we use the shift and add approach, there is another way to do the reduction that is easier than performing this long division. Note that the shift and add method requires that the accumulator be shifted left at each stage. This left shift is the same as multiplying by two. The simplification is to reduce the value within range after each shift rather than waiting until the end.

You might think that means more divisions rather than fewer. However, consider the result of the computation 2 * A. If the most significant bit of A is 0, we know that there *cannot* be an overflow so the result will already be in range. If the most significant bit is 1, we know that there *will* be an overflow. Because we know the result overflows, it needs to be reduced to get back to a byte value. We also know that the range of possible values after the shift will be 100000000 to 111111110. This means that the result of dividing by 100011011 must *always* be 1 and the remainder will be the result we want. Because we know the result of the division is 1, we can get that wanted remainder simply by subtracting 100011011 from the shifted value. So now we have a simple rule for computing 2 * A:

if (most significant bit 1) A = A shifted left 1
else A = (A shifted left 1) XOR 00011011   (A.17)

In the second case, the XOR accomplished the "subtract 100011011" operation for the byte value.

Now we have a long multiplication rule that works for all cases. The shift operation in Figure A.8 is replaced by the formula in (A.17). Each intermediate step as well as the final result is guaranteed to be within the GF(256) field; in other words, the result of the multiplication is always a single byte. The long multiplication has been achieved by a short sequence of XOR operations and shifts that are easily implemented in digital systems.

Conclusion

This section introduces mathematics that may be unfamiliar to you. The arguments seem logical, but you may be left feeling that the operations are puzzling and nonintuitive. However, the benefit of this type of mathematics is an amazing simplification in the way multiplication is implemented. It makes the design and implementation of encryption systems, which often rely on many multiplications, much more practical in the real world.

Steps in the AES Encryption Process

The encryption process uses a set of specially derived keys called **round keys**. These are applied, along with other operations, on an array of data that holds exactly one block of data—the data to be encrypted. This array we call the state array.

You take the following steps to encrypt a 128-bit block:

1. Derive the set of round keys from the cipher key.
2. Initialize the state array with the block data (plaintext).
3. Add the initial round key to the starting state array.
4. Perform nine rounds of state manipulation.
5. Perform the tenth and final round of state manipulation.
6. Copy the final state array out as the encrypted data (ciphertext).

The reason that the rounds have been listed as "nine followed by a final tenth round" is because the tenth round involves a slightly different manipulation from the others.

The block to be encrypted is just a sequence of 128 bits. AES works with byte quantities so we first convert the 128 bits into 16 bytes. We say "convert," but, in reality, it is almost certainly stored this way already. Operations in RSN/AES are performed on a two-dimensional byte array of four rows and four columns. At the start of the encryption, the 16 bytes of data, numbered $D_0 - D_{15}$, are loaded into the array as shown in Table A.5.

Each round of the encryption process requires a series of steps to alter the state array. These steps involve four types of operations called:

- SubBytes
- ShiftRows

Table A.5 Initial Value of the State Array

D_0	D_4	D_8	D_{12}
D_1	D_5	D_9	D_{13}
D_2	D_6	D_{10}	D_{14}
D_3	D_7	D_{11}	D_{15}

- MixColumns
- XorRoundKey

The details of these operations are described shortly, but first we need to look in more detail at the generation of the Round Keys, so called because there is a different one for each round in the process.

Round Keys

The cipher key used for encryption is 128 bits long. Where this key comes from is not important here; refer to Chapter 10 on key hierarchy and how the temporal encryption keys are produced. The cipher key is already the result of many hashing and cryptographic transformations and, by the time it arrives at the AES block encryption, it is far removed from the secret master key held by the authentication server. Now, finally, it is used to generate a set of eleven 128-bit round keys that will be combined with the data during encryption. Although there are ten rounds, eleven keys are needed because one extra key is added to the initial state array before the rounds start. The best way to view these keys is an array of eleven 16-byte values, each made up of four 32-bit words, as shown in Table A.6.

To start with, the first round key $Rkey_0$ is simply initialized to the value of the cipher key (that is the secret key delivered through the key hierarchy). Each of the remaining ten keys is derived from this as follows.

Table A.6 Round Key Array

	32 bits	32 bits	32 bits	32 bits
$Rkey_0$	W_0	W_1	W_2	W_3
$Rkey_1$	W_0	W_1	W_2	W_3
$Rkey_2$	W_0	W_1	W_2	W_3
$Rkey_3$	W_0	W_1	W_2	W_3
$Rkey_4$	W_0	W_1	W_2	W_3
$Rkey_5$	W_0	W_1	W_2	W_3
$Rkey_6$	W_0	W_1	W_2	W_3
$Rkey_7$	W_0	W_1	W_2	W_3
$Rkey_8$	W_0	W_1	W_2	W_3
$Rkey_9$	W_0	W_1	W_2	W_3
$Rkey_{10}$	W_0	W_1	W_2	W_3

For each of the round keys $Rkey_1$ to $Rkey_{10}$, words W_1, W_2, W_3 are computed as the sum[1] of the corresponding word in the previous round key and the preceding word in the current round key. For example, using XOR for addition:

$$Rkey_5{:}W_1 \ = \ Rkey_4{:}W_1 \quad XOR \quad Rkey_5{:}W_0,$$
$$Rkey_8{:}W_3 \ = \ Rkey_7{:}W_3 \quad XOR \quad Rkey_8{:}W_2 \quad \text{and so on.}$$

The rule for the value of W_0 is a little more complicated to describe, although still simple to compute. For each round key $Rkey_1$ to $Rkey_{10}$, the value of W_0 is the sum of three 32-bit values:

- The value of W_0 from the previous round key
- The value of W_3 from the previous round key, rotated right by 8 bits
- A special value from a table called Rcon

Thus, we write:

$$Rkey_i{:}W_0 \ = \ Rkey_{(i-1)}{:}W_0 \quad XOR \quad (Rkey_{(i-1)}{:}W_3 >>> 8) \quad XOR \quad Rcon[i]$$

where $W >>> 8$ means rotate right 8—for example (in hexadecimal) 1234 becomes 4123 and $Rcon[i]$ is an entry in Table A.7.

Table A.7 Values in Rcon

i	Rcon(i)
1	2
2	4
3	8
4	16
5	32
6	64
7	128
8	27
9	54
10	108

---

1. Using finite field arithmetic.

There is a good reason why the sequence of this table suddenly breaks off from 128 to 27. It is because of the way finite fields overflow, as described in the previous section.

Although the algorithm for deriving the round keys seems rather complicated, you will notice that no difficult computations have been performed and it is not at all computationally intensive. Also note that, after the first, each key is generated sequentially and based on the previous one. This means that it is possible to generate each round key just in time before it is needed in the encryption computation. Alternatively, if there is plenty of memory, they can be derived once at the start and stored for use with each subsequent AES block.

Computing the Rounds

Having described how the round keys are derived, we can now return to the operations used in computing each round. Earlier we mentioned that four operations are required called:

- SubBytes
- ShiftRows
- MixColumns
- XorRoundKey

Each one of these operations is applied to the current state array and produces a new version of the state array. In all but the rarest cases, the state array is changed by the operation. The details of each operation are given shortly.

In the first nine rounds of the process, the four operations are performed in the order listed. In the last (tenth) round, the MixColumns operation is not performed and only the SubBytes, ShiftRows, and XorRoundKey operations are done.

SubBytes

This operation is a simple substitution that converts every byte into a different value. AES defines a table of 256 values for the substitution. You work through the 16 bytes of the state array, use each byte as an index into the 256-byte substitution table, and replace the byte with the value from the substitution table. Because all possible 256 byte values are present in the table, you end up with a totally new result in the state array, which can be restored to its original contents using an inverse substitution table. The contents of the substitution table are not arbitrary; the entries are computed using a mathematical formula but most implementations will simply have the substitution table stored in memory as part of the design.

ShiftRows

As the name suggests, ShiftRows operates on each row of the state array. Each row is rotated to the right by a certain number of bytes as follows:

- 1st Row: rotated by 0 bytes (i.e., is not changed)
- 2nd Row: rotated by 1 byte
- 3rd Row: rotated by 2 bytes
- 4th Row: rotated by 3 bytes

As an example, if the ShiftRows operation is applied to the stating state array shown in Table A.8, the result is shown in Table A.9.

MixColumns

This operation is the most difficult, both to explain and perform. Each column of the state array is processed separately to produce a new column. The new column replaces the old one. The processing involves a matrix multiplication. If you are not familiar with matrix arithmetic, don't get to concerned—it is really just a convenient notation for showing operations on tables and arrays.

The MixColumns operation takes each column of the state array C_0 to C_3 and replaces it with a new column computed by the matrix multiplication shown in Figure A.2.

Table A.8 Effect of ShiftRows Operation—Start State

D_0	D_4	D_8	D_{12}
D_1	D_5	D_9	D_{13}
D_2	D_6	D_{10}	D_{14}
D_3	D_7	D_{11}	D_{15}

Table A.9 Effect of ShiftRows Operation—End State

D_0	D_4	D_8	D_{12}
D_{13}	D_1	D_5	D_9
D_{10}	D_{14}	D_2	D_6
D_7	D_{11}	D_{15}	D_3

Figure A.2 MixColumns Operation

The new column is computed as follows:

$$C'_0 = 02 * C_0 + 01 * C_1 + 01 * C_2 + 03 * C_3$$
$$C'_1 = 03 * C_0 + 02 * C_1 + 01 * C_2 + 01 * C_3$$
$$C'_2 = 01 * C_0 + 03 * C_1 + 02 * C_2 + 01 * C_3$$
$$C'_3 = 01 * C_0 + 01 * C_1 + 03 * C_2 + 02 * C_3$$

Remember that we are not using normal arithmetic—we are using finite field arithmetic, which has special rules and both the multiplications and additions can be implemented using XOR.

XorRoundKey

After the MixColumns operation, the XorRoundKey is very simple indeed and hardly needs its own name. This operation simply takes the existing state array, XORs the value of the appropriate round key, and replaces the state array with the result. It is done once before the rounds start and then once per round, using each of the round keys in turn.

Decryption

As you might expect, decryption involves reversing all the steps taken in encryption using *inverse* functions:

- InvSubBytes
- InvShiftRows
- InvMixColumns

XorRoundKey doesn't need an inverse function because XORing twice takes you back to the original value. InvSubBytes works the same way as SubBytes but uses a different table that returns the original value. InvShiftRows involves rotating left instead of right and InvMixColumns uses a different constant matrix to multiply the columns.

The order of operation in decryption is:

1. Perform initial decryption round:
   XorRoundKey
   InvShiftRows
   InvSubBytes
2. Perform nine full decryption rounds:
   XorRoundKey
   InvMixColumns
   InvShiftRows
   InvSubBytes
3. Perform final XorRoundKey

The same round keys are used in the same order.

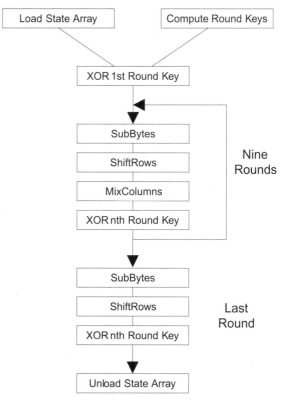

Figure A.3   Summary of AES/RSN Encryption

Summary of AES

Now we have seen all the steps needed to take a 128-bit block of data and transform it into ciphertext. We also looked at the reverse process for decryption. The process of encryption can be summarized as shown in Figure A.3. The mathematics behind the algorithm is rather hard to understand for nonmathematicians and we have focused on *how* rather than *why* in this book. If you are interested in such matters, it is probably worth reading the theoretical papers of looking at the book that specialize in cryptography. What is interesting, however, is the way in which all the operations are based on byte values and operations that are simple to implement in digital logic gates. AES achieves the goal of being both secure and practical for real systems.

B Appendix

Example Message Modification

This appendix describes the process needed to modify a WEP-encrypted packet and ensure that the CRC for the packet remains valid, in other words, the bit-flipping attack.

Assume that a sender wishes to send a message to a recipient, and that he wishes to use a CRC to detect errors during transmission.

Let the message, $M(x)$, be the single ASCII letter N: $M(x) = 01001110$, and let the CRC generator be $G(x) = x3 + x2 + 1$, or 1101. To compute the CRC value, $M(x)$ is first multiplied by the degree of $G(x)$, which is 3. Because multiplication in $GF(2)$ is a left shift, we end up with $M'(x) = 01001110000$. This value is now divided by $G(x)$, and because division in $GF(2)$ is the XOR operation, the result is:

```
        _____
1101|  01001110000
       1101
       1001
       1101
         1001
         1101
          1001
          1101
           1000
           1101
            1010
            1101
             1110
             1101
               110
```

The long division results in a remainder of 110, which is now subtracted (subtraction in GF(2) is the XOR operation) from $M'(x)$ to obtain $P(x)$—the message that is sent: $P(x)=01001110110$.

Upon receipt of the message, the recipient divides it with $G(x)$. If the remainder of the division is 0, the message did not contain errors within the precision of the CRC.

Example Message Modification

For this example, we take the message above (ASCII 'N') and modify the message so it becomes an ASCII y and we still ensure that the ICV remains valid using the process described in Chapter 15.

Stating the problem: Given $P(x)= 01001110110$, derive $P'(x)=01111001XXX$ where XXX is a valid CRC.

First, the delta between the current message, $M(x)$, and the desired message, $N(x)$, is computed by the exclusive OR of the two values.

```
M(x) = 01001110
N(x) = 01111001
Δ(x) = 00110111
```

Now, the CRC is calculated for the delta value:

```
          ------------
1101 |00110111000
        1101
            1100
            1101
             010
```

The remainder of the division is the CRC of the delta. Now the delta and its CRC are exclusive OR'd with $P(x)$:

```
P(x)       01001110110
Δ(x)  ⊕ 00110111000
                    01111001110
CRC(Δ)              ⊕  010
P'(x)   01111001100
```

Now, P'(x) is shown to be a valid message; the remainder of the CRC calculation is 0.

```
        _____
1101 |  01111001100
        1101
            1000
        1101
          1011
          1101
            1101
            1101
                   0
```

Because the remainder of the CRC calculation is 0, *P'(x)* has a valid CRC and the message has been successfully modified.

C
Appendix

Verifying the Integrity of Downloaded Files

Recently, a trend has occurred in which a malicious Trojan horse is hidden in popular open source programs. The authors of the programs do *not* do this. Instead, it is done by attackers modifying the source at distribution points such as ftp download sites. The best way to ensure you don't install software that has been modified after the authors created the ZIP or TAR file is to check either the MD5 message digest or the GPG signature of the files you download. The latter is significantly better than the former because the attacker could have easily changed the MD5 value as well.

In this appendix, we walk through the process of verifying the code you download.

Checking the MD5 Digest

Checking the MD5 digest value is easy if you're on a UNIX system. Most of the modern systems now have a command md5sum. Md5sum computes the MD5 digest value for the file name entered at the command line. Thus, you check the digest of the recent OpenSSL distribution with the following command:

```
bash-2.05$ md5sum openssl-0.9.7-beta4.tar.gz
43cf89b428fbdd7873b5aae2680cd324  openssl-0.9.7-beta4.tar.gz
```

The output of MD5sum is the 128-byte MD5 digest in hexadecimal of the file, or files, you entered on the command line. You must check that value with the value that would be contained in openssl-0.9.7-beta4.tar.gz.md5. The two values should be identical. If you're lazy and are familiar with the UNIX command line, you can also do:

```
md5sum TARBALL | awk '{print $1;}' | cmp - TARBALL.md5
```

If you don't get any output from the above command, then the digests match.

Checking the GPG Signature

An MD5 digest isn't foolproof. As mentioned before, an attacker could also change the value stored in the digest file so it always matches. A far better way to ensure the integrity of files you download is to check the digital signature of the file downloaded.

Checking the signature requires that you have either PGP (www.pgp.com) or GPG (www.gnupg.org) installed on one of your systems. You'll also need the public key of the creator of the signature.

Here's how you would go about checking the integrity on our openssl file.

```
bash-2.05$ gpg openssl-0.9.7-beta4.tar.gz.asc
gpg: Signature made Tue Nov 19 05:15:12 2002 EST using RSA key ID E06D2CB1
gpg: Can't check signature: public key not found
bash-2.05$
```

We ran GPG on the signature file, but we don't have the public key for the signer. So, we have to find the key at a keyserver using the key ID 0xE06D2CB1. The easiest way to do that is to go to www.keyserver.net and enter the key ID into the window, as shown in Figure C.1, making sure to enter "0x" before the key ID. In this case, we're entering "0xE06D2CB1".

If a key exists in the server with the ID you entered, you'll see it displayed as the result of your query. The answer to our query is shown in Figure C.2.

In this case, you'll see that Richard Levitte is the owner of the public key associated with the key ID 0xE06D2CB1. Now, you need to make sure that Richard Levitte is authorized to sign the file you downloaded. To answer this question, we simply look at the list of developer team members for OpenSSL on their home page, and we see that Richard Levitte is a member of the development team. Ideally, the team should also put their OpenPGP fingerprints on this page to verify that the Richard Levitte associated with the public key we found is in fact the Richard Levitte associated with the OpenSSL project.

Once we're happy that we have the correct key, we can view an ASCII representation of it and cut and paste the key into a file we can import into our Open-

Figure C.1 Public Key Server

PGP application. The ASCII representation of Richard Levitte's key is shown in Figure C.3.

Now, assuming that we saved a copy of the ASCII representation in the file levitte.asc, we import the key into our public key ring with the command:

```
bash-2.05$ gpg --import levitte.asc
gpg: key E06D2CB1: public key imported
gpg: Total number processed: 1
gpg:              imported: 1  (RSA: 1)
```

Now that we've loaded the proper key into our public key ring, we can verify the integrity, or authenticity, of the file we downloaded.

```
bash-2.05$ gpg openssl-0.9.7-beta4.tar.gz.asc
gpg: Signature made Tue Nov 19 05:15:12 2002 EST using RSA key ID E06D2CB1
```

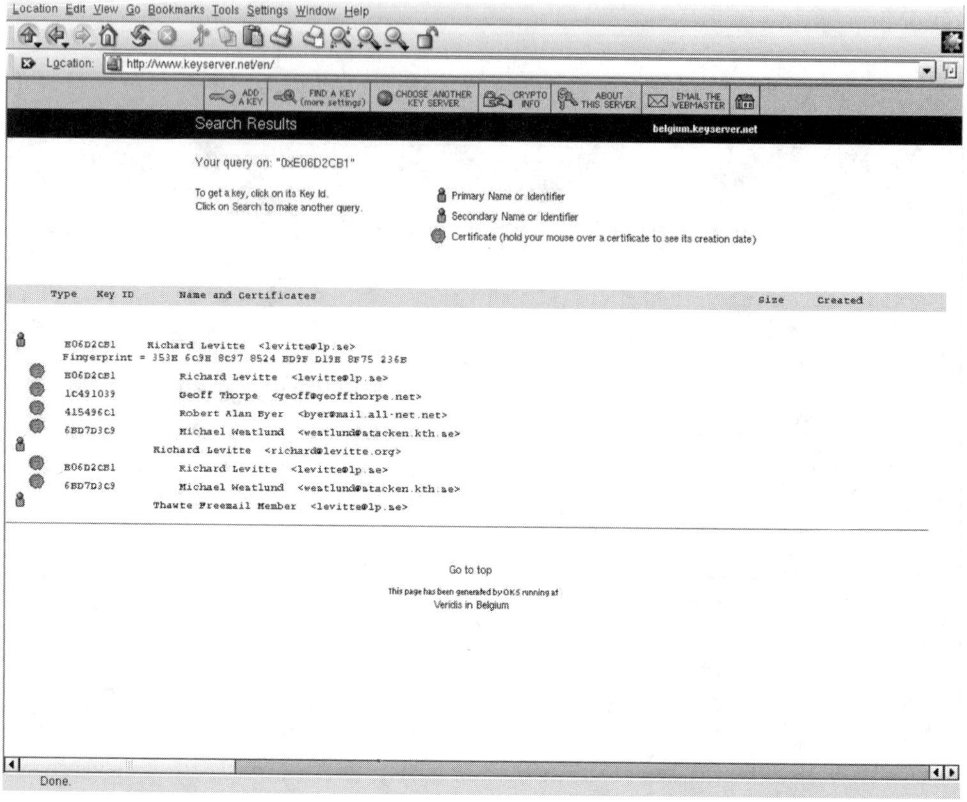

Figure C.2   Results of a Key ID Search

```
gpg: Good signature from "Richard Levitte <richard@levitte.org>"
gpg:               aka "Richard Levitte <levitte@lp.se>"
gpg: checking the trustdb
gpg: no ultimately trusted keys found
gpg: WARNING: This key is not certified with a trusted signature!
gpg:          There is no indication that the signature belongs to the
owner.
Fingerprint: 35 3E 6C 9E 8C 97 85 24  BD 9F D1 9E 8F 75 23 6B
```

You'll see that the signature of the file verified correctly. But there's a warning message. The warning is just telling us that Richard Levitte's public key certificate isn't signed by anyone we trust.

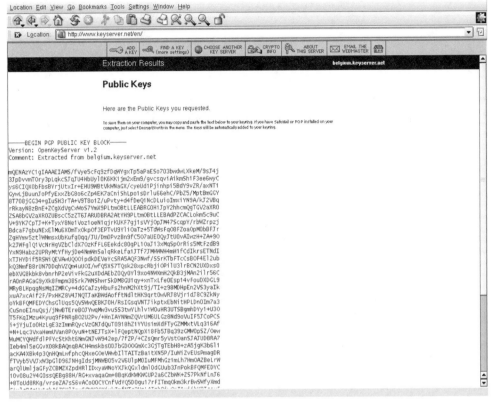

Figure C.3 ASCII Representation of Public Key

Acronyms

ACK	Acknowledge
ADSL	Asynchronous Digital Subscriber Line
AES	Advanced Encryption Standard
AP	Access Point
AS	Authentication Server
ATM	Automatic Teller Machine
BSS	Basic Service Set
CBC	Cipher Block Chaining
CCM	Counter Mode—CBC MAC
CCMP	Counter Mode—CBC MAC Protocol
CHAP	Challenge Handshake Authentication Protocol
CRC	Cyclic Redundancy Check
DA	Destination Address
DHCP	Dynamic Host Configuration Protocol
DoS	Denial of Service
EAP	Extensible Authentication Protocol
EAPOL	EAP Over LAN
EKE	Encrypted Key Exchange
ESS	Extended Service Set
GMK	Group Master Key
GPS	Global Positioning System
GSM	Groupe Spécial Mobile
GSSAPI	Generic Security Service Application Program Interface
GTK	Group Transient Key
HMAC	Hash Message Authentication Code

IAKERB	Initial and Pass-Through Authentication Using Kerberos V5
IANA	Internet Assigned Numbers Authority
IBSS	Independent Basic Service Set
ICMP	Internet Control Message Protocol
ICV	Integrity Check Value
IEEE	Institute of Electrical and Electronics Engineers
IETF	Internet Engineering Task Force
IMSI	International Mobile Subscriber Identity
IP	Internet Protocol
ISO	International Standards Organization
ISP	Internet Service Provider
IT	Information Technology
IV	Initialization Vector
KDC	Key Distribution Center
LAN	Local Area Network
LEAP	Light EAP (Cisco)
LLC	Link Layer Control
MAC	Medium Access Control (the meaning used in this book)
MAC (alt)	Message Authentication Code (cryptographic community use)
MIC	Message Integrity Code
MPDU	MAC Protocol Data Unit
MSDU	MAC Service Data Unit
NAK	Negative Acknowledge
NAS	Network Access Server
NIST	National Institute of Standards and Technology
PAE	Port Access Entity
PAP	Password Authentication Protocol
PC	Personal Computer
PDA	Personal Digital Assistant
PEAP	Protected EAP
PKI	Public Key Infrastructure
PLCP	Physical Layer Convergence Protocol
PIN	Personal Identification Number

PMK	Pairwise Master Key
PN	Packet Number
POP	Point of Presence
PPP	Point to Point Protocol
PRF	Pseudo Random Function
PTK	Pairwise Transient Key
PRNG	Pseudo Random Number Generator
USB	Universal Serial Bus
RA	Receiver Address
RADIUS	Remote Authentication Dial-In Service
RFC	Request For Comment
RH	RSN Header
RSN	Robust Security Network
SA	Source Address
SIM	Subscriber Identity Module
SRP	Secure Remote Password
SSID	Service Set Identifier
SSL	Secure Socket Layer
STA	Wireless Station
TA	Transmitter Address
TGi	IEEE 802.11 Task Group 'i'
TGS	Ticket Granting Service
TGT	Ticket Granting Ticket
TKIP	Temporal Key Integrity Protocol
TLS	Transport Layer Security
TSC	TKIP Sequence Counter
VPN	Virtual Private Network
WEP	Wired Equivalent Privacy
WPA	Wi-Fi Protected Access

References

Abaddon. July 2002. *Airjack*. http://802.11ninja.org,

Aboba, B., and D. Simon. 2001. IEEE 802.11 security and 802.1X. IEEE 802.11-00/034r1.

Abraham, D., G. Dolan, G. Double, and J. Stevens. 1991. Transaction security system. *IBM Systems Journal* 39:206–229.

Advanced Encryption Standard (AES). 2002. Technical Report FIPS 197. U.S. National Institute of Standards.

air. www.sourceforge.net/projects/airsnort.

Anderson, R. 2001. *Security Engineering*. New York: John Wiley and Sons.

Arbaugh, W.A. May 2001. An inductive chosen plaintext attack against WEP/WEP2. www.cs.umd.edu/waa/wepwep2-attack.html.

Arbaugh, W. A., W. L. Fithen, and John McHugh. 2000. Windows of vulnerability: a case study analysis. *IEEE Computer* 33(12):52–59.

Arbaugh, W. A., N. Shankar, and J. Wan. 2001. Your 802.11 network has no clothes. In *Proceedings of the First IEEE International Conference on Wireless LANs and Home Networks*. Pp. 131–144.

Arbaugh, W. A., N. Shankar, J. Wan, and K. Zhang. 2002. Your 802.11 network has no clothes. *IEEE Wireless Communications Magazine* 9(6):44–51.

N. Asokan, V. Niemi, and K. Nyberg. 2002. Man-in-the-Middle. In *Tunnelled Authentication Protocols, Cryptology ePrint Archive, Report* 2002/163. www.eprint.iacr.org/2002/163.

Bellare, M., J. Kilian, and P. Rogaway. 2000. The security of the cipher block chaining message authentication code. *Journal of Computer and System Sciences* 61(3):362–399.

Bellovin, S. M., and M. Merritt. 1991. Limitations of the Kerberos authentication system. In *USENIX Conference Proceedings*. Dallas, TX: USENIX. Pp. 253–267.

Bellovin, S. M., and M. Merritt. 1992. Encrypted key exchange: password-based protocols secure against dictionary attacks. In *Proceedings of the IEEE Symposium on Research in Security and Privacy.* Pp. 72–84.

Bishop, M. 2002. *Computer Security: Art and Science*, 1ˢᵗ ed. Boston: Addison-Wesley.

Blunk, L., and J. Vollbrecht. 1998. *PPP Extensible Authentication Protocol (EAP).* Technical Report RFC 2284. IETF.

Borisov, N, I. Goldberg, and D. Wagner. 2001. Intercepting mobile communications: the insecurity of 802.11. In *Proceedings of the Seventh Annual International Conference on Mobile Computing and Networking.* Pp. 180–188.

Cheswick, W., S. Bellovin, and A. Rubin. 2003. *Firewalls and Internet Security*, 2ⁿᵈ ed. Boston: Addison-Wesley.

Computer Emergency Response Team. October 2000. Windows based DDoS agent. http://www.cert.org/incident_notes/IN-2000-01.html.

Daemen, J., and V. Rijmen. 2000. *Smart Card Research and Applications*, The Block Cipher Rijndael. New York: Springer-Verlag. Pp. 288–296.

Daemen, J., and V. Rijmen. 2001. Rijndael, the advanced encryption standard. *Dr. Dobb's Journal*, 26(3):137–139.

Davie, B., L. Peterson, and D. Clark. 1999. *Computer Networks: A Systems Approach*, 2ⁿᵈ ed. San Francisco, CA: Morgan Kaufmann.

Dierks, T., and C. Allen. 1999. *The TLS Protocol.* Technical Report RFC 2246, IETF.

eth. www.ethereal.com.

Ferguson, Michael N. An Improved MIC for 802.11 WEP, 2002. Document number IEEE 802.11-02/020r0. Available from http://grouper.ieee.org/groups/802/11/Documents/DocumentHolder/2-020.zip

Fluhrer, S., I. Mantin, and A. Shamir. 2001. Weaknesses in the key scheduling algorithm of RC4. In *Eighth Annual Workshop on Selected Areas in Cryptography.*

Hassell, J. 2003. *RADIUS: Securing Public Access to Private Resources.* Cambridge, MA: O'Reilly and Associates.

Hopper, D. I. Secret Service agents probe wireless networks in Washington. www.securityfocus.com/news/899.

IEEE. 1997. LAN MAN standards of the IEEE Computer Society: wireless LAN medium access control (MAC) and physical layer(PHY) specification. *IEEE Standard 802.11.*

IEEE. 2001. Standards for local and metropolitan area networks: Standard for port based network access control. *IEEE Draft P802.1X/D11.*

Jonsson, J. 2002. On the security of CTR + CBC-MAC. In *SAC 2002 - Ninth Annual Workshop on Selected Areas of Cryptography.*

Kocher, P., J. Jaffe, and B. Jun. 1999. Differential power analysis. *Lecture Notes in Computer Science* 1666:388-397.

Krawczyk, H., M. Bellare, and R. Canetti. 1997. *HMAC: Keyed-Hasing for Message Authentication.* Technical Report RFC 2104. IETF.

Mantin, I., and A. Shamir. 2001. A practical attack on broadcast RC4. In *Proceedings of FSE 2001.*

Menezes, A. J., P. C. Van Oorschot, and S. A. Vanstone, eds. 1996. *Handbook of Applied Cryptography.* New York: CRC Press.

Mishra, A., and W. A. Arbaugh. 2002. *An Initial Security Analysis of the IEEE 802.1X Standard.* Technical Report CS-TR-4328. College Park: University of Maryland.

Neuman, B. C., and T. Ts'o. 1994. Kerberos: an authentication service for computer networks. *IEEE Communications Magazine* 32(9):33–38.

Neumann, P. G. *Computer-Related Risks.* 1995. Reading: Addison-Wesley.

Norris, M., and Steve Pretty. 2000. *Designing the Total Area Network: Intranets, VPNS and Enterprise Networks Explained.* New York: John Wiley and Sons.

Petroni, N. L., Jr., and W. A. Arbaugh. 2003. The dangers of mitigating security design flaws: a wireless case study. *IEEE Security and Privacy Magazine* 1(1):28–36.

Pfleeger, C. P., S. L. Pfleeger, and W. H. Ware. 2002. *Security in Computing,* 3rd ed. Upper Saddle River, NJ: Prentice Hall PTR.

Poulsen, K. 2001. War driving by the bay. www.securityfocus.com/news/192. Dallas Con Information Security Conference.

Rogaway, P., M. Bellare, J. Black, and T. Krovetz. 2001. OCB: a block-cipher mode of operation for efficient authenticated encryption. In *ACM Conference on Computer and Communications Security.* Pp. 196–205.

Rescorla, E. 2001. *SSL and TLS.* Boston: Addison-Wesley.

Rivest, R. 2001. RSA security response to weaknesses in key scheduling algorithm of RC4. www.rsasecurity.com/rsalabs/technotes/wep.html.

Rivest, R., A. Shamir, and L. Adleman. 1979. *On Digital Signatures and Public Key Cryptosystems.* Technical Report MIT/LCS/TR-212. Cambridge, MA: MIT Laboratory for Computer Science.

Salkever, A. 2000. Hollywood vs. the hackers vs. free speech. www.businessweek.com/bwdaily/dnflash/aug2000/nf20000825_720.htm.

Schneier, B. 1996. *Applied Cryptography,* 2nd ed. New York: John Wiley & Sons.

Shamir, A., and I. Mantin. 2001. A practical attack on broadcast RC4. In *Proceedings of Fast Software Encryption*. Pp. 152–164.

Simon, D., and B. Aboba. 1999. *PPP EAP TLS Authentication Protocol*. Technical Report RFC 2716, IETF.

Simpson, W. 1996. *PPP Challenge Handshake Authentication Protocol (CHAP)*. Technical Report RFC 1994, IETF.

Spitzner, L. 2002. *Honeypots: Tracking Hackers*. Boston: Addison-Wesley.

Stoll, C. 1989. *The Cuckoo's Egg*. New York: Doubleday.

Stubblefield, A., J. Ioannidis, and A. D. Rubin. 2002. Using the Fluhrer, Mantin, and Shamir attack to break WEP. In *Network and Distributed System Security Symposium (NDSS)*.

U.S. Government Accounting Office. May 1998. Information Security Management, Learning from Leading Organizations. www.gao.gov/cgi-bin/getrpt?GAO-01-376G.

U.S. National Security Agency. 1999. Venona project. www.nsa.gov/docs/venona/index.html.

Vernam, G. S. 1926. Cipher printing telegraphy systems for secret wire and radio telegraphic communications. *Journal of the AIEE* 45:109–115.

Viega, J., M. Messier, and P. Chandra. 2002. *Network Security with OpenSSL*. Cambridge, MA: O'Reilly and Associates.

Walker, J. 2000. Unsafe at any key size; an analysis of the WEP encapsulation. *IEEE 802.11-00/362*.

Thomas Wu. 1998. The Secure Remote Password Protocol. In *Proceedings of the 1998 Internet Society Network and Distributed System Security Symposium*, San Diego, CA. Pp. 97–111.

Index

A

Access control. *See also* EAP
  authentication and, 313–314
  as confidentiality mechanism, 313–314
  for data integrity, 314
  for hotspots, 295–296
  IEEE 802.1X for, 122–129, 360
  in IEEE 802.11, 320
    attacks against, 329–330
  importance of, 117–120
  steps in, 118
  in WEP, weaknesses in, 93
Access control layer, 111, 112, 112*f*
Access control list (ACL)
  as confidentiality mechanism, 313
  in IEEE 802.11, 320
  weakness of, 330
Access point (AP)
  access control layer in, 111
  association with, 54–55, 56, 280
  authentication of
    in LEAP, 185
    in temporal key computation, 205–207
  authentication server in, 128, 179*f*
  authenticator in, 128, 184
  bogus, 39
  Cisco, configuring, 376–382, 377*f*–383*f*
  constructing, 374–376
  disassociation from, 56, 280–281
    group keys and, 208
  as firewall, 356
  GMK created by, 209–210
  during group key distribution, 209

GTK derived by, 209
hardware for, 374
for hotspots, 295–296, 299–300
hubs and, 53
IEEE 802.1X and, 137
key hierarchy and, in mixed environments, 212
key mapping keys and, 83
in LEAP
  authentication of, 185
  authenticator in, 184
location of, 299
logical ports in, 127–128, 128*f*
man-in-the-middle attack against, 38–39
manufacturer of, in MAC address, 36
MIC failure at, 251
Michael implementation on, 237
multicasts and, 208
password for, 369–370
PMK delivery to, 202
RADIUS server configured for, 369–370
roaming among, 56, 283–284
as service, ticket for, 179–180
snooping, 36
software for, 375–376
speeds supported by, 62–63
ticket for, 181–182, 182*f*
in untrusted zone, 30
upgrading to WPA, 357–358
in Wi-Fi LANs, 127
wireless LAN layer in, 111
Access-Accept message, in RADIUS, 140

425

Access-Challenge message, in RADIUS, 140, 144–145
Access-Reject message, in RADIUS, 140, 144–145
Access-Request message, in RADIUS, 140
ACL. *See* Access control list
Active attacks
  accomplishments of, 40
  definition of, 34
  passive monitoring and, 22, 31–32
Active key
  for default keys, 79
  for key mapping keys, 83
Addition, in finite field arithmetic, 389–390, 392, 392*t*, 393*t*
Address resolution protocol. *See* ARP
Addresses, in data frame, 56–57
Ad-hoc mode, 285–289
  definition of, 53–54, 280
  vs. infrastructure mode, 280
  operation of, 285–286
  for RSN, 107
Advanced Encryption Standard. *See* AES
AES (Advanced Encryption Standard) cipher
  vs. CCMP, 261–262
  cipher key in, 399
  decryption with, 403–404
  encryption with, 398–404
  in IEEE 802.11i, 261–263
  Information Elements and, 282
  message authenticity and, 264–265
  modes of operation in, 264–269
  overview of, 264–269, 387–404, 405*f*
  Rijndael algorithm in, 264
  RSN and, 106, 261–262
  symmetric nature of, 313
  vs. TKIP, 261
AES-CCMP
  group key hierarchy for, 213*f*
  group temporal keys for, 211
  key hierarchy in, 211
  legacy hardware and, 234
  pairwise key hierarchy for, 213*f*
  pairwise temporal keys for, 211
Affirmation, 12

Airjack, 352–353
Airport hotspots, 303
AirSnort, 27, 351–352, 351*f*
Algorithm number, in authentication message, 72, 72*f*
Algorithmic attacks, on keys, 47–48
Analog signal, digital bit conversion to, 64
Analysis, in attack process, 349–350
ANonce
  definition of, 206
  in four-way handshake, 217, 221
Anonymity services, 308
Antenna. *See* Radio frequency section
AP. *See* Access point
Arithmetic, finite field. *See* Finite field arithmetic
ARP (address resolution protocol)
  in FMS attack, 325
  spoofing
    in man-in-the-middle attacks, 332–333
    VLAN and, 357
AS. *See* Authentication server
Association
  ad-hoc operation and, 286
  definition of, 55
  management messages for, in WPA/RSN, 281
  network access and, 55*n*
Association request message
  in association process, 56, 281–282
  definition of, 55
  Information Elements in, 282
Association response message
  in association process, 56
  definition of, 55
Assumptions
  hackers and, 16
  in IVs, 96–97
  in security, 15–16
Asymmetric encryption, 151–153
  as confidentiality mechanism, 312–313
Asymmetric key, 151–153. *See also* Private key; Public key
  symmetric key and, combining, 155

Attack(s). *See also specific types*
  classification of, 34
  collection in, 348–349
  execution of, 350–351
  goals of, 338
  on keys, 40–48
  without keys, 35–40
  planning for, 346–348
  process of, 338–351, 339*f*
  reconnaissance for, 338–344
  technical approach of, 33
  types of, 33
Attack tools, for war driving, 339–344, 340*f*,
    341*f*, 342*f*, 344*f*, 345*f*
Attributes
  in EAP messages, 145
  in LEAP, 185
  in RADIUS messages, 142–144, 144*t*
Authenticate request message, 54
Authenticated data, in MPDU encryption, 274
Authenticated encryption scheme, 269
Authentication. *See also* Guarantee;
    Preauthentication
  access control and, 313–314
  of access point, in LEAP, 185
  of cellular phones, 189–196
  certificates for, in TLS, 158
  definition of, 18
  for dial-in users, 120–122
  in EAP, 121
  in EAP over RADIUS, 145*f*, 146
  format of, 72, 72*f*
  group keys and, 209
  in GSM network, 192–193, 192*f*
  in hotspots, by hotspot controller,
    300–302
  of identity, 9, 314
  in IEEE 802.1X, 135–137, 360
  in IEEE 802.11, 321
    attacks against, 330–331
  as integrity mechanism, 314
  for key access, 109
  management frames in, 70, 71*f*
    in shared key authentication, 321
    in WPA/RSN, 281

  master, for master access ticket, 170
  of messages
    AES and, 264–265
    in authorization process, 129
    in CCM, 268
    modes of operation for, 264–269
  methods for
    choosing, 150, 182–183
    upper-layer (*See* Upper-layer
      authentication methods)
    in WPA, 183
  mutual
    in shared key authentication, 321
    for wireless networks, 91
  of network, with GSM, 194
  of nonencrypted data, 268
  open
    in IEEE 802.11, 321
    in WPA/RSN, 281
  in PPP, 120–121, 140
  preshared keys for, 131
  privacy and, 187
    separation of, 107
  private (*See* PEAP)
  purpose of, 70
  in RADIUS server configuration,
    372–373
  serial, 131
  of server, in PEAP, 187
  SIM cards for, 193
  ticket for, 179–180
  timesavings from, 72
  in WEP, 69–72, 71*f*
    weaknesses in, 90–92
Authentication key, 91
Authentication layer, 111, 112–113, 112*f*
Authentication server (AS). *See also*
    Authorizer
  in access point, 128, 179*f*
  in access point configuration, 376–379, 378*f*
  authenticator communication with,
    RADIUS for, 126, 178
  definition of, confusion about, 138
  in dial-in network, 121
  FreeRADIUS for, 361, 368–374

Authentication server *continued*
  for hotspots, 302
  in IEEE 802.1X, 123, 125
    in authentication sequence, 135, 135*f*
    vs. authenticator, 130
  Information Elements and, 282
  infrastructure for, 359–360
  in KDC, 171–172, 171*f*
  keys sent from, 146–147
  in LEAP, 184, 185
  location of, 125, 126*f*
  for network domains, 170
  ports and, 123
  in preauthentication, 285
  RADIUS server as, 139
  remote, 125, 126*f*
  in ticket-granting service, 172
  tickets and, 176
Authenticator.
  in access control, 118
  in access point, 128, 184
  in ad-hoc operation, 287, 287*f*
  in authentication sequence, 135–137
  authentication server communication
    with, RADIUS for, 126, 178
  in four-way handshake, nonce generated
    by, 206
  in IEEE 802.1X, 123, 125
    vs. authentication server, 130
    EAP in, 124
    MAC addresses for, 133
  in LEAP, 184
  port associated with, 123
  port state and, in IEEE 802.1X, 124
  in RADIUS message format, 142
  TLS and, 165
Authorization
  definition of, 18
  message authentication in, 129
  in RADIUS server configuration, 372
Automatic key management, 313

B

Base phase, of inductive chosen plaintext
  attack, 326

Baseband. *See* MODEM
Beacon
  about, 55
  access point manufacturer in, 36
  in ad-hoc operation, 286
  in association process, 281–282
  definition of, 54
  format of, 61–63, 62*f*
  Information Elements in, 282
  SSID in, 62, 62*f,* 330
Beacon interval, 61–62, 62*f*
Billing, for hotspots, 295–296
Binary number, in finite field arithmetic,
  388–389
Birthday paradox, 97
Block cipher, 73, 313
Broadcast, pairwise keys and, 208
Broadcast address, 58
Broadcast data, 200
Broadcast messages, 82, 299–300
Brute force attack
  on keys, 45
  Michael vulnerability to, 237
  temporal keys and, 226
bsd-airtools, 347–348, 351–352
Burst-ack, TSC and, 241

C

Calendar/clock, for nonce value,
  224–225
Canalization
  of deployed network, 357–359, 358*f*
  of wireless LAN, 356
Capabilities information, in beacon format,
  62, 62*f*
Capability bits, 282
CBC (cipher block chaining), for message
  authentication, 268
CBC-MAC
  in CCM, 268
  definition of, 268
  for MIC computation, 274–276
  first block of, 274–275, 275*f*
CCM mode
  about, 267–269

CBC-MAC in, 268
counter mode in, 268
CCMP (Counter Mode-CBC MAC
    Protocol)
  vs. AES, 261–262
  implementation of, 272–273, 272*f*
  message flow in, 270*f*
  MIC in, computation of, 274–276, 275*f*
  MPDU in, encryption of, 269–274
  in RSN, 269–278
CCMP header, 270–272, 272*f*
  in MDPU encryption, 273–274
Cellular phones
  authentication of, 189–196
  computers and, 189–190
  security of, 190
  Wi-Fi LAN access provided by, 296
Certificate(s), 155, 158. *See also* Client
    certificates; Public key; Public key
    certificates; Server certificates
Certificate authority
  creating, with OpenSSL, 364–365
  definition of, 153–154
Certification, of public keys, 153–155
Certification authority, 108. *See also*
    Certificate authority
Challenge
  in CHAP, 140, 141
  in GSM authentication, 191
  in shared-key authentication, 330–331
Challenge text
  in authentication message, 72, 72*f*
  definition of, 71
  in shared key authentication, 321
Change connection state, in TLS handshake,
    163–164
Channels, 54, 63
CHAP, for PPP authentication, 140–141,
    141, 141*f*
Checksum, 235–236. *See also* MIC
Checkword, 38–39, 40
Cipher
  in AES encryption, 399
  assumed knowledge of, 44
  definition of, 43, 43*f*

Cipher block chaining. *See* CBC
Cipher suite
  definition of, 159
  finished message and, 164
  pending state and, 164
  in TLS handshake, 159–160
Ciphertext
  in AES encryption, 398
  in challengetext, 71
  in counter mode, 266–267
  definition of, 43, 43*f*
  modification of, 94–95
  in RC4, distinguisher for, 322–323
  in stream cipher, 73
  in WEP, 92
Cisco LEAP. *See* LEAP
Client authentication, in TLS handshake,
    161
Client certificates
  creating, with OpenSSL, 365–369
  PKI for, 360
  in RADIUS server configuration, 373
  in TLS, 158
  in TLS handshake, 161–162
    verification of, 162–163
  in TLS over EAP handshake, 167
Client hello message, 159, 167
Client key exchange, 162
Closed network, 320–321, 330
Code field
  in EAP message format, 131–132, 132*f*
  in RADIUS message format, 142
Coffee shop hotspots, 303–304
Collection, in attack process, 348–349
Computers, cellular phones and, 189–190
Computing power, encryption and, 14
Confidentiality
  in IEEE 802.11, 316–321
  mechanisms for, 312–314
Connection state
  changing, 158, 158*f* (*See also* Change
    connection state)
  current *vs.* pending, 158
  pending, in TLS handshake, 163–164
  for record protocol, 157–158

Control frames
  definition of, 55
  in network coordination, 280
Conventional security architecture. *See*
    Security architectures, traditional
Convolutional coding, 64
"Cottage hotspots," 304–305
Counter, 265–267
  initialization of, 267, 276
  MIC and, 276
  in MPDU decryption, 277
  for nonce value, 225
Counter mode
  about, 265–267, 266*f*
  in CCM, 268
  counter in, 265–267, 276
  MPDU encryption in, 276
Counter Mode-CBC MAC protocol. *See*
    CCMP
Countermeasures
  definition of, 237
  for Michael, 237, 249–252
    denial-of-service attack and, 335–336
CRC. *See* Cyclic redundancy check
Credit card, as certificate, 161
Cryptanalysis, 13
Cryptographic algorithm. *See* Cipher
Cryptographic quality, 209–210
Cryptographic systems, flaws in, publication
    of, 27
Cryptography
  as confidentiality mechanism, 312–313
  definition of, 312
  finite field arithmetic in, 388
Customer service, for hotspots, 295–296
Cyclic redundancy check (CRC)
  finite field arithmetic in, 388
  vs. ICV, 84–85
  security of, 318
  in transmission, 58
  in WEP, 318

D
DA (destination address), 58
Daeman, Joan, 264

Data
  in EAP message format, 132, 132*f*
  nonencrypted, authentication of, 268
  in PRF-*n* functions, 226
  reception of, in TKIP, 248–249, 248*f*
  transmission of
    in infrastructure mode, 56–57
    in TKIP, 246–248, 247*f*
Data compression, in TLS, 156
Data Encryption key, 203, 211
Data frame
  addresses in, 56–57
  definition of, 55
Data integrity, 314–316
Data Integrity key, 203
  for AES-CCMP, 211
Data rate, range and, 64
Deauthentication message
  in denial-of-service attack, 335, 352
  in man-in-the-middle attacks, 331–332
Decapsulation. *See* Decryption
Decryption. *See also* Encryption
  in AES, 403–404
  in CCMP, 272, 277–278
  counter mode and, 267
  of public key, private key in, 152
  RC4 for, 86, 317
  in TKIP, 246
Default keys
  about, 78–82, 78*f*
  active key for, 79
  changing, 79–83, 80*f*, 81*f*
  definition of, 77
  directional use of, 81–82
  for multicast traffic, 82–83
  multiple, 78–79
  for WEP keys, 320
Denial-of-Service (DoS) attack
  with Airjack, 352
  definition of, 35
  with Michael countermeasures, 252, 335–336
  prevention and, 334–336
  with replay attacks, 324
  TSC and, 246–247
  WPA cryptographic, 335–336

Derived keys, for authentication, 91

Destination address (DA), 58

Detection, attack sophistication and, 33

DHCP (Dynamic Host Control Protocol), plaintext from, 326

DHCP server, ticket for, 180, 182

Dial-in network, organization of, 121, 122*f*

Dial-in users, authentication for, 120–122

Dictionary, for inductive chosen plaintext attack, 327–328

Dictionary attack, 46–47
  against CHAP, 141
  Kerberos and, 170, 176
  PEAP and, 186
  against tickets, 178

Digital certificates
  for hotspot authentication, 302
  in Kerberos, 170
  in SSL, 155

Digital signature
  for data integrity, 315–316
  for file verification, 412–414, 413*f*, 414*f*, 415*f*

Directional key use, 81–82

Disassociation message
  to access point, 280–281
  in denial-of-service attack, 335
  group keys and, 208
  in roaming, 56

Distributed server, 138

Division, in finite field arithmetic, 391–392, 394

DLen field, in CBC-MAC first block, 274

Domain, network
  authentication servers for, 170
  separate, in Kerberos, 174–175

DoS. *See* Denial-of-Service (DoS) attack

Down-grade attack, 359

Draft documents, in IETF, 119

dwepcrack, for WEP key recovery, 347, 349–350, 349*f*, 350*f*

dwepdump, for packet collection, 347–349, 348*f*

Dynamic Host Control Protocol. *See* DHCP

E

EAP, Protected. *See* PEAP

EAP (Extensible Authentication Protocol)
  for access control, 118
  extensibility of, 132
  with GSS-API, 183
  Identity in, 130–131
  in IEEE 802.1X authenticator, 124
  IETF and, 119
  intent of, 121
  Kerberos proxy and, 181
  man-in-the-middle attacks and, 333
  PEAP and, 186, 187
  for PPP, 121
  principles of, 129–132
  privacy for (*See* PEAP)
  protocols and, 133
  in RADIUS server configuration, 370–371
  Type field in, 130
  weaknesses of, 187

EAP messages
  attributes in, 145
  EAPOL-Packet frame for sending, 134
  flow of, 135, 135*f*
  format of, 131–132, 166*f*
  in IEEE 802.1X, 138
  passing, with RADIUS, 138, 168
  purpose of, 129
  types of, 130

EAP over RADIUS, 144–146
  authentication in, 145*f*
  in LEAP, 186
  in WPA/RSN, 146

EAP Type field, 130

EAP-Cisco Wireless. *See* LEAP

EAP-Failure message, 130, 187

EAP-Identity message, 187

EAPOL (EAP over LAN)
  about, 133–134
  in IEEE 802.1X, 127, 133, 205
  in LEAP, 186
  in preauthentication, 285

EAPOL messages, 133–134, 134*f*

EAPOL-Key Encryption key, 203, 211

EAPOL-Key Integrity key, 203, 206, 211
EAPOL-Key messages, 134, 185
  for four-way handshake, 205
  for group key distribution, 208, 223
  for key exchange, in WPA, 214–217, 214*f*,
    215*t*, 216*f*, 216*t*
  protection of, in TKIP, 245
EAPOL-Logoff, 134
EAPOL-Packet frame, 133, 134
EAPOL-Start message, 133
EAPOL-Success message, 185
EAP-Request /Identity message, in TLS
  over EAP handshake, 166
EAP-Request message, 130, 166*f*
EAP-Request/Identity message, 130
EAP-Response message, 130, 166*f*
EAP-Response/Identity message, 130, 166
EAP-SIM. *See also* GSM authentication
  about, 193–196
  definition of, 155
  message flow for, 194–196, 195*f*
  pseudonyms in, 194–195
  status of, 196
EAP-Start message, 145, 145*f*
EAP-Success message, 130, 187, 196
EAP-TLS. *See* TLS over EAP
ECB (Electronic Code Block) mode, 265,
  266*f*
EKE protocol, zero knowledge password
  proofs in, 178
Electronic Code Block. *See* ECB
Element
  definition of, 60
  in management frame, 60–61
  proprietary, 61
  structure of, 61
E-mail, as plaintext sample, 45
Encryption. *See also* Asymmetric encryption;
  Public key encryption; Symmetric
  encryption
  ad-hoc operation and, 286
  in ARP spoofing, 333
  breaking, 14

  in CCM, 268–269
  in CCMP
    decryption and, 272
    of MPDU, 269–274, 271*f*
  computing power and, 14
  definition of, 19, 312
  nonce *vs.* PN for, 274–275
  object of, 13
  RC4 for, 73–74, 317
    phases in, 88
    weak keys in, 99–100
    in WEP, 86–88
  against snooping, 34
  temporal keys for, in pairwise key
    hierarchy, 206–207
  of tickets, 176
  in TKIP, 246, 247*f*, 248
  in TLS, 156
Encryption key, 91
  for access control, 93
  EAPOL messages and, 134
  session, in LEAP, 185
  WEP authentication and, 92
ESS. *See* Infrastructure mode
ESSID. *See* SSID
essid_jack, 352
Ethereal, 346, 346*f*, 350
Ethernet. *See also* Wired LAN
  MAC headers in, 58
Exclusive OR (XOR) operation, 87*f*
  in counter mode, 265–267
  in finite field arithmetic, 389–392
  in RC4 encryption, 87
  in WEP, 91–92, 320
Execution, of attack, 350–351
Extensible Authentication Protocol. *See* EAP

F
Failure message, in EAP, 130, 187
Ferguson, Niels, 236, 249
Finished message
  in TLS handshake, 164
  in TLS over EAP handshake, 167–168

Finite field arithmetic, 388–398. *See also*
    AES cipher
    addition in, 389–390, 392, 392*t*, 393*t*
    division in, 391–392, 394
    Galois field in, 392–397
    multiplication in, 390–391, 392–397,
        393*t*, 394*t*
    overflow in, 392–397
    shift operation in, 391–392
    subtraction in, 390
    XOR operation in, 389–392
Firewall
    personal, 305–306
    security guidelines and, 356
    in traditional security architecture,
        27–31
Firmware, in Wi-Fi LAN card, 233, 233*f*
Fixed field, in management frame, 60
Fixed key, weakness of, 74
Flags field
    in CBC-MAC first block, 274, 275
    in TLS over EAP, 166
Fluhrer, Scott, 242, 323
Fluhrer-Mantin-Shamir attack. *See* FMS
    attack
FMS (Fluhrer-Mantin-Shamir) attack, 238,
    323
    active implementation of, 325–326
    countering
        with IV filtering, 329
        weak keys and, 242–243
Footprinting. *See* Snooping
Forgery, of tickets, 176
Forwarded ticket, 173–174, 175*f*
Four-way handshake
    EAPOL-Key descriptor and, 217–222
    in ESS network, joining, 282
    Information Element in, 283
    overview of, 205–207
    in preauthentication, 285
Fragmentation, of MSDU, 84, 237
Frame. *See also* Message(s)
    categories of, 55
    encrypting, 85–86

Frame formats
    general, 57–58, 58*f*
    in WEP, 83–84
FreeRADIUS
    for authentication server, 361, 368–374
    certificate for, 364–365
    compiling, 368–369
    configuration of, 369–374
    configuring connection to, 369–370
    downloading, 368
    testing, 374
Frequencies, 54, 63
Frequency hopping, 334
FTP, firewalls and, 306

G

Galois field GF(), 392–397
Generic Security Service Application
        Programming Interface. *See* GSS-API
GF(). *See* Galois field
GMK. *See* Group master key
GNonce, 224
GPG signature, for file verification,
        412–414, 413*f*, 414*f*, 415*f*
Group Encryption key, 210, 211
Group Integrity key, 210, 211
Group key(s)
    in ad-hoc operation, 288
    authentication and, 209
    in CCMP header, 271
    definition of, 200, 200*f*
    distribution of
        access point during, 209
        EAPOL-Key message for, 208, 223
        pairwise keys for, 208
    handshake for, 208–210, 223–224, 223*t*
    MIC attack against, 251
    in mixed environments, 212
    multiple, 209
    in preauthentication, 285
    in TKIP, 245
    updating of, 208, 224
Group key hierarchy
    about, 207–210

Group key hierarchy *continued*
    for AES-CCMP, 213*f*
    definition of, 201
    PRF-*n* functions and, 228
    for TKIP, 213*f*
Group master key (GMK), 209–210
Group messages, 82
Group transient key (GTK)
    delivery of, 224
    derivation of, 209, 210
    Key Data field in, 217
    PRNG for, 226
GSM authentication, 191–192, 192*f*. *See also*
        EAP-SIM
    identity in, 194
    SIM card for, 193–194
    status of, 196
    Wi-Fi LAN security and, 192–193
GSS-API (Generic Security Service
        Application Programming Interface)
    about, 182–183, 183*f*
    with EAP, 183
    proxy used with, 182
GTK. *See* Group transient key
Guarantee, 10

H

Hackers. *See also* Attack(s)
    about, 22–23
    assumptions and, 16
    definition of, 22–23
    motivations for, 23
Handshake
    four-way (*See* Four-way handshake)
    for group keys, 208–210, 223–224, 223*t*
    for pairwise keys (*See* Four-way
        handshake)
    in TLS, 159–164, 159*f*
        change connection state in, 163–164
        client certificate in, 161–162
            verification of, 162–163
        client key exchange, 162
        definition of, 159
        hello messages in, 159–161
        master key computation in, 162

    RSN and, 164–165
    server hello in, 160–161
    WPA and, 164–165
    in TLS over EAP, 166–168, 167*f*
Handshake protocol, in TLS, 157
Hardware
    for hotspots, 298
    legacy, 232, 239
Hardware assist
    weak keys and, 242
    in Wi-Fi LAN card, 233, 233*f*
Hash Message Authentication Code. *See*
        HMAC
Hashing, 162, 195, 314–316
HMAC (Hash Message Authentication
        Code), 220, 315
HMAC-MD5, 220
HMAC-SHA-1, 228
Home hotspots, 304–305
Honey pot networks, for attack detection,
        26
Host interface, in Wi-Fi LAN card, 232,
        233*f*
hostap, 375, 376
Hotel hotspots, 303
Hotspot(s)
    barriers to growth of, 294
    development of, 293–296
    organization of, 297–302
    public access through, definition of, 294
    security issues with, 296–297
    types of, 303–305
    user protection in, 305–308
Hotspot controllers
    for coffee shop-type operations, 304
    in hotspot organization, 300–302
    RADIUS and, 302
    SIM cards and, 302
Housley, Russ, 244
Hub, access points and, 53

I

IBSS (Independent Basis Service Set). *See*
        Ad-hoc mode
ICMP message, replaying, 39–40

ICV (integrity check value)
  in denial-of-service attack, 336
  hashing for, 163
  in IEEE 802.11, 238
  nonce in deriving, 143
  in shared key authentication, 321
  in TKIP, 235, 246, 248
  weakness of, 94–95
  in WEP, 84–85, 85*f*, 235
Identifier field
  in EAP message format, 132, 132*f*
  in RADIUS message format, 142
Identity
  authentication of, 9, 314
  certainty of, 8–9
  in EAP, 130–131
    snooping, 187
  encryption and, in Kerberos, 178
  in GSM authentication, 194
  in PEAP, 188–189
  proving, 11–12
  as special-purpose message, 131
Identity theft, from profit attacks, 25
IE. *See* Information Elements
IEEE 802.1AA, message authentication in,
    129
IEEE 802.1X, 127*f*
  about, 122–129
  for access control layer, 112
  for access point configuration, 376–382
  under ad-hoc mode, 287
  authentication in, 135–137
  authenticator in, 123, 125
    vs. authentication server, 130
    EAP in, 124
    MAC addresses for, 133
  on clients, 360–361
  EAP messages in, 138
  EAPOL in, 127, 133
  implementation of, 137–138
  in LEAP, 186
  man-in-the-middle attacks and, 333
  message authentication in, 129
  messages in, 135–137
  port security in, 123

preauthentication with, 283–285, 284*f*
RSN in, 119
in switched hub environment, 124–127,
    124*f*
in Wi-Fi LANs, 127–129
wireless and, 123
WPA and, 119, 360
IEEE 802.3. *See* Ethernet
IEEE 802.11. *See also* RSN
  about, 103–104
  authentication mechanisms in, 321
  channels for, 63–65
  committee for, 89, 103–104, 104*f*
  confidentiality mechanisms in, 316,
    322–329
  definition of, 6
  frame formats in, 57–58, 58*f*
  header in, key information in, 36
  integrity mechanisms in, 321
  key length and, 46
  MAC headers in, 58
  modes in, 53–54
  PMK delivery in, 202
  review of, 201
  security in (*See* WEP)
  security mechanisms in, 316, 322–331
  upper-layer authentication methods in,
    150
  vs. Wi-Fi, 104, 105*f*
  in Wi-Fi LAN card, 232
IEEE 802.11 header. *See* MAC header
IEEE 802.11a, 64
IEEE 802.11b, 62–63, 64
IEEE 802.11g, 63, 64
IEEE 802.11i. *See also* RSN
  about, 104–105
  ad-hoc operation in, 286–289
  AES in, 261–263
  OCB in, 269
  WPA and, 356–357
IETF (Internet Engineering Task Force), 119
IMSI. *See* International Mobile Subscriber
    Identity
Independent Basis Service Set (IBSS). *See*
    Ad-hoc mode

Inductive chosen plaintext attack, 326–329
  base phase of, 326
  cost of, 329
  inductive phase of, 326–329
  IV filtering and, 329
Information Elements (IE)
  capabilities passed in, 282
  in preauthentication, 285
  validating, 283
Information gathering. *See* Snooping
Infrastructure, for WPA network, deploying,
    360–361
Infrastructure mode (ESS)
  vs. ad-hoc mode, 280
  definition of, 53, 280
  joining, 280–282
  operation in, 54–57
  for RSN, 107
Initialization vector. *See* IV
Integrity
  of downloaded files, 411–414
  in IEEE 802.11, 321
  mechanisms for, 314–316
Integrity check value. *See* ICV
International Mobile Subscriber Identity
    (IMSI), 191–192, 194
Internet connection, for hotspots, 295–296
Internet Engineering Task Force (IETF), 119
Internet transactions, certification of, 153–154
IP address, obtaining
  from hotspot controller, 300–301
  Kerberos proxy and, 182
IP datagram service (UDP), hotspots and, 306
IP header, modification attack against, 34
IP network, RADIUS for, 138
IPsec
  for access point security, 376
  for VPNs, 307
Isolation
  of deployed network, 357–359
  of wireless LAN, 356
IV (initialization vector). *See also* Weak keys
  in CCM, 269
  definition of, 74
  in encrypted message, 85, 86*f*

filtering, 329
in IEEE 802.11, 318
incrementing, 238
in inductive chosen plaintext attack,
    327–328
MIC and, 246
in mixed key, 244, 255
MSDU and, in TKIP transmission,
    246–247
vs. nonce, 235
random generation of, 97
reuse of, 75, 96–99, 238
in shared key authentication, 321
in TKIP
  checking of, 246
  in data transmission, 246–247
  generation of, 246
  length of, 239–240
  selection of, 238
  use of, 238–243
in WEP, 74–76, 75*f,* 318
  length of, 239
  weakness in, 238
IV collision, 97–98
  per-packet key mixing and, 244
  in WEP, 324
IV space, in WEP, 324

K

Kc. *See* Session keys
KDC. *See* Key distribution center
Kerberos V5, 169–184
  cross-domain access in, 174–175
  dictionary attack and, 170, 176
  digital certificates in, 170
  with GSS-API, 183
  identity in, encryption and, 178
  passwords in, 170, 172
  in RSN, 178–184
  shared key in, 172
  switches and, 181–182*f*
  tickets in, 169–171
    format of, 177
    forwarded, 173–174, 175*f*
    proxy, 173, 174*f*

referral, 175
for services, 172–174, 177
weakness in, 184
Key(s). *See also* Passwords; *specific types*
access to, authentication for, 109
attacks against, 40–48
algorithmic, 47–48
by brute force, 45
dictionary method for, 46–47
wireless, 42–45
attacks without, 35–40
for authentication (*See* Authentication key)
burying, 41–42
capturing, value in, 95–96
changing, per-packet, 243
definition of, 17, 43, 43*f*
delivery of, to NAS, 146–147
direct attack against, 100–101
in IEEE 802.11 standard, 69
length of, brute force attack and, 45–46
in MIC, 236
for Michael, 238
in PRF-*n* functions, 226
in RSN, establishment and distribution of,
210
in security context, 108–110
storage of, in access point, 184
in tickets, 176
in upper-layer authentication, 151–155
in WPA, establishment and distribution of,
210
Key Data field
in four-way handshake, 222
in WPA EAPOL-Key message, 215*t*, 217
Key derivation
dictionary attack and, 47
key expansion for, 226
for per-packet key mixing, 244
in WPA, 214–224
Key distribution center (KDC), ticket-
granting ticket and, 171–172, 171*f*
Key entropy, 18, 45
Key expansion, for key derivation, 226
Key hierarchy

in AES-CCMP, 211
group (*See* Group key hierarchy)
in mixed environments, 212
pairwise (*See* Pairwise key hierarchy)
in RSN, 109
Key Information field, in WPA EAPOL-Key
message, 215*t*, 216*f*, 216*t*
Key management
as confidentiality mechanism, 313
in IEEE 802.11, 320
Key mapping keys
about, 78*f*, 82–83
active key for, 83
definition of, 78
Key mapping tables, for key management, 320
Key mixing. *See* Per-packet key mixing
Key pair, 312. *See also* Private key; Public
key
Key Sequence Start field, in four-way
handshake, 222
Key server, for file verification, 412–414,
413*f*–415*f*
Key setup, in RC4 encryption, 88, 317
Key stream
generation of, 88
pseudorandom, 87, 88, 242
in RC4 encryption, 86–87
weakness in, 99–100
in WEP, 91–92
Keyed cryptographic hash, MIC built with,
315
Key-generating, 202
KeyID bits
in CCMP header, 272
definition of, 82
in encrypted message, 85, 86*f*
KeyID field, during key change, 209
Kismet, for war driving, 341–344, 342*f*,
344*f*, 345*f*

L

LAN. *See* Wi-Fi LAN; Wired LAN; Wireless
LAN
Layer(s), network, 51–53, 52*f*

Layer 2, in denial-of-service attack, 334–335
LEAP
  about, 184–186
  authentication server in, 185
  importance of, 155
  message flow for, 185, 186*f*
  shared key in, 185
  type number for, 186
Legacy hardware
  AES and, 232
  IV length and, 239
  TKIP and, 232
Length field
  in attribute format, 142
  in EAP message format, 132, 132*f*
  in RADIUS message format, 142
  in TLS over EAP, 166
Length included flag, 166
Letter-swapping, dictionary attack and, 47
Linear method, 95
Link layer, in ARP spoofing, 333
Linux, for access point, 376
Liveness
  in CHAP, 141
  in one-time passwords, 41
  in temporal keys, 203–204
  in TLS client hello, 160
Logon passwords
  hacking, 25
  need for, by attackers, 32

M
MAC (medium access control) address
  for access control, 93
  in access control lists, 320, 330
  access point manufacturer in, 36
  in ad-hoc operation, 288
  in attack, 351
  for authentication, 71
  filtering, 351, 359
  in GTK, 210
  for IEEE 802.1X authenticators, 133
  masquerading, 59
  in mixed key, 244, 255

  in pairwise key hierarchy, 204, 206
  in PRF-*n* functions, 226
  visibility of, 59
  wireless adapter manufacturer in, 36
MAC (message authentication code). *See*
    MIC
MAC header
  about, 58–60
  addresses in, 58
  encryption and, 268
  in MDPU encryption, 273–274
  modification of, 59–60
  in pairwise key selection, 277
MAC layer, in denial-of-service attack,
    334–335
MAC protocol data unit. *See* MPDU
MAC section, in Wi-Fi LAN card, 232–234,
    233*f*
MAC service data unit. *See* MSDU
Management frames, 59–60
  in authentication phase, 70, 71*f*
  definition of, 55
  in denial-of-service attack, 335
  in man-in-the-middle attacks, 331–332
  in network coordination, 280
  in shared-key authentication, 330
  types of, 60
  in WPA/RSN, 281
Man-in-the-middle attack
  about, 37–40, 38*f*
  access point in, 185
  details of, 331–333, 332*f*
  monkey_jack for, 352–353
  problems from, 333
Mantin, Itsik, 242, 322–323
Mantin Shamir Bias Flaw, 322–323
Manual key management, 313, 320
Masquerading attack
  definition of, 34–35
  with MAC addresses, 59
  for server access, 32
Master access ticket, 170, 171
Master authentication, for master access
    ticket, 170

Master key. *See also* Pairwise master key (PMK)
  in authentication, 109–110
  computing, in TLS handshake, 162
  dictionary attack and, 47
  exposure of, 91
  generation of, 165
  nonce in, 162–163
  protection of, 163
  in tickets, 176
  for TKIP, 243
  in WPA/RSN, 165
Maximum transmission unit (MDU)
    recovery, 327–328, 327*f*, 328*f*
MD5 (Message Digest algorithm), 220
  in digital signatures, 315–316
  for file verification, 411–412
Medium access control. *See* MAC
Message(s). *See also* Frame; *specific types*
  authentication of
    AES and, 264–265
    in authorization process, 129
    in CCM, 268
    modes of operation for, 264–269
  in CCMP, flow of, 270*f*
  conversion of, to fixed-length blocks (*See*
    Modes of operation)
  decoding, with checkword, 40
  in EAP, 129
    attributes in, 145
    EAPOL-Packet frame for sending, 134
    flow of, 135, 135*f*
    format of, 131–132, 166*f*
    in IEEE 802.1X, 138
    passing, with RADIUS, 138, 168
    types of, 130
  in EAPOL
    format of, 134, 134*f*
    types of, 133–134
  in EAP-SIM, 194–196, 195*f*
  integrity of (*See* Message integrity)
  in LEAP, 185, 186*f*
  modification attack against, 34
    detection of, 94–95
    example of, 407–409

  identity and, 10–11, 10*f*
  on-the-fly, 37
  store-and-forward, 37–40
  privacy of, 95–101
  in RADIUS, 140–142
    attributes in, 142–144
    changing purpose of, 142
    format of, 142–143, 142*f*
  replaying, 39–40
    WEP and, 93–94
  reply of, preventing, 143
  signing, 152–153
  special purpose, 130–131
  timing of, 37
  in TLS over EAP, format of, 166, 166*f*
Message (A), in four-way handshake, 206,
    217–218, 217*f*
Message (B), in four-way handshake, 206,
    218–220, 219*t*
Message (C), in four-way handshake,
    206–207, 221–222, 221*t*
Message (D), in four-way handshake, 207,
    222, 222*t*
Message digest algorithm. *See* MD5
Message integrity
  Michael for, 249–255
  in TKIP, 235
Message integrity code. *See* MIC
MIC (message integrity code)
  attack with, 250
  CBC for, 268
  in CCMP
    computation of, 271, 274–276, 275*f*
    counter and, 276
    in MAC header, 270
  computation of, 220
    in CCMP, 271, 274–276, 275*f*
    data in, 252–253, 253*f*
    Michael for, 236–238, 249, 252–255
    in TKIP, 236
  countermeasures against, 250
  for data integrity, 315
  failure of
    at access point, 251

MIC (message integrity code) *continued*
  at mobile device, 250–251
  in four-way handshake, 206–207, 219, 221
  IV and, 246
  vs. MAC, 236
  in Michael, 236–238, 249, 252–255
  in TKIP
    checking of, 246
    computation of, 236
    in data reception, 249
    in data transmission, 246–247
    generation of, 246
  verifying, in MPDU decryption, 277
Michael
  about, 236–238
  algorithm in, 249, 254–255
  brute force attacks and, 237
  countermeasures for, 237, 249–252
    denial-of-service attack and, 252,
      335–336
  details of, 249–255
  key for, 238
  for MIC computation, 236–238, 249,
    252–255
  MSDUs and, 237–238
Milner, Marius, 341
MiniStumbler, for war driving, 341, 341*f*
Mixed keys. *See also* Per-packet key mixing
  in TKIP
    components of, 244, 255
    for IV length, 239–240
  weak keys and, 259
Mobile device. *See also* Cellular phones
  as authenticator, 287, 287*f*
  broadcasts and, 208
  configuration of, 381–382, 382*f*, 383*f*
  IEEE 802.1X in, 137
  Information Elements and, 282
  joining infrastructure mode, 280–282
  man-in-the-middle attack against, 38–39
  MIC failure at, 250–251
  PMK for, 201
  as supplicant, 201, 286–287, 287*f*

MODEM
  for digital bit conversion, 64
  in Wi-Fi LAN card, 232, 233*f*
Modes of operation
  in AES, 264–269
  definition of, 264
Modification attacks. *See also* Man-in-the-
    middle attack
  definition of, 34
  detection of, in WEP, 94–95
  example of, 407–409
  with MAC header, 59–60
  prevention of, for data integrity, 314
  against tickets, 176
  with WEP messages, 324–325
Monitoring, passive, 22, 31–32
monkey_jack, for man-in-the-middle
    attacks, 352–353
More fragments flag, 166
MPDU (MAC protocol data unit), 84
  in CCMP
    decryption of, 277–278
    encryption of, 269–271, 271*f*, 273–277,
      274*f*
    MAC header for, 270–271
  vs. MSDU, 237
  TKIP and, 238
MSDU (MAC service data unit), 84
  IV and, in TKIP transmission, 246–247
  in Michael, 237–238, 249
  vs. MPDU, 237
MTU (maximum transmission unit)
    recovery, 327–328, 327*f*, 328*f*
Multicast, in mixed environments, 212
Multicast address, 58
Multicast data, 200
Multicast messages, 82, 251. *See also* Group
    messages
Multiparty barrier, to hotspot growth,
    294–296
Multiplication, in finite field arithmetic,
    390–391, 392–397, 393*t*, 394*t*
Mutable fields, in MAC header, 271

Mutual authentication
    in shared key authentication, 321
    for wireless networks, 91

N

NAK type value, 130–131
NAS. *See* Network access server
Netscape SSL. *See* SSL
NetStumbler, for war driving, 340–341, 340*f*
Network
    authentication of, with GSM authenti-
        cation, 194
    deployed, protecting, 357–359, 358*f*
    layers in, 51–53, 52*f*
Network access
    seeking, in attack, 338–339
    ticket for, 179–180
Network access server (NAS). *See also*
        Authenticator
    in dial-in network, 121
    key delivered to, 146–147
    in RADIUS, 139
Network configuration, identification of, 350
Network domain
    authentication servers for, 170
    separate, in Kerberos, 174–175
Network name. *See* SSID
Network protocol
    EAP and, 133
    headers in, for plaintext sample, 44–45
    packet length and, 36–37
Network services, access to, tickets for,
        169–170
Nonce. *See also* Pre-master key; *specific nonces*
    in CBC-MAC first block, 274
    in CCM, 268
    for counter initialization, 267
    definition of, 151, 160
    in GTK, 210
    vs. IV, 235
    for liveness, in temporal keys, 204
    in master key, 162–163
    for network authentication, 194
    vs. PN, for encryption, 274–275

PRNG for, 226
    in RADIUS, 142–143
    selection of, 224–225
    in temporal key generation, 204
Notification message (Notify)
    definition of, 60
    type value for, 130
Null key, 79

O

OCB, 269
OFDM (orthogonal frequency division
        multiplexing), 64
One-time passwords, 41, 131, 317–318
Open authentication
    in IEEE 802.11, 321
    in WPA/RSN, 281
Open security, 69
Open Source projects. *See also*
        FreeRADIUS; OpenSSL
    for access point, 374–376
    for WPA network, 361–382
OpenBSD, for access point, 375–376
OpenPGP key server, for file verification,
        412–414, 413*f*, 414*f*, 415*f*
OpenSSL
    compiling, 362
    configuring, 363
    downloading, 362
    for public key certificates, 361–364
Operating systems
    hacking tools and, 337
    IEEE 802.1X supplicants in, 137
    security services and, 183
Orthogonal frequency division multiplexing
        (OFDM), 64
Overflow, in finite field arithmetic, 392–397

P

Packet collection, in attack, 347–349
Packet length
    network protocol and, 36–37
    in TLS over EAP, 166
Packet number. *See* PN

Pairwise key(s)
  in ad-hoc operation, 287–288
  in decryption, 277
  definition of, 200, 200*f*
  exchange of (*See* Four-way handshake)
  expansion of, PRNG for, 226
  for group key distribution, 208
  Information Elements and, 282
  Key Data field of, 217
  MIC attack against, 251
  in mixed environments, 212
  in TKIP, 245
Pairwise key hierarchy
  about, 201–207
  for AES-CCMP, 213*f*
  definition of, 200–201
  temporal keys in, computing, 203–204,
    204*f*
  for TKIP, 212*f*
Pairwise master key (PMK)
  in access point authentication, 205–207
  creation of, 202–203
  definition of, 201
  delivery of, to access point, 202
  generation of, 202–203
Pairwise transient key (PTK), 203
PAP, for PPP authentication, 140–141, 140*f*
Passive attacks, 34
Passive monitoring, active attacks and, 22,
    31–32
Passwords. *See also* Key(s)
  for access point, 369–370
  in attributes, 142–143
  in CHAP, 141
  definition of, 17
  in Kerberos, 170, 172
  master (*See* Master key)
  one-time, 41, 131, 317–318
  in PAP, 140–141
  protection with, 41
  for server
    hacking, 25
    need for, by attackers, 32
  for shared directories, 305
  ticket-granting ticket protection with, 172

PEAP (Protected EAP)
  about, 186–189
  definition of, 155
  identity in, 188–189
  man-in-the-middle attacks and, 334
  phases of, 187–189
  status of, 189
Pending connection state, in TLS handshake,
    163–164
Per-packet key mixing
  details of, 255–259
  in TKIP, 239–240, 240*f*, 243–245
    algorithm for, 255–256, 257–259
    IV collision and, 244
    key derivation in, 244
    phases in, 244–245, 255–259
    substitution table for, 256–257
PGP (Pretty Good Privacy)
  for file verification, 412–414, 413*f*, 414*f*,
    415*f*
  public key encryption with, 152
Physical Layer Convergence Protocol. *See*
    PLCP
Ping packet, in MTU recovery, 327
PKI (public key infrastructure), 152, 312
  for client certificates, 360
  vs. OpenSSL, 362
Plaintext
  capturing, value in, 96
  in challengetext, 71
  definition of, 43, 43*f*
  in inductive chosen plaintext attack,
    326–329
  knowledge of, 44
  in MDPU encryption, in CCMP,
    273–274
  sample of, 44–45
  in stream cipher, 73
  in WEP, 91–92
Planning, in attack process, 346–348
PLCP (Physical Layer Convergence
    Protocol) header, in transmission, 57–58
PMK. *See* Pairwise master key
PN (packet number)
  in CCMP header, 272

in CCMP implementation, 273
in MPDU decryption, 277
vs. nonce, for encryption, 274–275
Point of presence (POP), 121, 122
Point-to-point protocol. *See* PPP
Policy, *vs.* protocol, 12
Polynomials, in finite field arithmetic, 388–389
POP (point of presence), 121, 122
Port
    authentication server and, 123
    authenticator associated with, 123
    definition of, 123
    logical, in access point, 127–128, 128*f*
Port security, in IEEE 802.1X, 123
Port state, control over, in IEEE 802.1X, 124
Power save flags (TIM), in beacon format, 62*f*, 63
PPP (Point-to-point protocol)
    authentication in, 120–121, 140
    for dial-up access, 120–121
    EAP for, 121
Preamble, in transmission, 57
Preauthentication, with IEEE 802.1X, 283–285, 284*f*
Pre-master key, 162, 167
Preshared key(s)
    in ad-hoc operation, 287
    for authentication, 131
    definition of, 201
    Information Elements and, 282
    PMK and, 202
Preshared key mode, for WPA, 358
Pretty Good Privacy. *See* PGP
PRF-*n* functions, 226–229
Priority field, in CBC-MAC first block, 275
Privacy, message, 95–101
    authentication and, 187
        separation of, 107
    in WEP security, 72–83
Private key
    in digital signatures, 315–316
    generation of, 152
    in public key decryption, 152, 312–313
PRNG. *See* Pseudorandom number generator

Probe request message, 56, 281–282
Probe response message, 282
Probing, 56
Profit attacks, 25–26
Protected EAP. *See* PEAP
Protocol. *See* Network protocol; Security protocol
Proxy Kerberos application server, for tickets, 180, 181*f*
Proxy ticket, 173, 174*f*
Pseudonym, in EAP-SIM, 194–195
Pseudorandom bytes, security of, 318
Pseudorandom generation algorithm, in RC4, 317
Pseudorandom key stream, 87, 88, 242
Pseudorandom number generator (PRNG)
    for key expansion, 226
    in shared key authentication, 321
    in WPA/RSN, 226–229
Pseudorandom stream
    in inductive chosen plaintext attack, 326
    in shared-key authentication, 331
PTK (Pairwise transient key), 203
Public key, 151–152
    in asymmetric cryptography, 152, 312–313
    certification of, 153–155, 158
    distribution of, 153
    generation of, 152
Public key certificates
    creating, 364–368
    installation of, 379–381, 380*f*, 381*f*
    OpenSSL for, 361–374
    TLS over EAP and, 360
Public key encryption
    in certificate, 158
    in digital signatures, 315–316
    with PGP, 152
    public key in, 152
Public key infrastructure. *See* PKI
Public wireless access, 294

R

RA (receiver address), 58
Radio components, in wireless network, 63–65

Radio frequencies, 54, 63
Radio frequency section
    definition of, 64
    in Wi-Fi LAN card, 232, 233*f*
Radio parameters, in beacon format, 62*f*, 63
Radio spectrum, control of, 63–64
RADIUS (Remote Authentication Dial-In
        User Service)
    about, 138–147
    for access control, 118
    attributes for, 143–144
    for authenticator/authentication server
            communication, 126, 168, 178
    EAP message passed by, 138, 168
    extensions to, 144
    hotspot controllers and, 302
    for IEEE 802.1X support, 126
    intent of, 139
    mechanics of, 140–144
    messages in, 140–142
        attributes in, 142–144
        changing purpose of, 142
        format of, 142–143, 142*f*
    PMK delivery by, 202
    for POP authentication, 121
    in RSN, 146–147
    specifications for, 139–140
    support in, 139
    in WPA, 146–147
RADIUS server. *See also* FreeRADIUS
    in access point configuration, 376–379,
            378*f*
    as authentication server, 139, 185
    certificate for, 364–365
    configuration connection to, 369–370
    definition of, 138
    managing, 360
    for WPA network, 360
Random challenge (RAND), in GSM
        authentication, 191
Range, data rate and, 64
RC4 algorithm. *See also* Stream cipher
    about, 86–87
    for decryption, 86, 317

for encryption, 73–74, 317
    phases in, 88
    weak keys in, 99–100
    in WEP, 86–88
    flaws in, 322–323
    in IEEE 802.11, 316–321
    phases in, 316–317
    pseudorandom stream from, 242
    symmetric nature of, 313
    in WEP, 318, 318*f*
Reassociation message, 56
Receiver address (RA), 58
Reconnaissance, in attack process, 338–344
Record protocol, in TLS, 157
Redundant server, 138
Referral tickets, in Kerberos, 175
Remote Authentication Dial-In User
        Service. *See* RADIUS
Remote users
    virtual private network for, 28, 28*f*
    Wi-Fi LAN users as, 29–30, 30*f*
Replay, 39–40
    prevention of
        with CCMP header, 271
        with MIC, 207
        with nonce, 143
        in TKIP, 240–242
        WEP and, 93–94, 240, 324
    purpose of, 240
Replay window, in TKIP, 241
Request, handling, with layers, 52–53, 52*f*
Request for Comments. *See* RFC
Request message, in EAP, 130
Response message, in EAP, 130
Reuse
    of IVs, 75, 96–99, 238
    of packets, CCMP and, 273
Revenge attacks, 25–26
Revocation, of certificates, 154
RFC (Request for Comments), 119
RFC 1321. *See* MD5
RFC 1510. *See* Kerberos V5
RFC 2104. *See* HMAC
RFC 2284. *See* PPP

RFC 2716. *See* TLS over EAP
RFC 2743. *See* GSS-API
RFC 2869, RADIUS extensions in, 144
Rijmen, Vincent, 264
Rijndael algorithm, in AES, 264, 387
Roaming, 56, 283–284, 286
Robust security network. *See* RSN
Rogaway, Phil, 269
Round key, in AES encryption, 387,
    398–401, 399*t*, 400*t*
RSA public key algorithm, 313
RSN (robust security network). *See also*
    IEEE 802.11i; WPA
  about, 105
  AES and, 106, 261–262
  authentication in, 281
  CCMP in, 269–278
  cellular authentication converted to, 193
  in IEEE 802.1X, 119
  Information Elements for, 282
  joining under, 280–282
  Kerberos in, 178–184
  keys in, 108–110
    establishment and distribution of, 210
  master key in, generation of, 165
  nonce counter and, 225
  PRNG functions in, 226–229
  vs. proprietary solutions, 356, 359
  RADIUS in, 146–147
  security context for, 107–108
  security layers for, 110–113
  security model for, 179*f*
  with TLS authentication, 114, 115*f*
  TLS handshake and, 165
  WPA and, 106–107, 356–357

S
SA (source address), 58
S-box, for key mixing, 256–257
Scanners, about, 23–24
Scanning, 54
Script kiddies, 22
Secret key. *See* Key(s)
Secure Socket Layer (SSL), 156. *See also* TLS

Security. *See also* WEP
  in ad-hoc mode, 280
  assumptions in, 15–16
  basic mechanisms for, 311–316
  of cellular phones, 190
  definition of, 7
  goal of, 7–8
  humans in, 41
  in IEEE 802.11, 316, 322–331
  principles of, 8–16
  terms in, 17–19
Security architectures
  design guidelines for, 355–357
  for RSN, 106
  traditional, 21, 27–31, 28*f*
  for WPA, 106
Security context
  ad-hoc networks and, 285–289
  establishing, 107–108
    with certificates, 154
    in WPA/RSN, 146
  keys in, 108–110
  management of, 111
  for RSN, 107–108
  ticket-granting ticket for, 172
Security layers
  implementation of, 111–113
  for wireless LANs, 110–113, 112*f*
Security protocol
  definition of, 17
  dictionary attack and, 47
  in IEEE 802.11, 57
  vs. policy, 12
Security services, operating systems and, 183
Security session, in TLS, 160
Self-synchronization, 68–69
Serial authentication, 131
Server(s)
  authentication of, in PEAP, 187
  logon passwords for
    hacking, 25
    need for, by attackers, 32
Server certificates
  creating, with OpenSSL, 364–365

Server certificates *continued*
    in TLS, 155–156
    in TLS handshake, 161
Server Hello Done message, in TLS
    handshake, 161
Server hello message
    in TLS handshake, 160–161
    in TLS over EAP handshake, 167
Server-based infrastructure, for WPA, 358
Server-based keys, 201
Service tickets, in Kerberos, 172–174
    expiration of, 173
    obtaining, 177
    session keys in, 177
    vs. ticket-granting ticket, 173
Session encryption key, in LEAP, 185
Session ID, in TLS server hello, 160
Session keys. *See also* Temporal keys
    in EAP-SIM authentication, 195–196
    in GSM authentication (Kc), 191,
        193–194
    in mixed key, 244, 255
    in service tickets, 177
    in ticket-granting ticket, 176
    for TKIP, 243
    in TLS, 158
SHA1, 315–316. *See also* HMAC-SHA-1
Shamirand, Adi, 242, 322–323
Shared file systems, hotspots and, 305
Shared key. *See also* Passwords
    definition of, 69
    in Kerberos, 172
    in LEAP, 185
Shared-key authentication
    in IEEE 802.11, 321, 322*f*
        attacks against, 330–331
    for security, 359
Shift operation, in finite field arithmetic,
    391–392
Shipley, Pete, war driving and, 32
Signature
    for data integrity, 315–316
    for messages, 152–153

SIM cards
    cracking, 42
    definition of, 190
    hotspots and, 299, 302
    use of, 190–191
    for Wi-Fi LAN authentication, 193
Smart cards. *See also* SIM cards
    cracking, 42
    for key distribution, 77
SNonce
    definition of, 206
    generation of, 218
Snooping
    definition of, 34
    of EAP-Identity message, 187
    without keys, 36–37
Software, hotspots and, 298
Source address (SA), 58
Source integrity. *See* Authentication
Spoofing, of EAP message, 187
Spread spectrum transmission, 3, 334
SRES, 191, 195–196
SRP protocol, zero knowledge password
    proofs in, 178
SSID
    in ad-hoc operation, 286
    in beacon format, 62, 62*f,* 330
    closed network and, 330
    determination of, with Airjack, 352
    snooping, 36
SSL (Secure Socket Layer), 156. *See also* TLS
Standards. *See also* IEEE *entries*
    relationships of, 113–114, 115*f*
Start flag, 166
State array, in AES encryption, 398,
    401–403, 402*t*
Status code, in authentication message, 72,
    72*f*
Store-and-forward attack. *See* Man-in-the-
    middle attack
Stream cipher, 73, 73*f,* 85, 313
Subscribers, in hotspot organization,
    298–299

Subscriptions, for hotspots, 295–296
Substitution table, for key mixing, 256–257
Subtraction, in finite field arithmetic, 390
Success message
    in EAP, 130, 187
    in TLS over EAP handshake, 168
Sulmicki, Adam, 374
Supplicant
    in access control, 118
    in access point configuration, 379
    in ad-hoc operation, 286–287, 287*f*
    in four-way handshake, 206
    IEEE 802.1X, 123, 137, 360–361
    in LEAP, 184
    open source, 376
    in Wi-Fi LANs, 127
Supported data rates, in beacon format,
    62–63, 62*f*
Switch
    access control with, 124
    Kerberos and, 181–182*f*
    logical, in Wi-Fi LANs, 128
Switched hub environment, IEEE 802.1X
    in, 124–127, 124*f*
Symmetric algorithm, 73. *See also* Block
    cipher; Stream cipher
Symmetric encryption, as confidentiality
    mechanism, 312, 313
Symmetric key, 151
    asymmetric keys and, combining, 155
    in TLS, 158

T
TA (transmitter address), 58
Targeted attack, reconnaissance for,
    338–339. *See* War driving
TCP/IP packets, in hotspots, 306
Temporal Authenticator RX MIC key, 246
Temporal Authenticator TX MIC key, 246
Temporal Encryption key, 245
Temporal Key Integrity Protocol. *See* TKIP
Temporal keys. *See also* Session keys
    in ad-hoc operation, 288
    for AES-CCMP, 211

brute force attacks and, 226
computing, 225–229, 226*f*
definition of, 109
in group key hierarchy
    in PRF-*n* functions, 226
    types of, 210
in pairwise key hierarchy
    computing, 203–204, 204*f*, 206, 221
    for encryption, 206–207
    liveness in, 203–204
    types of, 203
for TKIP, 245–246
Text string, in PRF-*n* functions, 226
TGS (Ticket-granting service), in KDC,
    171–172, 171*f*
TGT. *See* Ticket-granting ticket
Threat model, 17
Ticket(s)
    for access point, 181–182, 182*f*
    for authentication, 179–180
    authentication server and, 176
    definition of, 169–171
    dictionary attacks against, 178
    encryption of, 176
    format of, 177
    forwarded, 173–174, 175*f*
    in Kerberos, 169–171
    key in, 176
    master, 170, 171
    master key in, 176
    modification of, 176
    for network access, 179–180
    operation of, 176–178
    proxy, 173, 174*f*
    proxy Kerberos application server for, 180,
        181*f*
    referral, in Kerberos, 175
    service, in Kerberos, 172–174, 177
Ticket-granting service (TGS), in KDC,
    171–172, 171*f*
Ticket-granting ticket (TGT)
    vs. master ticket, 171
    obtaining, 171–172, 176–177
    protection of, 172

Ticket-granting ticket (TGT) *continued*
    with proxy, 181
    for security context, 172
    service tickets *vs.*, 173
Timestamp, in beacon, 61–62, 62*f*
TKIP (Temporal Key Integrity Protocol)
    vs. AES, 261
    in data reception, 248–249, 248*f*
    in data transmission, 246–248, 247*f*
    development of, 105–106
    group key hierarchy for, 213*f*
    ICV in, 235
    implementation of, 245–249
    Information Elements and, 282
    IV in, 238–243
    keys for, 211, 245
    MIC computation in, Michael for,
        236–238
    MPDU and, 238
    for multicasts, in mixed environments,
        212
    objective of, 231
    overview of, 234–243
    pairwise key hierarchy for, 212*f*
    per-packet key mixing in, 239–240, 240*f*,
        243–245
        algorithm for, 255–256, 257–259
        IV collision and, 244
        key derivation in, 244
        phases in, 244–245, 255–259
        substitution table for, 256–257
    replay window in, 241–242
    for WEP weaknesses, 231
    WEP weaknesses solved by, 234–235,
        234*t*, 235*t*
TKIP sequence counter. *See* TSC
TLS (Transport Layer Security)
    about, 155–169
    authentication in
        certificates for, 158
        in RSN, 114, 115*f*
    functions of, 156–158
    handshake in (*See* handshake)
    layers in, 157, 157*f*

PEAP and, 186, 187
    security session in, 160
    summary of, 169
    Tunneled (*See* TTLS)
    Type field in, 166
TLS over EAP, 129, 165–168
    handshake in, 166–168, 167*f*
    messages in, format of, 166, 166*f*
    packet length in, 166
    type number for, 130
    for WPA, 360
Tokens
    in access control, 118
    affirmation with, 12, 70
Traditional security architecture. *See*
        Security architectures, traditional
Traffic analysis, in snooping, 36–37
Transaction sequence, in authentication
        message, 72, 72*f*
Transitional security network (TSN), 105
Transmission
    about, 57–58
    encryption of, with CCMP, 270–271
    in TKIP, 246–248, 247*f*
Transmitter address (TA), 58
Transport Layer Security. *See* TLS
Triplet
    in GSM authentication (Kc), 191
    multiple, 194–195
    in RSN authentication, 194
Trojan viruses, hotspots and, 305
Trusted zone
    hotspots and, 296
    in traditional security architecture, 27–31,
        28*f*
TSC (TKIP sequence counter)
    in denial-of-service attack, 336
    denial-of-service attack and, 246–247
    duplicate, 241
    for replay prevention, 240–242
    in TKIP reception, 248
TSN (transitional security network), 105
TTLS (Tunneled TLS) over EAP, 129
Tunnel, for EAP negotiation, 187

Type field
    in attribute format, 142
    in EAP, 130
        in message format, 132, 132*f*
    in TLS, 166
Type number
    for LEAP, 186
    for TLS over EAP, 130

U
UDP (IP datagram service), hotspots and, 306
Ultimate SubSeven Logging tool, 26
Ultrawide-band systems, 334
Unicast address, 58
Unicast data, 199
Unicast messages, 82, 251
Untrusted zone
    access points in, 30
    hotspots and, 296
    in traditional security architecture, 27–31, 28*f*
    wireless users in, 29, 29*f*
Upper-layer authentication methods
    definition of, 149
    EAP and, 129
    in IEEE 802.11, 150
    keys in, 151–155
    preshared keys and, 201
    roaming and, 284
    server-based keys and, 201
    in WPA, 150
User(s). *See also* Mobile device
    dial-in, 120–122
    hotspot, 298–299, 305–308
    layer interaction with, 52
    Wi-Fi, 29–30, 29*f*, 30*f*

V
Vernam cipher, 89, 317
Virtual private network (VPN)
    about, 306–308
    deployment issues with, 28
    details about, 307–308

hotspot controllers and, 301
purpose of, 306
for remote users, 28, 28*f*
server capacity in, 30
for Wireless LAN, 29–30
VLAN, for isolation, 357
VPN. *See* Virtual private network

W
Walker, Jesse, 96
War chalking, 32
War driving, 32
    gaming attackers and, 24
    honeypots and, 26
    SSID broadcasts and, 36
    tools for, 339–344, 340*f*, 341*f*, 342*f*, 344*f*, 345*f*
    in Wi-Fi LAN reconnaissance, 25
Weak keys. *See also* FMS attack
    avoiding, 243
    collection of, 348
    definition of, 100
    finding, 243
    key mixing and, 259
    in RC4, 99–100, 242
    TKIP and, 239
    in WEP, 239, 242
Web site, as plaintext sample, 45
WEP (Wired Equivalent Privacy)
    absence of, attack against, 346, 346*f*
    in access point configuration, 376–379, 378*f*, 379*f*
    AirSnort and, 27
    authentication in, 69–72, 71*f*
    CRC in, 318
    disabling, 359
    gaming attacks against, 24–25
    ICV in, 84–85, 85*f*, 235
    Information Elements and, 282, 283
    initialization vector in, 74–76, 75*f*
    IV collision in, 324
    IV in, 74–76, 75*f*, 318
        length of, 239
        weakness in, 238

WEP (Wired Equivalent Privacy) *continued*
  IV space in, 324
  keys in (*See* WEP keys)
  mechanics of, 83–89
  modification attacks against, 324–325
  objectives for, 68
  in OpenBSD, 375
  privacy in, 72–83
  RC4 in, 316–321, 318*f*
  for security, 359
  upgrading (*See* TKIP)
  weak keys in, 239, 242, 323
  weaknesses in, 89–101, 238
    fixing (*See* TKIP)
  XORing in, 91–92, 320
WEP Datagram Format, in IEEE 802.11,
    319–320, 319*f*
WEP keys, 76–83, 76*t*. *See also* Default keys;
    Key mapping keys
  changing, 359
  characteristics of, 76–77
  directional use of, 81–82
  distribution of, 77
  recovery of
    AirSnort for, 351–352
    dwepcrack for, 347, 349–350, 349*f*, 350*f*
  terminology for, 76, 76*t*
  vs. TKIP keys, 243
  weaknesses in, 99–100
White-list sites, 301
Whiting, Doug, 244
wicontrol, 375
Wi-Fi
  about, 3–4
  definition of, 6
  vs. IEEE 802.11 standard, 104, 105*f*
  products using, 4
Wi-Fi LAN
  authentication in, GSM and, 192–193
  cellular connection to, 191
  coordinating, 279–282
  gaming attacks against, 24–25
  IEEE 802.1X in, 127–129
  logical ports in, 127–128, 128*f*

man-in-the-middle attack against, 38–40
  security layers for, 110–113, 112*f*
  in traditional security architecture, 28–31
  in trusted zone, 30–31
  unprotected, 24
  in untrusted zone, 29–30
  vulnerabilities in, 21–32
Wi-Fi LAN card
  in access point construction, 375
  components of, 232–234, 233*f*
  upgrading to WPA, 357–358
Wi-Fi Protected Access. *See* WPA
Windows XP (Microsoft), in access point
    configuration, 379
Wired Equivalent Privacy. *See* WEP
Wired LAN
  in hotspots, 300
  man-in-the-middle attack against, 38
  for preauthentication, 284–285
  tapping into, 30–31
  wireless access points and, 30
  wireless connection to (*See* Infrastructure
    mode)
Wireless access, public, 294
Wireless adapter, manufacturer of, snooping,
    36
Wireless communications, denial-of-service
    attack and, 252
Wireless device. *See* Mobile device
Wireless equipment
  choosing, 359
  upgrading, to WPA, 357–358, 359
Wireless Internet Service Provider model,
    for hotspots, 295
Wireless LAN. *See also* Wi-Fi LAN
  canalization of, 356
  definition of, 6
  IEEE 802.1X and, 123, 137
  isolation of, 356
  mutual authentication for, 91
  organization of, 53–54
  powering down, 359
  security layers for, 110–113, 112*f*
  utility of, 358–359

Wireless LAN layer, 111, 112*f*
wlan_jack, for denial-of-service attack, 352
WPA (Wi-Fi Protected Access)
  about, 105–106
  AirSnort and, 27
  attributes in, 143
  authentication in, 183, 281
  deployment of, 359
  in IEEE 802.1X, 119
  IEEE 802.11i and, 356–357
  Information Elements for, 282
  infrastructure for, deploying, 360–361
  joining under, 280–282
  key exchange in, 214–217, 214*f*, 215*t*,
    216*f*, 216*t*
  keys in
    derivation of, 214–224
    establishment and distribution of, 210
  master key in, generation of, 165
  nonce counter and, 225
  PMK delivery in, 202

  preshared key mode for, 358
  PRNG functions in, 226–229
  vs. proprietary solutions, 356
  RADIUS in, 146–147
  RSN and, 106–107, 356–357
  server-based infrastructure in, 358
  TLS handshake and, 165
  upper-layer authentication methods in,
    150
WRAP, 269

X

XOR. *See* Exclusive OR operation
XorRoundKey operation, in AES
  encryption, 403
Xsupplicant, 376

Z

Zero knowledge password proofs, 178
Zombie computers, in denial-of-service
  attacks, 35

Register
Your Book
at www.awprofessional.com/register

You may be eligible to receive:
- Advance notice of forthcoming editions of the book
- Related book recommendations
- Chapter excerpts and supplements of forthcoming titles
- Information about special contests and promotions throughout the year
- Notices and reminders about author appearances, tradeshows, and online chats with special guests

Contact us

If you are interested in writing a book or reviewing manuscripts prior to publication, please write to us at:

Editorial Department
Addison-Wesley Professional
75 Arlington Street, Suite 300
Boston, MA 02116 USA
Email: AWPro@aw.com

Visit us on the Web: http://www.awprofessional.com